THE
BOOK

Suzuki
GSX-R600 and 750
Service and Repair Manual

by Matthew Coombs

Models covered

(3553-9AD3-288)

GSX-R600V, W, X and Y. 600cc. 1997 to 2000
GSX-R750T, V, W and X. 749cc. 1996 to 1999

ABCDE
FGHIJ

© Haynes Publishing 2004

A book in the **Haynes Service and Repair Manual Series**

ISBN **1 84425 061 X**

British Library Cataloguing in Publication Data
A catalogue record for this book is available from the British Library

Library of Congress Control Number **2003105793**

Printed in the USA

Haynes Publishing
Sparkford, Yeovil, Somerset BA22 7JJ, England

Haynes North America, Inc
861 Lawrence Drive, Newbury Park, California 91320, USA

Editions Haynes
4, Rue de l'Abreuvoir,
92415 COURBEVOIE CEDEX, France

Haynes Publishing Nordiska AB
Box 1504, 751 45 UPPSALA, Sweden

Contents

LIVING WITH YOUR SUZUKI GSX-R

Introduction

Daily (pre-ride) Checks

MAINTENANCE

Routine maintenance and Servicing

Contents

REPAIRS AND OVERHAUL

Engine, transmission and associated systems

Chassis components

Electrical system

Wiring diagrams

REFERENCE

Index

Suzuki
Every Which Way

by Julian Ryder

From Textile Machinery to Motorcycles

Suzuki were the second of Japan's Big Four motorcycle manufacturers to enter the business, and like Honda they started by bolting small two-stroke motors to bicycles. Unlike Honda, they had manufactured other products before turning to transportation in the aftermath of World War II. In fact Suzuki has been in business since the first decade of the 20th-Century when Michio Suzuki manufactured textile machinery.

The desperate need for transport in post-war Japan saw Suzuki make their first motorised bicycle in 1952, and the fact that by 1954 the company had changed its name to Suzuki Motor Company shows how quickly the sideline took over the whole company's activities. In their first full manufacturing year, Suzuki made nearly 4500 bikes and rapidly expanded into the world markets with a range of two-strokes.

Suzuki didn't make a four-stroke until 1977 when the GS750 double-overhead-cam across-the-frame four arrived. This was several years after Honda and Kawasaki had established the air-cooled four as the industry standard, but no motorcycle epitomises the era of what came to be known as the Universal

The T500 two-stroke twin

One of the later GT750 'kettle' models with front disc brakes

50 cc racer won six of the eight world titles chalked up by Suzuki during the 1960s as well as providing Mitsuo Itoh with the distinction of being the only Japanese rider to win an Isle of Man TT. Mr Itoh still works for Suzuki, he's in charge of their racing program.

Europe got the benefit of Suzuki's two-stroke expertise in a succession of air-cooled twins, the six-speed 250 cc Super Six being the most memorable, but the arrival in 1968 of the first of a series of 500 cc twins which were good looking, robust and versatile marked the start of mainstream success.

So confident were Suzuki of their two-stroke expertise that they even applied it to the burgeoning Superbike sector. The GT750 water-cooled triple arrived in 1972. It was big, fast and comfortable although the handling and stopping power did draw some comment. Whatever the drawbacks of the road bike, the engine was immensely successful in Superbike and Formula 750 racing. The roadster has its devotees, though, and is now a sought-after bike on the classic Japanese scene. Do not refer to it as the Water Buffalo in such company. Joking aside, the later disc-braked versions were quite civilised, but the audacious idea of using a big two-stroke motor in what was essentially a touring bike was a surprising success until the fuel crisis of the mid-'70s effectively killed off big strokers.

The same could be said of Suzuki's only real lemon, the RE5. This is still the only mass-produced bike to use the rotary (or Wankel) engine but never sold well. Fuel consumption in the mid-teens allied to frightening complexity and excess weight meant the RE5 was a non-starter in the sales race.

Japanese motorcycle better than the GS. So well engineered were the original fours that you can clearly see their genes in the GS500 twins that are still going strong in the mid-1990s. Suzuki's ability to prolong the life of their products this way means that they are often thought of as a conservative company. This is hardly fair if you look at some of their landmark designs, most of which have been commercial as well as critical successes.

Two-stroke Success

Early racing efforts were bolstered by the arrival of Ernst Degner who defected from the East German MZ team at the Swedish GP of 1961, bringing with him the rotary-valve secrets of design genius Walter Kaaden. The new Suzuki 50 cc racer won its first GP on the Isle of Man the following year and winning the title easily. Only Honda and Ralph Bryans interrupted Suzuki's run of 50 cc titles from 1962 to 1968.

The arrival of the twin-cylinder 125 racer in 1963 enabled Hugh Anderson to win both 50 and 125 world titles. You may not think 50 cc racing would be exciting - until you learn that the final incarnation of the thing had 14 gears and could do well over 100 mph on fast circuits. Before pulling out of GPs in 1967 the

Suzuki's GT250X7 was an instant hit in the popular 250 cc 'learner' sector

The GS400 was the first in a line of four-stroke twins

Development of the Four-stroke range

When Suzuki got round to building a four-stroke they did a very good job of it. The GS fours were built in 550, 650, 750, 850, 1000 and 1100 cc sizes in sports, custom, roadster and even shaft-driven touring forms over many years. The GS1000 was in on the start of Superbike racing in the early 1970s and the GS850 shaft-driven tourer was around nearly 15 years later. The fours spawned a line of 400, 425, 450 and 500 cc GS twins that were essentially the middle half of the four with all their reliability. If there was ever a criticism of the GS models it was that with the exception of the GS1000S of 1980, colloquially known as the ice-cream van, the range was visually uninspiring.

They nearly made the same mistake when they launched the four-valve-head GSX750 in 1979. Fortunately, the original twin-shock version was soon replaced by the 'E'-model with Full-Floater rear suspension and a full set of all the gadgets the Japanese industry was then keen on and has since forgotten about, like 16-inch front wheels and anti-dive forks. The air-cooled GSX was like the GS built in 550, 750 and 1100 cc versions with a variety of half, full and touring fairings, but the GSX that is best remembered is the Katana that first appeared in 1981. The power was provided by an 1000 or 1100 cc GSX motor, but wrapped around it was the most outrageous styling package to come out of Japan. Designed by Hans Muth of Target Design, the Katana looked like nothing seen before or since. At the time there was as much anti feeling as praise, but now it is rightly regarded as a classic, a true milestone in motorcycle design. The factory have even started making 250 and 400 cc fours for the home market with the same styling as the 1981 bike.

Just to remind us that they'd still been building two-strokes for the likes of Barry Sheene, in 1986 Suzuki marketed a road-going version of their RG500 square-four racer which had put an end to the era of the four-stroke in 500 GPs when it appeared in 1974. In 1976 Suzuki not only won their first 500 title with Sheene, they sold RG500s over the counter and won every GP with them - with the exception of the Isle of Man TT which the works riders boycotted. Ten years on, the RG500 Gamma gave road riders the nearest experience they'd ever get to riding a GP bike. The fearsome beast could top 140 mph and only weighed 340 lb - the other alleged GP replicas were pussy cats compared to the Gamma's man-eating tiger.

The RG only lasted a few years and is already firmly in the category of collector's item; its four-stroke equivalent, the GSX-R, is still with us and looks like being so for many years. You have to look back to 1985 and its launch to realise just what a revolutionary step the GSX-R750 was: quite simply it was the first race replica. Not a bike dressed up to look like a race bike, but a genuine racer with lights on, a bike that could be taken straight to the track and win.

The first GSX-R, the 750, had a completely new motor cooled by oil rather than water and an aluminium cradle frame. It was sparse, a little twitchy and very, very fast. This time Suzuki got the looks right, blue and white bodywork based on the factory's racing colours and endurance-racer lookalike twin headlights. And then came the 1100 - the big GSX-R got progressively more brutal as it chased the Yamaha EXUP for the heavyweight championship.

And alongside all these mould-breaking designs, Suzuki were also making the best looking custom bikes to come out of Japan,

The GS750 led the way for a series of four cylinder models

Later four-stroke models, like this GSX1100, were fitted with 16v engines

the Intruders; the first race replica trail bike, the DR350; the sharpest 250 Supersports, the RGV250; and a bargain-basement 600, the Bandit. The Bandit proved so popular they went on to build 1200 and 750 cc versions of it. I suppose that's predictable, a range of four-stroke fours just like the GS and GSXs. It's just like the company really, sometimes predictable, admittedly - but never boring.

No Compromise

In the techno wars of super-sports motor-cycling, GSX-R is a name that gets respect. The original 1985 oil-cooled version wasn't just a winner straight out of the crate it was revolutionary. The 1996 version wasn't so obviously path-breaking but it was still a winner. It's just that the twin-beam aluminium frame and water-cooled motor made it look a bit like the competition from Honda (FireBlade) and Kawasaki (ZX-7R). But you couldn't see what made it so different: weight – or rather lack of it. The first of the new-generation 750 Suzukis weighed in at just 179 kg (395 lb) thanks to ultra-thin materials, hollow swinging arm castings, composite-coated cylinders doing away with the need for liners, drilled fasteners, and a host of other detail tweaks. For comparison, a ZX-7R weighed in at 203 kg and a FireBlade at 183 kg (dry weights).

The big saving on the motor's architecture was the camchain drive on the left end of the

Suzuki's GSX-R range represented their cutting edge sports bikes

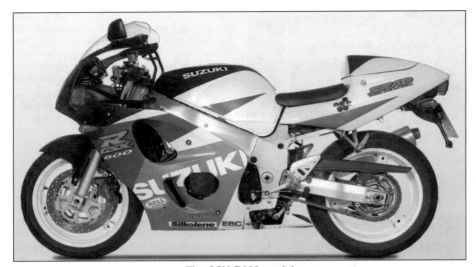

The GSX-R600 model

crank doing away with the need for one main bearing. Only when you stood it next to other 750s of the day did you realise how small it was and understood what Suzuki meant when they said they'd used lessons learnt from Kevin Schwantz's 500 in building the GSX-R. the relationship goes deeper than the characteristic rounded shape of the seat hump.

Not surprisingly, the GSX-R750 was the nearest thing you could buy to a racer for the roads despite the fact it was half the price of Honda's Superbike homologation special, the RC45. Suzuki didn't have a homologation special, like the RC45 or Yamaha's new R7, the standard, mass-produced roadbike did the job. Which tells you just how much of a racer it is. Not surprisingly, it was quick but it didn't suffer fools gladly, in fact it didn't suffer fools at all. This was a cutting-edge motorcycle in every way demanding concentration and application from its rider.

The only surprise was that this high-tech missile still sported carburettors. We had to wait until 1998 for fuel-injection. It also got a

larger airbox and a revised exhaust system to go with the new intake system plus a higher, more bulbous screen and an hydraulic steering damper. It was also one of the first bikes to use the latest trick bit of automotive electronics, the high-tension coil built into what look like giant spark-plug caps, thus doing away with separate coils bolted to the frame. The result was a cleaner pick-up through the rev-range plus a little more top end, but most road riders would have been hard pushed to spot the difference. The fuel injection was really there for the World Superbike Championship, but the works bikes didn't use it until 1999. When they did, Suzuki got its first wins since 1989.

The Supersports 600 class got its first GSX-R in 1997, and true-to-type it was the lightest, shortest, twitchiest bike in the class and became the hottest 600 on the race track. Jon Crawford won the 1998 British Championship on one and Fabrizio Pirovano won the 1998 World Supersport Series that runs alongside the World Superbike Championship.

On the road the GSX-R600 was just like the

750 only more so, standing out from its competition even more than the 750 did as the raciest bike in its class. It even looked like a scaled down 750 and like its bigger brother breathed through carburettors. On the road its lack of midrange and ultra-sensitive handling made it the hardest bike in its class to live with. Unless, of course, you buy a bike to use at track days.

Acknowledgements

Our thanks are due to GT Motorcycles of Mudford, Yeovil, who supplied the machines featured in the illustrations throughout this manual. We would also like to thank NGK Spark Plugs (UK) Ltd for supplying the colour spark plug condition photos and the Avon Rubber Company for supplying information on tyre fitting.

The introduction 'Every Which Way' was written by Julian Ryder. Kel Edge supplied the rear cover photograph.

About this manual

The aim of this manual is to help you get the best value from your motorcycle. It can do so in several ways. It can help you decide what work must be done, even if you choose to have it done by a dealer; it provides information and procedures for routine maintenance and servicing; and it offers diagnostic and repair procedures to follow when trouble occurs.

We hope you use the manual to tackle the work yourself. For many simpler jobs, doing it yourself may be quicker than arranging an appointment to get the motorcycle into a dealer and making the trips to leave it and pick it up. More importantly, a lot of money can be saved by avoiding the expense of the shop that must pass on to you to cover its labour and overhead costs. An added benefit is the sense of satisfaction and accomplishment that you feel after doing the job yourself.

References to the left or right side of the motorcycle assume you are sitting on the seat, facing forward.

We take great pride in the accuracy of information given in this manual, but motorcycle manufacturers make alterations and design changes during the production run of a particular motorcycle of which they do not inform us. No liability can be accepted by the authors or publishers for loss, damage or injury caused by any errors in, or omissions from, the information given.

Illegal Copying

The GSX-R750 model

Model development

GSX-R600

● The GSX-R600V was introduced in January 1997.

● The engine was a liquid cooled four-cylinder with double overhead camshafts driven by chain from the right-hand end of the crankshaft, based on the GSX-R750 unit. Carburettor air intake was via the SRAD (Suzuki Ram Air Direct) system. The crankcases were of the three-piece 'cassette' design with separate cylinder block.

● Drive was transmitted to the six-speed gearbox via a multi-plate clutch with single diaphragm spring, and to the rear wheel by chain and sprockets.

● PAIR (pulse air supply) and EVAP systems were fitted to California models

● The chassis comprised a twin-spar aluminium alloy frame, a bolt-on rear subframe and box-section swingarm. Front suspension was by conventional, two-way adjustable telescopic forks and rear suspension was by a rising rate, three-way adjustable mono-shock.

● Braking was by twin disc with four piston calipers at the front and a single disc with a twin piston caliper at the rear.

● The GSX-R600V was available in pearl white and deep blue, pearl black and metallic grey, or pearl black and candy red.

● The GSX-R600W was introduced in December 1997. Internal engine modifications included reshaped inlet ports and waisted inlet valves to enhance the airflow efficiency in conjunction with the increased size of the air filter housing and lengthened carburettor inlet funnels. The exhaust downpipes were lengthened and the silencer was enlarged in diameter to reduce exhaust pressure.

● An adjustable compression damping control was added to the front forks, the front discs were made thicker to avoid warping under heavy braking and the rear sprocket increased one tooth in size to improve acceleration.

● The GSX-R600W was available in pearl white and deep blue, metallic charcoal and silver, or candy orange and black.

● The GSX-R600X was introduced in November 1998. Minor detail changes included modifications to the cam chain adjuster, clutch friction plates and engine oil cooler. The bike was available in pearl white and deep blue, candy black or pearl yellow.

● The GSX-R600Y was introduced in November 1999. Minor detail changes were made to the starter motor and a security plate was fitted to the engine oil filter. The colour schemes remained unchanged.

GSX-R750

● The GSX-R750T was introduced in January 1996.

● The engine was a liquid cooled four-cylinder with double overhead camshafts driven by chain from the right-hand end of the crankshaft. Carburettor air intake was via the SRAD (Suzuki Ram Air Direct) system. The crankcases were of the three-piece 'cassette' design with separate cylinder block.

● Drive was transmitted to the six-speed gearbox via a multi-plate clutch with single diaphragm spring, and to the rear wheel by chain and sprockets.

● PAIR (pulse air supply) and EVAP systems were fitted to California models

● The chassis comprised a twin-spar aluminium alloy frame, a bolt-on rear subframe and braced, box-section swingarm. Front suspension was by upside-down, three-way adjustable forks and rear suspension was by a rising rate, three-way adjustable mono-shock.

● Braking was by twin disc with six piston calipers at the front and a single disc with a twin piston caliper at the rear.

● The GSX-R750T was available in pearl white and deep blue, pearl black and metallic grey, or pearl black and candy red.

● The GSX-R750V was introduced in January 1997. Minor detail changes included revised dimensions for the lower, rear engine mounting bolt, adjusting bolt and locknut and upper rear suspension mounting bracket. The design of the piston oil jets was modified. The bike was available in pearl white and deep blue or pearl black, red and silver metallic.

● The GSX-R750W was introduced in November 1997. Engine tuning and revised transmission ratios combined with new fuel injection and digital-direct ignition systems to improve engine power delivery and acceleration. Cam timing and inlet valve lift were modified, the size of the air filter housing was increased and a flapper valve in the housing optimised throttle response and cylinder charging. The exhaust system was redesigned to improve mid-range power.

● The performance of the two-stage fuel injection system was controlled by an ECU (electronic control unit) which was fed information from various sensors on the machine. The ECU was able to calculate the ideal fuel/air mixture dependent on engine performance and data relating to intake air pressure, ambient temperature and altitude. The system had a self-diagnostic mode for problem analysis.

● Modifications to the chassis included a revised manufacturing process for the swingarm pivot section and a higher specification rear shock designed to maintain damping performance as internal oil temperature rose. A steering damper was fitted to the front forks and the front discs were made thicker to avoid warping under heavy braking.

● The GSX-R750W was available in pearl white and deep blue, pearl black and metallic grey, or pearl black and candy orange.

● The GSX-R750X was introduced in December 1998. Minor detail changes included modifications to the cam chain adjuster and engine oil cooler. The bike was available in pearl white and deep blue, candy black and pearl red or pearl black and metallic silver.

Performance data sourced from Motor Cycle News road test features. See the MCN website for up-to-date biking news.

MCN www.motorcyclenews.com

Performance data

Maximum power

GSX-R600	95 bhp (70.8 kW) @ 12,000 rpm
GSX-R750T and V	116 bhp (86.5 kW) @ 11,500 rpm
GSX-R750W and X	118 bhp (88 kW) @ 12,000 rpm

Maximum torque

GSX-R600	46.2 lbf ft (62.6 Nm) @ 9750 rpm
GSX-R750	56 lbf ft (75.9 Nm) @ 9700 rpm

Power-to-weight ratio (approximate)

GSX-R600	0.53 bhp per kg
GSX-R750T and V	0.63 bhp per kg
GSX-R750W and X	0.71 bhp per kg

Top speed

GSX-R600	158 mph (254 km/h)
GSX-R750T and V	168 mph (270 km/h)
GSX-R750W and X	174.8 mph (281 km/h)

Acceleration

GSX-R600
Time taken to cover a 1/4 mile from a standing start	11.0 secs
Terminal speed after 1/4 mile	118 mph (190 km/h)

GSX-R750T and V
Time taken to cover a 1/4 mile from a standing start	10.9 secs
Terminal speed after 1/4 mile	123 mph (198 km/h)

GSX-R750W and X
Time taken to cover a 1/4 mile from a standing start	10.5 secs
Terminal speed after 1/4 mile	132.5 mph (212 km/h)

Average fuel consumption

Miles per gallon, Miles per litre, Litres per 100 km

GSX-R600	36 mpg, 7.9 mpl, 7.8 l/100 km
GSX-R750T and V	33 mpg, 7.3 mpl, 8.5 l/100 km
GSX-R750W and X	35 mpg, 7.7 mpl, 8.1 l/100 km
Fuel tank capacity (all models)	18 litres (3.96 Imp gal)

Fuel tank range

GSX-R600	142 miles (228 km)
GSX-R750T and V	130 miles (209 km)
GSX-R750W and X	138 miles (222 km)

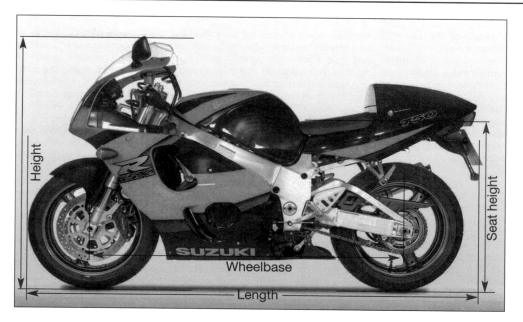

Bike spec

Weights and dimensions

Wheelbase
GSX-R600V . . . . .1390 mm
GSX-R600W, X and Y . . . . .1385 mm
GSX-R750T and V . . . . .1400 mm
GSX-R750 W and X . . . . .1395 mm

Overall length
GSX-R600V, W, X and Y . . . . .2065 mm
GSX-R750T and V . . . . .2055 mm
GSX-R750W and X . . . . .2065 mm

Overall height
GSX-R600V . . . . .1135 mm
GSX-R600W, X and Y . . . . .1165 mm
GSX-R750T and V . . . . .1135 mm
GSX-R750W and X . . . . .1165 mm

Overall width . . . . .720 mm
Seat height . . . . .830 mm
Ground clearance . . . . .130 mm

Dry weight
GSX-R600 (UK and US models) . . . . .174 kg
GSX-R600 (California model) . . . . .175 kg
GSX-R750 (UK and US models) . . . . .179 kg
GSX-R750 (California model) . . . . .180 kg

Engine

Type . . . . .Liquid cooled, in-line 4-cylinder

Capacity
GSX-R600 . . . . .600 cc
GSX-R750 . . . . .749 cc

Bore
GSX-R600 . . . . .65.5 mm
GSX-R750 . . . . .72 mm

Stroke
GSX-R600 . . . . .44.5 mm
GSX-R750 . . . . .46.0 mm

Compression ratio
GSX-R600 . . . . .12.0:1
GSX-R750 . . . . .11.8:1

Camshafts . . . . .DOHC, chain driven
Valves . . . . .4 valves per cylinder

Fuel system

GSX-R600 .4 x Mikuni BDSR36 carburettors
GSX-R750
GSX-R750T and V models . . . . .4 x Mikuni BDSR39 carburettors
GSX-R750W and X models .Fuel injection

Clutch .Wet multi-plate, hydraulically operated
Transmission . . . . .6 speed constant mesh

Final drive
Chain
GSX-R600 .RK 525SMOZ2 (108 links)
GSX-R750T and V . . . . .RK 50MFOZ1 (108 links)
GSX-R750W and X . . . . .RK 525ROZ2 (108 links)
Sprockets
GSX-R600X and Y . . . . .16 tooth front/45 tooth rear
GSX-R600V and W . . . . .16 tooth front/46 tooth rear
GSX-R750T and V . . . . .16 tooth front/43 tooth rear
GSX-R750W and X . . . . .16 tooth front/44 tooth rear

Chassis

Type . . . . .Twin spar, aluminium alloy
Rake . . . . .24.0°
Trail . . . . .96.0 mm

Front suspension
GSX-R600 . . . . .Adjustable telescopic forks
GSX-R750 . . . . .Adjustable upside-down forks
Travel . . . . .120 mm
Adjustments . .Spring pre-load, compression and rebound damping

Rear suspension
Type . . . . .Rising rate with monoshock
Wheel travel . . . . .133 mm
Adjustments . .Spring pre-load, compression and rebound damping

Tyre sizes
Front . . . . .120/70 ZR 17 58W
Rear
GSX-R600 . . . . .180/55 ZR 17 73W
GSX-R750 . . . . .190/50 ZR 17 73W

Brakes
Front
GSX-R600 . . . .2 x 320 mm discs with Tokico four-piston calipers
GSX-R750 . . . . .2 x 285 mm discs with Tokico six-piston calipers
Rear . . . . .1 x 220 mm disc with two-piston caliper

Professional mechanics are trained in safe working procedures. However enthusiastic you may be about getting on with the job at hand, take the time to ensure that your safety is not put at risk. A moment's lack of attention can result in an accident, as can failure to observe simple precautions.

There will always be new ways of having accidents, and the following is not a comprehensive list of all dangers; it is intended rather to make you aware of the risks and to encourage a safe approach to all work you carry out on your bike.

Asbestos

● Certain friction, insulating, sealing and other products - such as brake pads, clutch linings, gaskets, etc. - contain asbestos. Extreme care must be taken to avoid inhalation of dust from such products since it is hazardous to health. If in doubt, assume that they do contain asbestos.

Fire

● Remember at all times that petrol is highly flammable. Never smoke or have any kind of naked flame around, when working on the vehicle. But the risk does not end there - a spark caused by an electrical short-circuit, by two metal surfaces contacting each other, by careless use of tools, or even by static electricity built up in your body under certain conditions, can ignite petrol vapour, which in a confined space is highly explosive. Never use petrol as a cleaning solvent. Use an approved safety solvent.

● Always disconnect the battery earth terminal before working on any part of the fuel or electrical system, and never risk spilling fuel on to a hot engine or exhaust.

● It is recommended that a fire extinguisher of a type suitable for fuel and electrical fires is kept handy in the garage or workplace at all times. Never try to extinguish a fuel or electrical fire with water.

Fumes

● Certain fumes are highly toxic and can quickly cause unconsciousness and even death if inhaled to any extent. Petrol vapour comes into this category, as do the vapours from certain solvents such as trichloroethylene. Any draining or pouring of such volatile fluids should be done in a well ventilated area.

● When using cleaning fluids and solvents, read the instructions carefully. Never use materials from unmarked containers - they may give off poisonous vapours.

● Never run the engine of a motor vehicle in an enclosed space such as a garage. Exhaust fumes contain carbon monoxide which is extremely poisonous; if you need to run the engine, always do so in the open air or at least have the rear of the vehicle outside the workplace.

The battery

● Never cause a spark, or allow a naked light near the vehicle's battery. It will normally be giving off a certain amount of hydrogen gas, which is highly explosive.

● Always disconnect the battery ground (earth) terminal before working on the fuel or electrical systems (except where noted).

● If possible, loosen the filler plugs or cover when charging the battery from an external source. Do not charge at an excessive rate or the battery may burst.

● Take care when topping up, cleaning or carrying the battery. The acid electrolyte, evenwhen diluted, is very corrosive and should not be allowed to contact the eyes or skin. Always wear rubber gloves and goggles or a face shield. If you ever need to prepare electrolyte yourself, always add the acid slowly to the water; never add the water to the acid.

Electricity

● When using an electric power tool, inspection light etc., always ensure that the appliance is correctly connected to its plug and that, where necessary, it is properly grounded (earthed). Do not use such appliances in damp conditions and, again, beware of creating a spark or applying excessive heat in the vicinity of fuel or fuel vapour. Also ensure that the appliances meet national safety standards.

● A severe electric shock can result from touching certain parts of the electrical system, such as the spark plug wires (HT leads), when the engine is running or being cranked, particularly if components are damp or the insulation is defective. Where an electronic ignition system is used, the secondary (HT) voltage is much higher and could prove fatal.

Remember...

✗ **Don't** start the engine without first ascertaining that the transmission is in neutral.

✗ **Don't** suddenly remove the pressure cap from a hot cooling system - cover it with a cloth and release the pressure gradually first, or you may get scalded by escaping coolant.

✗ **Don't** attempt to drain oil until you are sure it has cooled sufficiently to avoid scalding you.

✗ **Don't** grasp any part of the engine or exhaust system without first ascertaining that it is cool enough not to burn you.

✗ **Don't** allow brake fluid or antifreeze to contact the machine's paintwork or plastic components.

✗ **Don't** siphon toxic liquids such as fuel, hydraulic fluid or antifreeze by mouth, or allow them to remain on your skin.

✗ **Don't** inhale dust - it may be injurious to health (see Asbestos heading).

✗ **Don't** allow any spilled oil or grease to remain on the floor - wipe it up right away, before someone slips on it.

✗ **Don't** use ill-fitting spanners or other tools which may slip and cause injury.

✗ **Don't** lift a heavy component which may be beyond your capability - get assistance.

✗ **Don't** rush to finish a job or take unverified short cuts.

✗ **Don't** allow children or animals in or around an unattended vehicle.

✗ **Don't** inflate a tyre above the recommended pressure. Apart from overstressing the carcass, in extreme cases the tyre may blow off forcibly.

✔ **Do** ensure that the machine is supported securely at all times. This is especially important when the machine is blocked up to aid wheel or fork removal.

✔ **Do** take care when attempting to loosen a stubborn nut or bolt. It is generally better to pull on a spanner, rather than push, so that if you slip, you fall away from the machine rather than onto it.

✔ **Do** wear eye protection when using power tools such as drill, sander, bench grinder etc.

✔ **Do** use a barrier cream on your hands prior to undertaking dirty jobs - it will protect your skin from infection as well as making the dirt easier to remove afterwards; but make sure your hands aren't left slippery. Note that long-term contact with used engine oil can be a health hazard.

✔ **Do** keep loose clothing (cuffs, ties etc. and long hair) well out of the way of moving mechanical parts.

✔ **Do** remove rings, wristwatch etc., before working on the vehicle - especially the electrical system.

✔ **Do** keep your work area tidy - it is only too easy to fall over articles left lying around.

✔ **Do** exercise caution when compressing springs for removal or installation. Ensure that the tension is applied and released in a controlled manner, using suitable tools which preclude the possibility of the spring escaping violently.

✔ **Do** ensure that any lifting tackle used has a safe working load rating adequate for the job.

✔ **Do** get someone to check periodically that all is well, when working alone on the vehicle.

✔ **Do** carry out work in a logical sequence and check that everything is correctly assembled and tightened afterwards.

✔ **Do** remember that your vehicle's safety affects that of yourself and others. If in doubt on any point, get professional advice.

● If in spite of following these precautions, you are unfortunate enough to injure yourself, seek medical attention as soon as possible.

Identifying model years

The procedures in this manual identify the bikes by model code. The model code (eg GSX-R**V**) is printed on the identification plate or label, which is located on the right-hand frame spar close to the steering head. The model code and production year can also be determined from the frame serial numbers as follows:

UK models

Model, code and year	Frame number	Carburettor number
GSX-R600V (1997)	JS1AD111400100001 - on	34EO
GSX-R600W (1998)	JS1AD111400101736 - on	34E6
GSX-R600X (1999)	JS1AD111400103985 - on	34E6
GSX-R600Y (2000)	JS1AD111400106281 - on	34E6
GSX-R750T (1996)	JS1GR7DA000500001 - on	33EO
GSX-R750V (1997)	JS1GR7DA000504678 - on	33EO
GSX-R750W (1998)	JS1GR7DA000507570 - on	Not applicable
GSX-R750X (1999)	JS1GR7DA000511803 - on	Not applicable

US models

Model, code and year	Frame number	Carburettor number
GSX-R600V (1997)	JS1GN78A V2100001 - on	34E1/34E3 (US/CALIF)
GSX-R600W (1998)	JS1GN78A W2100001 - on	34E7/34E9 (US/CALIF)
GSX-R600X (1999)	JS1GN78A X2100001 - on	34EC/34EE (US/CALIF)
GSX-R600Y (2000)	JS1GN78A Y2100001 - on	34EC/34EE (US/CALIF)
GSX-R750T (1996)	JS1GR7DA T2100001 - on	33E1/33E7 (US/CALIF)
GSX-R750V (1997)	JS1GR7DA V2100001 - on	33E1/33E7 (US/CALIF)
GSX-R750W (1998)	JS1GR7DA W2100001 - on	Not applicable
GSX-R750X (1999)	JS1GR7DA X2100001 - on	Not applicable

The frame serial number or VIN (Vehicle Identification Number) is stamped into the right-hand side of the steering head. The engine number is stamped into the back of the crankcase. Both of these numbers should be recorded and kept in a safe place so they can be furnished to law enforcement officials in the event of a theft. Where applicable, the carburettor number is stamped into the body of each carburettor.

The frame serial number, engine serial number and carburettor identification number should also be kept in a handy place (such as with your driving licence) so they are always available when purchasing or ordering parts for your machine.

Buying spare parts

Once you have found all the identification numbers, record them for reference when buying parts. Since the manufacturers change specifications, parts and vendors (companies that manufacture various components on the machine), providing the ID numbers is the only way to be reasonably sure that you are buying the correct parts.

Whenever possible, take the worn part to the dealer so direct comparison with the new component can be made. Along the trail from the manufacturer to the parts shelf, there are numerous places that the part can end up with the wrong number or be listed incorrectly.

The two places to purchase new parts for your motorcycle – the accessory store and the franchised dealer – differ in the type of parts they carry. While dealers can obtain virtually every part for your motorcycle, the accessory dealer is usually limited to normal high wear items such as shock absorbers, spark plugs, various engine gaskets, cables, chains, brake parts, etc. Rarely will an accessory outlet have major suspension components, cylinders, transmission gears, or cases.

Used parts can be obtained for roughly half the price of new ones, but you can't always be sure of what you're getting. Once again, take your worn part to the breaker (wrecking yard) for direct comparison.

Whether buying new, used or rebuilt parts, the best course is to deal directly with someone who specialises in parts for your particular make.

The engine number is stamped into the back of the crankcase

The identification plate or label is on the right-hand frame spar close to the steering head

The frame number is stamped on the right-hand side of the steering head

Note: *The daily (pre-ride) checks outlined in the owner's manual covers those items which should be inspected on a daily basis.*

1 Engine/transmission oil level check

Before you start:
✔ Start the engine and allow it to reach normal operating temperature.
Caution: Do not run the engine in an enclosed space such as a garage or workshop.
✔ Stop the engine and support the motorcycle in an upright position, using an auxiliary stand if required. Allow it to stand undisturbed for a few minutes to allow the oil level to stabilise. Make sure the motorcycle is on level ground.

Bike care:
● If you have to add oil frequently, you should check whether you have any oil leaks. If there is no sign of oil leakage from the joints and gaskets the engine could be burning oil (see *Fault Finding*).

The correct oil
● Modern, high-revving engines place great demands on their oil. It is very important that the correct oil for your bike is used.
● Always top up with a good quality oil of the specified type and viscosity and do not overfill the engine.

Oil type	API grade SF or SG (minimum) motor oil
Oil viscosity	SAE 10W40

1 Wipe the oil level window in the clutch cover so that it is clean.

2 With the motorcycle held vertical, the oil level should lie between the 'F' and 'L' lines.

3 If the level is below the 'L' line, remove the filler cap from the top of the clutch cover.

4 Top the engine up with the recommended grade and type of oil, to bring the level up to the 'F' line on the window. Do not overfill.

2 Coolant level check

 Warning: DO NOT remove the radiator pressure cap to add coolant. Topping up is done via the coolant reservoir tank filler. DO NOT leave open containers of coolant about, as it is poisonous.

Before you start:
✔ Make sure you have a supply of coolant available (a mixture of 50% distilled water and 50% corrosion inhibited ethylene glycol anti-freeze is needed).

✔ Support the motorcycle in an upright position, using an auxiliary stand if required, whilst checking the level. Make sure the motorcycle is on level ground.

Bike care:
● Use only the specified coolant mixture. It is important that anti-freeze is used in the system all year round, and not just in the winter. Do not top the system up using only water, as the system will become too diluted.

● Do not overfill the reservoir tank. If the coolant is significantly above the 'F' level line at any time, the surplus should be siphoned or drained off to prevent the possibility of it being expelled out of the overflow hose.

● If the coolant level falls steadily, check the system for leaks (see Chapter 1). If no leaks are found and the level continues to fall, it is recommended that the machine is taken to a Suzuki dealer for a pressure test.

1 The coolant reservoir is located on the inside of the left-hand fairing side panel. The coolant 'F' and 'L' level lines (arrowed) are on the back of the reservoir.

2 If the coolant level is not between the 'F' and 'L' lines, remove the left-hand fairing side panel (see Chapter 8), then remove the reservoir filler cap.

3 Top the coolant level up with the recommended coolant mixture, using a funnel to avoid spillage. Fit the cap securely, then install the fairing side panel.

3 Brake fluid level checks

Warning: Brake hydraulic fluid can harm your eyes and damage painted surfaces, so use extreme caution when handling and pouring it and cover surrounding surfaces with rag. Do not use fluid that has been standing open for some time, as it absorbs moisture from the air which can cause a dangerous loss of braking effectiveness.

Before you start:

✔ Support the motorcycle in an upright position, using an auxiliary stand if required, and turn the handlebars until the top of the front brake master cylinder is as level as possible.

✔ The rear master cylinder reservoir is located behind the seat cowling on the right-hand side of the machine.

✔ If topping up is necessary, make sure you have the correct hydraulic fluid. DOT 4 is recommended.

✔ Wrap a rag around the reservoir being worked on to ensure that any spillage does not come into contact with painted surfaces.

✔ Access to the rear reservoir cap screws is restricted by the seat cowling. Remove the cowling to access the screws (see Chapter 8).

Bike care:

● The fluid in the front and rear brake master cylinder reservoirs will drop slightly as the brake pads wear down.

● If any fluid reservoir requires repeated topping-up this is an indication of an hydraulic leak somewhere in the system, which should be investigated immediately.

● Check for signs of fluid leakage from the hydraulic hoses and components – if found, rectify immediately.

● Check the operation of both brakes before taking the machine on the road; if there is evidence of air in the system (spongy feel to lever or pedal), it must be bled as described in Chapter 7.

1 The front brake fluid level is visible through the reservoir body – it must be between the UPPER and LOWER level lines.

2 If the level is below the LOWER level line, remove the reservoir cap clamp screw (arrowed), then unscrew the cap and remove the diaphragm plate and the diaphragm.

3 Top up with new clean DOT 4 brake fluid, until the level is just below the UPPER level line. Do not overfill the reservoir, and take care to avoid spills (see **Warning** above).

4 Ensure that the diaphragm is correctly seated before installing the plate and cap. Tighten the cap and the clamp screw securely.

5 The rear brake fluid level is visible by looking through the translucent body of the reservoir - the fluid level must be between the UPPER and LOWER level lines.

6 If the level is below the LOWER level line, remove the seat cowling (see Chapter 8). Unscrew the two bolts securing the fuel tank bracket to the frame and swing the bracket upwards.

7 Unscrew the reservoir cover screws and remove the cover and diaphragm.

8 Top up with new clean DOT 4 brake fluid, until the level is just below the UPPER level line. Do not overfill the reservoir, and take care to avoid spills (see **Warning** above).

9 Ensure that the diaphragm is correctly seated before installing the cover. Tighten the cover screws securely, then install the tank bracket and seat cowling (see Chapter 8).

4 Tyre checks

The correct pressures

● The tyres must be checked when **cold**, not immediately after riding. Note that low tyre pressures may cause the tyre to slip on the rim or come off. High tyre pressures will cause abnormal tread wear and unsafe handling.

● Use an accurate pressure gauge.

● Proper air pressure will increase tyre life and provide maximum stability and ride comfort.

Tyre pressures (cold)	
Front	36 psi (2.50 Bar)
Rear	36 psi (2.50 Bar)

Tyre care

● Check the tyres carefully for cuts, tears, embedded nails or other sharp objects and excessive wear. Operation of the motorcycle with excessively worn tyres is extremely hazardous, as traction and handling are directly affected.

● Check the condition of the tyre valve and ensure the dust cap is in place.

● Pick out any stones or nails which may have become embedded in the tyre tread. If left, they will eventually penetrate through the casing and cause a puncture.

● If tyre damage is apparent, or unexplained loss of pressure is experienced, seek the advice of a tyre fitting specialist without delay.

1 Check the tyre pressures when the tyres are **cold** and keep them properly inflated.

2 Measure tread depth at the centre of the tyre using a tread depth gauge.

3 Tyre tread wear indicator bar and its location marking (usually either an arrow, a triangle or the letters TWI) on the sidewall (arrowed).

Tyre tread depth

● At the time of writing UK law requires that tread depth must be at least 1 mm over 3/4 of the tread breadth all the way around the tyre, with no bald patches. Many riders, however, consider 2 mm tread depth minimum to be a safer limit. The manufacturer's recommended minimum tread depth is given below.

● Many tyres now incorporate wear indicators in the tread. Identify the triangular pointer or 'TWI' mark on the tyre sidewall to locate the indicator bar and renew the tyre if the tread has worn down to the bar.

Minimum tyre tread depths	
Front	1.6 mm
Rear	2.0 mm

5 Suspension, steering and final drive checks

Drive chain
● Check that the drive chain slack isn't excessive, adjust if necessary (see Chapter 1).
● If the chain looks dry, lubricate it (see Chapter 1).

Suspension and Steering
● Check that the front and rear suspension operates smoothly without binding.
● Check that the suspension is adjusted as required.

● Check that the steering moves smoothly from lock-to-lock.

6 Legal and safety checks

Lighting and signalling
● Take a minute to check that the headlight, taillight, brake light, instrument lights and turn signals all work correctly.
● Check that the horn sounds when the switch is operated.
● A working speedometer graduated in mph is a statutory requirement in the UK.

Safety
● Check that the throttle grip rotates smoothly and snaps shut when released, in all steering positions. Also check for the correct amount of freeplay (see Chapter 1).
● Check that the engine shuts off when the kill switch is operated.
● Check that sidestand return spring holds the stand securely up when retracted.

Fuel
● This may seem obvious, but check that you have enough fuel to complete your journey. If you notice signs of fuel leakage, rectify the cause immediately.
● Ensure you use the correct grade unleaded fuel – see Chapter 4 Specifications.

Chapter 1
Routine maintenance and Servicing

Contents

Degrees of difficulty

| Easy, suitable for novice with little experience | | Fairly easy, suitable for beginner with some experience | | Fairly difficult, suitable for competent DIY mechanic | | Difficult, suitable for experienced DIY mechanic | | Very difficult, suitable for expert DIY or professional |

Specifications

Engine/transmission

Valve clearances (COLD engine)
  Inlet valves . . . . 0.10 to 0.20 mm
  Exhaust valves . . . . 0.20 to 0.30 mm
Spark plugs
  Type
    Standard . . . . NGK CR9E or Nippondenso U27ESR-N
    For cold climate (below 5°C) . . . . NGK CR8E or Nippondenso U24ESR-N
    For extended high speed riding . . . . NGK CR10E or Nippondenso U31ESR-N
  Electrode gap . . . . 0.7 to 0.8 mm
Engine idle speed
  UK GSX-R600 models . . . . 1200 ± 100 rpm
  US GSX-R600 models . . . . 1300 ± 100 rpm
  All GSX-R750 models . . . . 1200 ± 100 rpm
Clutch release mechanism screw (see text) . . . . 1/4 turn out
Cylinder compression
  Standard . . . . 156 to 213 psi (11 to 15 Bar)*
  Minimum . . . . 128 psi (9 Bar)*
  Maximum difference between cylinders . . . . 28 psi (2 Bar)*
Oil pressure (with engine warm) . . . . 28 to 71 psi (2.0 to 5.0 Bar) at 3000 rpm, oil at 60°C

Note: If all cylinders record less than the standard (even if they are above the minimum), or if the difference between any two cylinders is greater than the maximum, or if any one cylinder is less than the minimum, the engine should be overhauled.

Frame and cycle parts

Drive chain	
Freeplay	20 to 30 mm
Stretch limit (21 pin length – see text)	319.4 mm
Fuel level	
GSX-R600	15.5 ± 0.5 mm
GSX-R750T and V	15.7 ± 0.5 mm
Freeplay adjustments	
Clutch cable	
GSX-R600 models	10 to 15 mm
GSX-R750 models	3 to 13 mm
Throttle cables	
GSX-R600V models, GSX-R750T and V models	
Accelerator cable	0.5 to 1.0 mm
Decelerator cable	0.5 to 1.0 mm
GSX-R600W and X models, GSX-R750W and X models	
Accelerator cable	2 to 4 mm
Decelerator cable	zero freeplay (see text)
Rear brake pedal height	55 mm
Tyre pressures (cold) and tread depth	see *Daily (pre-ride) checks*

Recommended lubricants and fluids

Drive chain lubricant	Heavy engine oil (40 or 50 weight), or aerosol chain lubricant suitable for O-ring chains
Engine/transmission oil type	API grade SF or SG (minimum) motor oil
Engine/transmission oil viscosity	SAE 10W40
Engine/transmission oil capacity	
Oil change	2.6 litres
Oil and filter change	2.8 litres
Following engine overhaul – dry engine, new filter	3.5 litres
Coolant type	50% distilled water, 50% corrosion inhibited ethylene glycol anti-freeze
Coolant capacity	2.55 litres
Brake fluid	DOT 4

Miscellaneous

Steering head bearings	Lithium-based multi-purpose grease
Wheel bearings (unsealed)	Lithium-based multi-purpose grease
Swingarm pivot bearings	Lithium-based multi-purpose grease
Suspension linkage bearings	Lithium-based multi-purpose grease
Bearing seal lips	Lithium-based multi-purpose grease
Gearchange lever/rear brake pedal/footrest pivots	Lithium-based multi-purpose grease
Front brake lever and clutch lever pivots	10W40 motor oil
Cables	Cable lubricant or 10W40 motor oil
Sidestand pivot and spring hook	Lithium-based multi-purpose grease
Throttle grip	Multi-purpose grease or dry film lubricant

Torque settings

Rear axle nut	100 Nm
Spark plugs	12 Nm
Engine/transmission oil drain plug	28 Nm
Steering stem nut	90 Nm
Fork clamp bolts	23 Nm
Exhaust downpipe clamp bolts	23 Nm
Silencer mounting bolts	23 Nm
Brake hose banjo bolts	23 Nm
Main oil gallery plug	40 Nm

Note: *Always perform the pre-ride inspection at every maintenance interval (in addition to the procedures listed). The intervals listed below are the intervals recommended by the manufacturer for each particular operation during the model years covered in this manual. Your owner's manual may have different intervals for your model.*

Daily (pre-ride)

☐ See *'Daily (pre-ride) checks'* at the beginning of this manual.

After the initial 600 miles (1000 km)

Note: *This check is usually performed by a Suzuki dealer after the first 600 miles (1000 km) from new. Thereafter, maintenance is carried out according to the following intervals of the schedule.*

Every 600 miles (1000 km)

☐ Check, adjust and lubricate the drive chain (Section 1)

Every 4000 miles (6000 km) or 6 months

Carry out all the items under the Daily (pre-ride) checks and the 600 mile (1000 km) check, plus the following:

☐ Clean the air filter element (Section 2)
☐ Check the spark plugs (Section 3)
☐ Check the fuel hoses, EVAP hoses (California models), and fuel system components (Section 4)
☐ Change the engine oil (Section 5)
☐ Check and adjust the engine idle speed (Section 6)
☐ Check throttle/choke cable operation and freeplay (Section 7)
☐ Check the operation of the clutch (Section 8)
☐ Check the cooling system (Section 9)
☐ Check for drive chain wear and stretch (Section 10)
☐ Check the brake pads for wear (Section 11)
☐ Check the operation of the brakes, and for fluid leakage (Section 12)
☐ Check the tyre and wheel condition, and the tyre tread depth (Section 13)
☐ Check the tightness of all nuts and bolts (Section 14)
☐ Check and lubricate the sidestand, lever pivots and cables (Section 15)

Every 7500 miles (12,000 km) or 12 months

Carry out all the items under the 4000 mile (6000 km) check, plus the following:

☐ Renew the spark plugs (Section 16)
☐ Check carburettor or throttle body synchronisation (Section 17)
☐ Check the steering head bearing freeplay (Section 18)
☐ Check the front and rear suspension (Section 19)
☐ Check the tightness of the exhaust system bolts (Section 20)

Every 11,000 miles (18,000 km) or 18 months

Carry out all the items under the 4000 mile (6000 km) check, plus the following:

☐ Renew the air filter element (Section 21)
☐ Change the engine oil and renew the oil filter (Section 22)

Every 15,000 miles (24,000 km) or 24 months

Carry out all the items under the 7500 mile (12,000 km) check, plus the following:

☐ Check the valve clearances (Section 23)

Every two years

☐ Change the brake fluid (Section 24)
☐ Change the coolant (Section 25)

Every four years

☐ Renew the brake hoses (Section 26)
☐ Renew the fuel hoses and EVAP hoses (California models) (Section 27)

Non-scheduled maintenance

☐ Check the headlight aim (Section 28)
☐ Check the wheel bearings (Section 29)
☐ Change the front fork oil (Section 30)
☐ Check the cylinder compression (Section 31)
☐ Check the engine oil pressure (Section 32)
☐ Re-grease the steering head bearings (Section 33)
☐ Re-grease the swingarm and suspension linkage bearings (Section 34)
☐ Renew the brake master cylinder and caliper seals (Section 35)

Component locations – right-hand side

1 Rear brake fluid reservoir
2 Front brake fluid reservoir
3 Radiator pressure cap
4 Engine/transmission oil filter
5 Engine/transmission oil drain plug
6 Engine/transmission oil level sightglass
7 Engine/transmission oil filler
8 Rear brake pedal height adjuster

Component locations – left-hand side

1 Clutch cable upper adjuster
2 Steering head bearing adjuster
3 Air filter

4 Idle speed adjuster
5 Fuel filter
6 Battery

7 Clutch cable lower adjuster
8 Clutch release mechanism adjuster
9 Coolant reservoir

1 This Chapter is designed to help the home mechanic maintain his/her motorcycle for safety, economy, long life and peak performance.
2 Deciding where to start or plug into the routine maintenance schedule depends on several factors. If the warranty period on your motorcycle has just expired, and if it has been maintained according to the warranty standards, you may want to pick up routine maintenance as it coincides with the next mileage or calendar interval. If you have owned the machine for some time but have never performed any maintenance on it, then you may want to start at the nearest interval and include some additional procedures to ensure that nothing important is overlooked. If you have just had a major engine overhaul, then you may want to start the maintenance routine from the beginning. If you have a used machine and have no knowledge of its history or maintenance record, you may desire to combine all the checks into one large service initially and then settle into the maintenance schedule prescribed.

3 Before beginning any maintenance or repair, the machine should be cleaned thoroughly, especially around the oil filter, spark plugs, valve cover, side panels, carburettors, etc. Cleaning will help ensure that dirt does not contaminate the engine and will allow you to detect wear and damage that could otherwise easily go unnoticed.
4 Certain maintenance information is sometimes printed on decals attached to the motorcycle. If the information on the decals differs from that included here, use the information on the decal.

Every 600 miles (1000 km)

---

1   Drive chain – check, adjustment, cleaning and lubrication

Check

1 A neglected drive chain won't last long and can quickly damage the sprockets. Routine chain adjustment and lubrication isn't difficult and will ensure maximum chain and sprocket life.
2 To check the chain, place the bike on its sidestand and shift the transmission

1.3 Measuring drive chain freeplay

into neutral. Make sure the ignition switch is OFF.
3 Push up on the bottom run of the chain and measure the slack midway between the two sprockets, then compare your measurement to that listed in this Chapter's Specifications **(see illustration)**. As the chain stretches with wear, adjustment will periodically be necessary (see below). Since the chain will rarely wear evenly, roll the bike forwards so that another section of chain can be checked; do this several times to check the entire length of chain.
4 In some cases where lubrication has been neglected, corrosion and galling may cause the links to bind and kink, which effectively shortens the chain's length. Such links should be thoroughly cleaned and worked free. If the chain is tight between the sprockets, rusty or kinked, it's time to fit a new one (see Chapter 6). If you find a tight area, mark it with felt pen or paint, and repeat the measurement after the bike has been ridden. If the chain's still tight in the same area, it may be damaged or worn. Because a tight or kinked chain can damage the transmission output shaft bearing, it's a good idea to renew it.
Caution: If the machine is ridden with excessive slack in the drive chain, the chain could contact the frame and swingarm, causing severe damage.

5 Check the entire length of the chain for damaged rollers, loose links and pins, and missing O-rings. Fit a new chain if damage is found. **Note:** *Never install a new chain on old sprockets, and never use the old chain if you install new sprockets – renew the chain and sprockets as a set.*

Adjustment

6 Rotate the rear wheel until the chain is positioned with the tightest point at the centre of its bottom run. If available, raise the rear wheel off the ground using an auxiliary stand or support.
7 On US models, remove the split pin from the rear axle nut.
8 Slacken the rear axle nut **(see illustration)**.
9 Slacken the adjuster locknut on each side of the swingarm, then turn the adjuster bolts evenly until the amount of freeplay specified at the beginning of the Chapter is obtained at the centre of the bottom run of the chain **(see illustration)**. Following chain adjustment, check that the back of each chain adjuster block is in the same position in relation to the marks on the swingarm **(see illustration)**. It is important each adjuster aligns with the same notch; if not, the rear wheel will be out of alignment with the front.
10 Tighten the axle nut to the torque setting specified at the beginning of the Chapter **(see**

1.8 Remove the split pin (US models), then slacken the axle nut (arrowed)

1.9a Slacken the locknut (A) and turn the adjuster bolt (B) as required

1.9b Make sure the blocks are in the same position relative to the notches on each side of the swingarm

illustration). Tighten the chain adjuster locknuts securely **(see illustration 1.9a)**. On US models, fit a new split pin through the axle nut and bend the ends of the pin securely.

Cleaning and lubrication

11 If required, wash the chain in paraffin (kerosene), then wipe it off and allow it to dry, using compressed air if available. If the chain is excessively dirty it should be removed from the machine and allowed to soak in the paraffin (see Chapter 6).
Caution: Don't use petrol (gasoline), solvent or other cleaning fluids which might damage the internal sealing properties of the chain. Don't use high-pressure water. The entire process shouldn't take longer than ten minutes – if it does, the O-rings in the chain rollers could be damaged.
12 For routine lubrication, the best time to lubricate the chain is after the motorcycle has been ridden. When the chain is warm, the lubricant will penetrate the joints between the

1.10 Tighten the axle nut to the specified torque

side plates better than when cold. **Note:** *Suzuki specifies heavy engine oil (40 or 50 weight) or an aerosol drive chain lubricant suitable for O-ring chains only; do not use a chain lube which may contain solvents that could damage the O-rings.* Apply the lubricant to the area where the side plates overlap – not the middle of the rollers **(see illustration)**.

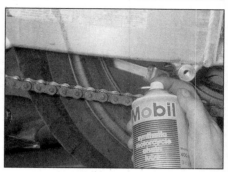

1.12 Applying an aerosol chain lubricant

> **HAYNES HiNT**
> *Apply the lubricant to the top of the lower chain run, so centrifugal force will work the oil into the chain when the bike is moving. After applying the lubricant, let it soak in a few minutes before wiping off any excess.*

Every 4000 miles (6000 km) or 6 months

2 Air filter – cleaning

Caution: If the machine is continually ridden in dusty conditions, the filter should be cleaned more frequently.
1 Raise the fuel tank (see Chapter 4).
2 Remove the air filter cover screws and lift off the cover **(see illustration)**. Withdraw the filter from the housing **(see illustration)**.
3 Tap the filter on a hard surface to dislodge any dirt. If compressed air is available, use it to clean the element, directing the air from the outside **(see illustration)**. If the element is torn or extremely dirty, install a new one.
4 Install the filter by reversing the removal procedure. Make sure the filter is properly seated, and the O-ring around the underside of the cover is located in its groove. When fitting the cover, locate the tabs at the back in the slots in the housing **(see illustration)**.
5 Remove the drain cover(s) from the bottom of the air filter housing. Allow any fluid to drain, then install the cover(s).

3 Spark plug gaps – check and adjustment

1 Make sure your spark plug socket is the correct size before attempting to remove the plugs – a suitable one is supplied in the motorcycle's tool kit which is stored under the passenger seat. Make sure the ignition is switched OFF.

2 To access the spark plugs, remove the air filter housing (see Chapter 4).
3 Clean the area around the plug caps to prevent any dirt falling into the spark plug channels. Check that the cylinder location is

2.2a Remove the screws (arrowed) and the cover . . .

2.3 Clean the element using compressed air directed from the outside

marked on each plug lead or connector and mark them accordingly if not.
4 On GSX-R750T and V models, pull the spark plug cap off each spark plug.
5 On all other models, disconnect the ignition

2.2b . . . and lift out the filter

2.4 Locate the tabs on the back of the cover in the slots in the housing

3.5a Disconnect the wiring connector . . .

3.5b . . . then pull the coil/plug cap off the spark plug

3.6 Removing a spark plug using the tool supplied in the bike's toolkit

coil/plug cap wiring connectors **(see illustration)**. Pull the coil/cap off each spark plug **(see illustration)**.

6 Clean the area around the base of the plugs to prevent any dirt falling into the engine. Using either the plug removing tool supplied in the bike's toolkit or a deep socket type wrench, unscrew the plugs from the cylinder head **(see illustration)**. Lay each plug out in relation to its cylinder; if any plug shows up a problem it will then be easy to identify the troublesome cylinder.

7 Inspect the electrodes for wear. Both the centre and side electrodes should have square edges and the side electrodes should be of uniform thickness. Look for excessive deposits and evidence of a cracked or chipped insulator around the centre electrode. Compare your spark plugs to the colour spark plug reading chart at the end of this manual. Check the threads, the washer and the ceramic insulator body for cracks and other damage.

8 If the electrodes are not excessively worn, and if the deposits can be easily removed with a wire brush, the plugs can be re-gapped and re-used (if no cracks or chips are visible in the insulator). If in doubt concerning the condition of the plugs, install new ones – the expense is minimal.

9 Cleaning spark plugs by sandblasting is permitted, provided you clean the plugs with a high flash-point solvent afterwards.

10 Before installing the plugs, make sure they are the correct type and heat range and check the gap between the electrodes **(see illustrations)**. Compare the gap to that specified and adjust as necessary. If the gap must be adjusted, bend the side electrodes only and be very careful not to chip or crack the insulator nose **(see illustration)**. Make sure the washer is in place before installing each plug.

11 Since the cylinder head is made of aluminium, which is soft and easily damaged, thread the plugs into the head turning the tool by hand **(see illustration)**. Once the plugs are finger-tight, tighten them to the torque setting specified at the beginning of the Chapter. If a torque wrench is not available, tighten them an extra 1/4 to 1/2 turn. Do not over-tighten them.

> **HAYNES HINT**
> *As the plugs are quite recessed, slip a short length of hose over the end of the plug to use as a tool to thread it into place. The hose will grip the plug well enough to turn it, but will start to slip if the plug begins to cross-thread in the hole – this will prevent damaged threads.*

12 Reconnect the spark plug caps or coils/caps, making sure they are securely connected to the correct cylinder **(see illustration 3.5b)**. Where appropriate, connect the coil/cap wiring connectors **(see illustration 3.5a)**.

13 Install the air filter housing (see Chapter 4).

> **HAYNES HINT**
> *Stripped plug threads in the cylinder head can be repaired with a thread insert – see 'Tools and Workshop Tips' in the Reference section.*

4 Fuel system – check

> ⚠ *Warning: Petrol (gasoline) is extremely flammable, so take extra precautions when you work on any part of the fuel*

3.10a A wire type gauge is recommended to measure the spark plug electrode gap

3.10b A blade type feeler gauge can also be used

3.10c Adjust the electrode gap by bending the side electrode only, as indicated by the arrows

3.11 Thread the plug as far as possible by hand

4.2 Fuel valve mounting bolts (A) and assembly screws (B), fuel pump mounting bolts (C)

4.7 Check and clean the strainer (arrowed) as described

system. Don't smoke or allow open flames or bare light bulbs near the work area, and don't work in a garage where a natural gas-type appliance is present. If you spill any fuel on your skin, rinse it off immediately with soap and water. When you perform any kind of work on the fuel system, wear safety glasses and have a fire extinguisher suitable for a Class B type fire (flammable liquids) on hand.

Check

1 Raise the fuel tank (see Chapter 4) and check the tank, the fuel valve or pressure regulator, the fuel hoses, and on California models the EVAP system hoses (see Chapter 4), for signs of leakage, deterioration or damage; in particular check that there is no leakage from the fuel hoses. Renew any hoses which are cracked or deteriorated.

2 On GSX-R600 and GSX-R750T and V models, if the fuel valve is leaking from between it and the fuel pump mounting plate, tighten the mounting bolts **(see illustration)**. If leakage persists, remove the valve (see Chapter 4) and renew the O-ring. If the valve itself is leaking, tighten the assembly screws. If leakage persists, a new one must be fitted (see Chapter 4). If there is leakage from between the fuel pump mounting plate and the tank, tighten the mounting bolts. If leakage persists, remove the pump and fit a new gasket (see Chapter 4).

3 On GSX-R750W and X models, if there is leakage from between the fuel pump mounting plate and the tank, tighten the mounting bolts. If leakage persists, remove the pump and fit a new gasket (see Chapter 4).

4 If the carburettor gaskets are leaking, the carburettors should be disassembled and rebuilt using new gaskets and seals (see Chapter 4).

Filter renewal

5 Cleaning and/or renewal of the fuel strainer (GSX-R600 and GSX-R750T and V models) or

strainer and filter (GSX-R750W and X models) is advised after a particularly high mileage has been covered. It is also necessary if fuel starvation is suspected.

6 Remove the fuel pump (see Chapter 4).

7 On GSX-R600 and GSX-R750T and V models, clean the strainer and check it for holes **(see illustration)**. Fit a new one if any are found. Blow it through and dry it using compressed air, if available.

8 On GSX-R750W and X models, remove the screw securing the pump cover and remove it, noting how it fits. Before removing the filter, note which way up it fits and be sure to install the new one the same way round, as the direction of flow is important. Release the clamps securing the hoses to the filter and detach the hoses, then remove the screws securing the filter to the pump, noting how the slit in the bracket locates over the raised section on the mounting. Also clean the strainer and check it for holes. Fit a new one if any are found. Blow it through and dry it using compressed air, if available.

Fuel level check – GSX-R600 and GSX-R750T and V models,

9 A check can be made of the fuel level in the carburettors without the need to remove and dismantle the carburettors to measure the float height. To perform the check, a special tool is needed (Pt. No. 09913-10760), which consists of a calibrated gauge and some hose. Alternatively a short length of clear fuel hose and a ruler will suffice.

10 Make sure the bike is on level ground and place it on an auxiliary stand, but making sure both wheels are on the ground. Adjust the position of the bike as necessary until the carburettors are level. This is fundamental to the accuracy of the test. Use a spirit level to ensure accuracy.

11 Install the gauge or the fuel hose over the end of the drain nozzle on the bottom of the float chamber of the first carburettor **(see illustration 4.14)**. Unscrew the drain screw on

the bottom of the float chamber a couple of turns or until fuel flows into the hose. Make sure all air is bled from the hose by flicking it at the lowest point.

12 Start the engine and run it for a few minutes to ensure the float chambers are full of fuel, then leave it idling.

13 Hold the gauge or hose against the side of the carburettor so that it is vertical.

14 When the fuel level in the hose has settled, check that the distance between the fuel level and the point shown on the carburettor body is as specified at the beginning of the Chapter **(see illustration)**. Turn off the engine.

15 On completion, tighten the drain screw. Invert the gauge and drain the fuel into a suitable container, then remove the hose from the nozzle. Check the other carburettors in the same way.

16 If the fuel level in any carburettor is incorrect, remove the carburettors, then remove the float chambers and adjust the float height as described in Chapter 4.

4.14 Check that the distance between the top of the fuel in the tube and the point shown on the carburettors is as specified

5 Engine/transmission – oil change

⚠️ **Warning: Be careful when draining the oil, as the exhaust pipes, the engine, and the oil itself can cause severe burns.**

1 Consistent routine oil and filter changes are the single most important maintenance procedure you can perform on a motorcycle. The oil not only lubricates the internal parts of the engine, transmission and clutch, but it also acts as a coolant, a cleaner, a sealant, and a protectant. Because of these demands, the oil takes a terrific amount of abuse and should be renewed often with new oil of the recommended grade and type. Saving a little money on the difference in cost between a good oil and a cheap oil won't pay off if the engine is damaged. The oil filter should be changed with every second oil change (see Section 22).

2 Before changing the oil, warm up the engine so the oil will drain easily.

3 Put the motorcycle on its sidestand, and position a clean drain tray below the engine. Unscrew the oil filler cap from the clutch cover to vent the crankcase and to act as a reminder that there is no oil in the engine **(see illustration)**.

4 Next, unscrew the oil drain plug from the sump on the bottom of the engine and allow the oil to flow into the drain tray **(see illustrations)**. Hold the bike upright while the oil is draining. Check the condition of the sealing washer on the drain plug and discard it if it is in any way damaged or worn. To remove the washer from the plug, it will probably be necessary to cut it off **(see illustration)**.

HAYNES HINT *To help determine whether any abnormal or excessive engine wear is occurring, place a strainer between the engine and the drain tray so that any debris in the oil is filtered out and can be examined. If there are flakes or chips of metal in the oil, then something is drastically wrong internally and the engine will have to be disassembled for inspection and repair. If there are pieces of fibre-like material in the oil, the clutch is experiencing excessive wear and should be checked*

5 When the oil has completely drained, fit the plug into the sump, using a new sealing washer if necessary, and tighten it to the torque setting specified at the beginning of the Chapter **(see illustrations)**. Avoid overtightening, as damage to the sump will result.

6 Refill the engine to the proper level using the recommended type and amount of oil (see *Daily (pre-ride) checks*). With the motorcycle held vertical, the oil level should lie between the 'F' and 'L' lines on the inspection window (see *Daily (pre-ride) checks*). Install the filler cap **(see illustration 5.3)**. Start the engine and let it run for two or three minutes (make sure that the oil pressure warning display and the warning light extinguish after a few seconds). Shut it off, wait a few minutes, then check the oil level. If necessary, add more oil to bring the level up to the 'F' line on the window. Check around the drain plug for leaks.

HAYNES HINT *Saving a little money on the difference between good and cheap oils won't pay off if the engine is damaged as a result.*

7 The old oil drained from the engine cannot be re-used and should be disposed of properly. Check with your local refuse disposal company, disposal facility or environmental agency to see whether they will accept the used oil for recycling. Don't pour used oil into drains or onto the ground.

OIL CARE
FOLLOW THE CODE
OIL BANK LINE
0800 66 33 66

Note: It is antisocial and illegal to dump oil down the drain. To find the location of your local oil recycling bank, call this number free.

In the USA, note that any oil supplier must accept used oil for recycling.

5.3 Unscrew the oil filler cap

5.4a Unscrew the oil drain plug (arrowed) . . .

5.4b . . . and allow all the oil to drain

5.4c To remove the old sealing washer, cut it off

5.5a Install the drain plug, using a new sealing washer if necessary . . .

5.5b . . . and tighten it to the specified torque

6.3 Idle speed adjuster (arrowed)

7.3a On GSX-R600V models and GSX-R750T and V models, pull the cable out of the socket and measure the free travel (A)

7.3b On GSX-R600W and X models and GSX-R750W and X models, twist the throttle and measure the amount of free rotation (B)

6 Idle speed –
check and adjustment

1 The idle speed should be checked and adjusted before and after the carburettors or throttle bodies are synchronised (balanced) and when it is obviously too high or too low. Before adjusting the idle speed, make sure the valve clearances and spark plug gaps are correct (see Sections 23 and 3). Also, turn the handlebars back-and-forth and see if the idle speed changes as this is done. If it does, the throttle cables may not be adjusted correctly, or may be worn out. This is a dangerous condition that can cause loss of control of the bike. Be sure to correct this problem before proceeding (see Section 7).
2 The engine should be at normal operating temperature, which is usually reached after 10 to 15 minutes of stop and go riding. Place the motorcycle on its sidestand, and make sure the transmission is in neutral.
3 The idle speed adjuster is located inside the left-hand fairing side panel **(see illustration)**. With the engine idling, adjust the idle speed by turning the adjuster screw until the idle speed listed in this Chapter's Specifications is obtained. Turn the screw clockwise to increase idle speed, and anti-clockwise to decrease it.

4 Snap the throttle open and shut a few times, then recheck the idle speed. If necessary, repeat the adjustment procedure.
5 If a smooth, steady idle can't be achieved, the fuel/air mixture may be incorrect (see Chapter 4) or the carburettors/throttle bodies may need synchronising (see Section 17).

7 Throttle and choke cables –
check

Throttle cables

1 Make sure the throttle grip rotates easily from fully closed to fully open with the front wheel turned at various angles. The grip should return automatically from fully open to fully closed when released.
2 If the throttle sticks, this is probably due to a cable fault. Remove the cables (see Chapter 4) and lubricate them (see Section 15). Install the cables, making sure they are correctly routed. If this fails to improve the operation of the throttle, the cables must be renewed. Note that in very rare cases the fault could lie in the carburettors or throttle bodies, rather than the cables, necessitating their removal and inspection of the throttle linkage (see Chapter 4).
3 With the throttle operating smoothly, check

for a small amount of freeplay before the throttle opens and compare the amount to that listed in this Chapter's Specifications. On GSX-R600V models and GSX-R750T and V models, freeplay is measured in terms of the amount of free movement the outer cables have in their sockets in the adjusters before they become tight **(see illustration)**. On GSX-R600W and X models and GSX-R750W and X models, freeplay is measured in terms of the amount of throttle (twistgrip) rotation before the throttle opens **(see illustration)**. If it's incorrect, adjust the cables to correct it.
4 To adjust the cables to GSX-R600V models and GSX-R750T and V models, loosen the lockring on the decelerator (throttle closing) cable adjuster, and turn the adjuster until the specified amount of freeplay is obtained (see this Chapter's Specifications) **(see illustration)**. Retighten the lockring. Now repeat the procedure for the accelerator (throttle opening) cable.
5 To adjust the cables on GSX-R600W and X models and GSX-R750W and X models, loosen the lockring on the decelerator (throttle closing) cable adjuster and turn the adjuster fully in **(see illustration 7.4)**. Now loosen the lockring on the accelerator (throttle opening) cable and turn the adjuster until the specified amount of freeplay is obtained (see this Chapter's Specifications), then retighten the lockring. Now turn the decelerator (throttle closing) cable adjuster out until a resistance can just be felt – at this point all the freeplay has been taken up. Do not turn the adjuster out any further than the point at which the resistance is felt. Tighten the lockring.
6 If the adjusters have reached their limit, or if major adjustment is required, reset them so that the freeplay is at a maximum (ie the adjusters are fully turned in), then raise the fuel tank and, if required for improved access, remove the air filter housing (see Chapter 4), and adjust the cables at the carburettor/throttle body end. Slacken the adjuster locknuts, then turn the adjusters until the specified amount of freeplay is obtained (see Step 3), then tighten the locknuts **(see illustrations)**. Further adjustments can now

7.4 Accelerator cable (A), decelerator cable (B). Adjuster locknut (C), adjuster (D)

7.6a Accelerator cable (A), decelerator cable (B). Adjuster locknut (C), adjuster (D) - carburettor models

7.6b Accelerator cable (A), decelerator cable (B). Adjuster locknut (C), adjuster (D) - fuel injection models

7.9 Choke cable adjuster locknut (A) and adjuster (B)

8.1 Measuring clutch cable freeplay

be made at the throttle end. If the cables cannot be adjusted as specified, install new ones (see Chapter 4).

 Warning: Turn the handlebars all the way through their travel with the engine idling. Idle speed should not change. If it does, the cable may be routed incorrectly. Correct this condition before riding the bike.

7 Check that the throttle twistgrip operates smoothly and snaps shut quickly when released.

Choke cable

8 If the choke does not operate smoothly this is probably due to a cable fault. Remove the cable (see Chapter 4) and lubricate it (see Section 15). Install the cable, making sure it is correctly routed.

9 Check for a small amount of freeplay in the cable before the choke opens and adjust it if necessary using the adjuster at the lever end of the cable. Slacken the locknut, then turn the adjuster as required until a small amount of freeplay is evident, then retighten the locknut **(see illustration)**. If this fails to improve the operation of the choke, the cable must be renewed. Note that in very rare cases the fault could lie in the carburettors rather than the cable, necessitating the removal of the carburettors and inspection of the choke valves (see Chapter 4).

10 On GSX-R750W and X models, the choke cable is also adjustable at the throttle body end, and is done so in the same way as the throttle cables (see Step 6 and **illustration 7.6b**)

8 Clutch – check

Cable adjustment

1 Periodic adjustment of the clutch cable is necessary to compensate for wear in the clutch plates and stretch of the cable. Check that the amount of freeplay at the clutch lever end is within the specifications listed at the beginning of the Chapter **(see illustration)**. If adjustment is required, it can be made at either the lever end of the cable or at the clutch end.

2 To adjust the freeplay at the lever, turn the adjuster in or out until the required amount of freeplay is obtained **(see illustration)**. To increase freeplay, turn the adjuster clockwise (in). To reduce freeplay, turn the adjuster anti-clockwise (out).

3 If all the adjustment has been taken up at the lever, reset the adjuster (turn it fully in) to give the maximum amount of freeplay, then set the correct amount of freeplay using the

adjuster at the clutch end of the cable (Step 4). Subsequent adjustments can then be made using the lever adjuster only.

4 To adjust the freeplay at the clutch end of the cable, slacken the locknut on the adjuster on the top of the sprocket cover and turn the adjuster until the specified amount of freeplay is obtained **(see illustration)**. To increase freeplay, turn the adjuster clockwise (in). To reduce freeplay, turn the adjuster anti-clockwise (out). Tighten the locknut securely. To improve access to the adjuster, remove the left-hand fairing side panel (see Chapter 8) and displace the coolant reservoir (see Chapter 3).

Release mechanism adjustment

Note: *Clutch plate wear can be compensated for by adjusting the release mechanism set in the sprocket cover. If it is impossible to eliminate clutch drag or slip with cable adjustment, set the release mechanism freeplay as follows.*

5 Turn the adjuster at the lever end of the cable fully in **(see illustration 8.2)**. This creates slack in the cable.

6 Remove the left-hand fairing side panel (see Chapter 8) and displace the coolant reservoir (see Chapter 3). Remove the rubber cover from the clutch release mechanism set in the engine sprocket cover **(see illustration)**.

7 Slacken the locknut on the release mechanism adjuster screw, then unscrew the

8.2 Turn the adjuster as required

8.4 Slacken the locknut (A) and turn the adjuster (B) as required

8.6 Remove the rubber cover . . .

8.7 . . . then slacken the locknut and turn the adjuster screw as described

9.6 Remove the radiator pressure cap as described

adjuster screw a few turns **(see illustration)**. Now turn the adjuster screw in until resistance is felt, then back it off 1/4 turn. When doing this, counter-hold the locknut as shown to prevent it from tightening and locking the adjuster.

8 Now counter-hold the adjuster screw to prevent it turning and tighten the locknut. Refit the rubber cover.

9 Slacken the locknut on the adjuster on the top of the sprocket cover and turn the adjuster until the specified amount of freeplay is obtained **(see illustration 8.4)**. To increase freeplay, turn the adjuster clockwise (in). To reduce freeplay, turn the adjuster anti-clockwise (out). Tighten the locknut securely.

10 Set the correct amount of freeplay at the lever by adjusting the cable as described in Steps 1 to 4.

9 Cooling system – check

Warning: The engine must be cool before beginning this procedure.

1 Check the coolant level (see *Daily (pre-ride) checks*).

2 Remove the fairing side panels (see Chapter 8). The entire cooling system should be checked for evidence of leakage. Examine each rubber coolant hose along its entire length. Look for cracks, abrasions and other damage. Squeeze each hose at various points. They should feel firm, yet pliable, and return to their original shape when released. If they are damaged, dried out, cracked or hard, renew them (see Chapter 3).

3 Check for evidence of leaks at each cooling system joint and around the bottom of the water pump, which is on the left-hand side of the engine. Tighten the hose clips carefully to prevent future leaks. If the pump is leaking, refer to Chapter 3 and check it.

4 Check the radiator for leaks and other damage. Leaks in the radiator leave tell-tale scale deposits or coolant stains on the outside of the core below the leak. If leaks are noted, remove the radiator (see Chapter 3) and have it repaired or renew it.

Caution: Do not use a liquid leak stopping compound to try to repair leaks.

5 Check the radiator fins for mud, dirt and insects, which may impede the flow of air through the radiator. If the fins are dirty, remove the radiator (see Chapter 3) and clean it using water or low pressure compressed air directed through the fins from the backside. If the fins are bent or distorted, straighten them carefully with a screwdriver. If the air flow is restricted by bent or damaged fins over more than 30% of the radiator's surface area, renew the radiator.

6 Remove the pressure cap from the radiator filler neck by turning it anti-clockwise until it reaches a stop. If you hear a hissing sound (indicating there is still pressure in the system), wait until it stops. Now press down on the cap and continue turning the cap until it can be removed **(see illustration)**. Check the condition of the coolant in the system. If it is rust-coloured or if accumulations of scale are visible, drain, flush and refill the system with new coolant (See Section 25). Check the cap seal for cracks and other damage. If in doubt about the pressure cap's condition, have it tested by a Suzuki dealer or renew it with a new one. Install the cap by turning it clockwise until it reaches the first stop then push down on the cap and continue turning until it can turn no further.

7 Check the antifreeze content of the coolant with an antifreeze hydrometer. Sometimes coolant looks like it's in good condition, but might be too weak to offer adequate

protection. If the hydrometer indicates a weak mixture, drain, flush and refill the system (see Section 25).

8 Start the engine and let it reach normal operating temperature, then check for leaks again. As the coolant temperature increases, the fan should come on automatically and the temperature should begin to drop. If it does not, refer to Chapter 3 and check the fan, the fan switch and fan circuit carefully.

9 If the coolant level is consistently low, and no evidence of leaks can be found, have the entire system pressure checked by a Suzuki dealer.

10 Drive chain – wear and stretch check

1 Check the entire length of the chain for damaged rollers, loose links and pins, and missing O-rings. Fit a new chain if damage is found. **Note:** *Never install a new chain on old sprockets, and never use the old chain if you install new sprockets – renew the chain and sprockets as a set.*

2 The amount of chain stretch be measured and compared to the stretch limit specified at the beginning of the Chapter. On US models, remove the split pin from the rear axle nut, then on all models slacken the axle nut **(see illustration 1.8)**. Slacken the adjuster locknut on each side of the swingarm, then turn the adjuster bolts evenly until the chain is tight **(see illustration 1.9a)**. Measure along the bottom run the length of 21 pins (from the centre of the 1st pin to the centre of the 21st pin) and compare the result with the service limit specified at the beginning of the Chapter **(see illustration)**. Rotate the rear wheel so that several sections of the chain are measured, then calculate the average. If the chain exceeds the service limit it must be renewed (see Chapter 5). **Note:** *Never install a new chain on old sprockets, and never use the old chain if you install new sprockets – renew the chain and sprockets as a set.* Refer to Section 1 and reset the correct amount of chain freeplay, then tighten the axle nut and adjuster bolt nuts and on US models install a

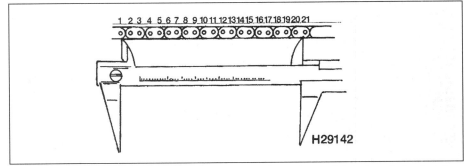

10.2 Measure the distance between the 1st and 21st pins to determine chain stretch

new split pin to secure the axle nut (bend the split pin ends securely).

3 Remove the front sprocket cover (see Chapter 6). Check the teeth on the front and rear sprockets for wear **(see illustration)**.

4 Inspect the drive chain slider on the swingarm for excessive wear and renew it if worn (see Chapter 6).

11 Brake pads – wear check

1 Each brake pad has wear indicator cutouts or a line that can be viewed without removing the pads from the caliper. On the front brake caliper, unscrew the two bolts securing the pad spring and remove the spring – the pad wear indicator cutouts are visible by looking at the top edge of the pads **(see illustrations)**. On the rear brake caliper, remove the caliper cover by levering it off with a screwdriver – the pad wear lines are visible by looking up at the bottom edge of the pads from under the caliper **(see illustrations)**.

DIRECTION OF ROTATION

ENGINE SPROCKET WORN TOOTH

REAR SPROCKET WORN TOOTH

0618H

10.3 Check the sprockets in the areas indicated to see if they are worn excessively

TOOL TiP *Checking the rear brake pads is much easier if you use a mirror.*

2 If the pads are worn to or beyond the base of the grooves, new ones must be installed. If the pads are dirty or if you are in doubt as to the amount of friction material remaining, remove them for inspection (see Chapter 7). **Note:** *Some after-market pads may use different indicators to those on the original equipment as shown.*

3 Refer to Chapter 7 for details of fitting new pads.

11.1a Unscrew the bolts (arrowed) and remove the pad spring

11.1b Front brake pad wear cutouts (arrowed)

11.1c Remove the rear caliper's cover

11.1d Using a mirror to check the rear brake pad wear – these pads are worn down to the wear indicator lines

12.3 Flex the brake hoses and check for cracks, bulges and leaking fluid

12.5 Rear brake light switch (arrowed)

12.6 Adjusting the front brake lever span

12 Brake system – check

1 A routine general check of the brake system will ensure that any problems are discovered and remedied before the rider's safety is jeopardised.
2 Check the brake lever and pedal for loose connections, improper or rough action, excessive play, bends, and other damage. Renew any damaged parts with new ones (see Chapter 6).
3 Make sure all brake fasteners are tight. Check the brake pads for wear (see Section 11) and make sure the fluid level in the reservoirs is correct (see *Daily (pre-ride) checks*). Look for leaks at the hose connections and check for cracks in the hoses **(see illustration)**. If the lever or pedal is spongy, bleed the brakes (see Chapter 7).
4 Make sure the brake light operates when the front brake lever is pulled in. The front brake light switch is not adjustable. If it fails to operate properly, check it (see Chapter 9).
5 Make sure the brake light is activated just before the rear brake takes effect. The switch is mounted on the inside of the frame on the right-hand side, above the brake pedal. If

adjustment is necessary, hold the switch and turn the adjuster nut on the switch body until the brake light is activated when required **(see illustration)**. If the brake light comes on too late, turn the ring clockwise. If the brake light comes on too soon or is permanently on, turn the ring anti-clockwise. If the switch doesn't operate the brake light, check it (see Chapter 9).
6 The front brake lever has a span adjuster which alters the distance of the lever from the handlebar **(see illustration)**. Pull the lever away from the handlebar and turn the adjuster dial until the setting which best suits the rider is obtained. Align the setting number with the arrow on the lever.
7 Check the position of the rear brake pedal. The distance between the top of the end of the brake pedal and the top of the rider's footrest should be as specified at the beginning of the Chapter **(see illustration)**. If the pedal height is incorrect, or if you want to adjust it to suit your own preference, slacken the locknut on the master cylinder pushrod, then turn the pushrod using a spanner on the hex at the top of the rod until the pedal is at the correct height **(see illustration)**. Tighten the locknut securely. Adjust the rear brake light switch after adjusting the pedal height (see Step 5).

13 Wheels and tyres – general check

Wheels

1 Cast wheels are virtually maintenance free, but they should be kept clean and checked periodically for cracks and other damage. Also check the wheel runout and alignment (see Chapter 7). Never attempt to repair damaged cast wheels; they must be renewed if damaged.

Tyres

2 Check the tyre condition and tread depth thoroughly – see *Daily (pre-ride) checks*. Check the valve rubber for signs of damage or deterioration and have it renewed if necessary by a tyre fitting specialist. Also, make sure the valve stem cap is in place and tight.

14 Nuts and bolts – tightness check

1 Since vibration of the machine tends to loosen fasteners, all nuts, bolts, screws, etc.

12.7a Rear brake pedal height measurement

12.7b Slacken the pushrod locknut (A) and turn the pushrod as required using the hex (B)

should be periodically checked for proper tightness.

2 Pay particular attention to the following:

Spark plugs
Engine oil drain plug
Gearchange pedal bolt
Footrest, footrest bracket and stand bolts
Engine mounting bolts
Shock absorber mounting bolts and
  suspension linkage bolts
Handlebar bolts
Front axle nut and clamp bolt
Front fork clamp bolts (top and bottom
  yoke)
Rear axle nut
Swingarm pivot nut
Brake caliper mounting bolts
Brake hose banjo bolts and caliper bleed
  valves
Brake disc bolts and rear sprocket nuts
Exhaust system bolts/nuts (see Section 20)

3 If a torque wrench is available, use it along with the torque specifications at the beginning of this, or other, Chapters.

15 Stand, lever pivots and cables – lubrication

Pivot points

1 Since the controls, cables and various other components of a motorcycle are exposed to the elements, they should be lubricated

15.3a Lubricating a cable with a cable oiler clamp. Make sure the tool seals around the inner cable

periodically to ensure safe and trouble-free operation.

2 The footrests, clutch and brake levers, brake pedal, gearchange lever linkage and sidestand pivots should be lubricated frequently. In order for the lubricant to be applied where it will do the most good, the component should be disassembled (see Chapter 6). However, if an aerosol chain lubricant is being used, it can be applied to the pivot joint gaps and will usually work its way into the areas where friction occurs. If motor oil or light grease is being used, apply it sparingly as it may attract dirt (which could cause the controls to bind or wear at an accelerated rate). **Note:** *One of the best lubricants for the control lever pivots is a dry-film lubricant (available from many sources by different names).*

15.3b Lubricating a cable with a makeshift funnel and motor oil

Cables

3 To lubricate the cables, disconnect the relevant cable at its upper end, then lubricate the cable with a cable oiler clamp, or if one is not available, using the set-up shown **(see illustrations)**. See Chapter 4 for the choke and throttle cable removal procedures, and Chapter 2 for the clutch cable.

Every 7500 miles (12,000 km) or 12 months

Carry out all the items under the 4000 mile (6000 km) check, plus the following:

16 Spark plugs – renewal

1 Remove the old spark plugs as described in Section 3 and install new ones.

17 Carburettors/throttle bodies – synchronisation

   Warning: Petrol (gasoline) is extremely flammable, so take extra precautions when you work on any part of the fuel system. Don't smoke or allow open flames or bare light bulbs near the work area, and don't work in a garage where a natural gas-type appliance is present. If you spill any fuel on your skin, rinse it off immediately with soap and water. When you perform any kind of work on the fuel system, wear safety glasses and have a

fire extinguisher suitable for a Class B type fire (flammable liquids) on hand.
Warning: Take great care not to burn your hand on the hot engine unit when accessing the gauge take-off points on the inlet manifolds. Do not allow exhaust gases to build up in the work area; either perform the check outside or use an exhaust gas extraction system.

1 Carburettor or throttle body synchronisation is simply the process of adjusting the carburettors or throttle bodies so they pass the same amount of fuel/air mixture to each cylinder. This is done by measuring the vacuum produced in each cylinder. Carburettors or throttle bodies that are out of synchronisation will result in decreased fuel mileage, increased engine temperature, less than ideal throttle response and higher vibration levels. Before synchronising the carburettors or throttle bodies, make sure the valve clearances are correct.

2 To properly synchronise the carburettors or throttle bodies, you will need a set of vacuum gauges or calibrated tubes to indicate engine vacuum. The equipment used should be suitable for a four cylinder engine and come

complete with the necessary adapters and hoses to fit the take off points. **Note:** *Because of the nature of the synchronisation procedure and the need for special instruments, most owners leave the task to a Suzuki dealer.*

3 Start the engine and let it run until it reaches normal operating temperature, then shut it off.

4 On GSX-R600 models, remove the fuel tank (see Chapter 4). On W, X and Y models, displace the solenoid mounting bracket from the bottom of the No. 1 carburettor **(see illustration)**.

17.4a Remove the screws securing its bracket and displace the solenoid

17.4b Disconnect the fuel valve vacuum hose (A) and remove the blanking screws (B)

17.4c Fit the adapters . . .

17.4d . . . and connect the hoses to them

Disconnect the fuel valve vacuum hose from the take-off stub on no. 3 inlet manifold and remove the blanking screws from the take-off points of the remaining manifolds **(see illustration)**. Thread the vacuum gauge hose adapters into the take-off points, then connect the gauge hoses to the adapters **(see illustrations)**. Make sure they are a good fit because any air leaks will result in false readings.

5 On GSX-R750T and V models, remove the air filter housing and displace the carburettors from the inlet manifolds – there is no need to disconnect any cables or hoses (see Chapter 4). Disconnect the vacuum hose from the take-off stub on no. 4 carburettor body and remove the blanking caps from the take-off points on the remaining carburettors. The take-off points are located on the engine side of the carburettors, and are positioned at about the 10 o'clock position (when viewed from the front), just behind the rims where the carburettors fit into the inlet manifolds on the cylinder head. Connect the gauge hoses to the take-off stubs. Make sure they are a good fit because any air leaks will result in false readings. Fit the carburettors back into the manifolds and tighten the clamp screws (see Chapter 4).

Caution: On GSX-R750 models, the carburettors/throttle bodies are synchronised with the air filter housing removed. To negate the possibility of drawing dirt into the engine, it is advisable to cut up an old pair of stockings and fit a circle of the material over each inlet and secure it with an elastic band or cable tie. The material acts as a filter.

6 On GSX-R750W and X models, disconnect the IAT (inlet air temperature) sensor wiring connector, then remove the sensor from the air filter housing and reconnect the wiring **(see illustration)**. Also remove the screw securing the IAP (inlet air pressure) sensor to the housing and displace the sensor **(see illustration)**. Remove the air filter housing (see Chapter 4). Disconnect the vacuum hose from the take-off stub on .no. 4 throttle body and plug its end **(see**

illustration). Also remove the blanking caps from the take-off stubs of the remaining throttle bodies. Connect the gauge hoses to the take-off stubs. Make sure they are a good fit because any air leaks will result in false readings.

7 Arrange a temporary fuel supply, either by using a small temporary tank or by using extra long fuel pipes to the now remote fuel tank. Alternatively, position the tank on a suitable base on the motorcycle, taking care not to scratch any paintwork, and making sure that the tank is safely and securely supported. Start the engine and increase the idle speed to 1750 rpm on carburettor models and

1200 rpm on fuel injected models, using the idle speed adjuster screw **(see illustration 6.3)**. If using vacuum gauges fitted with damping adjustment, set this so that the needle flutter is just eliminated but so that they can still respond to small changes in pressure.

8 The vacuum readings for all of the cylinders should be the same **(see illustration)**. If the vacuum readings vary, proceed as follows.

9 On GSX-R600 and 750T and V models, the carburettors are balanced by turning the synchronising screws situated in-between each carburettor, in the throttle linkage **(see**

17.6a Disconnect the wiring connector (A), then slacken the nut (B) and unscrew the IAT sensor

17.6b Remove the screw (arrowed) and displace the sensor, leaving it connected

17.6c Disconnect the vacuum hose (A) and remove the blanking caps (B)

17.8 Carburettor/throttle body synchronisation gauge set-up

17.9 Carburettor synchronising screws (arrowed) – air filter housing shown removed for clarity

17.10 Throttle body air screws (A), synchronising screws (B)

illustration). Note: *Do not press on the screws whilst adjusting them, otherwise a false reading will be obtained.* First synchronise no. 3 carburettor to no. 4 using the right-hand synchronising screw until the readings are the same. Then synchronise no. 1 carburettor to no. 2 using the left-hand screw. Finally synchronise nos. 1 and 2 carburettors to nos. 3 and 4 using the centre screw. When all the carburettors are synchronised, open and close the throttle quickly to settle the linkage, and recheck the gauge readings, readjusting if necessary.

10 On GSX-R750W and X models, if the vacuum difference between the throttle bodies is less than 20 mmHg, use the air screws located above the take-off point on each throttle body for fine adjustment – each air screw should be set at about 1/2 a turn out from its seat **(see illustration)**. If the vacuum difference is greater than 20 mmHg, check that each air screw is correctly set at about 1/2 turn out, then balance the throttle bodies by turning the synchronising screws situated in-between each body, in the throttle linkage. **Note:** *Do not press on the screws whilst adjusting them, otherwise a false reading will be obtained.* When using the synchronising screws, first synchronise no. 3 body to no. 4 using the left-hand synchronising screw (as shown in the illustration) until the readings are the same. Then synchronise no. 1 body to no. 2 using the right-hand screw. Finally synchronise nos. 1 and 2 bodies to nos. 3 and 4 using the centre screw. When all the bodies are synchronised, open and close the throttle quickly to settle the linkage, and recheck the gauge readings, readjusting if necessary.

11 When the adjustment is complete, recheck the vacuum readings, then adjust the idle speed by turning the adjuster screw until the idle speed listed in this Chapter's Specifications is obtained. Stop the engine.

12 On GSX-R750T and V models, displace the carburettors from the inlet manifolds. On all models remove the gauge hoses, and on GSX-R600 models the adapters, then fit the fuel valve vacuum hose onto no. 3 inlet manifold (600 models) or the vacuum hose onto no. 4 carburettor/throttle body (750 models) and the take-off blanking screws or caps onto the others.

13 On GSX-R600 models, detach the temporary fuel supply. Install the carburettors, solenoid mounting bracket, air filter housing and fuel tank as required by your model, in a reverse of the removal procedure.

18 Steering head bearings – freeplay check and adjustment

1 Steering head bearings can become dented, rough or loose during normal use of the machine. In extreme cases, worn or loose steering head bearings can cause steering wobble – a condition that is potentially dangerous.

Check

2 Support the motorcycle in an upright position using an auxiliary stand. Raise the front wheel off the ground either by having an assistant push down on the rear or by placing a support under the engine (first remove the fairing side panels (see Chapter 8)). On models equipped with a steering damper, disconnect one end to allow free movement of the steering.

3 Point the front wheel straight-ahead and slowly move the handlebars from side-to-side. Any dents or roughness in the bearing races will be felt and the bars will not move smoothly and freely.

4 Next, grasp the fork sliders and try to move them forward and backward **(see illustration)**. Any looseness in the steering head bearings will be felt as front-to-rear movement of the forks. If play is felt in the bearings, adjust the steering head as follows. Reconnect the steering damper, where applicable.

> **HAYNES HiNT**
> *Freeplay in the fork due to worn fork bushes can be misinterpreted for steering head bearing play – do not confuse the two.*

Adjustment

5 Although not essential, it is wise to raise the fuel tank to avoid the possibility of damage should a tool slip while adjustment is being made (see Chapter 4).

6 Slacken the steering stem nut, then slacken the fork clamp bolts in the bottom yoke **(see illustrations)**.

18.4 Checking for play in the steering head bearings

18.6a Slacken the steering stem nut (arrowed) . . .

18.6b . . . and the clamp bolt (arrowed) for each fork in the bottom yoke

18.7a Slacken the locknut . .

18.7b . . . then turn the adjuster nut as described until the bearings are correctly set

7 Using a slim C-spanner or a suitable drift located in one of the notches, slacken the adjuster locknut **(see illustration)**. Now, slacken the adjuster nut slightly by tapping the drift with a hammer, until pressure is just released, then tighten it until all freeplay in the forks is removed, yet the steering is able to move freely from side to side **(see illustration)**. The object is to set the adjuster nut so that the bearings are under a very light loading, just enough to remove any freeplay.

Caution: Take great care not to apply excessive pressure because this will cause premature failure of the bearings.

8 If the bearings cannot be set up properly, or if there is any binding, roughness or notchiness, they will have to be removed for inspection or renewal (see Chapter 6).

9 With the bearings correctly adjusted, tighten the locknut securely against the adjuster ring, making sure the adjuster does not turn as you do so. Now tighten the steering stem nut and the fork clamp bolts in the bottom yoke to the torque settings specified at the beginning of the Chapter.

10 Check the bearing adjustment as described above and re-adjust if necessary.

19 Suspension – check

1 The suspension components must be maintained in top operating condition to ensure rider safety. Loose, worn or damaged suspension parts decrease the motorcycle's stability and control.

Front suspension

2 While standing alongside the motorcycle, apply the front brake and push on the handlebars to compress the forks several times. See if they move up-and-down smoothly without binding. If binding is felt, the forks should be disassembled and inspected (see Chapter 6).

3 Inspect the area above (GSX-R600) or below (GSX-R750) the dust seal for signs of oil leakage, then carefully lever off the dust seal using a flat-bladed screwdriver and inspect the area around the fork seal **(see illustrations)**. If leakage is evident, the seals must be renewed (see Chapter 6).

4 Check the tightness of all suspension nuts and bolts to be sure none have worked loose, referring to the torque settings specified at the beginning of Chapter 6.

Rear suspension

5 Inspect the rear shock for fluid leakage and tightness of its mountings. If leakage is found, a new shock must be installed (see Chapter 6).

6 With the aid of an assistant to support the bike, compress the rear suspension several times. It should move up and down freely without binding. If any binding is felt, the worn or faulty component must be identified and

renewed. The problem could be due to either the shock absorber, the suspension linkage components or the swingarm components.

7 Support the motorcycle using an auxiliary stand so that the rear wheel is off the ground. Grab the swingarm and rock it from side to side – there should be no discernible movement at the rear **(see illustration)**. If there's a little movement or a slight clicking can be heard, check the tightness of all the rear suspension mounting bolts and nuts, referring to the torque settings specified at the beginning of Chapter 6, and re-check for movement. Next, grasp the top of the rear wheel and pull it upwards – there should be no discernible freeplay before the shock absorber begins to compress **(see illustration)**. Any freeplay felt in either check

19.3a Lever up the dust seal . . .

19.3b . . . and check for signs of oil leakage

19.7a Checking for play in the swingarm bearings

19.7b Checking for play in the suspension linkage bearings

indicates worn bearings in the suspension linkage or swingarm, or worn shock absorber mountings. The worn components must be renewed (see Chapter 6).

8 To make a more accurate assessment of the swingarm bearings, remove the rear wheel (see Chapter 7) and the bolt securing the suspension linkage rods to the linkage arm (see Chapter 6). Grasp the rear of the swingarm with one hand and place your other hand at the junction of the swingarm and the frame. Try to move the rear of the swingarm from side-to-side. Any wear (play) in the bearings should be felt as movement between the swingarm and the frame at the front. If there is any play, the swingarm will be felt to move forward and backward at the front (not from side-to-side). Next, move the swingarm up and down through its full travel. It should move freely, without any binding or rough spots. If any play in the swingarm is noted or if the swingarm does not move freely, the bearings must be removed for inspection or renewal (see Chapter 6).

20.2a Tighten the downpipe bolts . . .

20.2b . . . and the middle and rear mounting bolts (arrowed) to the specified torque

20 Exhaust system bolts – tightness check

1 Remove the fairing side panels (see Chapter 8). Refer to Chapter 3 and remove the radiator mounting bolts, then displace the radiator to improve access to the exhaust downpipe bolts. It should not be necessary to disconnect any hoses or wiring, but check that no strain is placed on them. If required, remove the radiator completely.

2 Using a torque wrench, check that the exhaust downpipe clamp bolts and the silencer mounting bolts are tightened to the torque settings specified at the beginning of the Chapter **(see illustrations)**.

Every 11,000 miles (18,000 km) or 18 months

Carry out all the items under the 4000 mile (6000 km) check:

21 Air filter – renewal

1 Remove the old air filter as described in Section 2 and install a new one.

22 Engine/transmission – oil and oil filter change

 Warning: Be careful when draining the oil, as the exhaust pipes, the engine, and the oil itself can cause severe burns.

1 Remove the right-hand fairing side panel (see Chapter 8).

2 Drain the engine oil as described in Section 5, Steps 2 to 5.

3 Now place the drain tray below the oil filter, which is on the right-hand side of the engine at the front. On GSX-R600Y models, undo the bolt retaining the oil filter security plate and remove the plate, noting the rubber damper. On all models, unscrew the oil filter using a filter adapter, chain wrench or strap wrench and tip any residual oil into the drain tray **(see illustrations)**. Wipe any oil off the exhaust pipes to prevent too much smoke when you start it.

22.3a Unscrew the filter . . .

22.3b . . . and drain it into the tray

22.4a Smear some clean oil onto the seal . . .

22.4b . . . then thread the filter onto the cooler . . .

4 Smear clean engine oil onto the rubber seal of the new filter, then manoeuvre it into position and screw it onto the engine by hand until the seal just seats **(see illustrations)**. Now tighten it a further two whole turns using a filter adapter, or if one is not available, tighten the filter by hand **(see illustration)**. **Note:** *Although Suzuki specify two whole turns, on the models we stripped down the filter became very tight well before this, and*

tightening it further would possibly have damaged the filter. It is best to use your own judgement should the filter become very tight – the most important consideration is that the filter does not leak. On GSX-R600Y models, ensure the rubber damper is in place on the oil filter security plate, then install the plate and tighten the retaining bolt securely.
5 Refill the engine with the correct amount and type of oil as described in Section 5, Step 6.

22.4c . . . and tighten it as described

Every 15,000 miles (24,000 km) or 24 months

Carry out all the items under the 7500 mile (12,000 km) check:

23 Valve clearances – check and adjustment

Check

1 The engine must be completely cool for this maintenance procedure, so let the machine sit overnight before beginning.
2 Remove the spark plugs (see Section 3).
3 Remove the valve cover (see Chapter 2). The cylinders are identified by number, and are numbered 1 to 4 from left to right.
4 Make a chart or sketch of all valve positions so that a note of each clearance can be made against the relevant valve.
5 Unscrew the timing inspection plug and the centre plug from the starter clutch cover on the right-hand side of the engine **(see illustration)**. Discard the plug O-rings as new ones should be used. The engine can be turned using a 14 mm socket on the starter clutch bolt and turning it in a clockwise direction only **(see illustration 23.6a)**. Alternatively, place the motorcycle on an auxiliary stand so that the rear wheel is off the ground, select a high gear and rotate the rear wheel by hand in its normal direction of rotation.
6 Turn the engine until the scribe line on the starter clutch aligns with the notch in the timing inspection hole **(see illustration)**. **Note:** *Turn the engine in the normal direction of rotation (clockwise) only, viewed from the right-hand end of the engine.* Now, check the position of the notch in the left-hand end of each camshaft. If the notch in the inlet camshaft is facing down and the notch on the exhaust camshaft is at 8 o'clock, then no. 1 cylinder is at TDC on the compression stroke **(see illustration)**. If the notch on the inlet camshaft is facing up and the notch on the exhaust camshaft is at 2 o'clock, then no. 4 cylinder is at TDC on the compression stroke **(see**

illustration). If the marks are not positioned as required for the cylinders being checked, turn the crankshaft through 360° (one complete turn).
7 With no. 1 cylinder at TDC on the compression stroke, the following valves can be checked:
  a) No. 1, inlet and exhaust
  b) No. 2, exhaust
  c) No. 3, inlet

8 With no. 4 cylinder at TDC on the compression stroke, the following valves can be checked:
  a) No. 2, inlet
  b) No. 3, exhaust
  c) No. 4, inlet and exhaust
9 Insert a feeler gauge of the same thickness as the correct valve clearance (see Specifications) between the base of the camshaft lobe and the follower of each valve

23.5 Remove the timing inspection plug (A) and the centre plug (B)

23.6a Turn the engine clockwise using the bolt (A), until the timing mark (B) aligns with the notch (C)

23.6b When the notch (A) on the inlet camshaft is down and the notch (B) on the exhaust camshaft is at 8 o'clock, No. 1 cylinder is at TDC on the compression stroke

23.6c When the notch (A) on the inlet camshaft is up and the notch (B) on the exhaust camshaft is at 2 o'clock, No. 4 cylinder is at TDC on the compression stroke

23.9 Insert the feeler gauge as shown (arrowed) and measure the clearance

23.13a Lift out the follower . . .

23.13b . . . and retrieve the shim, which will probably be inside the follower

23.14 Measure the shim thickness using a micrometer

and check that it is a firm sliding fit – you should feel a slight drag when the you pull the gauge out **(see illustration)**. If not, use the feeler gauges to obtain the exact clearance. **Note:** *The inlet and exhaust valve clearances are different.* Record the measured clearance on the chart.

10 Rotate the engine so that the timing rotor turns through 360° and measure the valve clearance of the remaining valves using the method described in Step 9. **Note:** *Turn the engine in the normal direction of rotation (clockwise) only, viewed from the right-hand end of the engine.*

Adjustment

11 When all clearances have been measured and charted, identify whether the clearance on any valve falls outside that specified. If it does, the shim between the follower and the valve must be replaced with one of a thickness which will restore the correct clearance.

12 Shim renewal requires removal of the camshafts (see Chapter 2). There is no need to remove both camshafts if shims from only one side of the engine need replacing.

13 With the camshaft removed, remove the cam follower of the valve in question using either a magnet or a pair of pliers **(see illustration)**. Retrieve the shim from either the inside of the follower **(see illustration)**, or pick it out of the top of the valve, using either a magnet, a small screwdriver with a dab of grease on it (the shim will stick to the grease), or a pair of pliers **(see illustration 23.17a)**. Do not allow the shim to fall into the engine.

14 The shim size should be stamped on its face, however, it is recommended that the shim is measured to check that it has not worn **(see illustration)**. The size marking is in the form of a three figure number, e.g. 180 indicating that the shim is 1.800 mm thick.

MEASURED TAPPET CLEARANCE (mm)	PRESENT SHIM SIZE (mm)																				
	1.20	1.25	1.30	1.35	1.40	1.45	1.50	1.55	1.60	1.65	1.70	1.75	1.80	1.85	1.90	1.95	2.00	2.05	2.10	2.15	2.20
0.00-0.04			1.20	1.25	1.30	1.35	1.40	1.45	1.50	1.55	1.60	1.65	1.70	1.75	1.80	1.85	1.90	1.95	2.00	2.05	2.10
0.05-0.09		1.20	1.25	1.30	1.35	1.40	1.45	1.50	1.55	1.60	1.65	1.70	1.75	1.80	1.85	1.90	1.95	2.00	2.05	2.10	2.15
0.10-0.20	SPECIFIED CLEARANCE/NO ADJUSTMENT REQUIRED																				
0.21-0.25	1.30	1.35	1.40	1.45	1.50	1.55	1.60	1.65	1.70	1.75	1.80	1.85	1.90	1.95	2.00	2.05	2.10	2.15	2.20	2.20	
0.26-0.30	1.35	1.40	1.45	1.50	1.55	1.60	1.65	1.70	1.75	1.80	1.85	1.90	1.95	2.00	2.05	2.10	2.15	2.20			
0.31-0.35	1.40	1.45	1.50	1.55	1.60	1.65	1.70	1.75	1.80	1.85	1.90	1.95	2.00	2.05	2.10	2.15	2.20				
0.36-0.40	1.45	1.50	1.55	1.60	1.65	1.70	1.75	1.80	1.85	1.90	1.95	2.00	2.05	2.10	2.15	2.20					
0.41-0.45	1.50	1.55	1.60	1.65	1.70	1.75	1.80	1.85	1.90	1.95	2.00	2.05	2.10	2.15	2.20						
0.46-0.50	1.55	1.60	1.65	1.70	1.75	1.80	1.85	1.90	1.95	2.00	2.05	2.10	2.15	2.20							
0.51-0.55	1.60	1.65	1.70	1.75	1.80	1.85	1.90	1.95	2.00	2.05	2.10	2.15	2.20								
0.56-0.60	1.65	1.70	1.75	1.80	1.85	1.90	1.95	2.00	2.05	2.10	2.15	2.20									
0.61-0.65	1.70	1.75	1.80	1.85	1.90	1.95	2.00	2.05	2.10	2.15	2.20										
0.66-0.70	1.75	1.80	1.85	1.90	1.95	2.00	2.05	2.10	2.15	2.20											
0.71-0.75	1.80	1.85	1.90	1.95	2.00	2.05	2.10	2.15	2.20												
0.76-0.80	1.85	1.90	1.95	2.00	2.05	2.10	2.15	2.20													
0.81-0.85	1.90	1.95	2.00	2.05	2.10	2.15	2.20														
0.86-0.90	1.95	2.00	2.05	2.10	2.15	2.20															
0.91-0.95	2.00	2.05	2.10	2.15	2.20																
0.96-1.00	2.05	2.10	2.15	2.20																	
1.01-1.05	2.10	2.15	2.20																		
1.06-1.10	2.15	2.20																			
1.11-1.15	2.20																				

H31236

23.15a Shim selection chart – inlet valves

MEASURED TAPPET CLEARANCE (mm)	PRESENT SHIM SIZE (mm)																				
	1.20	1.25	1.30	1.35	1.40	1.45	1.50	1.55	1.60	1.65	1.70	1.75	1.80	1.85	1.90	1.95	2.00	2.05	2.10	2.15	2.20
0.05-0.09				1.20	1.25	1.30	1.35	1.40	1.45	1.50	1.55	1.60	1.65	1.70	1.75	1.80	1.85	1.90	1.95	2.00	2.05
0.10-0.14			1.20	1.25	1.30	1.35	1.40	1.45	1.50	1.55	1.60	1.65	1.70	1.75	1.80	1.85	1.90	1.95	2.00	2.05	2.10
0.15-0.19		1.20	1.25	1.30	1.35	1.40	1.45	1.50	1.55	1.60	1.65	1.70	1.75	1.80	1.85	1.90	1.95	2.00	2.05	2.10	2.15
0.20-0.30	SPECIFIED CLEARANCE/NO ADJUSTMENT REQUIRED																				
0.31-0.35	1.30	1.35	1.40	1.45	1.50	1.55	1.60	1.65	1.70	1.75	1.80	1.85	1.90	1.95	2.00	2.05	2.10	2.15	2.20	2.20	
0.36-0.40	1.35	1.40	1.45	1.50	1.55	1.60	1.65	1.70	1.75	1.80	1.85	1.90	1.95	2.00	2.05	2.10	2.15	2.20			
0.41-0.45	1.40	1.45	1.50	1.55	1.60	1.65	1.70	1.75	1.80	1.85	1.90	1.95	2.00	2.05	2.10	2.15	2.20				
0.46-0.50	1.45	1.50	1.55	1.60	1.65	1.70	1.75	1.80	1.85	1.90	1.95	2.00	2.05	2.10	2.15	2.20					
0.51-0.55	1.50	1.55	1.60	1.65	1.70	1.75	1.80	1.85	1.90	1.95	2.00	2.05	2.10	2.15	2.20						
0.56-0.60	1.55	1.60	1.65	1.70	1.75	1.80	1.85	1.90	1.95	2.00	2.05	2.10	2.15	2.20							
0.61-0.65	1.60	1.65	1.70	1.75	1.80	1.85	1.90	1.95	2.00	2.05	2.10	2.15	2.20								
0.66-0.70	1.65	1.70	1.75	1.80	1.85	1.90	1.95	2.00	2.05	2.10	2.15	2.20									
0.71-0.75	1.70	1.75	1.80	1.85	1.90	1.95	2.00	2.05	2.10	2.15	2.20										
0.76-0.80	1.75	1.80	1.85	1.90	1.95	2.00	2.05	2.10	2.15	2.20											
0.81-0.85	1.80	1.85	1.90	1.95	2.00	2.05	2.10	2.15	2.20												
0.86-0.90	1.85	1.90	1.95	2.00	2.05	2.10	2.15	2.20													
0.91-0.95	1.90	1.95	2.00	2.05	2.10	2.15	2.20														
0.96-1.00	1.95	2.00	2.05	2.10	2.15	2.20															
1.01-1.05	2.00	2.05	2.10	2.15	2.20																
1.06-1.10	2.05	2.10	2.15	2.20																	
1.11-1.15	2.10	2.15	2.20																		
1.16-1.20	2.15	2.20																			
1.21-1.25	2.20																				

H31237

23.15b Shim selection chart – exhaust valves

Shims are available in 0.05 mm increments from 1.200 to 2.200 mm. If the shim thickness is less than its denomination, this must be taken into account when selecting a new shim.

15 Using the appropriate shim selection chart, find where the measured valve clearance and existing shim thickness values intersect and read off the shim size required **(see illustrations)**. **Note:** *If the existing shim is marked with a number not ending in 0 or 5, round it up or down as appropriate to the nearest number ending in 0 or 5 so that the chart can be used.* **Note:** *If the required renewal shim is greater than 2.20 mm (the largest available), the valve is probably not seating correctly due to a build-*up of carbon deposits and should be checked and cleaned or resurfaced as required (see Chapter 2).

16 Obtain the correct thickness shims from your Suzuki dealer. Where the required thickness is not equal to the available shim thickness, round off the measurement to the nearest available size.

17 Obtain the replacement shim, then lubricate it with engine oil or molybdenum disulphide oil (a 50/50 mixture of molybdenum disulphide grease and engine oil) and fit it into its recess in the top of the valve, with the size marking on each shim facing up **(see illustration)**. Check that the shim is correctly seated, then lubricate the follower with engine oil or molybdenum disulphide oil and install it onto the valve **(see illustration)**. Repeat the process for any other valves as required, then install the camshafts (see Chapter 2).

18 Rotate the crankshaft several turns to seat the new shim(s), then check the clearances again.

19 Install all disturbed components in a reverse of the removal sequence. Use a new O-ring on the centre plug and a new sealing washer on the timing inspection plug and smear the O-ring and the plug threads with engine oil or molybdenum disulphide oil (a 50/50 mixture of molybdenum disulphide grease and engine oil) **(see illustration)**.

23.17a Fit the shim into the recess in the top of the valve . . .

23.17b . . . then install the follower

23.19 Use a new O-ring and sealing washer on the centre and inspection plugs

Every two years

24 Brakes – fluid change

1 The brake fluid should be changed at the prescribed interval or whenever a master cylinder or caliper overhaul is carried out. Refer to the brake bleeding section in Chapter 7, noting that all old fluid must be pumped from the fluid reservoir and hydraulic line before filling with new fluid.

HAYNES HiNT Old brake fluid is invariably much darker than new fluid, making it easy to see when all old fluid has been expelled from the system.

25 Cooling system – draining, flushing and refilling

⚠ **Warning: Allow the engine to cool completely before performing this maintenance operation. Also, don't allow antifreeze to come into contact with your skin or the painted surfaces of the motorcycle. Rinse off spills immediately with plenty of water. Antifreeze is highly toxic if ingested. Never leave antifreeze lying around in an open container or in puddles on the floor; children and pets are attracted by its sweet smell and may drink it. Check with local authorities (councils) about disposing of antifreeze. Many communities have collection centres which will see that antifreeze is disposed of safely. Antifreeze is also combustible, so don't store it near open flames.**

Draining

1 Remove the fairing side panels (see Chapter 8). Remove the pressure cap by turning it anti-clockwise until it reaches a stop. If you hear a hissing sound (indicating there is still pressure in the system), wait until it stops. Now press down on the cap and continue turning the cap until it can be removed **(see illustration 9.6)**.

2 Position a suitable container beneath the water pump on the left-hand side of the engine. Slacken the clamp securing the radiator hose to the front of the water pump and release the cable tie, then pull the hose off its union and allow the coolant to completely drain from the system **(see illustrations)**. Also remove the reservoir cap, then detach the hose from the bottom of the reservoir and drain the coolant **(see illustration)**. Reconnect the hose after the reservoir has drained.

Flushing

3 Flush the radiator with clean tap water by inserting a garden hose in the radiator filler neck. Allow the water to run through until it is clear and flows cleanly out of the drain holes. If the radiator is extremely corroded, remove it (see Chapter 3) and have it cleaned professionally.

4 Now reconnect the radiator hose to the water pump and fill the system with clean water, then drain it again. Reconnect the hose and tighten the clamp.

5 Fill the cooling system with clean water mixed with a flushing compound. Make sure the flushing compound is compatible with aluminium components, and follow the manufacturer's instructions carefully. Fit the pressure cap.

6 Start the engine and allow it to reach normal operating temperature. Let it run for about ten minutes.

7 Stop the engine. Let it cool for a while, then cover the pressure cap with a heavy rag and turn it anti-clockwise to the first stop, releasing any pressure that may be present in the system. Once the hissing stops, push down on the cap and remove it completely.

8 Drain the system once again.

9 Fill the system with clean water, fit the radiator cap and repeat the procedure in Steps 6 to 8.

Refilling

10 Fit the radiator hose onto the water pump and tighten the clamp securely, then fit the cable tie **(see illustration 25.2a)**.

11 Fill the system with the proper coolant mixture (see this Chapter's Specifications) **(see illustration)**. Note: *Pour the coolant in slowly to minimise the amount of air entering the system.*

12 When the system is full (all the way up to the top of the radiator filler neck), install the pressure cap. Also top up the coolant reservoir to the 'F' level line (see *Daily (pre-ride) checks*).

13 Start the engine and allow it to idle for 2 to 3 minutes. Flick the throttle twistgrip part open 3 or 4 times, so that the engine speed rises to approximately 4000 – 5000 rpm, then stop the engine. Any air trapped in the system should have bled back to the radiator filler neck.

14 Let the engine cool then remove the pressure cap as described in Step 1. Check that the coolant level is still up to the radiator filler neck. If it's low, add the specified mixture until it reaches the top of the filler neck. Refit the cap.

15 Check the coolant level in the reservoir and top up if necessary.

16 Check the system for leaks.

17 Do not dispose of the old coolant by pouring it down the drain. Instead pour it into a heavy plastic container, cap it tightly and take it into an authorised disposal site or service station – see **Warning** at the beginning of this Section.

25.2a Slacken the clamp (A) and release the cable tie (B) . . .

25.2b . . . then detach the hose and drain the system

25.2c Detach the hose and drain the reservoir

25.11 Fill the system with the specified coolant mixture

Every four years

26 Brake hoses – renewal

1 The hoses will in time deteriorate with age and should be renewed regardless of their apparent condition.
2 Refer to Chapter 7 and disconnect the brake hoses from the master cylinders and calipers. Always renew the banjo union sealing washers and tighten the banjo union bolts to the specified torque setting.

27 Fuel hoses and EVAP hoses – renewal

⚠️ **Warning: Petrol (gasoline) is extremely flammable, so take extra precautions when you work on any part of the fuel system. Don't smoke or allow open flames or bare light bulbs near the work area, and don't work in a garage where a natural gas-type appliance is present. If you spill any fuel on your skin, rinse it off immediately with soap and water. When you perform any kind of work on the fuel system, wear safety glasses and have a fire extinguisher suitable for a Class B type fire (flammable liquids) on hand.**

1 The fuel delivery, return (injection models) and vacuum hoses should be renewed regardless of their condition. On California models, also renew the emission control system hoses (see Chapter 4).
2 Refer to Chapter 4 and raise or remove the fuel tank and remove the air filter housing. Disconnect the fuel hoses from the fuel tank, valve and from the carburettors or injector rail and pressure regulator as appropriate, noting the routing of each hose and where it connects. It is advisable to make a sketch of the various hoses before removing them to ensure they are correctly installed.
3 Secure each new hose to its unions using new clamps. Run the engine and check that there are no leaks before taking the machine out on the road.

Non-scheduled maintenance

28 Headlight aim – check and adjustment

Note: *An improperly adjusted headlight may cause problems for oncoming traffic or provide poor, unsafe illumination of the road ahead. Before adjusting the headlight aim, be sure to consult with local traffic laws and regulations – for UK models refer to MOT Test Checks in the Reference section.*
1 The headlight beam can adjusted both horizontally and vertically. Before making any adjustment, check that the tyre pressures are correct and the suspension is adjusted as required. Make any adjustments to the headlight aim with the machine on level ground, with the fuel tank half full and with an assistant sitting on the seat. If the bike is usually ridden with a passenger on the back, have a second assistant to do this.
2 Horizontal adjustment is made by turning the adjuster screw on the top outer corner of each headlight unit **(see illustration)**. Turn it clockwise to move the beam out (away from the centre of the bike), and anti-clockwise to move it in.
3 Vertical adjustment is made by turning the adjuster screw on the bottom outer corner of each headlight unit **(see illustration 28.2)**. Turn it clockwise to move the beam down, and anti-clockwise to move it up.

29 Wheel bearings – check

1 Wheel bearings will wear over a period of time and result in handling problems.

2 Support the motorcycle upright using an auxiliary stand so that the wheel being checked is off the ground. Check for any play in the bearings by pushing and pulling the wheel against the hub **(see illustration)**. Also rotate the wheel and check that it rotates smoothly.
3 If any play is detected in the hub, or if the wheel does not rotate smoothly (and this is not due to brake or transmission drag), the wheel bearings must be removed and inspected for wear or damage (see Chapter 7).

30 Front forks – oil change

1 Fork oil degrades over a period of time and loses its damping qualities. Refer to Chapter 6 for front fork removal, oil draining and refilling, following the relevant steps. The forks do not need to be completely disassembled.

28.2 Horizontal beam adjuster (A), vertical beam adjuster (B)

31 Cylinder compression – check

1 Among other things, poor engine performance may be caused by leaking valves, incorrect valve clearances, a leaking head gasket, or worn pistons, rings and/or cylinder walls. A cylinder compression check will help pinpoint these conditions and can also indicate the presence of excessive carbon deposits in the cylinder head.
2 The only tools required are a compression gauge (with a threaded adapter to suit the spark plug hole in the cylinder head) and a spark plug wrench. Depending on the outcome of the initial test, a squirt-type oil can may also be needed.
3 Make sure the valve clearances are correctly set (see Section 23) and that the cylinder head bolts are tightened to the correct torque setting (see Chapter 2).
4 Refer to *Fault Finding Equipment* in the

29.2 Checking for play in the wheel bearings

Reference section for details of the compression test, and to the Specifications at the beginning of this Chapter for the test data.

32 Engine – oil pressure check

1 The oil pressure warning display should flicker and the warning light come on when the ignition (main) switch is turned ON, and they extinguish after the engine is started – this serves as a check that the warning light bulb is sound. If the oil pressure light comes on whilst the engine is running, low oil pressure is indicated – stop the engine immediately and carry out an oil level check (see *Daily (pre-ride) checks*).

2 An oil pressure check must be carried out if the warning light comes on when the engine is running yet the oil level is good (Step 1). It can also provide useful information about the condition of the engine's lubrication system.

3 To check the oil pressure, a suitable gauge and adapter piece (which screws into the crankcase) will be needed. Suzuki provide a kit (pt nos. 09915-74510 and 09915-74540) for this purpose.

4 Warm the engine up to normal operating temperature then stop it.

5 Place a suitable container below the main oil gallery plug below the starter clutch cover on the right-hand side of the engine to catch any oil. Unscrew the plug and swiftly screw the adapter into the crankcase threads **(see illustration)**. Connect the gauge to the adapter. If much oil is lost, replenish it to the correct level before proceeding (see *Daily (pre-ride) checks*).

6 Start the engine and increase the engine speed to 3000 rpm whilst watching the gauge reading. The oil pressure should be similar to that given in the Specifications at the start of this Chapter.

7 If the pressure is significantly lower than the standard, either the pressure regulator is stuck open, the oil pump is faulty, the oil strainer or filter is blocked, or there is other engine damage. Begin diagnosis by checking the oil filter, strainer and regulator, then the oil pump (see Chapter 2). If those items check out okay, chances are the bearing oil clearances are excessive and the engine needs to be overhauled.

8 If the pressure is too high, either an oil passage is clogged, the regulator is stuck closed or the wrong grade of oil is being used.

9 Stop the engine and unscrew the gauge and adapter from the crankcase.

10 Install the main oil gallery plug using a new sealing washer, and tighten it to the torque setting specified at the beginning of the Chapter. Check the oil level (see *Daily (pre-ride) checks*).

33 Steering head bearings – lubrication

1 Over a period of time the grease will harden or may be washed out of the bearings by incorrect use of jet washes.

2 Disassemble the steering head for re-greasing of the bearings. Refer to Chapter 6 for details.

32.5 Main oil gallery oil plug (arrowed)

34 Rear suspension bearings – lubrication

1 Over a period of time the grease will harden or dirt will penetrate the bearings.

2 The suspension components are not equipped with grease nipples. Remove the swingarm and the suspension linkage as described in Chapter 6 for greasing of the bearings.

35 Brake caliper and master cylinder seals – renewal

1 Brake seals will deteriorate over a period of time and lose their effectiveness, leading to sticking operation or fluid loss, or allowing the ingress of air and dirt. Refer to Chapter 7 and dismantle the components for seal renewal.

Chapter 2
Engine, clutch and transmission

Contents

Degrees of difficulty

Easy, suitable for novice with little experience	**Fairly easy,** suitable for beginner with some experience	**Fairly difficult,** suitable for competent DIY mechanic	**Difficult,** suitable for experienced DIY mechanic	**Very difficult,** suitable for expert DIY or professional

Specifications – GSX-R600 models

General

Type	Four-stroke in-line four
Capacity	600 cc
Bore	65.5 mm
Stroke	44.5 mm
Compression ratio	12.0 to 1
Clutch	Wet multi-plate
Transmission	6-speed constant mesh
Final drive	Chain

Camshafts – V models

Inlet lobe height
  California models
    Standard .... 33.992 to 34.048 mm
    Service limit (min) .... 33.70 mm
  All other models
    Standard .... 35.992 to 36.048 mm
    Service limit (min) .... 35.70 mm
Exhaust lobe height
  Standard .... 35.292 to 35.348 mm
  Service limit (min) .... 35.00 mm
Journal diameter .... 23.959 to 23.980 mm
Journal holder diameter .... 24.012 to 24.025 mm
Journal oil clearance
  Standard .... 0.032 to 0.066 mm
  Service limit (max) .... 0.15 mm
Runout (max) .... 0.10 mm

Camshafts – W, X and Y models

Inlet lobe height
  California models
    Standard .... 33.980 to 34.048 mm
    Service limit (min) .... 33.68 mm
  All other models
    Standard .... 36.660 to 36.728 mm
    Service limit (min) .... 36.36 mm
Exhaust lobe height
  Standard .... 34.780 to 34.848 mm
  Service limit (min) .... 34.48 mm
Journal diameter .... 23.959 to 23.980 mm
Journal holder diameter .... 24.012 to 24.025 mm
Journal oil clearance
  Standard .... 0.032 to 0.066 mm
  Service limit (max) .... 0.15 mm
Runout (max) .... 0.10 mm

Valves, guides and springs

Valve clearances .... see Chapter 1
Inlet valve
  Head diameter .... 26.5 mm
  Stem diameter .... 4.475 to 4.490 mm
  Guide bore diameter .... 4.500 to 4.512 mm
  Stem-to-guide clearance .... 0.010 to 0.037 mm
  Stem deflection (max) – see text .... 0.35 mm
  Margin thickness (min) .... 0.5 mm
  Seat width .... 0.9 to 1.1 mm
  Head runout (max) .... 0.03 mm
  Stem runout (max) .... 0.05 mm
Exhaust valve
  Head diameter .... 22.0 mm
  Stem diameter .... 4.455 to 4.470 mm
  Guide bore diameter .... 4.500 to 4.512 mm
  Stem-to-guide clearance .... 0.030 to 0.057 mm
  Stem deflection (max) – see text .... 0.35 mm
  Margin thickness (min) .... 0.5 mm
  Seat width .... 0.9 to 1.1 mm
  Head runout (max) .... 0.03 mm
  Stem runout (max) .... 0.05 mm
Valve springs (inlet and exhaust)
  Free length limit (min)
    Inner spring .... 36.8 mm
    Outer spring .... 38.6 mm
  Spring tension
    Inner spring .... 29.9 mm with 4.5 kg load
    Outer spring .... 33.4 mm with 15.5 kg load

Cylinder block

Bore .... 65.500 to 65.515 mm
Warpage (max) .... 0.20 mm
Cylinder compression .... see Chapter 1

Cylinder head

Warpage (max) .... 0.20 mm

Pistons

Piston diameter (measured 15.0 mm up from skirt, at 90° to piston pin axis)	
Standard	65.470 to 65.485 mm
Service limit (min)	65.380 mm
Piston-to-bore clearance	0.025 to 0.035 mm
Piston pin diameter	
Standard	14.993 to 15.000 mm
Service limit (min)	14.980 mm
Piston pin bore diameter in piston	
Standard	15.002 to 15.008 mm
Service limit (max)	15.030 mm

Piston rings

Ring end gap (free)	
Top ring	
Standard	
V models	6.90 mm (approx.)
W models	6.20 mm (approx.)
X and Y models	5.40 mm (approx.)
Service limit (min)	
V models	5.50 mm
W models	4.90 mm
X and Y models	4.30 mm
2nd ring	
Standard	
V models	8.70 mm (approx.)
W models	8.00 mm (approx.)
X and Y models	5.90 mm
Service limit (min)	
V models	6.90 mm
W models	6.40 mm
X and Y models	4.70 mm
Ring end gap (installed)	
Top ring	
Standard	
V and W models	0.10 to 0.25 mm
X and Y models	0.08 to 0.20 mm
Service limit (max)	
All models	0.50 mm
2nd ring	
Standard	0.10 to 0.25 mm
Service limit (max)	0.50 mm
Ring thickness	
Top ring	0.97 to 0.99 mm
2nd ring	0.77 to 0.79 mm
Ring groove width in piston	
Top ring	1.01 to 1.03 mm
2nd ring	0.81 to 0.83 mm
Oil ring	1.51 to 1.53 mm
Ring-to-groove clearance	
Top ring (max)	0.18 mm
2nd ring (max)	0.18 mm

Clutch

Friction plate	
Quantity	9
Thickness	2.92 to 3.08 mm
Tab width (min) – V models	13.0 mm
Tab width – W, X and Y models	
Standard	13.7 to 13.8 mm
Service limit (min)	12.9 mm
Plain plate	
Quantity	8 (see text)
Warpage (max)	0.1 mm
Assembled clutch plate thickness	
W models	40.068 to 40.668 mm with 5 kg load (see text)
X and Y models	45.085 to 45.685 mm with 5 kg load (see text)
Diaphragm spring free height (min)	2.9 mm
Release mechanism screw	1/4 turn out

Lubrication system

Oil pressure	see Chapter 1	
Oil pump	**Standard**	**Service limit (max)**
Inner rotor tip-to-outer rotor clearance	0.10 mm	0.15 mm
Outer rotor-to-body clearance	0.15 to 0.22 mm	0.35 mm

Transmission

Gear ratios (no. of teeth) – V models
Primary reduction	1.756 to 1 (72/41T)
Final reduction	2.812 to 1 (45/16T)
1st gear	2.866 to 1 (43/15T)
2nd gear	2.058 to 1 (35/17T)
3rd gear	1.650 to 1 (33/20T)
4th gear	1.428 to 1 (30/21T)
5th gear	1.285 to 1 (27/21T)
6th gear	1.181 to 1 (26/22T)

Gear ratios (no. of teeth) – W, X and Y models
Primary reduction	1.756 to 1 (72/41T)
Final reduction	2.875 to 1 (46/16T)
1st gear	2.866 to 1 (43/15T)
2nd gear	2.052 to 1 (39/19T)
3rd gear	1.650 to 1 (33/20T)
4th gear	1.428 to 1 (30/21T)
5th gear	1.285 to 1 (27/21T)
6th gear	1.181 to 1 (26/22T)

Selector drum and forks

Selector fork-to-groove clearance	
Standard	0.1 to 0.3 mm
Service limit (max)	0.5 mm
Selector fork end thickness	4.8 to 4.9 mm
Selector fork groove width	5.0 to 5.1 mm

Crankshaft and bearings

Journal diameter	
Code A	33.992 to 34.000 mm
Code B	33.984 to 33.992 mm
Code C	33.976 to 33.984 mm
Main bearing oil clearance	
Standard – V models	0.020 to 0.044 mm
Standard – W, X and Y models	0.016 to 0.040 mm
Service limit (max) – all models	0.080 mm
Runout (max)	0.05 mm
Thrust bearing clearance	0.055 to 0.110 mm
Thrust bearing thickness	
Right-hand side	2.425 to 2.450 mm
Left-hand side	2.350 to 2.500 mm

Connecting rods

Small-end internal diameter	
Standard	15.010 to 15.018 mm
Service limit (max)	15.040 mm
Big-end side clearance	
Standard	0.1 to 0.2 mm
Service limit (max)	0.3 mm
Big-end width	20.95 to 21.00 mm
Crankpin width	21.10 to 21.15 mm
Big-end diameter	
Code 1	35.000 to 35.008 mm
Code 2	35.008 to 35.016 mm
Crankpin diameter	
Code 1	31.992 to 32.000 mm
Code 2	31.984 to 31.992 mm
Code 3	31.976 to 31.984 mm
Big-end oil clearance	
Standard	0.032 to 0.056 mm
Service limit (max)	0.08 mm

Torque wrench settings – see end of Specifications

Specifications – GSX-R750 models

General

Type	Four-stroke in-line four
Capacity	749 cc
Bore	72.0 mm
Stroke	46.0 mm
Compression ratio	11.8 to 1
Clutch	Wet multi-plate
Transmission	6-speed constant mesh
Final drive	Chain

Camshafts – T and V models

Inlet lobe height	
California models	
Standard	33.992 to 34.048 mm
Service limit (min)	33.70 mm
All other models	
Standard	36.502 to 36.558 mm
Service limit (min)	36.21 mm
Exhaust lobe height	
Standard	35.692 to 35.748 mm
Service limit (min)	35.40 mm
Journal diameter	23.959 to 23.980 mm
Journal holder diameter	24.012 to 24.025 mm
Journal oil clearance	
Standard	0.032 to 0.066 mm
Service limit (max)	0.15 mm
Runout (max)	0.10 mm

Camshafts – W and X models

Inlet lobe height	
Standard	36.660 to 36.728 mm
Service limit (min)	36.34 mm
Exhaust lobe height	
Standard	35.280 to 35.348 mm
Service limit (min)	34.98 mm
Journal diameter	23.959 to 23.980 mm
Journal holder diameter	24.012 to 24.025 mm
Journal oil clearance	
Standard	0.032 to 0.066 mm
Service limit (max)	0.15 mm
Runout (max)	0.10 mm

Cylinder head

Warpage (max)	0.20 mm

Valves, guides and springs

Valve clearances	see Chapter 1
Inlet valve	
Head diameter	29.0 mm
Stem diameter	4.475 to 4.490 mm
Guide bore diameter	4.500 to 4.512 mm
Stem-to-guide clearance	0.010 to 0.037 mm
Stem deflection (max) – see text	0.35 mm
Margin thickness (min)	0.5 mm
Seat width	0.9 to 1.1 mm
Head runout (max)	0.03 mm
Stem runout (max)	0.05 mm
Exhaust valve	
Head diameter	24.0 mm
Stem diameter	4.455 to 4.470 mm
Guide bore diameter	4.500 to 4.512 mm
Stem-to-guide clearance	0.030 to 0.057 mm
Stem deflection (max) – see text	0.35 mm
Margin thickness (min)	0.5 mm
Seat width	0.9 to 1.1 mm
Head runout (max)	0.03 mm
Stem runout (max)	0.05 mm

Valves, guides and springs (continued)

Valve springs (inlet and exhaust)
    Free length limit (min)
        Inner spring . . . .   36.8 mm
        Outer spring . . . .   38.6 mm
    Spring tension
        Inner spring . . . .   29.9 mm with 4.5 kg load
        Outer spring – T and V models . . . .   33.4 mm with 15.5 kg load
        Outer spring – W and X models . . . .   33.4 mm with 18.3 kg load

Cylinder block

Bore . . . .   72.000 to 72.015 mm
Warpage (max) . . . .   0.20 mm
Cylinder compression . . . .   see Chapter 1

Pistons

Piston diameter (measured 15.0 mm up from skirt, at 90° to piston pin axis)
    Standard – T and V models . . . .   71.955 to 71.970 mm
    Standard – W and X models . . . .   71.970 to 71.985 mm
    Service limit (min) . . . .   71.880 mm
Piston-to-bore clearance
    T and V models . . . .   0.040 to 0.050 mm
    W and X models . . . .   0.025 to 0.035 mm
Piston pin diameter
    Standard . . . .   15.995 to 16.000 mm
    Service limit (min) . . . .   15.980 mm
Piston pin bore diameter in piston
    Standard . . . .   16.002 to 16.008 mm
    Service limit (max) . . . .   16.030 mm

Piston rings

Ring end gap (free)
    Top ring
        Standard
            T and V models . . . .   6.90 mm (approx.)
            W and X models . . . .   7.20 mm (approx.)
        Service limit (min)
            T and V models . . . .   5.50 mm
            W and X models . . . .   5.70 mm
    2nd ring
        Standard
            T and V models . . . .   8.70 mm (approx.)
            W and X models . . . .   8.50 mm (approx.)
        Service limit (min)
            T and V models . . . .   6.90 mm
            W and X models . . . .   6.80 mm
Ring end gap (installed)
    Top ring
        Standard . . . .   0.10 to 0.25 mm
        Service limit (max) . . . .   0.50 mm
    2nd ring
        Standard . . . .   0.10 to 0.25 mm
        Service limit (max) . . . .   0.50 mm
Ring thickness
    Top ring . . . .   0.97 to 0.99 mm
    2nd ring . . . .   0.77 to 0.79 mm
Ring groove width in piston
    Top ring . . . .   1.01 to 1.03 mm
    2nd ring . . . .   0.81 to 0.83 mm
    Oil ring . . . .   1.51 to 1.53 mm
Ring-to-groove clearance
    Top ring (max) . . . .   0.18 mm
    2nd ring (max) . . . .   0.18 mm

Clutch

Friction plate
Quantity 10
Thickness . . . . 2.92 to 3.08 mm
Tab width (min) . . . . 13.0 mm
Plain plate
Quantity 9
Warpage (max) . . . . 0.1 mm
Assembled clutch plate thickness (W and X models) . . . . 45.05 to 45.65 mm with 5 kg load (see text)
Diaphragm spring free height (min) . . . . 2.9 mm
Release mechanism screw . . . . 1/4 turn out

Lubrication system

Oil pressure . . . . see Chapter 1
Oil pump – T and V models
Inner rotor tip-to-outer rotor clearance
Standard . . . . 0.10 mm
Service limit (max) . . . . 0.15 mm
Outer rotor-to-body clearance
Standard . . . . 0.15 to 0.22 mm
Service limit (max) . . . . 0.35 mm
Oil pump – W and X models
Inner rotor tip-to-outer rotor clearance (max) . . . . 0.20 mm
Outer rotor-to-body clearance (max) . . . . 0.35 mm

Transmission

Gear ratios (no. of teeth) – T and V models
Primary reduction . . . . 1.756 to 1 (72/41T)
Final reduction . . . . 2.687 to 1 (43/16T)
1st gear . . . . 2.866 to 1 (43/15T)
2nd gear . . . . 2.058 to 1 (35/17T)
3rd gear . . . . 1.650 to 1 (33/20T)
4th gear . . . . 1.428 to 1 (30/21T)
5th gear . . . . 1.260 to 1 (29/23T)
6th gear . . . . 1.120 to 1 (28/25T)
Gear ratios (no. of teeth) – W and X models
Primary reduction . . . . 1.756 to 1 (72/41T)
Final reduction . . . . 2.750 to 1 (44/16T)
1st gear . . . . 2.625 to 1 (42/16T)
2nd gear . . . . 1.950 to 1 (39/20T)
3rd gear . . . . 1.565 to 1 (36/23T)
4th gear . . . . 1.363 to 1 (30/22T)
5th gear . . . . 1.227 to 1 (27/22T)
6th gear . . . . 1.120 to 1 (28/25T)

Selector drum and forks

Selector fork-to-gear groove clearance
Standard . . . . 0.1 to 0.3 mm
Service limit (max) . . . . 0.5 mm
Selector fork end thickness . . . . 4.8 to 4.9 mm
Selector fork groove width in gears . . . . 5.0 to 5.1 mm

Crankshaft and bearings

Journal diameter
Code A . . . . 33.992 to 34.000 mm
Code B . . . . 33.984 to 33.992 mm
Code C . . . . 33.976 to 33.984 mm
Main bearing oil clearance
Standard – T and V models . . . . 0.020 to 0.044 mm
Standard – W and X models . . . . 0.016 to 0.040 mm
Service limit (max) – all models . . . . 0.080 mm
Runout (max) . . . . 0.05 mm
Thrust bearing clearance . . . . 0.055 to 0.110 mm
Thrust bearing thickness
Right-hand side . . . . 2.425 to 2.450 mm
Left-hand side . . . . 2.350 to 2.500 mm

Connecting rods

Small-end internal diameter	
Standard	16.010 to 16.018 mm
Service limit (max)	16.040 mm
Big-end side clearance	
Standard	0.1 to 0.2 mm
Service limit (max)	0.3 mm
Big-end width	20.95 to 21.00 mm
Crankpin width	21.10 to 21.15 mm
Big-end diameter	
Code 1	37.000 to 37.008 mm
Code 2	37.008 to 37.016 mm
Crankpin diameter	
Code 1	33.992 to 34.000 mm
Code 2	33.984 to 33.992 mm
Code 3	33.976 to 33.984 mm
Big-end oil clearance	
Standard	0.032 to 0.056 mm
Service limit (max)	0.08 mm

Torque wrench settings (all models)

Engine mountings	
Adjusting bolt	10 Nm
Adjusting bolt locknut	45 Nm
Upper and lower rear mounting bolt nuts	79 Nm
Right-hand and left-hand front mounting bolts	
GSX-R600 models	55 Nm
GSX-R750 models	79 Nm
Mounting lug pinchbolts	23 Nm
Oil cooler bolt	
GSX-R750X	70 Nm
All other models	73 Nm
Valve cover bolts	14 Nm
Cam chain tensioner mounting bolts	10 Nm
Cam chain tensioner and guide blade pivot bolts	10 Nm
Cam chain top guide bolts	10 Nm
Cam chain stopper bolt	14 Nm
Camshaft holder bolts	10 Nm
Oil pipe to camshaft holder banjo bolts	10 Nm
Cylinder head 10 mm bolts	
Initial setting	25 Nm
Final setting	43 Nm
Cylinder head 6 mm bolts	10 Nm
Oil hose to cylinder head banjo bolt	20 Nm
Cylinder block nuts	10 Nm
Coolant union to cylinder block bolts	10 Nm
Clutch nut	150 Nm
Gearchange mechanism locating pin in crankcase	19 Nm
Starter clutch bolt	54 Nm
Oil pressure regulator	28 Nm
Oil strainer housing bolts	12 Nm
Oil pick-up tube bolts	12 Nm
Oil sump bolts	14 Nm
Oil pump bolts	10 Nm
Crankshaft journal bolts (9 mm)	32 Nm
Crankcase bolts (8 mm)	24 Nm
Crankcase bolts (6 mm)	11 Nm
Oil hose banjo bolt to upper crankcase	20 Nm
Oil pipe banjo bolt to lower crankcase	25 Nm
Alternator oil jet	5 Nm
Selector drum stopper plate bolt	10 Nm
Connecting rod cap nuts	
Initial setting	35 Nm
Final setting	67 Nm

1 General information

The engine/transmission unit is a water-cooled in-line four. The valves are operated by double overhead camshafts which are chain driven off the crankshaft. The engine/transmission assembly is constructed from aluminium alloy. The crankcase divides horizontally into three parts.

The crankcase incorporates a wet sump, pressure-fed lubrication system which uses a gear-driven, dual-rotor oil pump, an oil filter and by-pass valve assembly, a relief valve and an oil pressure switch. The oil is routed around a cooler unit which is fed off the engine's cooling system.

Power from the crankshaft is routed to the transmission via the clutch, which is of the wet, multi-plate type with diaphragm springs, and is cable-operated. The transmission is a six-speed constant-mesh unit. Final drive to the rear wheel is by chain and sprockets.

2 Operations possible with the engine in the frame

The components and assemblies listed below can be removed without having to remove the engine/transmission assembly from the frame. If however, a number of areas require attention at the same time, removal of the engine/transmission is recommended.

Oil cooler
Valve cover
Cam chain tensioner and cam chain guides
Cam chain and cam chain tensioner blade
Camshafts
Cylinder head
Cylinder block, pistons and piston rings
Ignition rotor and pulse generator coil
*   assembly*
Clutch
Gearchange mechanism (external
*   components)*
Alternator
Starter clutch and idle gear
Oil sump, oil strainer and oil pressure relief
*   valve*
Oil pump
Starter motor

3 Operations requiring engine removal

It is necessary to remove the engine/transmission assembly from the frame and separate the crankcase halves to gain access to the following components.
Transmission shafts
Selector drum and forks
Crankshaft and bearings
Connecting rods and bearings

4 Major engine repair – general note

1 It is not always easy to determine when or if an engine should be completely overhauled, as a number of factors must be considered.
2 High mileage is not necessarily an indication that an overhaul is needed, while low mileage, on the other hand, does not preclude the need for an overhaul. Frequency of servicing is probably the single most important consideration. An engine that has regular and frequent oil and filter changes, as well as other required maintenance, will most likely give many miles of reliable service. Conversely, a neglected engine, or one which has not been run in properly, may require an overhaul very early in its life.
3 Exhaust smoke and excessive oil consumption are both indications that piston rings and/or valve guides are in need of attention, although make sure that the fault is not due to oil leakage.
4 If the engine is making obvious knocking or rumbling noises, the connecting rod and/or main bearings are probably at fault.
5 Loss of power, rough running, excessive valve train noise and high fuel consumption rates may also point to the need for an overhaul, especially if they are all present at the same time. If a complete tune-up does not remedy the situation, major mechanical work is the only solution.
6 An engine overhaul generally involves restoring the internal parts to the specifications of a new engine. The piston rings and main and connecting rod bearings are usually renewed during a major overhaul. Generally the valve seats are re-ground, since they are usually in less than perfect condition at this point. The end result should be a like new engine that will give as many trouble-free miles as the original.
7 Before beginning the engine overhaul, read through the related procedures to familiarise yourself with the scope and requirements of the job. Overhauling an engine is not all that difficult, but it is time consuming. Plan on the motorcycle being tied up for a minimum of two weeks. Check on the availability of parts and make sure that any necessary special tools, equipment and supplies are obtained in advance.
8 Most work can be done with typical workshop hand tools, although a number of precision measuring tools are required for inspecting parts to determine if they must be renewed. Often a dealer will handle the inspection of parts and offer advice concerning reconditioning and renewal. As a general rule, time is the primary cost of an overhaul so it does not pay to install worn or substandard parts.
9 As a final note, to ensure maximum life and minimum trouble from a rebuilt engine, everything must be assembled with care in a spotlessly clean environment.

5 Engine – removal and installation

Warning: The engine is very heavy. Removal and installation should be carried out with the aid of at least one assistant; personal injury or damage could occur if the engine falls or is dropped. If available, an hydraulic or mechanical floor jack can be used to support and lower or raise the engine.
Note: *Peg spanners are required to slacken and tighten the locknut and adjuster bolt on the lower rear engine mounting bolts If the Suzuki service tool (pt. no. 09940-14980) or a suitable peg spanner is not available, one will have to be obtained, or fabricated (see* **Tool Tip***).*
Note: *The rear engine mounting bolt nuts are self-locking, and Suzuki advise that they can only be used once, so new ones should be obtained before installing the engine.*
Note: *On GSX-R750 models, the lower rear mounting bolt, adjusting bolt and locknut were upgraded on V (1997) models onwards. Owners of T models should ask their dealer whether they advise fitting the new parts on their model when installing the engine, noting that they must be fitted as a set.*

Removal

1 Support the bike securely in an upright position using an auxiliary stand. Work can be made easier by raising the machine to a suitable working height on an hydraulic ramp or a suitable platform. Make sure the motorcycle is secure and will not topple over (see *Tools and Workshop Tips* in the Reference section).
2 If the engine is dirty, particularly around its mountings, wash it thoroughly before starting any major dismantling work. This will make work much easier and rule out the possibility of caked on lumps of dirt falling into some vital component.
3 Drain the engine oil and, if required, remove the oil filter (see Chapter 1).
4 Remove the seats, the fairing side panels and the lower fairing (see Chapter 8).
5 Disconnect the negative (-ve) lead from the battery (see Chapter 9). Also disconnect the earth wire and its connector **(see illustration)**.

5.5 Disconnect the earth lead (A) and the earth wire connector (B)

5.8a Disconnect the coil/cap wiring connectors . . .

5.8b . . . and on injection models the camshaft position sensor wiring connector (arrowed)

5.11a Coolant temperature sensor wiring connector (A) and hose clamp (B) – carburettor models

Release the earth lead from any clips or ties, then feed it through to the engine and coil it on the crankcase, noting its routing.

6 Remove the fuel tank and the air filter housing (see Chapter 4).

7 Remove the carburettors or throttle bodies according to model (see Chapter 4). Plug the engine inlet manifolds with clean rag.

8 On GSX-R750T and V models, pull the spark plug cap off each spark plug and secure the leads clear of the engine. On all other models, disconnect the ignition coil/plug cap wiring connectors, and on GSX-R750W and X models the camshaft position sensor wiring

5.11b Coolant temperature sensor wiring connectors (A) and hose clamp (B) – injection models

connector, and secure the wiring clear of the engine (see illustrations).

9 Remove the exhaust system (see Chapter 4).

10 Remove the radiator and the coolant reservoir (see Chapter 3).

11 Disconnect the coolant temperature sensor wiring connector(s) from the sensor(s) in the thermostat housing, then slacken the clamp securing the coolant hose to the housing and detach the hose – there is no need to draw the hose out of its hole in the frame (see illustrations). On fuel injected models, note which connector fits on which sensor (grey – left-facing sensor, brown – rear-facing sensor).

12 Pull back the rubber cover on the starter motor terminal and remove the screw (600 models) or nut (750 models) securing the lead to the motor (see illustration). Secure it clear of the engine.

13 Trace the ignition pulse generator wiring back from the top of the starter clutch cover on the left-hand side of the engine and disconnect it at the 2-pin connector with the black and green wires (see illustration). Release the wiring from any clips or ties, noting its routing, and coil it on top of the crankcase so that it does not impede engine removal.

14 Trace the neutral switch wiring back from

the bottom of the front sprocket cover and disconnect it at the 2-pin connector with the blue and pink wires (GSX-R600V and GSX-R750T and V models) or the 3-pin connector with the blue, pink and black/white wires (GSX-R600 W, X and Y and GSX-R750W and X models) (see illustration 5.13). Release the wiring from any clips or ties, noting its routing, and coil it on top of the crankcase so that it does not impede engine removal.

15 Trace the alternator wiring back from the top of the alternator cover on the left-hand side of the engine and disconnect it at the 3-pin connector with the three black wires (see illustration 5.13). Release the wiring from any clips or ties, noting its routing, and coil it on top of the crankcase so that it does not impede engine removal.

16 Trace the sidestand switch wiring back from the stand and disconnect it at the 2-pin connector with the green and black/white wires (see illustration 5.13). Release the wiring from any clips or ties, noting its routing, and position it clear so that it does not impede engine removal.

17 Trace the oil pressure switch wiring back from the switch on the right-hand side of the engine and disconnect it at the 1-pin connector with the green/yellow wire (see illustration). Coil it on top of the crankcase so that it does not impede engine removal.

5.12 Pull the rubber cover off the starter motor terminal and disconnect the lead

5.13 Pulse generator wiring connector (A), neutral switch wiring connector (B), alternator wiring connector (C), sidestand switch wiring connector (D)

5.17 Oil pressure switch wiring connector (arrowed)

5.20 Slacken the bolt (A) and swivel the guide to provide clearance to the lower rear mounting bolt (B) components

5.21a Unscrew and remove the locknut . . .

5.21b . . . and unscrew the adjusting bolt – the tool shown is the MacPherson strut tool

18 Remove the front sprocket cover and the sprocket (see Chapter 6). After removing the cover, separate the clutch cable from it (see Section 18).

19 At this point, position an hydraulic or mechanical jack under the engine with a block of wood between the jack head and sump. Make sure the jack is centrally positioned so the engine will not topple in any direction when the last mounting bolt is removed. Take the weight of the engine on the jack.

20 Slacken the bolt securing the engine breather hose guide to the underside of the frame on the right-hand side and swivel it round to provide clearance to the lower rear engine mounting bolt **(see illustration)**.

21 Unscrew the nut on the lower rear engine mounting bolt **(see illustration 5.20)**. Using either the Suzuki service tool *(pt. no. 09940-14980)*, a suitable peg spanner or a fabricated tool (see *Tool Tip*), unscrew the locknut on the adjusting bolt fitted in the right-hand side of the frame **(see illustration)**. Using a similar but smaller tool, slacken the adjusting bolt and unscrew it until it no longer protrudes from the inside of the frame, but do not remove it **(see illustration)**. Do not yet withdraw the mounting bolt.

22 Slacken the pinchbolt on the mounting lug for the upper rear mounting bolt, then unscrew the nut **(see illustration)**. Do not yet withdraw the mounting bolt.

Holes in the frame provide the best access for a socket extension on the bolt and nut.

23 Slacken the pinchbolts on the mounting lugs for the right-hand front mounting bolts, then unscrew and remove the bolts **(see illustration)**.

24 Unscrew and remove the left-hand front mounting bolts **(see illustration)**.

25 Make sure the engine is properly supported on the jack, and have an assistant support it as well. Withdraw the upper and lower rear engine mounting bolts **(see illustrations)**.

26 The engine can now be removed from the frame. Check that all wiring, cables and hoses

For the locknut, a peg spanner can be made by cutting an old 22 mm socket as shown – measure the width and depth of the slots in the locknut to determine the size of the castellations on the socket. If an old socket is not available, castellations can be welded onto a suitable nut. For the adjusting bolt, a similar tool must be made, though smaller. Alternatively, an automotive suspension strut tool, known as a MacPherson No. 1 Strut tool, can be used. This is available from Sykes Pickavant, pt. no. 08920170, along with other sizes. It is important to use a tool to which a torque wrench can be applied on installation, rather than using a drift to knock the nut and bolt loose.

5.22 Slacken the pinchbolt (A) and unscrew the nut (B)

5.23 Slacken the pinchbolts (A) and unscrew the right-hand front bolts (B)

5.24 Unscrew the left-hand front bolts (arrowed)

5.25a Withdraw the upper and lower rear mounting bolts (arrowed) . . .

5.25b . . . making sure the engine is properly supported

5.29 Fit the spacers into their sockets (arrowed)

5.31a Install the adjusting bolt if removed . . .

are disconnected and clear, then manoeuvre the engine out of the frame.

27 Remove the spacers for the right-hand front and upper rear mounting bolts, noting how they fit **(see illustration 5.29)**. If required, thread the adjusting bolt for the lower rear mounting out of the frame **(see illustration 5.31a)**.

28 The engine mounting bolt nuts are self-locking, and Suzuki advise that they can only be used once. Discard all the nuts and obtain new ones for installation.

Installation

29 Install the spacers for the right-hand front and upper rear mounting bolts, making sure their shouldered ends face the inside **(see illustration)**.

30 With the aid of an assistant place the engine unit on top of the jack and block of wood and carefully raise it into position in the frame, making sure the mounting bolt holes align. Also make sure no wires, cables or hoses become trapped between the engine and the frame.

31 If removed, thread the adjusting bolt for the lower rear mounting bolt into the right-hand side of the frame and tighten it finger-tight against the engine **(see illustration)**. Slide the lower rear mounting bolt through from the left-hand side, but do not yet fit either the adjusting bolt locknut or the new mounting bolt nut **(see illustration)**.

32 Slide the upper rear mounting bolt through from the left-hand side **(see illustration)**. Thread the new nut onto the bolt and tighten it finger-tight.

33 Install the right-hand front mounting bolts (55 mm) and tighten them finger-tight **(see illustration)**.

34 Install the left-hand front mounting bolts (45 mm) and tighten them finger-tight **(see illustration)**.

35 Tighten the adjusting bolt to the torque setting specified at the beginning of the Chapter using the tool as on removal **(see illustration)**. Make a reference mark between the adjusting bolt and the frame as a check against the bolt turning while the locknut is being tightened. Fit the locknut **(see illustration 5.21a)** and tighten it to the specified torque setting using the peg spanner or socket **(see illustration)**. Check that the reference marks still align – if they don't, repeat the installation and tightening

5.31b . . . then slide the lower rear mounting bolt through . . .

5.32 . . . followed by the upper rear bolt

5.33 Install the longer bolts into the right-hand side . . .

5.34 . . . and the shorter bolts into the left-hand side

5.35a Tighten the adjusting bolt . . .

5.35b . . . and then the locknut to the specified torque . . .

5.35c ... then fit the nut finger-tight

5.36a Tighten the bolts as described ...

5.36b ... to the specified torque settings

procedure. Thread the nut onto the mounting bolt and tighten it finger-tight **(see illustration)**.

36 Tighten the two nuts on the rear mounting bolts, then the left-hand front bolts, and then the right-hand front bolts, to the torque settings specified at the beginning of the Chapter. Best access to the upper rear bolt is via the holes in the frame, and it will probably be necessary to counter-hold the bolt while the nut is tightened **(see illustrations)**. Now tighten the pinchbolts on the mounting lugs for the upper rear and right-hand front mounting bolts to the specified torque setting **(see illustrations 5.22 and 23)**.

37 The remainder of the installation procedure is the reverse of removal, noting the following points.

a) Make sure all wires, cables and hoses are correctly routed and connected, and secured by the relevant clips or ties.

b) Adjust the throttle and clutch cable freeplay (see Chapter 1).

c) Adjust the drive chain (see Chapter 1).

d) Refill the engine with oil and coolant (see Chapter 1 and 'Daily (pre-ride) checks').

e) Prior to installing the fairing side panels start the engine and check that there is no coolant/oil leakage.

---

6 Engine disassembly and reassembly –
general information

Disassembly

1 Before disassembling the engine, the external surfaces of the unit should be thoroughly cleaned and degreased. This will prevent contamination of the engine internals, and will also make working a lot easier and cleaner. A high flash-point solvent, such as paraffin (kerosene) can be used, or better still, a proprietary engine degreaser such as Gunk. Use old paintbrushes and toothbrushes to work the solvent into the various recesses of the engine casings. Take care to exclude solvent or water from the electrical components and inlet and exhaust ports.

 Warning: The use of petrol (gasoline) as a cleaning agent should be avoided because of the risk of fire.

2 When clean and dry, arrange the unit on the workbench, leaving suitable clear area for working. Gather a selection of small containers and plastic bags so that parts can be grouped together in an easily identifiable manner. Some paper and a pen should be on hand to permit notes to be made and labels attached where necessary. A supply of clean rag is also required.

3 Before commencing work, read through the appropriate section so that some idea of the necessary procedure can be gained. When removing components it should be noted that great force is seldom required, unless specified. In many cases, a component's reluctance to be removed is indicative of an incorrect approach or removal method – if in any doubt, re-check with the text. In cases where fasteners have corroded, have a can of penetrating oil or WD40 available.

4 An engine support stand made from short lengths of 2 x 4 inch wood bolted together into a rectangle will help support the engine **(see illustration)**. The perimeter of the mount should be just big enough to accommodate the sump within it so that the engine rests on its crankcase.

5 When disassembling the engine, keep 'mated' parts together (including gears, cylinders, pistons, connecting rods, valves, etc. that have been in contact with each other

6.4 An engine support made from pieces of 2 x 4 inch wood

during engine operation). These 'mated' parts must be reused or renewed as an assembly.

6 Engine/transmission disassembly should be done in the following general order with reference to the appropriate Sections.

Remove the valve cover
Remove the cam chain tensioner and cam chain guide blades
Remove the camshafts
Remove the cylinder head
Remove the cylinder block
Remove the pistons
Remove the starter clutch
Remove the pulse generator coil assembly (see Chapter 5)
Remove the clutch
Remove the oil pump
Remove the gearchange mechanism
Remove the alternator (see Chapter 9)
Remove the starter motor (see Chapter 9)
Remove the oil sump
Separate the lower crankcase from the middle crankcase
Remove the transmission shafts/gears
Remove the selector drum and forks
Separate the middle and upper crankcases
Remove the crankshaft and connecting rods

Reassembly

7 Reassembly is accomplished by reversing the general disassembly sequence.

---

7 Oil cooler –
removal and installation

Note: *The oil cooler can be removed with the engine in the frame. If the engine has been removed, ignore the steps which do not apply.*

Removal

1 Remove the fairing side panels (see Chapter 8).

2 Drain the engine oil and remove the oil filter (see Chapter 1). Drain the cooling system (see Chapter 1), or have some means of blocking or clamping the hoses to avoid excessive loss of coolant.

7.3 Slacken the clamps (arrowed) and detach the coolant hoses

7.4 Unscrew the cooler bolt (arrowed) using a 30 mm socket

7.5a Fit the O-ring into the groove in the cooler

7.5b Locate the bracket over the lug (arrowed)

7.5c Tighten the cooler bolt to the specified torque

3 Slacken the clamp securing each hose to the cooler and detach the hoses **(see illustration)**.
4 Unscrew the cooler bolt using a 30 mm socket and remove the cooler **(see illustration)**, noting how the cutout in the bracket locates over the lug on the crankcase. Check the condition of the cooler O-ring – if it is in any way damaged, deformed or deteriorated a new one must be used.

Installation

5 Installation is the reverse of removal, noting the following:
  a) *Use a new O-ring if necessary, and smear it with clean engine oil. Make sure it seats in its groove* **(see illustration)**.
  b) *Locate the bracket on the cooler over the lug on the crankcase* **(see illustration)**. *Do not forget the washer with the bolt.*
  c) *Tighten the cooler bolt to the torque setting specified at the beginning of the Chapter* **(see illustration)**.
  d) *Make sure the coolant hoses are pressed fully onto their unions and are secured by the clamps* **(see illustration 7.3)**.
  e) *Fit a new oil filter and fill the engine with oil (see Chapter 1 and 'Daily (pre-ride) checks').*
  f) *Refill the cooling system if it was drained,*

or check the level in both the radiator and the reservoir and top up if necessary (see Chapter 1 and 'Daily (pre-ride) checks').

8 Valve cover – removal and installation

Note: *The valve cover can be removed with the engine in the frame. If the engine has been removed, ignore the steps which do not apply.*

Removal

1 Remove the fairing side panels (see Chapter 8).
2 Remove the fuel tank, air filter housing, and carburettors or throttle bodies according to model (see Chapter 4). Plug the engine inlet manifolds with clean rag.
3 On GSX-R750T and V models, pull the spark plug cap off each spark plug and secure the leads clear of the engine. On all other models, disconnect the ignition coil/plug cap wiring connectors and secure the wiring clear of the engine **(see illustration 5.8a)**. On GSX-R750W and X models, also disconnect the camshaft position sensor wiring connector **(see illustration 5.8b)**. Pull the coil/cap off each spark plug and remove them.

4 Unscrew the valve cover bolts and remove them along with their sealing washers **(see illustration)**. Check the condition of the sealing washers and renew them if necessary. It is a good idea to renew them as a matter of course.
5 Lift the valve cover off the cylinder head. If it is stuck, do not try to lever it off with a screwdriver. Tap it gently around the sides with a rubber hammer or block of wood to dislodge it. Remove the dowels from the cylinder head or cover if they are loose.

Installation

6 Check the valve cover gaskets for signs of

8.4 Valve cover bolts (arrowed)

8.7a **Make sure the gaskets sit in their grooves**

8.7b **Smear some adhesive into the cutouts**

8.8a **Make sure the cover locates onto the dowels (arrowed)**

damage or deterioration and renew them if necessary.

7 Clean the mating surface of the cylinder head with lacquer thinner, acetone or brake system cleaner. If new gaskets are being fitted, clean all traces of any adhesive from the gasket grooves in the valve cover, then apply a smear of a suitable adhesive (such as Suzuki Bond no. 1207B) into the grooves. Lay the gaskets onto the valve cover, making sure they fit correctly into the grooves **(see illustration)**. Also apply the adhesive to the cut-outs in the cylinder head where the gasket half-circles fit **(see illustration)**.

8 If removed, fit the dowels into the cylinder head. Position the cover on the cylinder head, making sure the gaskets stay in place and the cover locates correctly onto the dowels **(see illustration)**. Install the cover bolts, using new sealing washers if required, and tighten them to the torque setting specified at the beginning of the Chapter **(see illustration)**.

9 Install the remaining components in the reverse order of removal.

9 Cam chain, tensioner and blades – removal, inspection and installation

Note: *The cam chain tensioner and guide blades can be removed with the engine in the frame.*

Cam chain tensioner

Caution: Once you start to remove the tensioner bolts, you must remove the tensioner all the way and reset it before tightening the bolts. The tensioner extends itself and locks in place, so if you loosen the bolts partway and then retighten them, the tensioner or cam chain will be damaged.

Removal

1 On GSX-R600V and W models, and GSX-R750T, V and W models, remove the plug from the centre of the tensioner cap **(see illustration)**. On GSX-R600X and Y models and GSX-R750X models, unscrew the tensioner cap bolt.

2 Insert a flat-bladed screwdriver into the slot in the end of the tensioner, and turn it clockwise to lock the plunger **(see illustration)**. On GSX-R600X and Y models and GSX-R750X models, a special tool (Pt. No. 09917-62430) is available which keeps the tensioner locked, rather than having to hold the screwdriver to prevent the tensioner unlocking itself.

3 Unscrew the two tensioner mounting bolts and withdraw the tensioner from the back of the cylinder block **(see illustration)**.

4 Remove the gasket from the base of the tensioner or from the cylinder block and discard it as a new one must be used.

8.8b **Use new sealing washers on the bolts if necessary**

Inspection

5 Examine the tensioner components for signs of wear or damage.

6 Release the tensioner by turning the slotted end anti-clockwise with a screwdriver, or by removing the special tool, and check that the plunger moves freely in and out of the tensioner body **(see illustration 9.9)**.

7 If the tensioner or any of its components (except gaskets, screws, bolts etc) are worn or damaged, or if the plunger is seized in the body, a new tensioner must be installed – individual components are not available.

9.1 **Remove the plug or bolt from the tensioner . . .**

9.2 **. . . and turn the slotted end clockwise**

9.3 **Unscrew the bolts (arrowed) and remove the tensioner**

9.9 Release the plunger and push it all the way into the body

9.10a Fit the new gasket . . .

9.10b . . . and install the tensioner

9.12 Fit the plug or bolt and washer into the tensioner

Installation

8 Unscrew the centre plug from the starter clutch cover on the right-hand side of the engine **(see illustration 10.2)**. Discard the plug O-ring as a new one should be used. Turn the engine in a clockwise direction using a 14 mm socket on the starter clutch bolt **(see illustration 10.3a)**. Alternatively, place the motorcycle on an auxiliary stand so that the rear wheel is off the ground, select a high gear and rotate the rear wheel by hand in its normal direction of rotation. This removes all the slack between

the crankshaft and the camshaft in the front run of the chain and transfers it to the back run where it will be taken up by the tensioner.

9 Release the tensioner by turning the slotted end anti-clockwise and press the plunger all the way into the tensioner body, then lock the plunger in this position by turning the slotted end clockwise **(see illustration)**. On GSX-R600X and Y models and GSX-R750X models, a special tool (Pt. No. 09917-62430) is available which keeps the tensioner locked, rather than having to hold the screwdriver to prevent the tensioner unlocking itself.

10 Place a new gasket on the tensioner body, then install it in the engine **(see illustrations)**. Tighten the mounting bolts to the torque setting specified at the beginning of the Chapter.

11 Release the tensioner by turning the slotted end anti-clockwise, or on GSX-R600X and Y models and GSX-R750X models by removing the special tool or screwdriver **(see illustration 9.2)**.

12 On GSX-R600V and W models, and GSX-R750T, V and W models, fit the plug into the centre of the tensioner cap **(see illustration)**. On GSX-R600X and Y models and GSX-R750X models, fit a new sealing washer onto the cap

bolt. Install the cap bolt and tighten it securely.

13 It is advisable to remove the valve cover (see Section 8) and check that the cam chain is tensioned. If it is slack, the tensioner plunger did not release.

14 Fit the centre plug into the starter clutch cover using a new O-ring, and smear it and the threads with clean engine oil **(see illustration 10.32)**. If removed, install the valve cover (see Section 8).

Cam chain guides and tensioner blade

Removal

15 Remove the valve cover (see Section 8).

16 To remove the top cam chain guide, unscrew the two bolts securing it to the cylinder head **(see illustration)**.

17 To remove the front cam chain guide, first remove the cylinder head (see Section 11). Lift the front cam chain guide out of the front of the cam chain tunnel, noting which way round it fits and how it locates **(see illustration)**.

18 To remove the tensioner blade, first remove the inlet camshaft (see Section 10) and the starter clutch (see Section 20). Unscrew the tensioner blade pivot bolt, noting the washer that fits on the inside of the blade, and on X and Y

9.16 Unscrew the bolts (arrowed) and remove the top guide

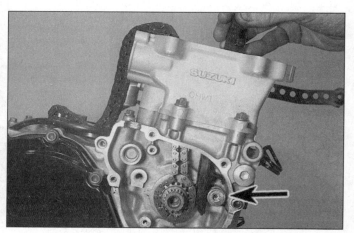

9.17 Lift the front guide out of the tunnel, noting how it hooks onto the pivot bolt (arrowed)

9.18a Unscrew the pivot bolt . . .

9.18b . . . then twist the blade and remove it. Note the washer on the inside

9.21 Make sure the lugs locate in the cutouts (arrowed)

models also on the outside **(see illustration)**. Twist the blade and lift it out of the back of the cam chain tunnel, noting which way round it fits and how it locates **(see illustration)**.

Inspection

19 Examine the sliding surface of the guides and blade for signs of wear or damage, and renew them if necessary. Check carefully for cracks in the blades and along the edges. Install new blades if necessary.

Installation

20 Install the tensioner blade into the back of the cam chain tunnel, making sure it is the correct way round. Apply a suitable non-permanent thread locking compound to the pivot bolt threads, making sure none gets on the pivot section, then install the bolt, not forgetting the washer(s) **(see illustration 9.18b)**, and tighten it to the torque setting specified at the beginning of the Chapter. Install the starter clutch (see Section 20) and the inlet camshaft (see Section 10).

21 Install the front guide blade into the front of the cam chain tunnel **(see illustration 9.17)**, making sure it locates correctly onto its pivot bolt seat and its lugs locate in their cut-outs **(see illustration)**. Install the cylinder head (see Section 11).

22 Install the top guide onto the cylinder head and tighten the mounting bolts to the torque setting specified at the beginning of the Chapter **(see illustration)**.

23 Install the valve cover (see Section 8).

Cam chain

Removal

24 If the tensioner and front guide blades are also being removed, do that first (see above). If not, remove the camshafts (see Section 10) and the starter clutch (see Section 20).

25 If the blades haven't been removed, unscrew their pivot bolts **(see illustrations 9.17 and 9.18a)**, noting the washers that fit on the inside, and on X and Y models on the outside of the tensioner blade as well, then push the bottom of each blade aside to provide clearance for the chain.

26 Unscrew and remove the cam chain stopper bolt **(see illustration)**. Discard the seal as a new one must be fitted.

9.22 Install the top guide and tighten the bolts to the specified torque

27 Slip the cam chain down the tunnel and off its sprocket on the crankshaft **(see illustration)**. If required, slide the cam chain sprocket/timing rotor off the crankshaft **(see illustration)**.

Installation

28 If removed, slide the cam chain sprocket/timing rotor onto the crankshaft, aligning the punchmark on the sprocket with that in the end of the shaft **(see illustration)**. Using a piece of wire hooked over at the end, draw the cam chain up the tunnel and slip the bottom onto its sprocket on the crankshaft, making sure it is properly engaged **(see illustration 9.27a)**. Wire the chain to another component to prevent it slipping back down the tunnel.

9.26 Remove the stopper bolt (arrowed) . . .

9.27a . . . then remove the chain . . .

9.27b . . . and if required, the sprocket/timing rotor

9.28 Make sure the punchmarks on the sprocket and crankshaft (arrowed) are aligned

9.29 Use a new sealing washer on the stopper bolt

10.2 Unscrew the centre plug (A) and the timing inspection plug (B)

10.3a Turn the engine clockwise using the bolt (A), until the timing mark (B) aligns with the notch (C)

29 Fit a new seal onto the cam chain stopper bolt, making sure its lipped side will face the engine, and smear it with clean oil **(see illustration)**. Install the bolt, making sure the shaft sits between the two runs of chain, and tighten it to the torque setting specified at the beginning of the Chapter.

30 If the tensioner and guide blades are in situ, apply a suitable non-permanent thread locking compound to the pivot bolt threads, making sure none gets on the pivot section, then install the bolts, not forgetting the washers **(see illustrations 9.17 and 9.18b)**, and tighten them to the torque setting specified at the beginning of the Chapter.

31 If removed, install the tensioner and guide blades (see above). Otherwise install the camshafts (see Section 10) and the starter clutch (see Section 20).

10 Camshafts – removal, inspection and installation

Note: *The camshafts can be removed with the engine in the frame.*

Removal

1 Remove the valve cover (see Section 8).
2 Unscrew the timing inspection plug and the centre plug from the starter clutch cover on the right-hand side of the engine **(see illustration)**. Discard the plug O-rings as new

ones should be used. The engine can be turned using a 14 mm socket on the starter clutch bolt and turning it in a clockwise direction only **(see illustration 10.3a)**. Alternatively, place the motorcycle on an auxiliary stand so that the rear wheel is off the ground, select a high gear and rotate the rear wheel by hand in its normal direction of rotation.

3 Turn the engine until the scribe line on the starter clutch aligns with the notch in the timing inspection hole and the number 1 arrow on the exhaust camshaft sprocket points forwards and is level with the top surface on the cylinder head **(see illustrations)**. **Note:** *Turn the engine in the normal direction of rotation (clockwise) only, viewed from the right-hand end of the engine.* If the number 3 arrow is pointing forwards, turn the engine through 360° until the scribe line again aligns with the notch – the number 1 arrow will now be correctly positioned. This is how the camshafts must be positioned for installation later.

4 Remove the cam chain tensioner and the cam chain top guide (see Section 9).
5 Unscrew the two oil pipe bolts, noting their different lengths, and remove the pipe, noting which way round it fits **(see illustration)**. Discard the sealing washers as new ones must be fitted.
6 Before disturbing the camshaft holders, check for identification markings. The inlet camshaft holder is marked IN, and the

10.3b Make sure the timing marks are as shown with the No. 1 arrow on the exhaust sprocket pointing forwards

exhaust camshaft holder is marked EX. These markings ensure that the holders can be matched up to their original camshaft on installation. If no markings are visible, mark your own using a felt pen.

7 Working on one camshaft at a time, unscrew the holder bolts evenly and a little at a time in a reverse of the numerical sequence marked on each holder until they are all loose **(see illustration)**. While slackening the bolts make sure that the holder is lifting squarely away from the cylinder head and is not sticking on the locating dowels. Remove the bolts, then lift off the camshaft holder, noting how it fits **(see illustration)**. Retrieve the dowels from either the holder or the cylinder head if they are loose. Slip the cam chain off

10.5 Unscrew the bolts and remove the oil pipe

10.7a Camshaft holder bolts (arrowed) – note the number cast next to each bolt

10.7b Remove the holder . . .

10.7c . . . then the camshaft

10.7d Note the identification mark on each camshaft

10.9 Remove each camshaft end bearing half ring retainer

the sprocket and lift the shaft out of the head (see illustration). The camshafts are marked for identification. The inlet camshaft is marked 'IN' and the exhaust camshaft is marked 'EX' (see illustration).

Caution: If the bolts are carelessly loosened and the holder does not come squarely away from the head, the holder is likely to break. If this happens the complete cylinder head assembly must be renewed; the holders are matched to the cylinder head and cannot be renewed separately. Also, a camshaft could break if the holder bolts are not slackened evenly and the pressure from a depressed valve causes the shaft to bend.

8 While the camshafts are out, either let the chain rest on the stopper bolt shaft, or wire it to another component to prevent it from dropping. Also, cover the top of the cylinder head with a rag to prevent foreign objects from falling into the engine.

9 Remove the two bearing half-ring retainers from the cylinder head or from the bearings on the camshafts, noting how they fit (see illustration).

Inspection

10 Inspect the bearing surfaces of the head and the holders and the corresponding journals on the camshaft. Look for score marks, deep scratches and evidence of

spalling (a pitted appearance) (see illustration).

11 Check the camshaft lobes for heat discoloration (blue appearance), score marks, chipped areas, flat spots and spalling (see illustration). Measure the height of each lobe with a micrometer and compare the results to the minimum lobe height listed in this Chapter's Specifications (see illustration). If damage is noted or wear is excessive, the camshaft must be renewed. Also check the condition of the cam followers in the cylinder head (see Section 13).

12 Check the amount of camshaft runout by supporting each end of the camshaft on V-blocks, and measuring any runout using a dial gauge. If the runout exceeds the specified limit the camshaft must be renewed.

> **HAYNES HiNT** *Refer to Tools and Workshop Tips in the Reference section for details of how to read a micrometer and dial gauge.*

13 The camshaft bearing oil clearance should now be checked. There are two possible ways of doing this, either by direct measurement (see Step 14) or by the use of a product known as Plastigauge (see Steps 15 to 18). If the Plastigauge method is used and the oil clearance is excessive, the direct method

will then have to be used to determine whether it is the camshaft or the holder that is worn.

14 If the direct measurement method is to be used, make sure the camshaft holder dowels are in position then fit the holders, making sure they are in their correct location (see Step 6). Tighten the holder bolts evenly and a little at a time in a criss-cross pattern to the torque setting specified at the beginning of the Chapter. Using telescoping gauges and a micrometer (see *Tools and Workshop Tips*), measure the journal holder diameter. Now measure the diameter of the camshaft journal with a micrometer (see illustration 10.18b). To determine the journal oil clearance, subtract the journal diameter from the holder diameter and compare the result to the clearance specified. If the clearance is greater than specified, compare the measurements of the camshaft journal and the holder to those specified and renew whichever component is beyond its limit.

15 If the Plastigauge method is to be used, clean the camshaft and the bearing surfaces in the cylinder head and camshaft holder with a clean lint-free cloth, then lay the camshafts in place in the cylinder head, positioning them so that their lobes face away from the followers, and so will not fully depress the valves when the holder is installed. Work on one camshaft at a time.

10.10 Check the journal surfaces of the camshaft for scratches or wear

10.11a Check the lobes of the camshaft for wear – here's an example of damage requiring camshaft repair or renewal

10.11b Measure the height of the camshaft lobes with a micrometer

10.16 Place a strip of Plastigauge on each bearing journal, parallel with the centreline

10.18a Compare the width of the crushed Plastigauge to the scale provided with it to obtain the clearance

10.18b Measure the cam bearing journal with a micrometer

16 Cut strips of Plastigauge and lay one piece on each bearing journal, parallel with the camshaft centreline (see illustration). Make sure the camshaft holder dowels are in position then fit the holder, making sure it is in its correct location (see Step 6). Tighten the holder bolts evenly and a little at a time in the correct numerical sequence as marked on the holder to the torque setting specified at the beginning of the Chapter. While doing this, don't let the camshaft rotate.

17 Now unscrew the bolts evenly and a little at a time in a criss-cross pattern, and carefully lift off the camshaft holder.

18 To determine the oil clearance, compare the crushed Plastigauge (at its widest point) on each journal to the scale printed on the Plastigauge container (see illustration). Compare the results to this Chapter's Specifications. If the oil clearance is greater than specified, measure the journal holder diameter using telescoping gauges and a micrometer (see Step 14) (see Tools and Workshop Tips). Now measure the diameter of the camshaft journal with a micrometer (see illustration). Compare the measurements of the camshaft holder and the journal to those specified and renew whichever component is beyond its limit.

19 Check the condition of the end bearing on each camshaft, referring to Tools and Workshop Tips (Section 5) in the Reference Section. If the bearings are worn, new camshafts must be installed as the bearings are not available separately.

20 Except in cases of oil starvation, the cam chain wears very little. If the chain has stretched excessively, which makes it difficult to maintain proper tension, renew it (see Section 9).

21 Check the sprockets for wear, cracks and other damage. If the sprockets are worn, the chain and the sprocket on the crankshaft are probably worn as well. If wear this severe is apparent, the entire engine should be disassembled for inspection. The camshaft sprockets are integral with the camshafts, while the crankshaft sprocket is available separately (see Section 9).

22 Check the cam chain guides and tensioner blade for wear or damage (see Section 9). If any is found, the chain may be worn out or improperly tensioned. Check the operation of the cam chain tensioner (see Section 9).

Installation

23 Fit each bearing half-ring retainer into its groove in the cylinder head (see illustration 10.9).

24 Make sure the bearing surfaces in the cylinder head, on the camshafts and in the holders are clean, then liberally apply

10.25 Lay the exhaust camshaft in the head, positioning it as described, and engage the chain with the sprocket

molybdenum disulphide oil (a 50/50 mixture of molybdenum disulphide grease and engine oil) to each of them. Also apply oil to the camshaft lobes and the followers.

25 Check that the cam chain is engaged around the sprocket teeth on the crankshaft and that the crankshaft is positioned as described in Step 3. Keeping the front run of the cam chain taut, lay the exhaust camshaft (identified by EX) (see illustration 10.7d) onto the cylinder head, positioning the camshaft so that the arrow marked 1 on the sprocket points forwards and is flush with the top of the cylinder head mating surface, and the arrow marked 2 points vertically upwards (see illustration 10.3b). Check that the bearing retainer locates into the groove in the bearing, and engage the chain on the sprocket teeth (see illustration).

26 Starting with the cam chain pin that is directly above the arrow marked 2 on the exhaust camshaft sprocket, count 15 pins along the chain towards the inlet side. Lay the inlet camshaft (identified by IN) onto the cylinder head, making sure the bearing retainer locates into the groove in the bearing, then engage the chain with the sprocket so that the arrow marked 3 on the sprocket aligns with the 15th pin (see illustrations).

27 Before proceeding further, check that everything aligns as described in Steps 3, 25 and 26. If it doesn't, the valve timing will be

10.26a Install the inlet camshaft as described . . .

10.26b ... and check that all the marks and the chain are aligned as shown

inaccurate and the valves could contact the pistons when the engine is turned over.

28 Make sure the camshaft holder dowels are in position then fit the holders, making sure they are in their correct locations (see Step 6) **(see illustration)**. Tighten the holder bolts evenly and a little at a time in the numerical sequence marked on each holder to the torque setting specified at the beginning of the Chapter **(see illustrations)**. Whilst tightening the bolts, make sure the holders are being pulled squarely down and

are not binding on the dowels. **Note:** *The camshaft holder bolts are of the high tensile type, indicated by a 9 mark on the bolt head. Don't use any other type of bolt.*
Caution: The camshaft is likely to break if it is tightened down onto the closed valves before the open valves. The holders are likely to break if they are not tightened down evenly and squarely.

29 With all caps tightened down, check that the valve timing marks still align (see Steps 3, 25 and 26). Check that each camshaft is not

pinched by turning the crankshaft a few degrees in each direction with a 14 mm socket on the starter clutch bolt.

30 Fit the oil pipe using new sealing washers, making sure the white paint mark on the pipe faces up, and tighten the bolts to the specified torque setting – the longer bolt fits on the exhaust side **(see illustration 10.5)**. If the cylinder head has been removed, pour approximately 50 cc of the specified engine oil into the oil pockets in the head.

31 Install the cam chain top guide and the cam chain tensioner (see Section 9).

32 Use a new O-ring on the centre plug and a new sealing washer on the timing inspection plug and smear the O-ring and the plug threads with engine oil or molybdenum disulphide oil (a 50/50 mixture of molybdenum disulphide grease and engine oil) **(see illustration)**.

33 Check the valve clearances and adjust them if necessary (see Chapter 1).

34 Install the valve cover (see Section 8).

11 Cylinder head – removal and installation

Caution: *The engine must be completely cool before beginning this procedure or the cylinder head may become warped.*
Note: *The cylinder head can be removed with the engine in the frame. If the engine has already been removed, ignore the steps which don't apply.*

Removal

1 Remove the exhaust system (see Chapter 4).
2 Remove the camshafts (see Section 10).
3 Obtain a container which is divided into sixteen compartments, and label each compartment with the location of its corresponding valve in the cylinder head and whether it belongs with an inlet or an exhaust valve. If a container is not available, use labelled plastic bags. Lift each cam follower out of the cylinder head using either a magnet or a pair of pliers and store it in its corresponding compartment in the container **(see illustration)**. Retrieve the shim from

10.28a Install the holders, making sure the dowels (arrowed) are installed ...

10.28b ... then install the bolts ...

10.28c ... and tighten them in sequence to the specified torque

10.32 Use a new O-ring and sealing washer on the centre and inspection plugs

11.3a Lift out the follower ...

11.3b . . . and retrieve the shim, which will probably be inside the follower

11.5 Unscrew the banjo bolt (arrowed) and detach the hose

11.10a Unscrew the 6 mm bolts (arrowed)

either the inside of the follower (see illustration) or pick it out of the top of the valve, using either a magnet, a small screwdriver with a dab of grease on it (the shim will stick to the grease), or a screwdriver and a pair of pliers (see illustration 11.27a). Do not allow the shim to fall into the engine.

4 Drain the cooling system (see Chapter 1). Either remove the thermostat (see Chapter 3), or disconnect the coolant temperature sensor wiring connector(s) from the sensor(s) in the thermostat housing, then slacken the clamp securing the coolant hose to the housing and detach the hose – there is no need to draw the hose out of its hole in the frame (see illustrations 5.11a and b). On fuel injected models, note which connector fits on which sensor (grey – left-facing sensor, brown – rear-facing sensor).

5 Unscrew the oil hose banjo bolt and detach the hose from the cylinder head (see illustration). Discard the sealing washers as new ones must be used.

6 On California models, unscrew the nuts securing the PAIR system pipes to the cylinder head and detach the pipes. Remove the gaskets and discard them as new ones must be fitted.

7 Slacken the pinchbolts on the mounting

lugs for the right-hand front engine mounting bolts, then unscrew and remove the bolts (see illustration 5.23).

8 Unscrew and remove the left-hand front engine mounting bolts (see illustration 5.24).

9 Unscrew and remove the camshaft stopper bolt (see illustration 9.26). Discard the seal as a new one must be fitted.

10 The cylinder head is secured by three 6 mm bolts and ten 10 mm bolts. First unscrew and remove the 6 mm bolts (see illustration). Now slacken the 10 mm bolts evenly and a little at a time in a **reverse** of their numerical sequence until they are all slack, then remove the bolts and their washers (see illustration).

11 Lift the head off the block, passing the cam chain down through the tunnel as you do (see illustration). If it is stuck, tap around the joint faces of the cylinder head with a soft-faced mallet to free the head. Do not attempt to free the head by inserting a screwdriver between the head and block – you'll damage the sealing surfaces.

12 Do not let the cam chain fall into the tunnel – secure it with a piece of wire or metal bar to prevent it from doing so. Remove the old cylinder head gasket and discard it. Stuff a clean rag into the cam chain tunnel to prevent any debris falling into the engine.

13 If they are loose, remove the dowel from each rear corner of the cylinder block. If either appears to be missing it is probably stuck in the underside of the cylinder head. If the engine is in the frame, also remove the spacers for the right-hand front engine mounting bolts for safekeeping, if required.

14 Check the cylinder head gasket and the mating surfaces on the cylinder head and block for signs of leakage, which could indicate warpage. Refer to Section 13 and check the flatness of the cylinder head.

15 Clean all traces of old gasket material from the cylinder head and block. If a scraper is used, take care not to scratch or gouge the soft aluminium. Be careful not to let any of the gasket material fall into the crankcase, the cylinder bores or the oil passages.

Installation

16 If removed, install the two dowels onto the cylinder block and, if the engine is in the frame, position the spacers for the right-hand front engine mounting bolts between the frame and the engine, making sure their shouldered ends face the engine. Lubricate the cylinder bores with engine oil.

17 Ensure both cylinder head and block mating surfaces are clean, then lay the new

11.10b Cylinder head 10 mm bolts (arrowed) – slacken them in reverse numerical order, and tighten them in the correct numerical order

11.11 Lift the cylinder head up off the block

11.17 Fit the new gasket, making sure it locates over the dowels (arrowed)

11.18 Install the head, passing the cam chain up through the tunnel as you do

11.19a Do not forget the washers with the cylinder head 10 mm bolts

head gasket in place on the cylinder block, making sure it locates over the dowels and all the holes are correctly aligned **(see illustration)**. Never re-use the old gasket.

18 Carefully lower the cylinder head onto the block **(see illustration)**. It is helpful to have an assistant to pass the cam chain up through the tunnel and slip a piece of wire through it to prevent it falling back into the engine. Keep the chain taut to prevent it becoming disengaged from the crankshaft sprocket.

19 Apply clean engine oil to the cylinder head 10 mm bolt washers, then install the bolts and tighten them finger-tight **(see illustration)**. Now tighten the 10 mm bolts in their correct numerical sequence **(see illustration 11.10b)** first to the initial torque setting specified at the

beginning of the Chapter, then tighten them in the same sequence to the final torque setting specified **(see illustration)**.

20 When the bolts are correctly torqued, install the 6 mm bolts and tighten them to the specified torque setting **(see illustration)**.

21 Fit a new seal onto the cam chain stopper bolt, making sure its lipped side will face the engine, and smear it with clean oil. Install the bolt, making sure the shaft sits between the two runs of chain, and tighten it to the torque setting specified at the beginning of the Chapter **(see illustration 9.29)**.

22 Install the left-hand front mounting bolts (45 mm) and tighten them to the specified torque setting **(see illustration 5.34)**.

23 Install the right-hand front engine

mounting bolts (55 mm) and tighten them to the specified torque setting **(see illustration 5.33)**. Now tighten the pinchbolts on the mounting lugs to the specified torque setting **(see illustration 5.23)**.

24 On California models, fit a new gasket onto each PAIR system pipe union, then fit the pipes and tighten the nuts securely.

25 Install the oil hose using new sealing washers on each side of the union and tighten the banjo bolt to the specified torque setting **(see illustration)**.

26 Either install the thermostat (see Chapter 3), or connect the coolant hose to the thermostat housing and tighten the clamp, then connect the wiring connector(s) to the sensor(s), depending on your removal procedure **(see illustrations 5.11a and b)**.

27 Lubricate each shim with engine oil or molybdenum disulphide oil (a 50/50 mixture of molybdenum disulphide grease and engine oil) and fit it into its recess in the top of the valve, with the size marking on each shim facing up **(see illustration)**. Check that the shim is correctly seated, then lubricate the follower with engine oil or molybdenum disulphide oil and install it onto the valve **(see illustration)**. **Note:** *It is most important that the shims and followers are returned to their original valves otherwise the valve clearances will be inaccurate.*

28 Install the camshafts (see Section 10).

29 Install the exhaust system (see Chapter 4). Fill the cooling system (see Chapter 1).

11.19b Tighten the bolts as described to the specified torque

11.20 Install the 6 mm bolts (arrowed) and tighten them to the specified torque

11.25 Use new sealing washers on each side of the hose union

11.27a Fit the shim into the recess in the top of the valve . . .

11.27b . . . then install the follower

12 Valves/valve seats/valve guides – servicing

1 Because of the complex nature of this job and the special tools and equipment required, most owners leave servicing of the valves, valve seats and valve guides to a professional.
2 The home mechanic can, however, remove the valves from the cylinder head, clean and check the components for wear and assess the extent of the work needed, and, unless a valve service is required, grind in the valves (see Section 13).
3 The dealer service department will remove the valves and springs, renew the valves and guides, recut the valve seats, check and renew the valve springs, spring retainers and collets (as necessary), renew the valve seals with new ones and reassemble the valve components. **Note:** *Suzuki recommends against grinding in the valves after the seats have been recut. The valve seat must be soft and unpolished in order for final seating to occur when the engine is first run.*
4 After the valve service has been performed, the head will be in like-new condition. When the head is returned, be sure to clean it again very thoroughly before installation on the engine to remove any metal particles or abrasive grit that may still be present from the valve service operations. Use compressed air, if available, to blow out all the holes and passages.

13 Cylinder head and valves – disassembly, inspection and reassembly

1 As mentioned in the previous section, valve servicing, valve seat re-cutting and valve guide renewal should be left to a Suzuki dealer. However, disassembly, cleaning and inspection of the valves and related components can be done (if the necessary special tools are available) by the home mechanic. This way no expense is incurred if the inspection reveals that overhaul is not required at this time.
2 To disassemble the valve components without the risk of damaging them, a valve spring compressor is absolutely necessary. This tool can usually be rented, but if it's not available, have a dealer handle the entire process of disassembly, inspection, service or repair (if required) and reassembly of the valves.

Disassembly

3 Before proceeding, arrange to label and store the valves along with their related components in such a way that they can be returned to their original locations without getting mixed up **(see illustration)**. A good way to do this is to use the same container as the followers and shims are stored in (see

Section 11), or to obtain a separate container which is divided into sixteen compartments, and to label each compartment with the identity of the valve which will be stored in it (ie number of cylinder, inlet or exhaust side, inner or outer valve). Alternatively, labelled plastic bags will do just as well.
4 If not already done, clean all traces of old gasket material from the cylinder head. If a scraper is used, take care not to scratch or gouge the soft aluminium.

> **HAYNES HINT** *Refer to Tools and Workshop Tips for details of gasket removal methods.*

5 Compress the valve spring on the first valve with a spring compressor, making sure it is correctly located onto each end of the valve assembly **(see illustrations)**. On the underside of the head make sure the plate on the compressor only contacts the valve and not the soft aluminium of the head – if the plate is too big for the valve, use a spacer between them **(see illustration)**. Do not compress the springs any more than is absolutely necessary. Remove the collets, using either needle-nose pliers, tweezers, a magnet or a screwdriver with a dab of grease on it **(see illustration)**. Carefully release the valve spring compressor and remove the spring retainer, noting which way up it fits, the springs, the spring seat, and the valve from the head **(see illustration 13.3)**. If the valve binds in the guide (won't pull through),

13.3 Valve components

1	*Collets*	*5*	*Spring seat*
2	*Spring retainer*	*6*	*Stem seal*
3	*Inner spring*	*7*	*Valve*
4	*Outer spring*		

push it back into the head and deburr the area around the collet groove with a very fine file or whetstone **(see illustration)**.
6 Repeat the procedure for the remaining valves. Remember to keep the parts for each valve together and in order so they can be reinstalled in the same location.

13.5a Compressing the valves using a valve spring compressor

13.5b Make sure the compressor is a good fit both on the top . . .

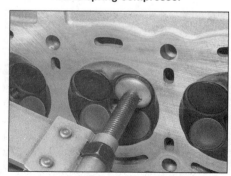

13.5c . . . and the bottom of the valve assembly

13.5d Use a spacer between the plate and the valve if the plate is too big

13.5e Remove the collets with needle-nose pliers, tweezers, a magnet or a screwdriver with a dab of grease on it

7 Once the valves have been removed and labelled, pull the valve stem seals off the top of the valve guides with pliers and discard them (the old seals should never be reused).
8 Next, clean the cylinder head with solvent and dry it thoroughly. Compressed air will speed the drying process and ensure that all holes and recessed areas are clean.
9 Clean all of the valve springs, collets, retainers and spring seats with solvent and dry them thoroughly. Do the parts from one valve at a time so that no mixing of parts between valves occurs.
10 Scrape off any deposits that may have formed on the valve, then use a motorised wire brush to remove deposits from the valve heads and stems. Again, make sure the valves do not get mixed up.

Inspection

11 Inspect the head very carefully for cracks and other damage. If cracks are found, a new head will be required. Check the cam bearing surfaces for wear and evidence of seizure. Check the camshafts for wear as well (see Section 10).
12 Inspect the outer surfaces of the cam followers for evidence of scoring or other damage. If a follower is in poor condition, it is probable that the bore in which it works is also damaged. Check for clearance between the followers and their bores. Whilst no specifications are given, if slack is excessive, renew the followers. If the bores are seriously out-of-round or tapered, the cylinder head and the followers must be renewed.
13 Using a precision straight-edge and a feeler gauge set to the warpage limit listed in the specifications at the beginning of the Chapter, check the head gasket mating surface for warpage **(see illustration)**. Refer to *Tools and Workshop Tips* in the Reference section for details of how to use the straight-edge.
14 Examine the valve seats in the combustion chamber. If they are pitted, cracked or burned, the head will require work beyond the scope of the home mechanic. Measure the valve seat width and compare it to this Chapter's Specifications **(see illustration)**. If it exceeds the service limit, or if it varies around its circumference, valve overhaul is required. If available, use Prussian blue to determine the

13.5f If the valve stem won't pull through the guide, deburr the area above the collet groove

extent of valve seat wear. Uniformly coat the seat with the Prussian blue, then install the valve and rotate it back and forth using a lapping tool. Remove the valve and check whether the ring of blue on the valve is uniform and continuous around the valve, and of the correct width as specified.
15 Clean the valve guides to remove any carbon build-up, then install each valve in its guide in turn so that its face is 10 mm above the seat. Mount a dial gauge against the side of the valve face and measure the amount of side clearance (wobble) between the valve stem and its guide in two perpendicular directions **(see illustration)**. If the clearance exceeds the limit specified, remove the valve and measure the valve stem diameter **(see illustration)**. Also measure the inside

13.13 Checking the cylinder head gasket face for distortion

13.14 Measure the valve seat width with a ruler (or for greater precision use a vernier caliper)

13.15a Measure the amount of 'wobble' as shown

13.15b Measure the valve stem diameter with a micrometer

13.15c Insert a small hole gauge into the valve guide and expand it so there's a slight drag when it's pulled out

13.15d Measure the small hole gauge with a micrometer

13.16a Valve head measurement points

A Head diameter   B Face width   C Seat width   D Margin thickness

diameter of the guide with a small hole gauge and micrometer **(see illustrations)**. Measure the guides at the ends and at the centre to determine if they are worn in a bell-mouth pattern (more wear at the ends). Subtract the stem diameter from the valve guide diameter to obtain the valve stem-to-guide clearance. If the stem-to-guide clearance is greater than listed in this Chapter's Specifications, renew whichever, of the components is worn beyond its specifications. If the valve guide is within specifications, but is worn unevenly, it should be renewed.

16 Carefully inspect each valve face for cracks, pits and burned spots. Measure the valve margin thickness and compare it to this Chapter's Specifications **(see illustrations)**. If

it exceeds the service limit, or if it varies around its circumference, valve overhaul is required.

17 Check the valve stem and the collet groove area for cracks **(see illustration)**. Rotate the valve and check for any obvious indication that it is bent. Check the end of the stem for pitting and excessive wear. The presence of any of the above conditions indicates the need for valve servicing. The stem end can be ground down, provided that the amount of stem above the collet groove after grinding is sufficient. When installing a valve whose end has been ground, check that the stem end protrudes above the collets.

18 Using V-blocks and a dial gauge, measure the valve stem runout and the valve head runout and compare the results to the specifications **(see illustration)**. If either

measurement exceeds the service limit specified, the valve must be discarded.

19 Check the end of each valve spring for wear and pitting. Measure the spring free length and compare it to that listed in the specifications **(see illustration)**. If any spring is shorter than specified it has sagged and must be renewed. Also place the spring upright on a flat surface and check it for bend by placing a ruler against it **(see illustration)**. If the bend in any spring is excessive, it must be renewed. The spring tension should also be checked by measuring the amount of weight needed to compress each spring to a particular length. If the weight required to compress the spring to the specified length is greater or less than the weight specified, the spring must be renewed.

20 Check the spring retainers and collets for obvious wear and cracks. Any questionable parts should not be reused, as extensive damage will occur in the event of failure during engine operation.

21 If the inspection indicates that no overhaul work is required, the valve components can be reinstalled in the head.

Reassembly

22 Unless a valve service has been performed, before installing the valves in the head they should be ground in (lapped) to ensure a positive seal between the valves and seats. **Note:** *Suzuki advise against grinding in the valves after the seats have been recut. The valve seat must be soft and unpolished in order for final seating to occur when the engine is first run.* This procedure requires coarse and fine valve grinding compound and

13.16b Measure the valve margin thickness as shown

13.17 Check the valve face (A), stem (B) and collet groove (C) for signs of wear and damage

13.18 Measure the valve stem runout (A) and the valve head runout (B)

13.19a Measure the free length of the valve springs

13.19b Check the valve springs for squareness

13.23 Apply the lapping compound very sparingly, in small dabs, to the valve face only

13.24a Rotate the valve grinding tool back and forth between the palms of your hands

13.24b The valve face and seat should show a uniform unbroken ring (arrowed) . . .

a valve grinding tool. If a grinding tool is not available, a piece of rubber or plastic hose can be slipped over the valve stem (after the valve has been installed in the guide) and used to turn the valve.

23 Apply a small amount of coarse grinding compound to the valve face, then slip the valve into the guide **(see illustration)**. **Note:** *Make sure each valve is installed in its correct guide and be careful not to get any grinding compound on the valve stem.*

24 Attach the grinding tool (or hose) to the valve and rotate the tool between the palms of your hands. Use a back-and-forth motion (as though rubbing your hands together) rather than a circular motion (ie so that the valve rotates alternately clockwise and anti-clockwise rather than in one direction only) **(see illustration)**. Lift the valve off the seat

and turn it at regular intervals to distribute the grinding compound properly. Continue the grinding procedure until the valve face and seat contact area is of uniform width and unbroken around the entire circumference of the valve face and seat **(see illustrations)**.

25 Carefully remove the valve from the guide and wipe off all traces of grinding compound. Use solvent to clean the valve and wipe the seat area thoroughly with a solvent soaked cloth.

26 Repeat the procedure with fine valve grinding compound, then repeat the entire procedure for the remaining valves.

27 Working on one valve at a time, install a new valve stem seal onto the valve guide. Use an appropriate size deep socket to push the seal over the end of the valve guide until it is felt to clip into place **(see illustration)**. Don't

twist or cock it, or it will not seal properly against the valve stem. Also, don't remove it again or it will be damaged.

28 Lay the spring seat in place in the cylinder head, with its shouldered side facing up so that it fits into the base of the springs (the spring seat can be identified from the spring retainer by its larger internal diameter – be sure not to mix up the two) **(see illustration 13.3)**.

29 Coat the valve stem with molybdenum disulphide grease, then install it into its guide, rotating it slowly to avoid damaging the seal **(see illustration)**. Check that the valve moves up and down freely in the guide. Next, install the inner and outer springs, with their closer-wound coils facing down into the cylinder head, followed by the spring retainer, with its shouldered side facing down so that it fits into the top of the springs **(see illustrations)**.

13.24c . . . and the seat (arrowed) should be the specified width all the way round

13.27 Press the valve stem seal into position using a suitable deep socket

13.29a Lubricate the valve stem and slide it into its guide

13.29b Fit the inner valve spring . . .

13.29c . . . and the outer valve spring, with their closer-wound coils facing down . . .

13.29d . . . then fit the spring retainer

13.30a A small dab of grease will help to keep the collets in place on the valve while the spring is released

30 Apply a small amount of grease to the collets to help hold them in place **(see illustration)**. Compress the spring with the valve spring compressor and install the collets **(see illustration)**. When compressing the spring, depress it only as far as is absolutely necessary to slip the collets into place. Make certain that the collets are securely locked in the retaining groove.

31 Repeat the procedure for the remaining valves. Remember to keep the parts for each valve together and separate from the other valves so they can be reinstalled in the same location.

32 Support the cylinder head on blocks so the valves can't contact the workbench top, then very gently tap each of the valve stems with a soft-faced hammer. This will help seat the collets in their grooves.

14.3 Hose clamp (A), union bolts (B)

14.4 Unscrew the nuts (arrowed)

13.30b Compress the springs and install the collets, making sure they locate in the groove

> **HAYNES HINT**
>
> *Check for proper sealing of the valves by pouring a small amount of solvent into each of the valve ports. If the solvent leaks past any valve into the combustion chamber area the valve grinding operation on that valve should be repeated.*

14 Cylinder block – removal, inspection and installation

Note: *The cylinder block can be removed with the engine in the frame.*

Removal

1 Remove the cylinder head (see Section 11).
2 Lift the cam chain front guide out of the front of the cam chain tunnel, noting which way round it fits and how it locates **(see illustration 9.17)**.
3 Either slacken the clamp securing the coolant hose to the union on the rear of the cylinder block and detach the hose, or unscrew the three bolts securing the coolant union to the block and detach the union, or do both if required **(see illustration)**. If the union is detached, discard the O-ring as a new one must be used. Also unscrew the bolts securing the radiator bracket to the front of the block and detach the bracket.

14.5 Lift the block up off the crankcase and pistons

4 Unscrew the nuts which secure the right-hand side of the block to the crankcase **(see illustration)**.
5 Hold the cam chain up and lift the cylinder block up off the crankcase, then pass the cam chain down through the tunnel **(see illustration)**. Do not let the chain fall into the crankcase. If the block is stuck, tap around the joint faces of the block with a soft-faced mallet to free it from the crankcase. Don't attempt to free the block by inserting a screwdriver between it and the crankcase – you'll damage the sealing surfaces. When lifting the block off the pistons, try not to let them fall against the crankcase as they become free. When the block is removed, stuff clean rags around the pistons to prevent anything falling into the crankcase.
6 Remove the dowels from the mating surface of the crankcase or the underside of the block if they are loose; be careful not to let them drop into the engine.
7 Remove the gasket and clean all traces of old gasket material from the cylinder block and crankcase mating surfaces. If a scraper is used, take care not to scratch or gouge the soft aluminium. Be careful not to let any of the gasket material fall into the crankcase or the oil passages.

Inspection

8 Check the cylinder walls carefully for scratches and score marks.
9 Using a precision straight-edge and a feeler gauge set to the warpage limit listed in the specifications at the beginning of the Chapter, check the block gasket mating surface for warpage. Refer to *Tools and Workshop Tips* in the Reference section for details of how to use the straight-edge. If warpage is excessive the block must be renewed.
10 Using telescoping gauges and a micrometer (see *Tools and Workshop Tips*), check the dimensions of each cylinder to assess the amount of wear, taper and ovality. Measure near the top (but below the level of the top piston ring at TDC), centre and bottom (but above the level of the oil ring at BDC) of the bore, both parallel to and across the crankshaft axis **(see illustration)**. Compare the results to the specifications at the beginning of the Chapter.

14.10 Measure the cylinder bore in the directions shown with a telescoping gauge, then measure the gauge with a micrometer

14.14 Fit the new gasket, locating it over the dowels (arrowed)

14.16 Lower the block and feed in the pistons and rings as described

14.18 Fit the nuts and tighten them down

11 If the precision measuring tools are not available, take the block to a Suzuki dealer or specialist motorcycle repair shop for assessment and advice.

12 If the cylinders are worn beyond the service limit, or badly scratched, scuffed or scored, the cylinder block must be renewed. The block material is not suitable for rebore, and thus Suzuki do not supply oversize pistons and rings. The cylinders are coated with Suzuki's SCEM (Suzuki Composite Electrochemical Material), a highly wear resistant nickel-silicon-carbide plating which should last the life of the engine. Note that the cylinder bores should not be honed.

Installation

13 Check that the mating surfaces of the cylinder block and crankcase are free from oil or pieces of old gasket. If removed, fit the dowels into the crankcase.

14 Remove the rags from around the pistons, then lay the new base gasket in place on the crankcase making sure it locates over the dowels and all the holes are correctly aligned **(see illustration)**. Never re-use the old gasket.

15 If required, install piston ring clamps onto the pistons to ease their entry into the bores as the block is lowered. This is not essential as each cylinder has a good lead-in enabling the piston rings to be hand-fed into the bore. If possible, have an assistant support the block while this is done.

> **HAYNES HiNT** *Rotate the crankshaft until the inner pistons (2 and 3) are uppermost and feed them into the block first. Access to the lower pistons (1 and 4) is easier since they are on the outside.*

16 Lubricate the cylinder bores, pistons and piston rings, and the connecting rod big- and small-ends, with clean engine oil, then lower the block down until the uppermost piston crowns fit into the bores **(see illustration)**. At this stage feed the cam chain up through the tunnel and secure it in place with a piece of wire to prevent it from falling back down.

17 Gently push down on the cylinder block, making sure the pistons enter the bores squarely and do not get cocked sideways. If piston ring clamps are not being used, carefully compress and feed each ring into the bore as the block is lowered. If necessary, use a soft mallet to gently tap the block down, but do not use force if the block appears to be stuck as the pistons and/or rings will be damaged. If clamps are used, remove them once the pistons are in the bore.

18 When the pistons are correctly installed in the cylinders, press the block down onto the base gasket, making sure it locates correctly onto the dowels. Install the two nuts and tighten them to the torque setting specified at the beginning of the Chapter (this will probably have to be done by feel as it is not actually

possible to get a socket and therefore a torque wrench onto the nuts) **(see illustration)**.

19 If removed, fit a new O-ring into the groove in the coolant union and smear it with grease, then attach the union and tighten the bolts to the specified torque setting **(see illustration 14.3)**. If detached, connect the hose to the union and secure it with the clamp. Also fit the radiator bracket onto the front of the block and tighten its bolts.

20 Install the front guide blade into the front of the cam chain tunnel **(see illustration 9.17)**, making sure it locates correctly onto its pivot bolt seat and its lugs locate in their cut-outs **(see illustration 9.21)**.

21 Install the cylinder head (see Section 11).

15 Pistons – removal, inspection and installation

Note: *The pistons can be removed with the engine in the frame.*

Removal

1 Remove the cylinder block (see Section 14).

2 Before removing the piston from the connecting rod, and if not already done, stuff a clean rag into the hole around the rod to prevent the circlips or anything else from falling into the crankcase. Use a sharp scriber or felt marker pen to write the cylinder identity on the crown of each piston (or on the inside of the skirt if the piston is dirty and going to be cleaned). Each piston should also have a triangle or punchmark on its crown which should point forwards **(see illustration 15.3b)**. If this is not visible, mark the piston accordingly so that it can be installed the correct way round.

3 Carefully prise out the circlip on one side of the piston using needle-nose pliers or a small flat-bladed screwdriver inserted into the notch **(see illustration)**. Push the piston pin out from the other side to free the piston from the connecting rod **(see illustration)**. Remove the other circlip and discard them as new ones must be used. When the piston has been removed, install its pin back into its bore so that related parts do not get mixed up. Rotate the crankshaft so that the best access is obtained for each piston.

15.3a Remove the circlip using pointed-nose pliers or a small screwdriver inserted in the notch . . .

15.3b . . . then push the pin out from the other side and withdraw it from the piston. Note the punchmark (arrowed) in each piston – it must face forward

15.5a Removing the piston rings using a ring removal and installation tool

 To prevent the circlip from pinging away or from dropping into the crankcase, pass a rod or screwdriver which has a diameter greater than the gap between the circlip ends, through the piston pin. This will trap the circlip if it springs out.

 If a piston pin is a tight fit in the piston bosses, soak a rag in boiling water then wring it out and wrap it around the piston – this will expand the alloy piston sufficiently to release its grip on the pin. If the piston pin is particularly stubborn, extract it using a drawbolt tool, but be careful to protect the piston's working surfaces – see Tools and Workshop Tips in the Reference section.

Inspection

4 Before the inspection process can be carried out, the pistons must be cleaned and the old piston rings removed.

5 Using your thumbs or a piston ring removal and installation tool, carefully remove the rings from the pistons **(see illustration)**. Do not nick or gouge the pistons in the process. Carefully note which way up each ring fits and in which groove as they must be installed in their original positions if being re-used. The upper surface of each ring is marked at one end **(see illustration)**. The top ring is identified by the letter R, and the second (middle) ring by the letters RN (though after-market rings may be differently marked). The rings can also be identified by their different cross-section shape.

6 Scrape all traces of carbon from the tops of the pistons. A hand-held wire brush or a piece of fine emery cloth can be used once most of the deposits have been scraped away. Do not, under any circumstances, use a wire brush mounted in a drill motor to remove deposits from the pistons; the piston material is soft and will be eroded away by the wire brush.

15.5b Note the letters, which must face up, and don't confuse the top ring with the second ring

7 Use a piston ring groove cleaning tool to remove any carbon deposits from the ring grooves. If a tool is not available, a piece broken off an old ring will do the job. Be very careful to remove only the carbon deposits. Do not remove any metal and do not nick or gouge the sides of the ring grooves.

8 Once the deposits have been removed, clean the pistons with solvent and dry them thoroughly. If the identification previously marked on the piston is cleaned off, be sure to re-mark it with the correct identity. Make sure the oil return holes below the oil ring groove are clear.

9 Carefully inspect each piston for cracks around the skirt, at the pin bosses and at the ring lands. Normal piston wear appears as even, vertical wear on the thrust surfaces of the piston and slight looseness of the top ring in its groove. If the skirt is scored or scuffed, the engine may have been suffering from overheating and/or abnormal combustion, which caused excessively high operating temperatures. The oil pump should be checked thoroughly. Also check that the circlip grooves are not damaged.

15.12 Measure the piston diameter with a micrometer at the specified distance from the bottom of the skirt

15.11 Measure the piston ring-to-groove clearance with a feeler gauge

10 A hole in the piston crown, an extreme to be sure, is an indication that abnormal combustion (pre-ignition) was occurring. Burned areas at the edge of the piston crown are usually evidence of spark knock (detonation). If any of the above problems exist, the causes must be corrected or the damage will occur again.

11 Measure the piston ring-to-groove clearance by laying each piston ring in its groove and slipping a feeler gauge in beside it **(see illustration)**. Make sure you have the correct ring for the groove (see Step 5). Check the clearance at three or four locations around the groove. If the clearance is greater than specified, renew both the piston and rings as a set. If new rings are being used, measure the clearance using the new rings. If the clearance is greater than that specified, the piston is worn and must be renewed.

12 Check the piston-to-bore clearance by measuring the bore (see Section 14) and the piston diameter. Make sure each piston is matched to its correct cylinder. Measure the piston 15.0 mm up from the bottom of the skirt and at 90° to the piston pin axis **(see illustration)**. Subtract the piston diameter from the bore diameter to obtain the clearance. If it is greater than the specified figure, the piston must be renewed (assuming the bore itself is within limits, otherwise a new cylinder block must be fitted).

13 Apply clean engine oil to the piston pin, insert it into the piston and check for any freeplay between the two **(see illustration)**.

15.13a Slip the pin (A) into the piston (B) and try to rock it back and forth. If it's loose, renew the piston and pin

Measure the pin external diameter and the pin bore in the piston and compare the measurements to the specifications at the beginning of the Chapter **(see illustrations)**. Repeat the measurements between the pin and the connecting rod small-end **(see illustration)**. Renew components that are worn beyond the specified limits.

Installation

14 Inspect and install the piston rings (see Section 16).

15 Lubricate the piston pin, the piston pin bore and the connecting rod small-end bore with clean engine oil or molybdenum disulphide oil (a 50/50 mixture of molybdenum disulphide grease and clean engine oil).

16 Install a new circlip in one side of the piston (do not re-use old circlips) **(see illustration)**. Line up the piston on its correct connecting rod, making sure the triangle or punchmark on the piston crown faces forwards, and insert the piston pin from the other side **(see illustration 15.3b)**. Secure the pin with the other new circlip. When installing the circlips, compress them only just enough to fit them in the piston, and make sure they are properly seated in their grooves with the open end away from the removal notch.

16 Piston rings –
inspection and installation

1 It is good practice to renew the piston rings when an engine is being overhauled. Before installing the new piston rings, the ring end gaps must be checked, both free and installed.

2 Lay out the pistons and the new ring sets so the rings will be matched with the same piston and cylinder during the end gap measurement procedure and engine assembly.

3 To measure the free end gap of each ring, lay the ring on a flat surface and measure the gap between the ends using a vernier caliper **(see illustration)**. Compare the results to the specifications at the beginning of the Chapter and renew any ring that is outside its service limit.

15.13b Measure the external diameter of the pin . . .

15.13d . . . and the internal diameter of the connecting rod small-end

4 To measure the installed end gap, insert the top ring into the top of the first cylinder and square it up with the cylinder walls by pushing it in with the top of the piston. The ring should be about 20 mm below the top edge of the cylinder. Slip a feeler gauge between the ends of the ring and compare the measurement to the specifications at the beginning of the Chapter **(see illustration)**.

5 If the gap is larger or smaller than specified, double check to make sure that you have the correct ring before proceeding.

6 If the gap is too small, it must be enlarged or the ring ends may come in contact with each other during engine operation, which can cause serious damage. The end gap can be increased by filing the ring ends very carefully with a fine file. When performing this

15.13c . . . the internal diameter of the bore in the piston . . .

15.16 Install the circlip, making sure it is properly seated in its groove, with the open end away from the notch

operation, file only from the outside in **(see illustration)**.

7 Excess end gap is not critical unless it exceeds the service limit. Again, double-check to make sure you have the correct rings for your engine and check that the bore is not worn.

8 Repeat the procedure for each ring that will be installed in the cylinders. Remember to keep the rings, pistons and cylinders matched up.

9 Once the ring end gaps have been checked/corrected, the rings can be installed on the pistons.

10 The oil control ring (lowest on the piston) is installed first. It is composed of three separate components, namely the expander and the upper and lower side rails. Slip the

16.3 Measuring piston ring free end gap

16.4 Measuring piston ring installed end gap

16.6 Ring end gap can be enlarged by clamping a file in a vice and filing the ring ends

16.10a Install the oil ring expander in its groove . . .

16.10b . . . and fit the side rails each side of it

expander into the groove, then install the upper side rail **(see illustration)**. Do not use a piston ring installation tool on the oil ring side rails as they may be damaged. Instead, place one end of the side rail into the groove between the expander and the ring land **(see illustration)**. Hold it firmly in place and slide a finger around the piston while pushing the rail into the groove. Next, install the lower side rail

16.12 Old pieces of feeler gauge blade can be used to guide the ring over the piston

in the same manner. Make sure the ends of the expander do not overlap.

11 After the three oil ring components have been installed, check to make sure that both the upper and lower side rails can be turned smoothly in the ring groove.

12 The upper surface of each compression ring is marked at one end **(see illustration 15.5b)**. The top ring is identified by the letter R, and the second (middle) ring by the letters RN (though after-market rings may be differently marked). The rings can also be identified by their different cross-section shape. Install the second (middle) ring next. Make sure that the identification letter near the end gap is facing up. Fit the ring into the middle groove in the piston. Do not expand the ring any more than is necessary to slide it into place. To avoid breaking the ring, use a piston ring installation tool **(see illustration 15.5a)** or old pieces of feeler gauge blades **(see illustration)**.

13 Finally, install the top ring in the same manner into the top groove in the piston. Make sure the identification letter near the end gap is facing up.

14 Once the rings are correctly installed, check they move freely without snagging and stagger their end gaps as shown **(see illustration)**.

17 Clutch – removal, inspection and installation

Note: *The clutch can be removed with the engine in the frame.*

Removal

Note: *It is advisable to order new diaphragm spring holder screws in advance of disassembling the clutch and renew them as a matter of course, as their size means they are easily damaged or stressed, even though it may not be apparent.*

1 Remove the fairing side panels (see Chapter 8). Drain the engine oil (see Chapter 1).

2 Working in a criss-cross pattern, evenly slacken the clutch cover bolts **(see illustration)**. Note which size bolts fit where, and that some bolts are fitted with sealing

16.14 When installing the rings, stagger their end gaps as shown

17.2 Clutch cover bolts (arrowed) – note the positions of the bolts with sealing washers (A)

17.3a Remove the circlip using a pair of internal circlip pliers . . .

17.3b . . . then remove the pressure plate lifter

17.4a Withdraw the pushrod end-piece along with the thrust washer and release bearing . . .

washers. Discard these washers as new ones should be used. Lift the cover away from the engine, being prepared to catch any residual oil which may be released as the cover is removed. Remove the gasket and discard it. Note the positions of the two locating dowels fitted to the crankcase and remove them for safe-keeping if they are loose.

3 Remove the circlip securing the pressure plate lifter inside the pressure plate and remove the lifter **(see illustrations)**.

4 Remove the thrust washer, release bearing and pushrod end-piece from either the back of the pressure plate or the end of the input shaft **(see illustration)**. If required, withdraw the clutch pushrod right-hand half from the input shaft **(see illustration)** – if a magnet is not available, it will have to be poked through from the other side using the left-hand half of the pushrod, requiring removal of the front sprocket cover, or the engine will have to be tipped on its side (if it is out of the frame).

5 Unstake the clutch nut using a suitable drift **(see illustration)**. To remove the clutch nut the input shaft must be locked using one of the following two methods:

a) If the engine is in the frame, engage 1st gear and have an assistant hold the rear brake on hard with the rear tyre in firm contact with the ground.

b) Use the Suzuki service tool (Pt. No. 09920-34820).

c) If the engine is out of the frame, fit a suitable ring spanner around the

transmission output shaft end (where the front sprocket fits) and counter-hold the shaft while slackening the nut.

d) If the engine has been, or is going to be, disassembled, use piston holders, or blocks of wood under the pistons and a metal bar through the pistons pins, to prevent the engine turning.

Unscrew the nut and remove the dished washer from the input shaft, noting which way round it fits **(see illustration)**.

6 Remove the three screws securing the diaphragm spring holder and remove the holder, noting how it fits **(see illustration)**. Take care to use the correct size screwdriver when removing these screws as the heads are easily rounded off. Also make sure that the

screws are removed immediately after the clutch nut, as they are not strong enough to hold the pressure of the diaphragm springs without the nut and will stretch. It is advisable to order new screws in advance of disassembling the clutch and renew them as a matter of course, as their small size means they are easily damaged or stressed, even though it may not be apparent.

7 Remove the two diaphragm springs, noting how they fit **(see illustrations 17.29c and b)**. If required, remove the spring seat from inside the pressure plate **(see illustration 17.29a)**.

8 Pull the clutch centre and the clutch friction and plain plates off the shaft as an assembly **(see illustration)**. If required, screw two M6

17.4b . . . and if required the right-hand half of the pushrod

17.5a Unstake the clutch nut using a suitable drift . . .

17.5b . . . then unscrew it, using one of the locking methods described, and remove the washer

17.6 Remove the three screws (arrowed) and withdraw the diaphragm spring holder

17.8 Grasp the clutch centre and pull it off with the plates

17.9 Withdraw the needle bearing and spacer from the centre of the housing . . .

17.10 . . . then remove the housing, noting how it engages with the primary drive gear

7.12 Turn the gear so the drive pin (A) is horizontal, then remove the circlip (B) and slide the gear and its washer(s) off the shaft

Inspection

13 After an extended period of service the clutch friction plates will wear and promote clutch slip. Measure the thickness of each friction plate and the width of their tabs using a vernier caliper **(see illustrations)**. If any plate has worn to or beyond the service limits given in the Specifications at the beginning of the Chapter, the friction plates must be renewed as a set. Also, if any of the plates smell burnt or are glazed, they must be renewed as a set.

14 The plain plates should not show any signs of excess heating (bluing). Check for warpage using a surface plate and feeler gauges **(see illustration)**. If any plate exceeds the maximum permissible amount of warpage, or shows signs of bluing, all plain plates must be renewed as a set.

15 On W, X and Y models, the total thickness of the assembled friction and plain plates should be measured. Wipe the oil off the plates, then assemble them in order on a surface plate (or a piece of plate glass). Place a 5 kg weight on the assembled plates, then measure their thickness **(see illustration)**. If it is less (or greater) than specified, and the thickness of each individual friction plate and warpage of each plain plate is within specifications, some of the No. 1 plain plates must be replaced with No. 2 plates (which are

17.13a Measure the thickness of the friction plates . . .

17.13b . . . and the width of their tabs

bolts into the threaded holes in the clutch centre and use them to pull the assembly off. Also remove the outer thrust washer from behind the clutch centre **(see illustration 17.24d)**.

9 Withdraw the needle roller bearing and spacer from the centre of the clutch housing **(see illustration)**. It may be necessary to pull the clutch housing part-way out and then push it back in order to expose the bearing and spacer.

10 Remove the clutch housing from the shaft, then remove the inner thrust washer **(see illustration and 17.23a)**. If required, the oil pump drive gear can be separated from the clutch housing by lifting it off the back of the primary driven gear **(see illustration 17.23b)**.

11 If required for either inspection or renewal, remove the clutch friction and plain plates from the clutch centre, followed by the anti-

judder spring and spring seat, noting which way round they fit **(see illustrations 17.25a)**. Keep the friction and plain plates in their original order (there are different types of each plate – keeping them in order will avoid confusion on reassembly).

12 If the engine is being completely disassembled or if the oil pump is being removed, turn the oil pump drive gear so that its drive pin is horizontal (this will prevent it from dropping out) **(see illustration)**. Remove the circlip from the end of the oil pump drive shaft, then remove the outer washer (where fitted) and the driven gear. Also remove the drive pin from the shaft, noting how it fits into the slot in the back of the gear, and the inner washer.

17.14 Check the plain plates for warpage

5 kg. load

H31241

17.15 Measure the total thickness of the assembled and weighted plates as shown

17.16 Measure the height of the inner edge of each diaphragm spring

17.19 Withdraw the pushrod and check it is straight. The oil seal retainer plate is secured by two bolts (arrowed)

slightly thicker), or vice versa if the total is too thick – (on 600X and Y models, a No. 3 plain plate, which is thinner than the No. 1 plate, is available) to bring the overall thickness to that specified. Up to four (750W and X models) or three (600W models) of the thicker plain plates can be used, and they should be the third to seventh (750) or third to sixth (600) plain plates fitted as counted from the outside (see Table). On 600X and Y models, one of the thicker plates can be used, and it should be the sixth or seventh plate as counted from the outside, and one of the thinner plates can be used, and it should be the first or second plate as counted from the outside.

16 Lay each diaphragm spring in turn on a surface plate (or a piece of plate glass) and measure the height of the inner edge of the spring **(see illustration)**. Renew the spring if the height measured is less than

the limit specified at the beginning of the Chapter.

17 Inspect the clutch assembly for burrs and indentations on the edges of the protruding tangs of the friction plates and/or slots in the edge of the housing with which they engage. Similarly check for wear between the inner tongues of the plain plates and the slots in the clutch centre. Wear of this nature will cause clutch drag and slow disengagement during gear changes, since the plates will snag when the pressure plate is lifted. With care, a small amount of wear can be corrected by dressing with a fine file, but if this is excessive the worn components should be renewed.

18 Check the pressure plate, release bearing, pushrod end piece and thrust washer for signs of roughness, wear or damage, and renew any parts necessary as necessary. Check that the pushrod is straight by rolling it on a flat surface.

19 To access the pushrod oil seal, remove the left-hand fairing side panel (see Chapter 8) and displace the coolant reservoir (see Chapter 3). Unscrew the gearchange lever linkage arm pinch bolt and remove the arm from the shaft, noting any alignment marks **(see illustration 18.2)**. If no marks are visible, make your own before removing the arm so that it can be correctly aligned with the shaft on installation. Disconnect the speedometer sensor wiring connector **(see illustration 18.3)**. Unscrew the bolts securing the front sprocket cover and remove the cover **(see illustration 18.4)**. Note the position of the dowels and remove them if loose. Withdraw the clutch pushrod left-hand half and check it for straightness by rolling it on a surface plate **(see illustration)**. Check the pushrod oil seal for signs of leakage and renew it if necessary. Unscrew the bolts securing the oil seal retainer plate and remove the plate (on T and V models, first remove the front sprocket (see Chapter 6). On W, X and Y models, it may also be necessary to remove the sprocket, depending on whether your tools allow you to access the lower bolt which is partially obscured by the chain). Lever out the old seal using a screwdriver, then drive a new seal squarely into place. Install the retainer plate and where removed, the engine sprocket (see Chapter 6).

20 Inspect the clutch release mechanism whilst the engine sprocket cover is removed **(see illustration)**. Check the mechanism for smooth operation and any signs of wear or damage. Unscrew the two bolts securing the mechanism to the cover and remove it for cleaning and re-greasing if required **(see illustration)**. Apply a dab of grease to the pushrod end **(see illustration 18.7b)**.

Installation

21 Remove all traces of old gasket from the crankcase and clutch cover surfaces.
22 If removed, slide the inner washer onto the oil pump drive shaft, then fit the drive pin into its hole in the shaft, making sure it is

	No. 1 plain plate	No. 2 plain plate	No. 3 plain plate	Total plates
GSX-R600W	5 to 8 plates	3 to 0 plates		8
GSX-R600X/Y	7 or 8 plates	1 or 0 plates	1 or 0 plates	8
GSX-R750W	5 to 8 plates	4 to 1 plates		9
GSX-R750X	5 to 8 plates	4 to 1 plates		9

17.20a Check the release mechanism for damage and smooth operation

17.20b The mechanism is secured in the cover by the two bolts (arrowed)

17.22a Fit the inner washer . . .

17.22b . . . and slide the drive pin into the shaft . . .

17.22c . . . then fit the gear onto the drive pin . . .

17.22d . . . and secure the assembly with the circlip

17.23a Slide the inner thrust washer onto the shaft with its flat side facing out

central (see illustrations). Locate the oil pump driven gear onto the shaft so that the drive pin locates into the slot in the back of the gear, then install the outer washer (where fitted) and secure the assembly with the circlip, making sure it is properly seated in its groove (see illustrations).

23 Slide the inner thrust washer, with its flat surface facing out, onto the end of the input shaft (see illustration). If removed, fit the oil pump drive gear onto the primary driven gear on the back of the clutch housing, making sure the shouldered inner section faces the housing and the flat side faces the engine (see illustrations).

24 Lubricate the needle roller bearing and spacer with clean engine oil. Slide the clutch housing onto the shaft, making sure it engages correctly with the teeth on the primary drive gear and the oil pump driven gear, then support it in position and slide the spacer and needle roller bearing onto the shaft and into the middle of the housing (see illustrations). Slide the outer thrust washer onto the shaft (see illustration).

25 Install the spring seat and anti-judder spring onto the clutch centre (see illustration), noting that the anti-judder spring must be fitted the correct way round, with its outer edge raised off the spring seat (see illustration). Slide the clutch centre onto the shaft splines (see illustration).

26 On T and V models, before building up the plates in the clutch housing, identify the single

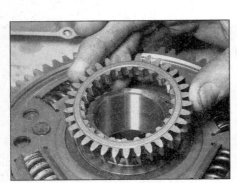

17.23b Fit the oil pump drive gear onto the back of the housing . . .

17.23c . . . making sure it is the correct way round

17.24a Engage the clutch housing with the primary drive and oil pump driven gears . . .

17.24b . . . then slide the spacer . . .

17.24c . . . and the needle bearing into the centre of the housing . . .

17.24d . . . followed by the outer thrust washer

17.25a Install the spring seat and the spring . . .

17.25b . . . making sure they are correctly fitted . . .

friction plate that has a larger internal diameter than the rest, and the one (600 models) or two (750 models) plain plates that are slightly thicker than the rest. The friction plate with the larger internal diameter is fitted first and locates over the anti-judder spring and seat. The thicker plain plate(s) is fourth out of eight to be fitted on 600 models, and are fifth and sixth out of nine to be fitted on 750 models.

27 On W, X and Y models, before building up the plates in the clutch housing, identify the single friction plate that has a larger internal diameter than the rest, and on 600X and Y models the friction plate that has a green paint mark on it (original equipment only). The friction plate with the larger internal diameter is fitted first and locates over the anti-judder spring and seat. On 600X and Y models, the painted friction plate fits last, and its tabs locate in the shallow slots in the housing, rather than in the deep slots with the rest of the friction plates. Also refer to Step 15 and identify the different plain plates and fit them as described.

28 Coat each clutch plate with clean engine, then build up the plates in the clutch housing, starting with the friction plate (with the larger internal diameter), then a plain plate and alternating friction and plain plates (not forgetting the order) until all are installed **(see illustrations)**.

29 If removed, install the diaphragm spring seat into the pressure plate **(see illustration)**. Fit the pressure plate into the clutch centre, then install the two diaphragm springs, making sure their higher inner edges face out **(see illustrations)**.

17.25c . . . then slide the clutch centre on the shaft

17.28a Install the first friction plate with the larger internal diameter . . .

17.28b . . . followed by a plain plate . . .

17.28c . . . followed by a standard friction plate

17.29a Fit the diaphragm spring seat into the pressure plate if removed . . .

17.29b . . . then fit the pressure plate into the clutch centre

17.29c Fit the two diaphragm springs with their raised inner edges facing out

17.30a Fit the spring holder into the pressure plate . . .

17.30b . . . and secure it with the new screws

17.31a Install the dished washer with its raised inner edge facing out . . .

17.31b . . . then fit the clutch nut . . .

17.31c . . . and tighten it to the specified torque setting

30 Install the diaphragm spring holder and secure it with the three screws, preferably using new ones **(see illustrations)**. Tighten the screws evenly, taking care not to strip their threads as the screws are very small. Proceed to the next step immediately, as the screws are not strong enough to secure the spring holder against the pressure of the springs without the clutch nut, and consequently will stretch.

31 Fit the dished washer, with its raised inner edge facing out, onto the shaft, then install the clutch nut and, using the method employed on removal to lock the input shaft, tighten the nut to the torque setting specified at the beginning of the Chapter **(see illustrations)**. Stake the nut against the shaft using a punch to secure it **(see illustration)**.

32 If removed, lubricate the pushrod right-hand half and slide it into the end of the input shaft **(see illustration)**. Lubricate both sides of the release bearing and thrust washer with clean engine oil, then fit them onto the end of the pushrod end-piece and slide the assembly into the shaft as well **(see illustrations)**.

33 Install the pressure plate lifter and secure it with the circlip, making sure it is properly seated in its groove and that its sharper edge faces out **(see illustrations)**.

34 Apply a smear of sealant (Suzuki Bond 1207B or equivalent) to the area around the

17.31d Stake the nut against the shaft using a punch

17.32a Slide in the pushrod if removed . . .

17.32b . . . then fit the release bearing and thrust washer onto the pushrod end-piece . . .

17.32c . . . and slide that into the shaft

17.33a Install the pressure plate lifter . . .

17.33b ... and secure it with its circlip

17.34a Apply the sealant to the crankcase joints (arrowed)

17.34b Make sure the gasket locates correctly over the dowels (arrowed)

crankcase joints as shown **(see illustration)**. If removed, insert the clutch cover dowels into the crankcase, then place a new gasket onto the crankcase, making sure it locates correctly over the dowels **(see illustration)**.

35 Install the clutch cover and tighten its bolts evenly in a criss-cross sequence, making sure that new sealing washers are used on the front three bolts **(see illustration 17.2)**.

36 Refill the engine with oil (see Chapter 1). Install the fairing side panels (see Chapter 8).

37 Adjust the clutch release mechanism, followed by the clutch cable as described in Chapter 1.

18 Clutch cable – removal and installation

Removal

1 Remove the left-hand fairing side panel (see Chapter 8) and displace the coolant reservoir (see Chapter 3).

2 Unscrew the gearchange linkage arm pinch bolt and remove the arm from the shaft, noting any alignment marks **(see illustration)**. If no marks are visible, make your own before removing the arm so that it can be correctly aligned with the shaft on installation.

3 Trace the wiring from the speedometer

sensor on the front sprocket cover and disconnect it at the connector **(see illustration)**.

4 Unscrew the bolts securing the sprocket cover to the crankcase and move the cover aside **(see illustration)**. On W, X and Y models, note the rubber bushing for the gearchange shaft and remove it from the cover if required.

5 Bend out the tab in the cable retainer on the end of the release mechanism arm, then lift the arm and slip the cable end out of the retainer, noting how it fits **(see illustrations)**. Slacken the cable adjuster locknut on the top of the cover, then unscrew the adjuster and withdraw the cable from the cover **(see illustration)**.

6 Thread the clutch adjuster at the lever end fully into the lever bracket, then back it off

18.2 Unscrew the bolt (arrowed) and slide the arm off the shaft

18.3 Disconnect the speedometer sensor wiring connector

18.4 Sprocket cover bolts (arrowed)

18.5a Bend out the tab on the retainer ...

18.5b ... and free the cable end from the arm

18.5c Slacken the locknut (arrowed), then thread the adjuster out of the cover and withdraw the cable

18.6a With the slots in the adjuster and bracket aligned, pull the outer cable out of the adjuster, . . .

18.6b . . . the inner cable out of the bracket . . .

18.6c . . . and the cable end out of the lever

until its slot aligns with that in the lever bracket **(see illustration)**. Pull the outer cable end from the socket in the adjuster and release the inner cable from the lever **(see illustrations)**. Remove the cable from the machine, noting its routing.

> **HAYNES HINT**
> *Before removing the cable from the bike, tape the lower end of the new cable to the upper end of the old cable. Slowly pull the lower end of the old cable out, guiding the new cable down into position. Using this method will ensure the cable is routed correctly.*

18.7a Bend up the tab on the retainer to secure the cable end

18.8a Make sure the rotor (A) fits correctly into the sensor (B)

Installation

7 Installation is the reverse of removal, making sure the cable is correctly routed. Bend in the retainer to secure the cable end **(see illustration)**. Before installing the cover, check the clutch release actuating mechanism for smooth operation and any signs of wear or damage **(see illustration 17.20a)**. Unscrew the two bolts securing the mechanism to the cover and remove it for cleaning and re-greasing if required **(see illustration 17.20b)**. Apply a dab of grease to the pushrod end **(see illustration)**.

8 Make sure the dowels are either in the crankcase or the sprocket cover. Install the cover, making sure the speedometer

18.7b Smear some grease onto the end of the pushrod

18.8b Where fitted and if removed, fit the rubber bush for the gearchange shaft

rotor fits properly into the sensor and the dowels locate correctly, and tighten its bolts **(see illustration)**. On W, X and Y models, if removed, fit the rubber bushing for the gearchange shaft into the cover **(see illustration)**.

9 Slide the gearchange linkage arm onto the shaft, aligning the marks, and tighten the pinch bolt **(see illustration 18.2)**.

10 Reconnect the speedometer sensor wiring connector **(see illustration 18.3)**.

11 Adjust the amount of clutch lever freeplay (see Chapter 1).

19 Gearchange mechanism – removal, inspection and installation

Note: *The gearchange mechanism can be removed with the engine in the frame.*

Removal

1 Remove the fairing side panels (see Chapter 8) and the clutch (see Section 17). Displace the coolant reservoir (see Chapter 3).

2 Shift the transmission into neutral. Unscrew the gearchange linkage arm pinch bolt and remove the arm from the shaft, noting any alignment marks **(see illustration 18.2)**. If no marks are visible, make your own before removing the arm so that it can be correctly aligned with the shaft on installation.

3 Trace the wiring from the speedometer sensor on the front sprocket cover and disconnect it at the connector **(see illustration 18.3)**.

4 Unscrew the bolts securing the sprocket cover to the crankcase and move the cover aside **(see illustration 18.4)**. On W, X and Y models, note the rubber bushing for the gearchange shaft and remove it from the cover if required. The cover can be secured out of the way with the clutch cable still connected.

5 Remove the circlip from the left-hand end

19.5 Remove the circlip and washer

19.6 Withdraw the gearchange shaft from the engine, noting how it fits

19.7 Front cam guide plate (A), rear guide plate (B)

of the gearchange shaft and slide off the washer (see illustration).

6 Working on the right-hand side of the engine, note how the gearchange shaft centralising spring ends fit on each side of the locating pin in the crankcase, and how the eye in the shaft arm locates over the roller on the selector cam, then withdraw the gearchange shaft from the right-hand side of the engine (see illustration). If the washer does not come with the shaft, retrieve it from the engine. Remove the roller from the pin on the cam for safekeeping (see illustration 19.18b).

7 Remove the screw and the nut securing the front cam guide plate and the screw and locating pin securing the rear guide plate to the crankcase and remove them along with the spacers (one for each plate) (see illustration). A thread-locking compound is used on these screws during assembly, which may necessitate the use of an impact driver for removal.

8 The pawls are spring-loaded in the selector cam. Before withdrawing the cam, place a finger over each pawl to prevent them from springing out when the cam is withdrawn (see illustration). Remove the cam along with the pawls. Place the cam on a bench and carefully release the pawls, noting how they and their pins and springs fit in the cam.

9 Note how the stopper arm roller locates in the neutral detent in the stopper plate. If the selector drum is to be removed, or if required, remove the stopper arm return spring, noting how it fits, then unscrew the stopper arm stud and remove the arm and washer (see illustrations).

Inspection

10 Inspect the shaft centralising spring for fatigue, wear or damage. If any is found, it must be renewed. It is retained on the shaft by a circlip (see illustration 19.18a). Similarly check the stopper arm return spring.

11 Check the gearchange shaft for straightness and damage to the splines, and check for wear on the eye in the arm and the roller on the selector cam pin. If the shaft is bent you can attempt to straighten it, but if the splines or eye are damaged or worn the shaft must be renewed.

12 Check the condition of the shaft oil seal in the left-hand side of the crankcase. If it is damaged or deteriorated it must be renewed. Lever out the old seal and press or drive the new one squarely into place, with its lip facing inward, using a seal driver or suitable socket (see illustrations).

13 Check that the gearchange shaft needle bearings rotate freely and have no sign of

19.8 Press each pawl in and carefully withdraw the cam

19.9a Remove the return spring (arrowed), noting how it fits . . .

19.9b . . . then unscrew the stud (arrowed) and remove the arm

19.12a Lever out the old seal . . .

19.12b . . . and press the new one into place

19.13 Check the bearings (arrowed) –
there is another one behind the oil seal
(see illustration 19.12a)

19.15a Slide the arm and washer onto the
stud and install the assembly . . .

19.15b . . . then fit the return spring

freeplay between them and the crankcase **(see illustration)**. Renew the bearings if necessary. To renew them, first remove the oil seal (see Step 12), then draw them out of the crankcase, noting that once removed they cannot be re-used. Drive the new bearings into place, making sure they enter squarely. Refer to *Tools and Workshop Tips* in the Reference Section for more information on bearings and how to remove and install them.

14 Check the selector cam, pawls, pins and springs for wear and damage. Renew them if defects are found. Also check the stopper arm roller and the detents in the stopper plate for wear or damage. Check that the arm is a light fit on the bolt with no appreciable freeplay between them.

Installation

15 Slide the stopper arm and its washer onto the stopper arm bolt, making sure the cutout in the arm will face the front when installed **(see illustration)**. Apply a suitable non-permanent thread locking compound to the bolt threads and tighten it securely **(see illustration 19.9b)**. Fit the return spring, making sure the ends locate correctly against the cutout in the arm and the crankcase **(see illustration)**, and locate the roller onto the neutral detent in the stopper plate **(see illustration 19.9a)**.

16 Install the springs, pins and pawls in the selector cam as shown **(see illustrations)**. Make sure the rounded end of each pawl fits into the rounded cut-out in the cam, and that

the pins locate correctly in the cut-outs in the pawls, with the wider edge of the cut-out on the outside. It will be necessary to hold each pawl assembly in place while the cam is installed in the end of the selector drum **(see illustration)**. Install the selector cam with its roller pin positioned as shown so it will align with the eye in the gearchange shaft arm when it is installed **(see illustration 19.19a)**.

17 Apply a suitable non-permanent thread locking compound to the front and rear cam guide plate screws, nut and locating pin, then install the plates, not forgetting the spacers between the plates and the engine on the screw mountings, and tighten the screws and nut securely, and the locating pin to the torque setting specified at the beginning of the Chapter **(see illustrations)**.

19.16a Fit the spring into the hole . . .

19.16b . . . and the pin onto the spring . . .

19.16c . . . then locate the rounded end of
the pawl in the cutout

19.16d Press the pawls in against the pins
when installing the cam

19.17a Locate the spacer for the front
plate . . .

19.17b . . . then position the plate . . .

19.17c ... and fit the screw and nut

19.17d Fit the screw into the rear plate and slide the spacer on it ...

19.17e ... then install the plate and fit the locating pin

18 If removed, slide the centralising spring onto the gearchange shaft and locate the spring ends each side of the tab on the arm. Fit the circlip, making sure it locates in its groove, then slide on the washer **(see illustration)**. Fit the roller onto the pin on the selector cam **(see illustration)**.

19 Apply a smear of grease to the lip of the gearchange shaft seal in the left-hand side of the crankcase and smear clean engine oil over the gearchange shaft. Carefully guide the gearchange shaft into place, making sure the centralising spring ends locate correctly on each side of the pin in the crankcase, and locate the eye in the shaft arm over the roller on the selector cam **(see illustrations)**.

20 Install the washer and circlip onto the left-hand end of the gearchange shaft **(see illustrations)**.

21 Make sure the dowels are either in the crankcase or the sprocket cover. Install the cover, making sure the speedometer rotor fits properly into the sensor and the dowels locate correctly, and tighten its bolts **(see illustration 18.8a)**. On W, X and Y models, if removed, fit the rubber bushing for the gearchange shaft into the cover **(see illustration 18.8b)**.

22 Slide the gearchange linkage arm onto the shaft, aligning the marks, and tighten the pinch bolt **(see illustration 18.2)**. Check that the mechanism works correctly

23 Reconnect the speedometer sensor wiring connector **(see illustration 18.3)**.

24 Install the clutch (see Section 17), the coolant reservoir (see Chapter 3) and the fairing side panels (see Chapter 8).

20 Starter clutch and idle/ reduction gear – removal, inspection and installation

Note: *The starter clutch and idle/reduction gear assembly can be removed with the engine in the frame.*

Removal

1 Remove the right-hand fairing side panel (see Chapter 8).

2 Unscrew the bolts securing the

19.18a Make sure the return spring is correctly fitted and secured by the circlip

19.18b Fit the roller on the cam pin

19.19a Slide the shaft through ...

19.19b ... and locate the eye and return spring ends as shown

19.20a Slide on the washer ...

19.20b ... and fit the circlip

20.2 Idle/reduction gear cover bolts (arrowed) – note the bolt with the sealing washer (A)

20.3a Starter clutch cover bolts (arrowed) (W, X and Y models shown) – note the bolt with the sealing washer (A)

idle/reduction gear cover to the starter clutch cover, noting the sealing washer fitted on the lower front bolt, and remove the cover (see illustration). Remove the gasket and discard it. Note the position of the locating dowels and remove them for safe-keeping if loose. Remove the wave washer and outer thrust washer from the starter No. 1 idle/reduction gear shaft, then remove the gear with its bearing, noting which way round the gear fits, the inner thrust washer and the shaft (see illustrations 20.16d, c, b and a).

3 Now unscrew the bolts securing the starter clutch cover, noting the sealing washer fitted on the upper front bolt (see illustration). On T and V models, the cover has four bolts and one locating dowel, while on W, X and Y models the cover has five bolts and two dowels. Remove the cover, being prepared to catch any residual oil. Remove the gasket and discard it. Note the position of the dowel(s) and remove it/them for safe-keeping if loose. Remove the wave washer from the starter No. 2 idle/reduction gear shaft, then withdraw the shaft and remove the gear, noting which way round it fits (see illustration).

4 Before proceeding further, the operation of the starter clutch can be checked while it is in situ. Check that the gear on the back of the clutch is able to rotate freely anti-clockwise as you look at it, but locks when rotated clockwise.

5 To remove the starter clutch bolt it is necessary to stop the starter clutch and crankshaft from turning using one of the following methods, then unscrew the bolt and slide the starter clutch and its thrust washer off the end of the crankshaft.

a) If the engine is in the frame, engage 1st gear and have an assistant hold the rear brake on hard with the rear tyre in firm contact with the ground.

b) If the cylinder block has been removed, use a con-rod stopper or block of wood under the pistons.

c) The Suzuki service tool (Pt. No. 09920-34830), or a home-made equivalent made from two strips of steel, with a bolt through one end of each strip, and bolted together in the middle, can be used (by inserting the bolts into the holes in the starter clutch) to stop the clutch from

turning(see illustration). On some W models, the starter clutch design was changed, as was the special tool, however its part number has remained the same, so it is necessary to quote your engine number if ordering the tool. The engine numbers affected are R731-100043 to 101067, and R732-100007 to 100700. The tool for these models also requires spacers, Pt. No. 09180-08140.

6 Clean all old gasket and sealant from the cover and crankcase.

Inspection

7 With the clutch face down on a workbench, check that the gear rotates freely in a clockwise direction and locks against the rotor in an anti-clockwise direction (see illustration). If it doesn't, renew the starter clutch.

8 Withdraw the starter driven gear from the starter clutch. If it appears stuck, rotate it clockwise as you withdraw it to free it from the starter clutch.

9 Check the bearing surface of the starter driven gear hub and the condition of the

20.3b Remove the No. 2 idle/reduction gear assembly

20.5 Unscrewing the starter clutch bolt using the home-made tool described

20.7 With the clutch face down, the gear should rotate freely clockwise and should lock when turned anti-clockwise

20.9 Check the condition of the sprags (arrowed) and the corresponding surface on the gear hub

20.12 Fit the bearing and gear into the clutch

20.13a Slide on the thrust washer and clutch . . .

sprags inside the clutch body **(see illustration)**. If the bearing surface shows signs of excessive wear or the sprags are damaged, marked or flattened at any point, they should be renewed.

10 Remove the needle roller bearing from the centre of the starter clutch and from the centre of the No. 1 idle/reduction gear. Check the condition of the rollers and the cages and renew the bearing if any wear or damage is found, or if any roughness or stiffness is detected when the components are assembled and turned.

11 Examine the teeth of the starter idle/reduction gears and the corresponding teeth of the starter driven gear and starter motor drive shaft. Renew the gears and/or starter motor if worn or chipped teeth are discovered on related gears. Also check the idle/reduction gear shafts for damage, and check that the gears are not a loose fit on the shafts. Renew the shafts if necessary.

Installation

12 Lubricate the needle bearing and the hub of the starter driven gear with clean engine oil, then install the bearing and the gear into the clutch, rotating the gear clockwise as you do

20.13b . . . making sure the scribe line aligns with the punchmark . . .

so to spread the sprags and allow the hub of the gear to enter **(see illustration)**.

13 Slide the thrust washer and the starter clutch assembly onto the end of the crankshaft, aligning the scribe line on the clutch with the punchmark on the crankshaft end **(see illustrations)**. Apply a little clean engine oil to the starter clutch bolt and its washer, then install the bolt **(see illustration)**. Using the method employed on removal to stop the clutch from turning, tighten the bolt to the torque setting specified

20.13c . . . then install the bolt with its washer . . .

at the beginning of the Chapter **(see illustration)**.

14 Lubricate the No. 2 idle/reduction gear shaft with clean engine oil and slide it through the gear. Install the idle/reduction gear, making sure the smaller (14T) pinion faces inwards and meshes correctly with the teeth of the starter driven gear, and fit the wave washer onto the end of the shaft **(see illustration)**.

15 Apply a smear of sealant (Suzuki Bond 1207B or equivalent) to the area around the

20.13d . . . and tighten it to the specified torque

20.14 Install the No. 2 idle/reduction gear and shaft, not forgetting the wave washer (arrowed)

20.15a Apply some sealant to the crankcase joints (arrowed) . . .

20.15b . . . then locate the gasket onto the dowels (arrowed) . . .

20.15c . . . and install the cover

crankcase joints as shown (see illustration). If removed, insert the dowel(s) in the crankcase, then install the starter clutch cover using a new gasket, making sure it locates correctly onto the dowel(s) (see illustrations). Tighten the cover bolts evenly in a criss-cross sequence, making sure the sealing washer is installed on the upper front bolt (see illustration 20.3a).

16 Lubricate the No. 1 idle/reduction gear shaft with clean engine oil and fit it into its bore in the crankcase, then slide on the inner thrust washer (see illustrations). Lubricate the needle bearing and slide it into the gear, then slide the gear onto the shaft, making sure the smaller (14T) pinion faces inwards and meshes correctly with the teeth of the No. 2 gear outer pinion, and the larger pinion

meshes with the starter motor drive shaft (see illustration). Fit the outer thrust washer followed by the wave washer onto the end of the shaft (see illustration).

17 If removed, insert the dowels in the crankcase, then install the idle/reduction gear cover using a new gasket, making sure it locates correctly onto the dowels (see illustrations). Tighten the cover bolts evenly in a criss-cross sequence, making sure the sealing washer is installed on the lower front bolt (see illustration 20.2).

18 Check the engine/transmission oil level and top up if necessary (see Daily (pre-ride) checks).

19 Install the right-hand fairing side panel (see Chapter 8).

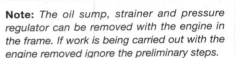

21 Oil sump, strainer and pressure regulator – removal, inspection and installation

Note: The oil sump, strainer and pressure regulator can be removed with the engine in the frame. If work is being carried out with the engine removed ignore the preliminary steps.

Removal

1 Remove the exhaust system (see Chapter 4).

2 Drain the engine oil (see Chapter 1).

3 Unscrew the sump bolts, slackening them evenly in a criss-cross sequence to prevent

20.16a Fit the shaft into its bore . . .

20.16b . . . then slide on the inner thrust washer

20.16c Fit the bearing into the gear and the gear onto the shaft . . .

20.16d . . . then fit the outer thrust washer and the wave washer

20.17a Locate the gasket onto the dowels (arrowed) . . .

20.17b . . . then install the cover

21.3 Sump bolts (arrowed) – note the positions of the bolts with the sealing washers (A)

21.4 Pick-up tube bolts (A), strainer housing bolts (B)

distortion, and remove the sump **(see illustration)**. Note the position of the bolts with the sealing washers. Discard the gasket as a new one must be used. Remove the two locating dowels from either the sump or the crankcase, if loose.

4 To access the oil strainer, unscrew the three bolts securing the oil pick-up tube to the strainer housing and remove the tube, the gasket and the strainer **(see illustration)**. Discard the gasket as a new one must be used.

5 To remove the complete strainer housing, unscrew the two bolts securing the housing to the underside of the crankcase **(see illustration 21.4)**. Discard the O-ring as a new one must be used.

6 If required, unscrew the oil pressure regulator from inside the sump and remove it **(see illustration)**.

7 Remove all traces of gasket from the sump and crankcase mating surfaces.

Inspection

8 Clean the sump, making sure all the oil passages are free of any debris.

9 Make sure the oil strainer is clean and remove any debris caught in the mesh, using compressed air if available. Inspect the strainer for any signs of wear or damage and renew it if necessary.

10 Clean the pressure regulator, and check that the plunger moves freely in its body. Inspect the pressure regulator for signs of wear or damage and renew it if necessary.

Installation

11 Install the oil pressure regulator and tighten it to the torque setting specified at the beginning of the Chapter **(see illustration 21.6)**.

12 To install the strainer housing, use a new O-ring and smear it with clean engine oil, then tighten the bolts to the specified torque setting **(see illustrations)**. If the engine is in the frame, it may be easier to locate the O-ring on the housing, rather than hope it will stay in place on the engine while the housing is fitted (though the oil should help it stick).

13 To install the strainer, position it on the housing, then install the pick-up tube using a

new gasket and tighten its bolts to the specified torque setting **(see illustrations)**. If the engine is in the frame, it may be easier to locate the gasket and the strainer on the pick-up tube, rather than hope they will stay in place on the housing while the tube is fitted.

14 If removed, fit the two locating dowels into the crankcase (if the engine has been removed and is positioned upside down on the work surface) or into the sump (if the

21.6 Oil pressure regulator (arrowed)

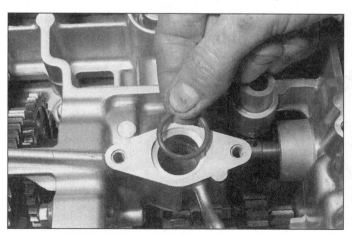

21.12a Fit a new O-ring into the groove . . .

21.12b . . . then install the housing and tighten the bolts to the specified torque

21.13a Fit the strainer . . .

21.13b . . . the gasket . . .

21.13c . . . and the pick-up tube

engine is in the frame). Lay a new gasket onto the crankcase or sump, making sure the holes in the gasket align correctly with the bolt holes, and that the gasket locates correctly onto the dowels **(see illustration)**.

15 Position the sump on the crankcase and install the bolts, using new sealing washers on the three right-hand rear corner bolts **(see illustration and 21.3)**. Tighten the bolts evenly in a criss-cross pattern to the specified torque setting.

16 Install the exhaust system (see Chapter 4), but do not yet fit the fairing side panels.

17 Fill the engine with the correct type and quantity of oil as described in Chapter 1. Start the engine and check that there are no leaks around the sump, then install the fairing side panels (see Chapter 8).

22 Oil pump – removal, inspection and installation

Note: *The oil pump can be removed with the engine in the frame.*

Removal

1 Remove the clutch (see Section 17). If not already done, turn the oil pump driven gear so that its drive pin is horizontal (this will prevent it from dropping out) **(see illustration 17.12)**. Remove the circlip from the end of the oil pump drive shaft, then remove the outer washer (where fitted) and the oil pump driven gear. Also remove the drive pin from the shaft, noting how it fits into the slot in the back of

the oil pump driven gear, and the inner washer.

2 Unscrew the three bolts securing the pump to the crankcase, then remove the pump **(see illustrations)**. Remove the O-ring and discard it as a new one must be used.

Inspection

3 Inspect the pump body for any obvious damage such as cracks or distortion, and check that the shaft rotates freely and without any side-to-side play or excessive endfloat.

4 Remove the screw on the inside of the pump cover and remove the cover **(see illustrations)**.

5 Withdraw the pump drive shaft along with the inner rotor, then remove the outer rotor from the

21.14 Locate the gasket onto the dowels (arrowed) . . .

21.15 . . . then install the sump

22.2a Unscrew the bolts (arrowed) . . .

22.2b . . . and withdraw the pump

22.4a Remove the screw (arrowed) . . .

22.4b . . . and lift off the cover

22.5 Withdraw the shaft and inner rotor, then remove the outer rotor

22.6 Look for scoring and wear, such as on this outer rotor

22.7 Measuring inner rotor tip-to-outer rotor clearance

pump body **(see illustration)**. Note how the pin locates through the shaft and in the notches in the inner rotor, and how the punchmarks on the rotors face out towards the pump cover. Clean all the components in solvent.

6 Inspect the pump body and rotors for scoring and wear **(see illustration)**. If any damage, scoring or uneven or excessive wear is evident, renew the pump (individual components are not available).

7 Measure the clearance between the inner rotor tip and the outer rotor with a feeler gauge and compare it to the maximum clearance listed in the specifications at the beginning of the Chapter **(see illustration)**. If the clearance measured is greater than the maximum listed, renew the pump.

8 Measure the clearance between the outer rotor and the pump body with a feeler gauge and compare it to the maximum clearance listed in the specifications at the beginning of the Chapter **(see illustration)**. If the clearance measured is greater than the maximum listed, renew the pump.

9 Check the pump drive and driven gears for wear or damage, and renew them as a set if necessary.

10 If the pump is good, make sure all the components are clean, then lubricate them with new engine oil.

11 Install the outer rotor into the pump body with the punchmark facing out towards the pump cover **(see illustration)**.

12 Fit the drive pin into the pump drive shaft,

then slide the inner rotor onto the round end of the shaft, making sure the drive pin ends fit into the notches in the inside of the rotor, and therefore the punchmark faces out **(see illustrations)**. Fit the shaft and inner rotor into the pump body **(see illustration)**.

13 Install the cover **(see illustration 22.4b)**, then apply a suitable non-permanent thread locking compound to the screw and tighten it securely **(see illustration)**.

Installation

14 Align the tabbed end of the pump drive shaft so that it will fit easily into the slot in the water pump shaft on installation. Fit a new O-ring onto the oil pump, then install the pump, wiggling the shaft if necessary to make it

22.8 Measuring outer rotor-to-body clearance

22.11 Fit the outer rotor into the body with the punchmark facing out

22.12a Fit the drive pin into the shaft . . .

22.12b . . . then slide the inner rotor onto the pin, locating the pin ends into the slots . . .

22.12c . . . then slide the shaft through the pump and fit the inner rotor in the outer rotor

22.13 Apply thread-lock to the cover screw

22.14a Fit the new O-ring into the grooves . . .

22.14b . . . then install the pump, making sure the tabbed end of the shaft is aligned as described

22.14c Apply a thread-lock to the pump bolts . . .

22.14d . . . and tighten them to the specified torque

locate in the water pump **(see illustrations)**. Apply a suitable non-permanent thread locking compound to the threads of the pump bolts and tighten them to the torque setting specified at the beginning of the Chapter **(see illustrations)**.

15 Slide the inner washer onto the oil pump drive shaft, then fit the drive pin into its hole in the shaft, making sure it is central **(see illustrations 17.22a and b)**. Locate the oil pump driven gear onto the shaft so that the drive pin locates into the slot in the back of the gear, then install the outer washer (where fitted) and secure the assembly with the circlip, making sure it is properly seated in its groove **(see illustrations 17.22c and d)**.

16 Install the clutch (see Section 17).

23 Crankcases – separation and reassembly

Note: *When the engine is upside down, referrals to the right and left-hand ends or sides of the transmission shafts or components are made as though the engine is the correct way up. Therefore the right-hand end of a shaft or side of a crankcase will actually be on your left as you look down onto the underside of the crankcase assembly.*

Separation

1 To access the transmission shafts and selector drum and forks, the lower crankcase must be separated from the middle crankcase. To access the crankshaft, connecting rods and bearings, the lower crankcase must be separated from the middle crankcase and the transmission shafts removed, then the middle crankcase must be separated from upper the crankcase.

2 To enable the crankcases to be separated, the engine must be removed from the frame (see Section 5).

Lower crankcase

3 Before the lower crankcase can be separated, remove the oil sump and the oil strainer housing (see Section 21). If the lower crankcase is being separated for removal of the transmission shafts, remove the clutch (see Section 17). If it is being separated to access

the selector drum and forks, the clutch can be left in situ, though the cover must be removed, and it is advisable to remove the clutch itself for ease of installation. If the selector drum and forks are being removed, first remove the gearchange mechanism (see Section 19) and the neutral switch (see Chapter 9).

4 If the lower crankcase is being separated as part of a complete engine overhaul, remove the oil cooler, then unscrew the bolts securing the cooler base and detach it from the crankcase. Discard the gasket as a new one must be used. Also remove the oil and water pumps (see Section 22 and Chapter 3 respectively), the oil pressure regulator (see Section 21), the gearchange mechanism (see Section 19), and the neutral and oil pressure switches (see Chapter 9). **Note:** *If required, all those components can be removed after the lower crankcase has been separated.* After separation, remove the selector drum and forks (see Section 27).

5 Slacken the clamp securing the coolant hose to the top of the water pump and detach the hose.

6 Unscrew the banjo bolts securing the oil pipe to the lower and upper crankcases and detach the hose **(see illustration)**. Discard the sealing washers as new ones must be used.

7 Unscrew the bolts securing the oil seal retainer plate and remove the plate **(see illustration)**.

8 Unscrew the seven bolts in the upper crankcase, noting the positions of the bolts with sealing washers **(see illustration)**. **Note:**

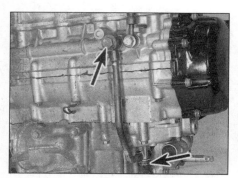

23.6 Unscrew the banjo bolts (arrowed) and remove the oil pipe

23.7 Unscrew the bolts (arrowed) and remove the plate

23.8 Unscrew the bolts (arrowed) in the upper and middle crankcase. The bolts (A) have copper sealing washers

23.11 Lift the lower crankcase up off the middle case

c) Cylinder head and cam chain front blade (Section 11).
d) Cylinder block (Section 14).
e) Pistons (Section 15).
f) Starter clutch and starter idle/reduction gear assembly (Section 20).
g) Ignition pulse generator coil (Chapter 5).
h) Alternator (Chapter 9).
i) Starter motor (Chapter 9).

23.10 Unscrew the lower crankcase bolts (arrowed). The bolts (A) have sealing washers

As each bolt is removed, store it in its relative position in a cardboard template of the crankcase halves. This will ensure all bolts are installed in the correct location on reassembly. Also note the washers fitted with certain bolts, and keep them with their bolts as different washers are used in different places.

9 Turn the engine upside down. Support it on wood blocks if required.

10 Unscrew the thirteen lower crankcase bolts, noting the positions of the bolts with sealing washers **(see illustration)**.

11 Carefully lift the lower crankcase off the middle, using a soft-faced hammer to tap around the joint to initially separate the halves if necessary **(see illustration)**. **Note:** *If the halves do not separate easily, make sure all fasteners have been removed. Do not try and separate the halves by levering against the crankcase mating surfaces as they are easily scored and will leak oil.* The lower crankcase half will come away with the oil pump, water pump and gearchange mechanism (unless

previously removed), and the selector drum and forks, leaving the transmission shafts in the middle crankcase.

12 Remove the three locating dowels from the crankcase if they are loose (they could be in either case), noting their locations **(see illustration 23.36)**. Also remove the five oil passage O-rings from the middle crankcase **(see illustration 23.37)**. Discard these as new ones must be used.

Middle crankcase

13 Before the middle crankcase can be separated, remove the starter clutch cover (see Section 20), the alternator cover (see Chapter 9), the lower crankcase (see above) and the transmission shafts (see Section 25). If the engine is being completely overhauled, remove the following components:
a) Cam chain tensioner, cam chain and tensioner blade (Section 9).
b) Camshafts (Section 10).

Note: *If the crankcases are being separated to remove the crankshaft leaving the connecting rods in place, the cylinder head and cylinder block can remain in situ. If this is the case, the connecting rods must be separated from the crankshaft before removing the crankshaft. However, if removal of the crankshaft with the connecting rod assemblies is intended, the cylinder head, cylinder block and pistons must be removed.*

14 Unscrew the nine upper crankcase bolts **(see illustration)**. Note the position of the earth (ground) cable and the bolt with sealing washer.

15 Turn the engine upside down. Support it on wood blocks if required.

16 Unscrew the six middle crankcase bolts, noting the positions of the bolts with wiring clips **(see illustration)**.

17 Working in a **reverse** of the tightening sequence shown and as cast into the casing **(see illustration)**, slacken each crankshaft journal bolt a little a time until they are all finger-tight, then remove the bolts. **Note:** *As

23.14 Unscrew the bolts (arrowed) in the upper crankcase. The bolt (A) has a sealing washer and (B) holds the earth lead

23.16 Unscrew the middle crankcase bolts (arrowed), noting the wiring clips (A) for the oil pressure switch

23.17 Crankshaft journal bolt TIGHTENING sequence. Slacken them in REVERSE order

23.18 Lift the middle crankcase up off the upper case

23.24 Make sure the dowels (arrowed) are installed in one of the cases. W and X models shown here – on T and V models the rearmost dowel is at the back of the case

each bolt is removed, store it in its relative position in a cardboard template of the crankcase halves. This will ensure all bolts are installed in the correct location on reassembly.
18 Carefully lift the middle crankcase off the upper, using a soft-faced hammer to tap around the joint to initially separate the halves if necessary **(see illustration)**. **Note:** *If the halves do not separate easily, make sure all fasteners have been removed. Do not try and separate the halves by levering against the crankcase mating surfaces as they are easily scored and will leak oil. The middle crankcase will come away by itself, leaving the crankshaft in the upper crankcase.*
19 Remove the three locating dowels from the crankcase if they are loose (they could be in either case), noting their locations **(see illustration 23.24)**.
20 Refer to Sections 24 to 30 for the removal

and installation of the components housed within the crankcases.

Reassembly

Middle crankcase

21 Remove all traces of sealant from the middle and upper crankcase mating surfaces.
22 Ensure that all components and their bearings are in place in the upper crankcase. Check that the crankshaft thrust bearings are correctly located, and that all oil jets have been installed, if removed.
23 Generously lubricate the crankshaft, particularly around the bearings, with clean engine oil, then use a rag soaked in high flash-

point solvent to wipe over the gasket surfaces of both cases to remove all traces of oil.
24 If removed, fit the three locating dowels into the upper crankcase **(see illustration)**.
25 Apply a small amount of suitable sealant (such as Suzuki Bond 1207B) to the mating surface of the middle crankcase **(see illustration)**.
Caution: Do not apply an excessive amount of sealant as it will ooze out when the case halves are assembled and may obstruct oil passages. Do not apply the sealant on or too close to any of the bearing inserts or surfaces.
26 Check again that all components are in position, particularly that the bearing shells are still correctly located in the middle crankcase. Carefully fit the middle crankcase onto the upper crankcase, making sure the dowels all locate correctly into the middle crankcase **(see illustration 23.18)**.
27 Check that the middle crankcase is correctly seated. **Note:** *The crankcase halves should fit together without being forced. If the casings are not correctly seated, remove the middle crankcase and investigate the problem. Do not attempt to pull them together using the crankcase bolts as the casing will crack and be ruined.*
28 Clean the threads of the 9 mm crankshaft journal bolts and insert them in their original locations **(see illustration)**. Secure all bolts finger-tight at first, then tighten the bolts a little at a time and in the numerical sequence shown, and as marked on the casing, to the torque setting specified at the beginning of the Chapter **(see illustration 23.17)**.
29 Turn the engine over. Install the nine upper crankcase bolts, not forgetting the sealing washer with the right-hand front bolt and the earth (ground) cable with the middle rear bolt (clean the terminal first) **(see illustration 23.14)**. Tighten the bolts evenly and a little at a time to the specified torque setting, working from the middle outwards.
30 Turn the engine over. Clean the threads of the six middle crankcase bolts and insert them in their original locations, not forgetting the wiring clips **(see illustration 23.16)**. Tighten the bolts evenly and a little at a time

23.25 Apply sealant to the shaded areas

H31243

23.28 Install the crankshaft journal bolts

to the specified torque setting, working from the middle outwards.

31 With all crankcase fasteners tightened, check that the crankshaft rotates smoothly and easily. If there are any signs of undue stiffness, tight or rough spots, or of any other problem, the fault must be rectified before proceeding further.

32 Install all other removed assemblies according to Step 13.

Lower crankcase

33 Remove all traces of sealant from the crankcase mating surfaces.

34 Ensure that all components and their bearings are in place in the middle and lower crankcases. Check that the transmission bearing locating pins and half-ring retainers are correctly located, and that the oil jet has been installed, if removed.

35 Generously lubricate the transmission shafts and the selector drum and forks, particularly around the bearings, with clean engine oil, then use a rag soaked in high flash-point solvent to wipe over the gasket surfaces of both cases to remove all traces of oil.

36 If removed, fit the three locating dowels into the middle crankcase **(see illustration)**. Make sure that the selector drum is in the neutral position.

37 Fit new O-rings into the oil passage holes in the middle crankcase **(see illustration)**.

38 Apply a small amount of suitable sealant (such as Suzuki Bond 1207B) to the mating surface of the lower crankcase **(see illustration)**.

23.36 Make sure the dowels (arrowed) are installed in one of the cases

23.37 Fit a new O-ring around each oil passage (arrowed)

Caution: Do not apply an excessive amount of sealant as it will ooze out when the case halves are assembled and may obstruct oil passages. Do not apply the sealant on or too close to any of the bearing inserts or surfaces.

39 Check again that all components are in position. Carefully fit the lower crankcase onto the middle crankcase, making sure the selector forks locate correctly into their grooves in the transmission shaft gears **(see illustration)**. Make sure the dowels all locate correctly into the lower crankcase.

40 Check that the lower crankcase is correctly seated. **Note:** *The crankcase halves should fit together without being forced. If the casings are not correctly seated, remove the lower crankcase and investigate the problem.*

Do not attempt to pull them together using the crankcase bolts as the casing will crack and be ruined.

41 Check that the transmission shafts rotate freely and independently in neutral.

42 Clean the threads of the thirteen lower crankcase bolts and insert them in their original locations, not forgetting the sealing washers with the specified bolts **(see illustration 23.10)**. Secure all bolts finger-tight only.

43 Turn the engine over. Clean the threads of the seven upper crankcase bolts and insert them in their original locations, not forgetting the copper sealing washers with the specified bolts **(see illustration 23.8)**. Tighten all the bolts evenly and a little at a time to the specified torque setting, working from the middle outwards.

44 Turn the engine over. Tighten the thirteen lower crankcase bolts evenly and a little at a time to the specified torque setting, working from the middle outwards **(see illustration 23.10)**.

45 With all crankcase fasteners tightened, check that the crankshaft and transmission shafts rotate smoothly and easily. Rotate the selector drum by hand and select each gear in turn whilst rotating the input shaft. Check that all gears can be selected and that the shafts rotate freely in every gear. If there are any signs of undue stiffness, tight or rough spots, or of any other problem, the fault must be rectified before proceeding further.

23.38 Apply sealant to the shaded areas

23.39 Make sure each selector fork locates in the groove in its gear pinion

23.46 Fit the retainer plate and tighten the bolts

23.47 Use new sealing washers on each side of each union

46 Install the oil seal retainer plate and tighten the bolts securely **(see illustration)**.
47 Fit the oil pipe onto the lower and upper crankcases, using new sealing washers on each side of the unions, and tighten the banjo bolts to the specified torque settings **(see illustration)**.
48 Install all other removed assemblies in the reverse of the sequence given in Steps 3 and 4. Use a new gasket on the oil cooler base.
49 Fit the coolant hose from the cylinder block onto the top union on the water pump and tighten the clamp securely.

24 Crankcases –
inspection and servicing

1 After the crankcases have been separated, remove all the components housed within them (if not already done), referring to the relevant Sections of this Chapter and to Chapter 9 for the oil pressure and neutral switches. Remove the transmission oil jet from the lower crankcase using a flat-bladed screwdriver **(see illustration)**. Remove the alternator oil jet from the upper crankcase using a suitable socket or spanner **(see illustration)**. Unscrew the bolts securing the piston oil jets in the upper crankcase and remove the jets, noting how

they fit – there are four of them. Remove the O-rings and discard them as new ones should be used.
2 The crankcases should be cleaned thoroughly with new solvent and dried with compressed air. All oil passages and oil jets should be blown out with compressed air.
3 All traces of old gasket sealant should be removed from the mating surfaces. Minor damage to the surfaces can be cleaned up with a fine sharpening stone or grindstone.
Caution: Be very careful not to nick or gouge the crankcase mating surfaces or oil leaks will result. Check the crankcases very carefully for cracks and other damage.
4 Small cracks or holes in aluminium castings may be repaired with an epoxy resin adhesive as a temporary measure. Permanent repairs can only be effected by argon-arc welding, and only a specialist in this process is in a position to advise on the economy or practical aspect of such a repair. If any damage is found that can't be repaired, renew the crankcase halves as a set.
5 Damaged threads can be economically reclaimed by using a diamond section wire insert, of the Heli-Coil type, which is easily fitted after drilling and re-tapping the affected thread.
6 Sheared studs or screws can usually be removed with screw extractors, which consist

of a tapered, left thread screw of very hard steel. These are inserted into a pre-drilled hole in the stud, and usually succeed in dislodging the most stubborn stud or screw.

> **HAYNES HiNT** *Refer to Tools and Workshop Tips for details of installing a thread insert and using screw extractors.*

7 Fit a new O-ring onto the base of each piston oil jet and smear it with clean engine oil. Push each jet into its bore in the upper crankcase, making sure the oil nozzle points up. Apply a suitable non-permanent thread locking compound to the jet bolts and tighten them securely. Fit the alternator oil jet in the upper crankcase and tighten it to the torque setting specified at the beginning of the Chapter. Screw the transmission oil jet into the lower crankcase.
8 Install all other components and assemblies, referring to the relevant Sections of this Chapter and to Chapter 9, before reassembling the crankcase halves.

25 Transmission shafts –
removal and installation

Note: *To remove the transmission shafts the engine must be removed from the frame and the lower crankcase separated.*
Note: *Referrals to the right and left-hand ends of the transmission shafts are made as though the engine is the correct way up, even though throughout this procedure it is upside down. Therefore the right-hand end of a shaft will actually be on your left as you look down onto the underside of the upper crankcase assembly.*

Removal

1 Separate the lower crankcase from the middle crankcase (see Section 23).
2 Remove the clutch pushrod oil seal from the left-hand end of the input shaft (see

24.1a Transmission oil jet location (arrowed)

24.1b Alternator oil jet

25.2a Remove the clutch pushrod oil seal . . .

25.2b . . . and if required, the output shaft oil seal

25.3 Lift each shaft out of the casing

25.4 Remove the half ring retainers (A) and the dowel pins (B)

illustration). If required, remove the oil seal from the left-hand end of the output shaft, noting how it fits **(see illustration).**

3 Lift the output shaft and input shaft out of the crankcase, noting their relative positions in the crankcase and how they fit together **(see illustration).** If they are stuck, use a soft-faced hammer and gently tap on the ends of the shafts to free them.

4 Remove the ball bearing half-ring retainers and the needle bearing dowel pins from the middle crankcase, noting how they fit **(see illustration).** If they are not in their slot or hole

25.7a Locate the pin (A) in the hole (B), . . .

in the crankcase, remove them from the bearings themselves on the shafts.

5 If required, the shafts can be disassembled and inspected for wear or damage (see Section 26).

Installation

6 Install the ball bearing half-ring retainers into their slots in the upper crankcase half, and install the needle bearing dowels into their holes **(see illustration 25.4).**

7 Lower the input shaft into position in the middle crankcase, making sure the hole in the needle bearing engages correctly with the dowel, the ball bearing locating pin faces forward and locates in its recess, and the groove in the bearing engages correctly with the half-ring retainer **(see illustrations).**

8 Lower the output shaft into position in the middle crankcase, making sure the hole in the needle bearing engages correctly with the dowel, the ball bearing locating pin faces back and locates in its recess, and the groove in the bearing engages correctly with the half-ring retainer **(see illustration).**

9 Smear the lips of the new output shaft oil seal with grease. Slide the oil seal onto the left-hand end of the output shaft **(see illustration 25.2b).** Smear the lips of the new clutch pushrod oil seal with grease. Fit the

seal against the left-hand end of the shaft **(see illustration 25.2a).**

10 Make sure both transmission shafts are correctly seated and their related pinions are correctly engaged.

Caution: If the ball bearing locating pins and half-ring retainers or needle bearing dowel pins are not correctly engaged, the crankcase halves will not seat correctly.

11 Position the gears in the neutral position and check the shafts are free to rotate easily and independently (ie the input shaft can turn whilst the output shaft is held stationary) before proceeding further.

12 Install the lower crankcase (see Section 23).

26 Transmission shafts – disassembly, inspection and reassembly

Note: *References to the right- and left-hand ends of the transmission shafts are made as though they are installed in the engine and the engine is the correct way up.*

1 Remove the transmission shafts from the middle crankcase (see Section 25). Always

25.7b . . . the bearing pin in its cutout (C), and the retainer in the groove (D)

25.8 Locate the bearing pin in its cutout (A) and the retainer in the groove (B)

26.1 Transmission shaft components

Numbers indicate gears

disassemble the transmission shafts separately to avoid mixing up the components **(see illustration)**.

Input shaft disassembly

 When disassembling the transmission shafts, place the parts on a long rod or thread a wire through them to keep them in order and facing the proper direction.

2 Remove the needle bearing and oil seal from the left-hand end of the shaft **(see illustrations 26.20b and a)**.
3 Reach behind the 6th gear pinion with circlip pliers, spread the circlip and slide it toward the 3rd/4th gear pinion **(see illustration 26.19e and d)**. Slide the 6th and 2nd gear pinions back to expose the snapring on the end of the shaft, then remove it and slide the 2nd and 6th gear pinions and the bush off the shaft **(see illustrations 26.19c, b and a, and 26.18b and a)**.

4 Remove the circlip securing the combined 3rd/4th gear pinion, then slide the pinion off the shaft **(see illustration 26.17b and a)**.
5 Remove the circlip securing the 5th gear pinion, then slide the 5th gear pinion and its bush off the shaft **(see illustrations 26.16c, b and a)**.
6 The 1st gear pinion is integral with the shaft.

Input shaft inspection

7 Wash all of the components in clean solvent and dry them off.
8 Check the gear teeth for cracking chipping, pitting and other obvious wear or damage. Any pinion that is damaged as such must be renewed.
9 Inspect the dogs and the dog holes in the gears for cracks, chips, and excessive wear especially in the form of rounded edges. Make sure mating gears engage properly. Renew the paired gears as a set if necessary.
10 Check for signs of scoring or bluing on the pinions, bushes and shaft. This could be caused by overheating due to inadequate

lubrication. Check that all the oil holes and passages are clear. Renew any damaged pinions or bushes.
11 Check that each pinion moves freely on the shaft or bush but without undue freeplay. Check that each bush moves freely on the shaft but without undue freeplay.
12 The shaft is unlikely to sustain damage unless the engine has seized, placing an unusually high loading on the transmission, or the machine has covered a very high mileage. Check the surface of the shaft, especially where a pinion turns on it, and renew the shaft if it has scored or picked up, or if there are any cracks. Damage of any kind can only be cured by renewal.
13 Check the ball bearing for play or roughness, and that it is a tight fit on the shaft. Renew the bearing if it is worn, loose or damaged, using a bearing puller to remove it. Install the bearing using a press or a length of tubing which bears only on the bearing's inner race. Install the needle roller bearing onto the shaft, and check it for play or roughness. Renew the bearing if it is worn or damaged.

26.16a Slide on the 5th gear pinion . . .

26.16b . . . and its bush . . .

26.16c . . . and secure them with the circlip

26.17a Slide on the 3rd/4th gear pinion . . .

26.17b . . . and its circlip, positioning it beyond its groove toward the 3rd/4th gear pinion

26.18a Slide on the bush, aligning the oil holes . . .

14 Check the needle bearing oil seal and renew it if it is damaged or deteriorated. Discard all the circlips and the snap-ring as new ones must be used.

Input shaft reassembly

15 During reassembly, apply molybdenum disulphide oil (a 50/50 mixture of molybdenum disulphide paste or grease and clean engine oil) to the mating surfaces of the shaft, pinions and bushes. When installing the circlips, do not expand the ends any further than is necessary. Install the stamped circlips so that their chamfered side faces the pinion it secures, ie so that its sharp edge faces the

direction of thrust load (see *correct fitting of a stamped circlip* illustration in Tools and Workshop Tips of the Reference section).
16 Slide the 5th gear pinion, with its dogs facing away from the integral 1st gear, onto the left-hand end of the shaft **(see illustration)**. Slide the 5th gear bush onto the shaft so that it fits into the pinion **(see illustration)**. Install the circlip, making sure that it locates correctly in the groove in the shaft **(see illustration)**.
17 Slide the combined 3rd/4th gear pinion onto the shaft, so that the larger (4th gear) pinion faces the 5th gear pinion dogs **(see illustration)**. Fit the circlip onto the shaft but

do not locate it in its groove – slide it past the groove and as far towards the 3rd/4th gear pinion as possible **(see illustration)**.
18 Slide the 6th gear pinion splined bush onto the shaft, with its shouldered end facing the circlip and aligning the oil hole in the bush with that in the shaft **(see illustration)**. Slide the 6th gear pinion onto the bush, with its dogs facing the dogs on the 3rd gear pinion **(see illustration)**.
19 Slide the 2nd gear pinion onto the shaft and secure it with the snap-ring, making sure it is properly seated in its groove **(see illustrations)**. Now slide the 6th and 2nd gear pinions along to expose the groove for the

26.18b . . . and slide the 6th gear pinion onto the bush

26.19a Slide on the 2nd gear pinion . . .

26.19b . . . and fit the snap-ring into its groove

26.19c Slide the 6th and 2nd gear pinions along . . .

26.19d . . . followed by the circlip . . .

26.19e . . . and fit it into its groove

26.20a Fit the oil seal . . .

26.20b . . . and the bearing

26.20c Check that the assembled shaft is as shown

3rd/4th gear pinion circlip, then move the circlip along the shaft and fit it into the groove **(see illustrations)**.

20 Apply some grease to the needle bearing oil seal. Slide the oil seal and the needle bearing onto the shaft end **(see illustrations)**. Check that all components have been correctly installed **(see illustration)**.

Output shaft disassembly

21 Remove the needle bearing and the thrust washer from the right-hand end of the shaft **(see illustration 26.1)**.

22 Slide the 1st gear pinion and its bush off the shaft, followed by the thrust washer and the 5th gear pinion.

23 Remove the circlip securing the 4th gear pinion, then slide the pinion and its splined bush off the shaft, followed by the thrust washer, the 3rd gear pinion and its bush.

24 Remove the circlip securing the 6th gear pinion, then slide the pinion off the shaft.

25 Remove the circlip securing the 2nd gear pinion, then slide the thrust washer, the 2nd gear pinion and its bush off the shaft.

Output shaft inspection

26 Refer to Steps 7 to 14 above.

Output shaft reassembly

27 During reassembly, apply molybdenum disulphide oil (a 50/50 mixture of molybdenum disulphide paste or grease and clean engine oil) to the mating surfaces of the shaft, pinions and bushes. When installing the circlips, do not expand the ends any further than is necessary. Install the stamped circlips so that their chamfered side faces the pinion it secures, ie so that its sharp edge faces the direction of thrust load (see *correct fitting of a stamped circlip* illustration in Tools and Workshop Tips of the Reference section) **(see illustration 26.1)**.

28 Slide the 2nd gear pinion (flat faces towards the bearing) and its bush onto the shaft, followed by the thrust washer, and secure it in place with the circlip, making sure it is properly seated in its groove.

29 Slide the 6th gear pinion onto the shaft with its selector fork groove facing away from the 2nd gear pinion, and secure it in place with the circlip, making sure it is properly seated in its groove.

30 Slide the 3rd gear pinion splined bush onto the shaft, with its shouldered side facing the circlip and aligning the oil hole in the bush with that in the shaft. Slide the 3rd gear pinion onto the bush so that its open side faces the 6th gear pinion.

31 Slide the thrust washer and the 4th gear pinion (open side facing away from the 3rd gear pinion) onto the shaft, then fit the 4th gear pinion bush into the pinion, aligning the oil hole in the bush with that in the shaft. Secure them in place with the circlip, making sure it is properly seated in its groove.

32 Slide the 5th gear pinion onto the shaft with its selector fork groove facing the 4th gear pinion, followed by the thrust washer.

33 Slide the 1st gear pinion (with its open side facing the 5th gear pinion) and its bush onto the shaft, followed by the thrust washer.

34 Slide the needle bearing onto the shaft end. Check that all components have been correctly installed.

27 Selector drum and forks – removal, inspection and installation

Note: *To remove the selector drum and forks the engine must be removed from the frame and the lower crankcase separated.*

Removal

1 Separate the lower crankcase from the middle crankcase (see Section 23). The selector drum and forks are housed inside the lower case. If not already done, remove the gearchange mechanism (see Section 19).

2 Before removing the selector forks, mark each fork for identification using a felt pen and note which way round they fit, as an aid to installation.

3 Supporting the selector forks, withdraw the fork shafts from the right-hand side of the crankcase and remove the forks **(see**

27.3 Withdraw the shafts and remove the forks

27.6 Withdraw the selector drum

illustration). Once removed from the crankcase, slide the forks back onto the shafts in their correct order and way round.

4 If not already done, remove the neutral switch (see Chapter 9).

5 If required, counter-hold the selector drum using a spanner on the flats on its left-hand end, then unscrew the stopper plate bolt and remove the plate, the washer and the two locating pins.

6 Slide the drum out of the right-hand side of the case (see illustration).

Inspection

7 Inspect the selector forks for any signs of wear or damage, especially around the fork ends where they engage with the groove in the pinion. Check that each fork fits correctly in its pinion groove. Check closely to see if the forks are bent. If the forks are in any way damaged they must be renewed.

8 With the fork engaged with its gear pinion groove, measure the fork-to-groove clearance using a feeler gauge, and compare the result to the specifications at the beginning of the Chapter (see illustration). If the clearance exceeds the service limit specified, measure the thickness of the fork ends and the width of the groove and compare the readings to the specifications (see illustrations). Renew whichever components are worn beyond their specifications.

9 Check that the forks fit correctly on their shaft. They should move freely with a light fit but no appreciable freeplay. Check that the fork shaft holes in the crankcases are not worn or damaged.

10 The selector fork shafts can be checked for trueness by rolling them along a flat surface. A bent rod will cause difficulty in selecting gears and make the gearshift action heavy. Renew the shafts if bent.

11 Inspect the selector drum grooves and selector fork guide pins for signs of wear or damage. If either components show signs of wear or damage they must be renewed.

12 Check that the selector drum bearings

rotate freely and have no sign of freeplay between them and the crankcase. A needle bearing is on the left-hand end (in the crankcase) and a caged ball bearing is on the right-hand end (on the selector drum). Renew the bearings if necessary. To renew the ball bearing, remove the stopper plate (if not already done – see Step 5) and slide it off the end of the selector drum. To renew the needle bearing, drift it out of the crankcase, noting that once it has been removed it cannot be re-used (see illustration). Draw or drive the new bearing into place, making sure it enters squarely. Refer to *Tools and Workshop Tips* in

the Reference Section for more information on bearings and how to remove and install them.

Installation

13 Slide the drum into position in the crankcase (see illustration 27.6).

14 If removed, fit the stopper plate locating pins into the end of the drum. Slide the washer and stopper plate onto the selector drum, making sure the holes in the plate locate onto the pins in the drum. Apply a suitable non-permanent thread locking compound to the stopper plate bolt threads, then tighten it to the torque setting specified

27.8a Measure the fork-to-groove clearance using a feeler gauge

27.8b Measure the thickness of the fork end . . .

27.8c . . . and the width of the groove

27.12 The needle bearing is in the crankcase

27.16a Position the front fork with its pin in the centre groove in the selector drum and slide the shaft through

27.16b Similarly install the rear forks

29.2 Measure the clearance between the outer thrust bearing and the crankshaft as shown

at the beginning of the Chapter, using a spanner on the selector drum flats to counter-hold it as on removal. Position the selector drum so that the neutral detent in the stopper plate, identifiable by its different outline to the other detents, is roughly aligned at the 2 o'clock position, so that the stopper arm locates onto it when it is later installed.

15 Install the neutral switch (see Chapter 9).

16 Lubricate each selector fork shaft with clean engine oil and slide them into the bores in the crankcase **(see illustrations)**. As each shaft is installed, fit each selector fork in turn, making sure it is in its correct location and the right way round (see Step 2), and that its guide pin locates in its track in the selector drum.

17 Install the gearchange mechanism (see Section 19).

18 Install the lower crankcase (see Section 23).

28 Main and connecting rod bearings – general information

1 Even though main and connecting rod bearings are generally renewed with new ones during the engine overhaul, the old bearings should be retained for close examination as they may reveal valuable information about the condition of the engine.

2 Bearing failure occurs mainly because of lack of lubrication, the presence of dirt or other foreign particles, overloading the engine and/or corrosion. Regardless of the cause of bearing failure, it must be corrected before the engine is reassembled to prevent it from happening again.

3 When examining the connecting rod bearings, remove them from the connecting rods and caps and lay them out on a clean surface in the same general position as their location on the crankshaft journals. This will enable you to match any noted bearing problems with the corresponding crankshaft journal.

4 Dirt and other foreign particles get into the engine in a variety of ways. It may be left in

the engine during assembly or it may pass through filters or breathers. It may get into the oil and from there into the bearings. Metal chips from machining operations and normal engine wear are often present. Abrasives are sometimes left in engine components after reconditioning operations, especially when parts are not thoroughly cleaned using the proper cleaning methods. Whatever the source, these foreign objects often end up embedded in the soft bearing material and are easily recognised. Large particles will not embed in the bearing and will score or gouge the bearing and journal. The best prevention for this cause of bearing failure is to clean all parts thoroughly and keep everything spotlessly clean during engine reassembly. Frequent and regular oil and filter changes are also recommended.

5 Lack of lubrication or lubrication breakdown has a number of interrelated causes. Excessive heat (which thins the oil), overloading (which squeezes the oil from the bearing face) and oil leakage or throw off (from excessive bearing clearances, worn oil pump or high engine speeds) all contribute to lubrication breakdown. Blocked oil passages will also starve a bearing and destroy it. When lack of lubrication is the cause of bearing failure, the bearing material is wiped or extruded from the steel backing of the bearing. Temperatures may increase to the point where the steel backing and the journal turn blue from overheating.

HAYNES HINT *Refer to Tools and Workshop Tips for bearing fault finding.*

6 Riding habits can have a definite effect on bearing life. Full throttle low speed operation, or labouring the engine, puts very high loads on bearings, which tend to squeeze out the oil film. These loads cause the bearings to flex, which produces fine cracks in the bearing face (fatigue failure). Eventually the bearing material will loosen in pieces and tear away from the steel backing. Short trip riding leads to corrosion of bearings, as insufficient engine

heat is produced to drive off the condensed water and corrosive gases produced. These products collect in the engine oil, forming acid and sludge. As the oil is carried to the engine bearings, the acid attacks and corrodes the bearing material.

7 Incorrect bearing installation during engine assembly will lead to bearing failure as well. Tight fitting bearings which leave insufficient bearing oil clearances result in oil starvation. Dirt or foreign particles trapped behind a bearing insert result in high spots on the bearing which lead to failure.

8 To avoid bearing problems, clean all parts thoroughly before reassembly, double check all bearing clearance measurements and lubricate the new bearings with clean engine oil during installation.

29 Crankshaft and main bearings – removal, inspection and installation

Note: *To remove the crankshaft the engine must be removed from the frame and the crankcases separated.*

Removal

1 Separate the middle crankcase from the upper crankcase (see Section 23).

2 Before removing the crankshaft check the thrust bearing clearance. The thrust bearings are located between the crank webs and the main bearing housing between cylinder Nos. 1 and 2. Push the crankshaft as far as it will go toward the left-hand (alternator) end (this eliminates play in the inner bearing). Insert a feeler gauge between the crankshaft and the outer thrust bearing and record the clearance **(see illustration)**. Compare the measurement with this Chapter's Specifications. If the clearance is excessive, refer to Steps 11 and 12 for selection of new bearings.

3 If the crankshaft only is being removed and the piston/connecting rod assemblies are staying in the engine, separate the connecting rods from the crankshaft (see Section 30) and gently push them to the top of the bores.

4 Remove the thrust bearings, noting how

29.4 Remove each thrust bearing, and do not mix them up

29.5 To remove a main bearing shell, push it sideways and lift it out

29.11 Measure the thickness of the inner thrust bearing

and where they fit – do not get the inner and outer bearings mixed up (note their different coloured ends) (see illustration).

Lift the crankshaft, together with the connecting rods if they haven't been separated, out of the upper crankcase. If the crankshaft appears stuck, tap it gently on each end using a soft-faced mallet.

5 The main bearing shells can be removed from their cut-outs by pushing their centres to the side, then lifting them out (see illustration). Keep the bearing shells in order.

6 If required and not already done, separate the connecting rods from the crankshaft (see Section 30).

Inspection

7 Clean the crankshaft with solvent, using a rifle-cleaning brush to scrub out the oil passages. If available, blow the crank dry with compressed air, and also blow through the oil passages. Check the cam chain sprocket for wear or damage. If any of the sprocket teeth are excessively worn, chipped or broken, the sprocket must be renewed. Similarly check the primary drive gear.

8 Refer to Section 28 and examine the main bearing shells. If they are scored, badly scuffed or appear to have been seized, new bearings must be installed. Always renew the main bearings as a set. If they are badly damaged, check the corresponding crankshaft journals. Evidence of extreme heat, such as discoloration, indicates that

lubrication failure has occurred. Be sure to thoroughly check the oil pump and pressure regulator as well as all oil holes and passages before reassembling the engine.

9 The crankshaft journals should be given a close visual examination, paying particular attention where damaged bearings have been discovered. If the journals are scored or pitted in any way a new crankshaft will be required. Note that undersizes are not available, precluding the option of re-grinding the crankshaft.

10 Place the crankshaft on V-blocks and check the runout at the main bearing journals using a dial gauge. Compare the reading to the maximum specified at the beginning of the Chapter. If the runout exceeds the limit, a new crankshaft must be installed.

Thrust bearing selection

11 If the thrust bearing clearance was excessive (see Step 2), measure the thickness of the inner thrust bearing, and compare the result to the specifications at the beginning of the Chapter (see illustration). If the thickness measured is below the service limit specified, the inner thrust bearing must be renewed. There is only one size of replacement inner bearing. Install the new inner bearing and check the clearance again (see Step 2). If the clearance is still excessive, or if the inner bearing was within specifications, select a new outer bearing as follows:

12 Remove the outer thrust bearing. Install

the inner bearing and push the crankshaft as far as it will go toward the left-hand (alternator) end to eliminate any clearance. Insert a feeler gauge between the crankshaft and the main bearing housing where the outer bearing fits, and record the clearance (see illustration). Using the table below, select a replacement outer thrust bearing according to the clearance measured. For example, if the clearance recorded was 2.495 mm, the bearing colour-code required is blue. Re-check the clearance with the new bearings (see Step 2).

Outer bearing clearance (bearing removed)	Bearing colour-code required
2.430 to 2.460 mm	Red
2.460 to 2.485 mm	Black
2.485 to 2.510 mm	Blue
2.510 to 2.535 mm	Green
2.535 to 2.560 mm	Yellow
2.560 to 2.585 mm	White

Main bearing shell selection

13 New bearing shells for the main bearings are supplied on a selected fit basis. Code numbers stamped on various components are used to identify the correct replacement bearings. The crankshaft main bearing journal size letters, one letter for each journal (either an A, B or C), are stamped on the outside of the crankshaft left-hand web (see illustration). The corresponding main bearing housing size letters (either an A or B), are

29.12 Measure the clearance between the crankshaft and the main bearing housing

29.13a Crankshaft journal size letters

29.13b Bearing housing size letters

29.14 The colour code is marked on the side of the shell

stamped into the rear of the upper crankcase **(see illustration)**. The first letter of each set of five is for the outer left-hand journal, the second for the inner left-hand, the third for the middle, the fourth for the inner right-hand, and the fifth for the outer right-hand journal. **Note:** *Referrals to left- and right-hand are made as though the engine is the correct way up. Do not confuse the two if the engine is upside down.*

14 A range of bearing shells is available. To select the correct bearing for a particular journal, using the table below cross-refer the main bearing journal size letter (stamped on the crank web) with the main bearing housing size letter (stamped on the crankcase) to determine the colour code of the bearing required. For example, if the journal code is C, and the housing code is B, then the bearing required is Yellow. The colour is marked on the side of the shell **(see illustration)**.

Crankcase housing code	Crankshaft journal code		
	A	**B**	**C**
A	Green	Black	Brown
B	Black	Brown	Yellow

Oil clearance check

15 Whether new bearing shells are being fitted or the original ones are being re-used,

the main bearing oil clearance should be checked before the engine is reassembled. Main bearing oil clearance is measured with a product known as Plastigauge.

16 Clean the backs of the bearing shells and the bearing housings in both crankcase halves.

17 Press the bearing shells into their cut-outs, ensuring that the tab on each shell engages in the notch in the crankcase **(see illustration)**. Make sure the bearings are fitted in the correct locations and take care not to touch any shell's bearing surface with your fingers.

18 Ensure the shells and crankshaft are clean and dry. Lay the crankshaft in position in the upper crankcase.

19 Cut several lengths of the appropriate size Plastigauge (they should be slightly shorter than the width of the crankshaft journals). Place a strand of Plastigauge on each (cleaned) journal **(see illustration)**. Make sure the crankshaft is not rotated.

20 Carefully lower the middle crankcase onto the upper, making sure it seats correctly **(see illustration 23.18)**. **Note:** *Do not tighten the crankcase bolts if the casing is not correctly seated.* Clean the threads of the 9 mm crankshaft journal bolts and insert them in their original locations **(see illustration 23.28)**. Secure all bolts finger-tight at first, then

tighten the bolts a little at a time and in the numerical sequence shown to the torque setting specified at the beginning of the Chapter **(see illustration 23.17)**. Make sure that the crankshaft is not rotated as the bolts are tightened.

21 Slacken each bolt in reverse sequence starting at number 10 and working backwards to number 1. Slacken each bolt a little at a time until they are all finger-tight, then remove the bolts. Carefully lift off the middle crankcase, making sure the Plastigauge is not disturbed.

22 Compare the width of the crushed Plastigauge on each crankshaft journal to the scale printed on the Plastigauge envelope to obtain the main bearing oil clearance **(see illustration)**. Compare the reading to the specifications at the beginning of the Chapter.

23 On completion carefully scrape away all traces of the Plastigauge material from the crankshaft journal and bearing shells; use a fingernail or other object which is unlikely to score them.

24 If the oil clearance falls into the specified range, no bearing shell replacement is required (provided they are in good condition). If the clearance is more than the standard range, but within the service limit, refer to the marks on the case and the marks on the crankshaft and select new bearing shells (see Steps 13 and 14). Install the new shells and check the oil clearance once again (the new shells may bring bearing clearance within the

29.17 Make sure the tabs on the shells locate in the notches in the bearing housings

29.19 Lay a strip of Plastigauge on each journal parallel to the crankshaft centreline

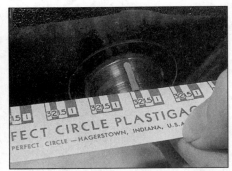

29.22 Measure the width of the crushed Plastigauge (be sure to use the correct scale – metric and imperial are included)

29.25 Measure the diameter of each crankshaft journal

29.30 Install the thrust bearings with their grooves toward the crankshaft web

30.2 Slip a feeler gauge between the connecting rod and the crank web to check side clearance

specified range). Always renew all of the shells at the same time.

25 If the clearance is still greater than the service limit listed in this Chapter's Specifications (even with new shells), the crankshaft journal is worn and the crankshaft should be renewed. Measure the diameter of each journal and compare the measurements to the specifications to confirm **(see illustration)**. By measuring the diameter at a number of points around each journal's circumference, you'll be able to determine whether or not the journal is out-of-round. Also take a measurement at each end of the journal, near the crank throws, as well as in the middle, to determine if the journal is tapered.

Installation

26 If removed with the crankshaft and separated from it, fit the connecting rods onto the crankshaft (see Section 30).

27 Clean the backs of the bearing shells and the bearing cut-outs in the upper and middle crankcases. If new shells are being fitted, ensure that all traces of the protective grease are cleaned off using paraffin (kerosene). Wipe the shells and crankcases dry with a lint-free cloth. Make sure all the oil passages and holes are clear, and blow them through with compressed air if it is available.

28 Lubricate each shell, preferably with molybdenum paste, molybdenum disulphide oil (a 50/50 mixture of molybdenum disulphide

paste or grease and clean engine oil), or if not available then with clean engine oil. Press the bearing shells into their locations. Make sure the tab on each shell engages in the notch in the casing **(see illustration 29.17)**. Make sure the bearings are fitted in the correct locations and take care not to touch any shell's bearing surface with your fingers.

29 Lower the crankshaft into position in the upper crankcase.

30 Install the thrust bearings into their correct locations (do not mix up the inner with the outer) between the crank webs and the main bearing housing between cylinder Nos. 1 and 2, making sure that the oil grooves face towards the crankshaft web **(see illustration)**.

31 If the crankshaft only was removed and the piston/connecting rod assemblies are in the engine, draw each connecting rod/piston down its bore and fit them onto the crankshaft (see Section 30).

32 Reassemble the crankcases (see Section 23).

30 Connecting rods – removal, inspection and installation

Note: *To remove the connecting rods the engine must be removed from the frame and the crankcases separated.*

Removal

1 Remove the cylinder block (see Section 14)

and, if required, the pistons (see Section 15), then separate the middle crankcase from the upper crankcase (see Section 23). **Note:** *If the crankshaft is being removed with the connecting rods attached, the pistons must be removed. If the crankshaft is being left in place, the pistons can remain on the connecting rods if no work is being carried out on them or the small ends.*

2 Before separating the rods from the crankshaft, measure the big-end side clearance on each rod with a feeler gauge **(see illustration)**. If the clearance on any rod is greater than the service limit listed in this Chapter's Specifications, measure the big-end and crankpin widths as described in Step 7.

3 Using paint or a felt marker pen, mark the relevant cylinder identity on each connecting rod and cap. Mark across the cap-to-connecting rod join and note which side of the rod faces the front of the engine to ensure that the cap and rod are fitted the correct way around on reassembly. Note that the number already across the rod and cap indicates size grade, not cylinder number, and that this number faces the rear of the engine **(see illustration)**.

4 Unscrew the cap bolts and separate the connecting rod, cap and both bearing shells from the crankpin **(see illustration)**. There are locating pins between each rod and cap. To help separation, before the bolts are fully unscrewed tap on the bolt heads to push the rod off the crank **(see illustration)**. Keep the

30.3 This number indicates the connecting rod bearing size and faces back – make your own marks to indicate cylinder number

30.4a Slacken and partially unscrew the cap bolts . . .

30.4b . . . then tap on the bolt heads to separate the rod from the crank

30.6 Slip the piston pin into the rod's small-end and check for freeplay between them

30.7a Measure the width of the connecting rod . . .

30.7b . . . and of the corresponding crankpin

rod, cap, bolts and (if they are to be reused) the bearing shells together in their correct positions to ensure correct installation.

Inspection

5 Check the connecting rods for cracks and other obvious damage.

6 If not already done (see Section 15), apply clean engine oil to the piston pin, insert it into the connecting rod small-end and check for any freeplay between the two **(see illustration)**. Measure the pin external diameter and the small-end bore diameter and compare the measurements to the specifications at the beginning of the Chapter **(see illustrations 15.13b and 15.13d)**. Renew components that are worn beyond the specified limits.

7 If the side clearance measured in Step 2 exceeds the service limit specified, measure the width of the connecting rod big-end and the width of the crankpin **(see illustrations)**. Compare the results to the specifications at the beginning of the Chapter, and renew whichever component exceeds those specifications.

8 Refer to Section 28 and examine the connecting rod bearing shells. If they are scored, badly scuffed or appear to have seized, new shells must be installed. Always renew the shells in the connecting rods as a set. If they are badly damaged, check the corresponding crankpin. Evidence of extreme heat, such as discoloration, indicates that

lubrication failure has occurred. Be sure to thoroughly check the oil pump and pressure regulator as well as all oil holes and passages before reassembling the engine.

9 Have the rods checked for twist and bend by a Suzuki dealer if you are in doubt about their straightness.

Bearing shell selection

10 New bearing shells for the big-end bearings are supplied on a selected fit basis. Codes stamped on various components are used to identify the correct replacement bearings. The crankpin journal size numbers are stamped on the crankshaft inner left web and will be either a 1, 2 or 3 **(see illustration)**. The number coming immediately after the L is for the outer left-hand big-end (cyl No. 1), the next number is for the inner left-hand big-end (cyl No. 2), the next for the inner right-hand (cyl No. 3) and the number coming before the R is for the outer right-hand big-end (cyl No. 4). The connecting rod size code is marked on the flat face of the connecting rod and cap and will be either a 1 or a 2 **(see illustration 30.3)**.

11 A range of bearing shells is available. To select the correct bearing for a particular big-end, using the table below cross-refer the crankpin journal size number (stamped on the web) with the connecting rod size letter (stamped on the rod) to determine the colour code of the bearing required. For example, if the connecting rod size is 2, and the crankpin

size is 3, then the bearing required is Yellow. The colour is marked on the side of the shell **(see illustration 29.14)**.

Connecting rod code	Crankpin code		
	1	2	3
1	Green	Black	Brown
2	Black	Brown	Yellow

Oil clearance check

12 Whether new bearing shells are being fitted or the original ones are being re-used, the connecting rod bearing oil clearance should be checked prior to reassembly.

13 Clean the backs of the bearing shells and the bearing locations in both the connecting rod and cap.

14 Press the bearing shells into their locations, ensuring that the tab on each shell engages the notch in the connecting rod/cap **(see illustration)**. Make sure the bearings are fitted in the correct locations and take care not to touch any shell's bearing surface with your fingers.

15 Cut a length of the appropriate size Plastigauge (it should be slightly shorter than the width of the crankpin). Place a strand of Plastigauge on the (cleaned) crankpin journal and fit the (clean) connecting rod, shells and cap **(see illustration 30.22)**. Make sure the cap is fitted the correct way around so the previously made markings align, and that the rod is facing the right way, and tighten the cap bolts in two stages, first to the initial torque setting specified at the beginning of the

30.10 Crankpin journal size numbers

30.14 Make sure the tab locates in the notch (arrowed)

30.19 Measure the width of the crankpin

30.22 Fit the caps onto the rods, making sure the pins locate correctly

30.23 Tighten the cap bolts as described to the specified torque settings

Chapter, and then to the final torque setting specified, whilst ensuring that the connecting rod does not rotate. Slacken the cap bolts and remove the connecting rod, again taking great care not to rotate the crankshaft.

16 Compare the width of the crushed Plastigauge on the crankpin to the scale printed on the Plastigauge envelope to obtain the connecting rod bearing oil clearance **(see illustration 29.22)**. Compare the reading to the specifications at the beginning of the Chapter.

17 On completion carefully scrape away all traces of the Plastigauge material from the crankpin and bearing shells using a fingernail or other object which is unlikely to score the shells.

18 If the clearance is within the range listed in this Chapter's Specifications and the bearings are in perfect condition, they can be reused. If the clearance is beyond the service limit, renew the bearing shells with new ones (see Steps 10 and 11). Check the oil clearance once again (the new shells may be thick enough to bring bearing clearance within the specified range). Always renew all of the shells at the same time.

19 If the clearance is still greater than the service limit listed in this Chapter's Specifications, measure the diameter of the crankpin journal with a micrometer and compare your findings with this Chapter's Specifications **(see illustration)**. Also, by measuring the diameter at a number of points around the journal's circumference, you'll be able to determine whether or not the journal is out-of-round. Also take a measurement at each end of the journal, near the crank throws, as well as in the middle, to determine if the journal is tapered.

20 If any journal has worn down past the limit, renew the crankshaft.

21 Repeat the bearing selection procedure for the remaining connecting rods.

Installation

22 Fit the bearing shells in the connecting rods and caps, aligning the notch in the bearing with the groove in the rod or cap **(see illustration 30.14)**. Lubricate the shells, preferably with molybdenum paste, molybdenum disulphide oil (a 50/50 mixture of molybdenum disulphide paste or grease and clean engine oil), or if not available

then with clean engine oil, and assemble each connecting rod on its correct crankpin so that the previously made matchmarks align and the connecting rod size letter is facing the rear of the engine **(see illustration)**. Tighten the bolts finger-tight at this stage. Check to make sure that all components have been returned to their original locations using the marks made on disassembly.

23 Tighten the bearing cap bolts in two stages, first to the initial torque setting specified at the beginning of the Chapter, and then to the final torque setting specified **(see illustration)**.

24 Check that the rods rotate smoothly and freely on the crankpin. If there are any signs of roughness or tightness, remove the rods and re-check the bearing clearance. Sometimes tapping the connecting rod cap bolts will relieve tightness, but if in doubt, recheck the clearances.

25 Install the remaining components and assemble the crankcases.

31 Initial start-up after overhaul

1 Make sure the engine oil level and coolant level are correct (see *Daily (pre-ride) checks*).

2 Pull the plug caps off the spark plugs and insert a spare spark plug into each cap. Position the spare plugs so that their bodies are earthed (grounded) against the engine. Turn on the ignition switch and crank the engine over with the starter until the oil pressure warning LED goes off (which indicates that oil pressure exists). Turn off the ignition. Remove the spare spark plugs and reconnect the plug caps.

3 Make sure there is fuel in the tank, then turn the fuel tap to the ON position and operate the choke.

4 Start the engine and allow it to run at a moderately fast idle until it reaches operating temperature.

 Warning: If the oil pressure warning LED doesn't go off, or it comes on while the engine is running, stop the engine immediately.

5 Check carefully for oil leaks and make sure the transmission and controls, especially the brakes, function properly before road testing the machine. Refer to Section 32 for the recommended running-in procedure.

6 Upon completion of the road test, and after the engine has cooled down completely, recheck the valve clearances (Chapter 1) and check the engine oil level (see *Daily (pre-ride) checks*).

32 Recommended running-in procedure

1 Treat the machine gently for the first few miles to make sure oil has circulated throughout the engine and any new parts installed have started to seat.

2 Even greater care is necessary if a new cylinder block or crankshaft has been installed. In the case of a new cylinder block, the bike will have to be run in as when new. This means greater use of the transmission and a restraining hand on the throttle until at least 500 miles (800 km) have been covered. There's no point in keeping to any set speed limit – the main idea is to keep from labouring the engine and to gradually increase performance up to the 500 mile (800 km) mark. These recommendations can be lessened to an extent when only a new crankshaft is installed. Experience is the best guide, since it's easy to tell when an engine is running freely. The maximum engine speed limitations in the table below, which Suzuki provide for new motorcycles, can be used as a guide.

3 If a lubrication failure is suspected, stop the engine immediately and try to find the cause. If an engine is run without oil, even for a short period of time, severe damage will occur.

Up to 500 miles (800 km)	6500 rpm max	Vary throttle position/speed
500 to 1000 miles (800 to 1600 km)	10,000 rpm max	Vary throttle position/speed. Use full throttle for short bursts
Over 1000 miles (1600 km)	13,500 rpm max	Do not exceed tachometer red line

Notes

Chapter 3
Cooling system

Contents

Degrees of difficulty

| Easy, suitable for novice with little experience | | Fairly easy, suitable for beginner with some experience | | Fairly difficult, suitable for competent DIY mechanic | 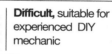 | Difficult, suitable for experienced DIY mechanic | | Very difficult, suitable for expert DIY or professional | |

Specifications

Coolant

Mixture type and capacity . . . . see Chapter 1

Pressure cap

Cap valve opening pressure . . . . 13.5 to 17.7 psi (0.95 to 1.25 Bar)

Fan switch

Cooling fan cut-in temperature . . . . approx. 105°C
Cooling fan cut-out temperature . . . . approx. 100°C

Coolant temperature sensor

Resistance
GSX-R600 and GSX-R750T and V models
  @ 50°C . . . . approx. 9.56 K-ohms
  @ 100°C . . . . approx. 2.78 K-ohms
  @ 120°C . . . . approx. 0.69 K-ohms
  @ 130°C . . . . approx. 0.50 K-ohms
GSX-R750W and X models
  @ 20°C . . . . approx. 2.450 K-ohms
  @ 50°C . . . . approx. 0.811 K-ohms
  @ 80°C . . . . approx. 0.318 K-ohms
  @ 110°C . . . . approx. 0.142 K-ohms
  @ 130°C . . . . approx. 0.088 K-ohms

Thermostat

Opening temperature . . . . 74.5 to 78.5°C
Valve lift . . . . 7 mm (min) @ 90°C

Torque settings

Cooling fan bolts	6 Nm
Cooling fan switch	
GSX-R600 and GSX-R750T and V models	17 Nm
GSX-R750W and X models	18 Nm
Coolant temperature gauge sensor	
GSX-R600 and GSX-R750T and V models	9 Nm
GSX-R750W and X models	18 Nm
Thermostat cover bolts	10 Nm
Radiator mounting bolts	6 Nm
Water pump impeller bolt	8 Nm
Water pump mounting bolts	6 Nm
Water pump cover screws	6 Nm
Coolant union to cylinder block bolts	10 Nm

1 General information

The cooling system uses a water/antifreeze coolant to carry away excess energy in the form of heat. The cylinders are surrounded by a water jacket from which the heated coolant is circulated by thermo-syphonic action in conjunction with a water pump, driven by the oil pump. The hot coolant from the engine flows via the thermostat to the radiator. The coolant then flows across the radiator core, where it is cooled by the passing air, to the water pump and back to the engine where the cycle is repeated.

A thermostat is fitted in the system to prevent the coolant flowing through the radiator when the engine is cold, therefore accelerating the speed at which the engine reaches normal operating temperature. A coolant temperature sensor mounted in the thermostat housing transmits to the temperature gauge on the instrument panel. A thermostatically-controlled cooling fan is also fitted to aid cooling in extreme conditions.

The complete cooling system is partially sealed and pressurised, the pressure being controlled by a valve contained in the spring-loaded pressure cap. By pressurising the coolant the boiling point is raised, preventing premature boiling in adverse conditions. The overflow pipe from the system is connected to a reservoir into which excess coolant is expelled under pressure. The discharged coolant automatically returns to the radiator when the engine cools.

⚠ **Warning:** *Do not remove the pressure cap from the radiator when the engine is hot. Scalding hot coolant and steam may be blown out under pressure, which could cause serious injury. When the engine has cooled, place a thick rag, like a towel over the pressure cap; slowly rotate the cap anti-clockwise to the first stop. This procedure allows any residual pressure to escape. When the steam has stopped escaping, press down on the cap while turning it anti-clockwise and remove it. Do not allow antifreeze to come in contact with your skin or painted surfaces of the motorcycle. Rinse off any spills immediately with plenty of water. Antifreeze is highly toxic if ingested. Never leave antifreeze lying around in an open container or in puddles on the floor; children and pets are attracted by its sweet smell and may drink it. Check with the local authorities about disposing of used antifreeze. Many communities will have collection centres which will see that antifreeze is disposed of safely.*

Caution: At all times use the specified type of antifreeze, and always mix it with distilled water in the correct proportion. The antifreeze contains corrosion inhibitors which are essential to avoid damage to the cooling system. A lack of these inhibitors could lead to a build-up of corrosion which would block the coolant passages, resulting in overheating and severe engine damage. Distilled water must be used as opposed to tap water to avoid a build-up of scale which would also block the passages.

2 Pressure cap – check

1 If problems such as overheating or loss of coolant occur, check the entire system as

3.2 Detach the breather hose (A) and the radiator hose (B) and drain the reservoir, then unscrew the bolts (C) and remove the reservoir

described in Chapter 1. The radiator cap opening pressure should be checked by a Suzuki dealer with the special tester required to do the job. If the cap is defective, renew it.

3 Coolant reservoir – removal and installation

Removal

1 The coolant reservoir is located on the inside of the left-hand fairing side panel. Remove the panel (see Chapter 8) for access.
2 Detach the breather/overflow hose from the top of the reservoir **(see illustration)**.
3 Place a suitable container underneath the reservoir, then release the clamp securing the radiator overflow hose to the base of the reservoir. Detach the hose and allow the coolant to drain into the container **(see illustration 3.2)**.
4 Unscrew the reservoir mounting screws, noting how the rear one secures the idle speed adjuster, and remove the reservoir **(see illustration 3.2)**.

Installation

5 Installation is the reverse of removal. Make sure the hoses are correctly installed and secured with their clamps. On completion refill the reservoir as described in *Daily (pre-ride) checks*.

4 Cooling fan and cooling fan switch – check and renewal

Cooling fan

Check

1 If the engine is overheating and the cooling fan isn't coming on, first check the cooling fan circuit fuse (see Chapter 9) and then the fan switch as described in Steps 9 to 16 below.
2 If the fan does not come on, (and the fan switch is good), the fault lies in either the cooling fan motor or the relevant wiring. Test all the wiring and connections as described in Chapter 9.
3 To test the cooling fan motor, remove the

4.3a It may be possible to access the connector from behind the radiator . . .

4.3b . . . although you may have to remove the air filter housing to access it (arrowed)

4.5 The fan assembly is secured by three bolts (arrowed)

fairing side panels (see Chapter 8). Disconnect the fan wiring connector **(see illustration)**. It may be possible to reach behind the radiator and access the connector by drawing the wiring down (removing the radiator mounting bolts and shifting it forward will help – see Section 7) **(see illustration)**, although if the connector is positioned behind the steering head under the air filter housing, it may be necessary to remove the air filter housing for access (see Chapter 4) **(see illustration)**. Using a 12 volt battery and two jumper wires, connect the battery to the terminals on the fan side of the wiring connector. Once connected the fan should operate. If it does not, and the wiring is all good, then the fan is faulty.

Renewal

 Warning: The engine must be completely cool before carrying out this procedure.

4 Remove the radiator (see Section 7).
5 Unscrew the three bolts securing the fan shroud and fan assembly to the radiator and remove the fan **(see illustration)**.
6 If required, remove the three screws on the front and separate the fan from the shroud.
7 Installation is the reverse of removal. Tighten the cooling fan bolts to the torque setting specified at the beginning of the Chapter.
8 Install the radiator (see Section 7).

Cooling fan switch

Check

9 If the engine is overheating and the cooling fan isn't coming on, first check the cooling fan circuit fuse (see Chapter 9). If the fuse is blown, check the fan circuit for a short to earth (see the wiring diagrams at the end of this book). If the fuse is good, proceed as follows.
10 On GSX-R600 and GSX-R750T and V models, remove the right-hand fairing side panel (see Chapter 8), and disconnect the wiring connector from the fan switch on the right-hand side of the radiator **(see illustration)**.
11 On GSX-R750W and X models, raise the fuel tank (see Chapter 4). Disconnect the

wiring connector from the fan switch on the thermostat cover **(see illustration)**.
12 Using a jumper wire, connect across the two terminals on the wiring connector. The fan should come on. If it does, the fan switch is defective and must be renewed. If it does not come on, the fan motor should be tested (see Step 3).
13 If the fan is on the whole time, disconnect the wiring connector. The fan should stop. If it does, the switch is defective and must be renewed. If it doesn't, check the wiring between the switch and the fan for a short to earth, and the fan itself.
14 If the fan works but is suspected of cutting in at the wrong temperature, a more comprehensive test of the switch can be made as follows.
15 Remove the switch (see Steps 17 to 20). Fill a small heatproof container with oil and place it on a stove. Connect the positive (+ve) probe of an ohmmeter to one terminal of the switch and the negative (-ve) probe to the other, and using some wire or other support suspend it in the oil so that just the sensing portion and the threads are submerged **(see illustration 5.2)**. Also place a thermometer capable of reading temperatures up to 110°C in the oil so that its bulb is close to the switch. **Note:** *None of the components should be allowed to directly touch the container.*
16 Initially the ohmmeter reading should be very high indicating that the switch is open (OFF). Heat the oil, stirring it gently.

 Warning: This must be done very carefully to avoid the risk of personal injury.

When the temperature reaches around 105°C the meter reading should drop to around zero ohms, indicating that the switch has closed (ON). Now turn the heat off. As the temperature falls below 100°C the meter reading should show infinite (very high) resistance, indicating that the switch has opened (OFF). If the meter readings obtained are different, or they are obtained at different temperatures, then the switch is faulty and must be renewed.

Renewal

 Warning: The engine must be completely cool before carrying out this procedure.

17 Drain the cooling system (see Chapter 1).
18 On GSX-R600 and GSX-R750T and V models, remove the right-hand fairing side panel (see Chapter 8), and disconnect the wiring connector from the fan switch on the right-hand side of the radiator **(see illustration 4.10)**.
19 On GSX-R750W and X models, raise the fuel tank (see Chapter 4). Disconnect the wiring connector from the fan switch on the thermostat cover **(see illustration 4.11)**.
20 Unscrew the switch and withdraw it.
21 Apply some grease to the O-ring. Install the switch and tighten it to the torque setting specified at the beginning of the Chapter. Take care not to overtighten the switch.

4.10 Disconnect the fan switch wiring connector (arrowed)

4.11 Disconnect the fan switch wiring connector (arrowed)

THERMOMETER SENDER UNIT

5.2 Coolant temperature sensor testing set-up

22 Reconnect the switch wiring and refill the cooling system (see *Daily (pre-ride) checks*). Lower the fuel tank and tighten its bolts securely.

5 Coolant temperature sensor – check and renewal

Check

1 Raise the fuel tank (see Chapter 4). The sensor is mounted in the thermostat housing, which is on the back of the cylinder head on the right-hand side.

2 Remove the sensor (see Steps 4 and 5 below). Fill a small heatproof container with oil and place it on a stove. Using an ohmmeter, on GSX-R600 and GSX-R750T and V models, connect the positive (+ve) probe of the meter to the terminal on the sensor, and the negative (-ve) probe to the body of the sensor. On GSX-R750W and X models, connect the positive (+ve) probe of the meter one terminal on the sensor, and the negative (-ve) probe to the other terminal. Using some wire or other support suspend the sensor in the oil so that just the sensing portion and the threads are submerged. Also place a thermometer capable of reading temperatures up to 140°C in the oil so that its bulb is close to the sensor **(see illustration)**. **Note:** *None of the components should be allowed to directly touch the container.*

3 Heat the oil, stirring it gently.

 Warning: This must be done very carefully to avoid the risk of personal injury.

As the temperature of the oil rises, the resistance of the sensor will fall. Check that the specified resistance is obtained at the correct temperature, as specified at the beginning of the Chapter. If the meter readings obtained are different, or they are obtained at different temperatures, then the sensor is faulty and must be renewed. If the readings are as specified, the fault could lie in the coolant temperature display circuit in the instrument cluster (see Chapter 9).

Renewal

 Warning: The engine must be completely cool before carrying out this procedure.

4 Drain the cooling system (see Chapter 1). Raise the fuel tank (see Chapter 4). The sensor is mounted in the thermostat housing, which is on the back of the cylinder head on the right-hand side.

5 Disconnect the sensor wiring connector **(see illustrations)**. Unscrew the sensor and remove it from the thermostat housing.

6 On GSX-R600 and GSX-R750T and V models, apply a smear of sealant to the threads of the sensor. On GSX-R750W and X models, make sure the washer is fitted and is in good condition. Thread the sensor into the thermostat housing and tighten it to the torque setting specified at the beginning of the Chapter. Connect the sensor wiring.

7 Refill the cooling system (see Chapter 1).

8 Lower the fuel tank and tighten its bolts securely.

6 Thermostat – removal, check and installation

Removal

 Warning: The engine must be completely cool before carrying out this procedure.

1 The thermostat is automatic in operation and should give many years service without requiring attention. In the event of a failure, the valve will probably jam open, in which case the engine will take much longer than normal to warm up. Conversely, if the valve jams shut, the coolant will be unable to circulate and the engine will overheat. Neither condition is acceptable, and the fault must be investigated promptly.

2 Drain the cooling system (see Chapter 1). Raise the fuel tank (see Chapter 4).

3 The thermostat is located in the thermostat housing, which is on the back of the cylinder head on the right-hand side. Disconnect the temperature sensor wiring connector, and on GSX-R750W and X models the fan switch wiring connector **(see illustrations 5.5a and b and 4.11)**.

4 Unscrew the two bolts securing the cover

5.5a Temperature sensor wiring connector (arrowed) – GSX-R600 and GSX-R750T and V models

5.5b Temperature sensor wiring connector (arrowed) – GSX-R750W and X models

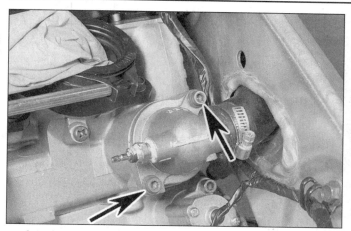

6.4a Unscrew the bolts (arrowed) and detach the cover . . .

6.4b . . . and remove the thermostat

and detach it **(see illustration)**. Withdraw the thermostat, noting how it fits **(see illustration)**.

Check

5 Examine the thermostat visually before carrying out the test. If it remains in the open position at room temperature, it should be renewed.

6 Suspend the thermostat by a piece of wire in a container of cold water, making sure it does not touch the bottom or sides. Place a thermometer in the water so that the bulb is close to the thermostat **(see illustration)**. Heat the water, noting the temperature when the thermostat opens, and compare the result with the specifications given at the beginning of the Chapter. Also check the amount the valve opens after it has been heated at 90°C for a few minutes and compare the measurement to the specifications. If the readings obtained differ from those given, the thermostat is faulty and must be renewed.

7 In the event of thermostat failure, as an emergency measure only, it can be removed

6.6 Thermostat testing set-up

and the machine used without it. **Note:** *Take care when starting the engine from cold as it will take much longer than usual to warm up.* Ensure that a new unit is installed as soon as possible.

Installation

8 Installation is the reverse of removal. Apply a smear of grease to the rubber seal on the

thermostat and install it with the bleed hole at the top **(see illustration)**. Make sure the thermostat seats correctly. Tighten the cover bolts to the torque setting specified at the beginning of the Chapter **(see illustration)**. Connect the wiring connector(s).

9 Refill the cooling system (see Chapter 1).

10 Lower the fuel tank and tighten its bolts securely.

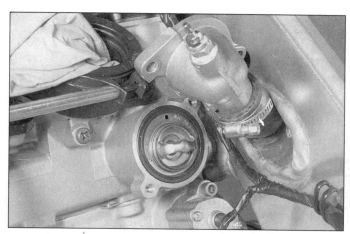

6.8a Fit the thermostat with the hole at the top . . .

6.8b . . . refit and tighten the bolts to the specified torque

7.2a Radiator hoses (A) and mounting bolts (B) – right-hand side

7.2b Radiator hose (A) and mounting bolt (B) – left-hand side

7.3 Remove the radiator

7 Radiator – removal and installation

Removal

Warning: The engine must be completely cool before carrying out this procedure.

1 Remove the fairing side panels (see Chapter 8) and drain the cooling system (see Chapter 1).

2 Slacken the clamps securing the main hoses to the top and bottom right-hand side and bottom left-hand side of the radiator and detach the hoses **(see illustrations)**. Also detach the reservoir hose from the filler neck. On GSX-R600 and GSX-R750T and V models, disconnect the fan switch wiring connector **(see illustration 4.10)**.

3 Unscrew the radiator mounting bolts and disconnect the fan wiring connector as it becomes accessible **(see illustration 4.3a)**; note that on GSX-R750W and X models the horn will be freed as the radiator top left-hand mounting bolt is removed. Remove the radiator **(see illustration)**.

4 If necessary, separate the cooling fan from the radiator (see Section 4).

5 Check the radiator for signs of damage and clear any dirt or debris that might obstruct air flow and inhibit cooling. If the radiator fins are badly damaged or broken the radiator must

be renewed. Also check the rubber mounting grommets, and renew them if necessary.

Installation

6 Installation is the reverse of removal, noting the following.
  a) Make sure the rubber grommets and collars are correctly installed with the mounting bolts **(see illustration)**.
  b) Make sure that the fan and fan switch (where applicable) wiring is correctly connected.
  c) Ensure the coolant hoses are in good condition (see Chapter 1), and are securely retained by their clamps, using new ones if necessary.
  d) On completion refill the cooling system as described in Chapter 1.

8 Water pump – check, removal and installation

Check

1 The water pump is located on the lower left side of the engine. Visually check the area around the pump for signs of leakage.

2 To prevent leakage of water from the cooling system to the lubrication system and vice versa, two seals are fitted on the pump shaft. The seal on the water pump side is of the mechanical type which bears on the rear

face of the impeller. The second seal, which is mounted behind the mechanical seal is of the normal feathered lip type. If on inspection there are signs of leakage, the seals must be removed and new ones installed. If you are not sure about their condition, remove the pump and check them visually, looking for signs of damage and leakage.

3 Remove the pump cover (see Step 10). Wiggle the water pump impeller back-and-forth and in-and-out, and spin it by hand. If there is excessive movement, or the pump is noisy or rough when turned, the drive shaft bearings must be renewed. If you are not sure about their condition, remove the pump and check them visually and mechanically, referring to *Tools and Workshop Tips* in the reference Section. Also check for corrosion or a build-up of scale in the pump body and clean or renew the pump as necessary.

Removal

4 Drain the coolant and the engine oil (see Chapter 1).

5 Remove the coolant reservoir (see Section 3).

6 Unscrew the gearchange linkage arm pinch bolt and remove the arm from the shaft, noting any alignment marks **(see illustration)**. If no marks are visible, make your own before removing the arm so that it can be correctly aligned with the shaft on installation.

7 Trace the wiring from the speedometer sensor on the front sprocket cover and disconnect it at the connector **(see illustration)**.

7.6 Make sure the grommets are in good condition and the collars are installed

8.6 Unscrew the bolt and slide the arm off the shaft

8.7 Disconnect the speedometer sensor wiring connector

8.8 Sprocket cover bolts (arrowed)

8.9 Slacken the clamps (arrowed) and detach the hoses

8.10 Pump screws (A), pump bolts (B)

8 Unscrew the bolts securing the sprocket cover to the crankcase and move the cover aside **(see illustration)**. On W and X models, note the rubber bushing for the gearchange shaft and remove it from the cover if required. The cover can be secured out of the way with the clutch cable still connected.

9 Slacken the clamps securing the coolant hoses to the pump cover and detach the hoses, noting which fits where **(see illustration)**.

10 To remove the pump cover, remove the two screws and the two bolts, noting the wiring clamp with the top bolt, and remove the cover **(see illustration)**. Discard the cover O-ring as a new one must be used.

11 To remove the pump body after removing the cover, carefully draw it out of the

8.11a Draw the pump out of the crankcase

crankcase, noting how it fits **(see illustration)**. Remove the O-ring from the rear of the pump body and discard it as a new one must be used **(see illustration)**.

12 To remove the whole pump as an assembly, unscrew the two bolts securing the pump assembly to the crankcase **(see illustration 8.10)** and carefully draw the pump out, noting how it fits **(see illustration)**. Remove the O-ring from the rear of the pump body and discard it as a new one must be used **(see illustration 8.11b)**. Separate the cover from the pump by removing the two screws if required.

Seal and bearing renewal

13 Remove the pump cover, then remove the pump (see above).

14 Counter-hold the impeller or pump drive shaft to prevent it from turning, then unscrew the impeller bolt, noting the washers, and remove the impeller **(see illustration)**. Remove the seal ring from the back of the impeller, and draw out the drive shaft from the rear of the pump body.

15 To renew the bearings, use a bearing puller (see *Tools and Workshop Tips* in the reference Section), and draw out the two bearings from the rear of the body. Once the bearings have been removed, they cannot be reused – new ones must be fitted.

16 To renew the seals, first remove the bearings (see above). Using a suitable socket

inserted into the rear of the pump body, drive out the seals together, noting which way round the oil seal fits. Discard them as new ones must be fitted.

17 Press or carefully drive the new mechanical seal into the front of the pump body using a suitable sized socket or seal driver.

18 Apply a smear of grease to the lips of the new oil seal. Press or carefully drive the new oil seal into the rear of the pump body so that it fits against the back of the mechanical seal – use a suitable sized socket or seal driver and make sure the seal is the correct way round. Take care not dislodge the mechanical seal by driving the oil seal too far in.

19 Press or drive the new bearings into the rear of the pump body, using a suitable sized socket or bearing driver. The smaller diameter bearing fits on the inside, and the larger one is on the outside. Drive the bearings in until they are properly seated.

20 Slide the narrow end of the drive shaft into the rear of the pump body and push it through until the shouldered sections are properly seated against their bearings. Fit the seal ring onto the back of the impeller, making sure the marked side of the ring faces the impeller, then fit the impeller onto the shaft. Counter-hold the impeller or shaft as before and tighten the impeller bolt (not forgetting its washers) to the torque setting specified at the beginning of the Chapter **(see illustration 8.14)**.

8.11b Remove and discard the O-ring

8.12 Unscrew the bolts and withdraw the pump

8.14 Counter-hold the shaft and unscrew the bolt

8.21 Fit a new O-ring into the groove in the pump body

8.22 Grease the O-ring and fit it into the cover

8.25a Make sure the rotor (A) fits correctly into the sensor (B)

Installation

21 Apply a smear of grease to the new pump body O-ring and fit it into the groove in the body **(see illustration)**. Slide the pump into the crankcase, aligning the slot in the impeller shaft with the tab on the oil pump shaft **(see illustration 8.11a)**.
22 To fit the cover, smear the new O-ring with grease and fit it into its groove in the cover **(see illustration)**.
23 Fit the cover onto the pump, then install the two bolts, not forgetting the wiring clamp with the top bolt, and the two screws and tighten them to the torque setting specified at the beginning of the Chapter **(see illustration 8.10)**.
24 If detached, attach the coolant hoses to the pump cover and secure them with their clamps **(see illustrations 8.9)**.
25 Make sure the dowels are either in the crankcase or the sprocket cover. Install the cover, making sure the speedometer rotor fits properly into the sensor and the dowels locate

correctly, and tighten its bolts **(see illustration)**. On W and X models, if removed, fit the rubber bushing for the gearchange shaft into the cover **(see illustration)**.
26 Slide the gearchange linkage arm onto the shaft, aligning the marks, and tighten the pinch bolt **(see illustration 8.6)**. Check that the mechanism works correctly
27 Reconnect the speedometer sensor wiring connector **(see illustration 8.7)**.
28 Install the coolant reservoir (see Section 3). Refill the cooling system and the engine oil (see Chapter 1).

---

9 Coolant hoses –
removal and installation

Removal

1 Before removing a hose, drain the coolant (see Chapter 1).

2 Use a screwdriver to slacken the larger-bore hose clamps, then slide them back along the hose and clear of the union spigot. The smaller-bore hoses are secured by spring clamps which can be expanded by squeezing their ears together with pliers.
Caution: The radiator unions are fragile. Do not use excessive force when attempting to remove the hoses.
3 If a hose proves stubborn, release it by rotating it on its union before working it off. If all else fails, cut the hose with a sharp knife then slit it at each union so that it can be peeled off in two pieces. Whilst this means renewing the hose, it is preferable to buying a new radiator.
4 The coolant inlet hose union on the cylinder block can be removed by unscrewing its bolts **(see illustration)**. If the union is removed, the O-ring must be renewed.

Installation

5 Slide the clips onto the hose and then work it on to its respective union.

> **HAYNES HINT** *If the hose is difficult to push on its union, it can be softened by soaking it in very hot water, or alternatively a little soapy water can be used as a lubricant.*

6 Rotate the hose on its unions to settle it in position before sliding the clamps into place and tightening them securely.
7 If the inlet union to the cylinder block has been removed, fit a new O-ring, then install the union and tighten the mounting bolts to the torque setting specified at the beginning of the Chapter **(see illustration 9.4)**.

8.25b Where fitted and if removed, fit the rubber bush for the gearchange shaft

9.4 The union is secured by three bolts (arrowed)

Chapter 4
Fuel and exhaust systems

Contents

Degrees of difficulty

Easy, suitable for novice with little experience	**Fairly easy,** suitable for beginner with some experience	**Fairly difficult,** suitable for competent DIY mechanic

| **Difficult,** suitable for experienced DIY mechanic | **Very difficult,** suitable for expert DIY or professional |

Specifications

Fuel

Grade	Unleaded, minimum 91 RON (Research Octane Number)
Fuel tank capacity (including reserve)	18 litres

Carburettors – GSX-R600V

Type	Mikuni BDSR36
Bore	36.5 mm
I.D. no.	
UK	34E0
US	34E1
California	34E3
Pilot jet	12.5
Needle jet	
UK	P-O
US and California	P-OM
Jet needle	
UK	5DH18-52-3
US and California	5DH20-53
Main jet	
Cylinder 1	125
Cylinders 2, 3 and 4	122.5
Pilot screw setting (turns out)	
UK	
Cylinders 1 and 4	3 1/2 turns out
Cylinders 2 and 3	2 1/2 turns out
US and California	Pre-set

Carburettors – GSX-R600V (continued)

Float height	7.0 ± 1.0 mm
Fuel level	15.5 ± 0.5 mm
Idle speed	see Chapter 1
Throttle position sensor resistance	3.5 to 6.5 K-ohms
Heater system resistance (UK models)	12 to 18 ohms

Carburettors – GSX-R600W

Type	Mikuni BDSR36
Bore	36.5 mm
I.D. no.	
UK	34E6
US	34E7
California	34E9
Pilot jet	12.5
Needle jet	
UK	P-O
US and California	P-OM
Jet needle	
UK	5DHZ31-3
US	5DHZ32
California	5DH20-53
Main jet	
Cylinders 1 and 4	135
Cylinders 2 and 3	132.5
Pilot screw setting (turns out)	
UK	
Cylinders 1 and 4	3 turns out
Cylinders 2 and 3	2 3/4 turns out
US and California	Pre-set
Float height	7.0 ± 1.0 mm
Fuel level	15.5 ± 0.5 mm
Idle speed	see Chapter 1
Throttle position sensor resistance	3.5 to 6.5 K-ohms
Heater system resistance (UK models)	12 to 18 ohms

Carburettors – GSX-R600X and Y

Type	Mikuni BDSR36
Bore	36.5 mm
I.D. no.	
UK	34E6
US	34EC
California	34EE
Pilot jet	12.5
Needle jet	
UK	P-O
US and California	P-OM
Jet needle	
UK	5DHZ31-3
US	5DH20-53
California	5DH20-53
Main jet	
UK	
Cylinders 1 and 4	135
Cylinders 2 and 3	132.5
US and California	
Cylinders 1 and 4	132.5
Cylinders 2 and 3	130
Pilot screw setting (turns out)	
UK	
Cylinders 1 and 4	3 turns out
Cylinders 2 and 3	2 3/4 turns out
US and California	Pre-set
Float height	7.0 ± 1.0 mm
Fuel level	15.5 ± 0.5 mm
Idle speed	see Chapter 1
Throttle position sensor resistance	3.5 to 6.5 K-ohms
Heater system resistance (UK models)	12 to 18 ohms

Carburettors – GSX-R750T and V

Type	Mikuni BDSR39
Bore	39 mm
I.D. no.	
UK	33EO
US	33E1
California	33E7
Pilot jet	12.5
Needle jet	
UK	P-O
US and California	P-OM
Jet needle	
UK	6E38-54-3
US	6E41-55
California	6E39-55
Main jet	
UK	
Cylinders 1 and 4	127.5
Cylinders 2 and 3	125
US and California	
Cylinders 1 and 4	127.5
Cylinders 2 and 3	125
Pilot screw setting (turns out)	
UK	
Cylinders 1 and 4	2 turns out
Cylinders 2 and 3	2 turns out
US and California	Pre-set
Float height	7.0 ± 1.0 mm
Idle speed	see Chapter 1
Throttle position sensor resistance	3.5 to 6.5 K-ohms
Heater system resistance (UK models)	12 to 18 ohms

Fuel injection system – GSX-R750W and X models

Operating pressure	41 psi
Inlet air control valve operating rpm	
Open	above 5400 rpm
Closed	below 5200 rpm
Inlet air control solenoid valve resistance	36 to 44 ohms
Fuel injector resistance	11 to 16 ohms @ 20ºC
Air screw setting	1/2 turn out
Camshaft position (CMP) sensor resistance	0.9 to 1.3 K-ohms
Camshaft position (CMP) sensor peak voltage	min. 0.8 V
Crankshaft position (CKP) sensor resistance	50 to 200 ohms
Crankshaft position (CKP) sensor peak voltage	min 0.5 V
Inlet air pressure (IAP) sensor input voltage	4.5 to 5.5 V
Inlet air pressure (IAP) sensor output voltage	approx. 2.85 V at idle
Throttle position (TP) sensor input voltage	4.5 to 5.5 V
Throttle position (TP) sensor resistance	
Closed	approx. 1.2 K-ohms
Open	approx. 4.4 K-ohms
Throttle position (TP) sensor output voltage	
Closed	approx. 1.1 V
Open	approx. 4.2 V
Engine coolant temperature (ECT) sensor input voltage	4.5 to 5.5 V
Engine coolant temperature (ECT) sensor resistance	2.3 to 2.6 K-ohms @ 20ºC
Inlet air temperature (IAT) sensor input voltage	4.5 to 5.5 V
Inlet air temperature (IAT) sensor resistance	2.2 to 2.7 K-ohms @ 20ºC
Atmospheric pressure (AP) sensor input voltage	4.5 to 5.5 V
Atmospheric pressure (AP) sensor output voltage	approx. 3.6 V @ 760 mmHg
Tip-over (TO) sensor resistance	60 to 64 K-ohms
Tip-over (TO) sensor voltage	approx. 2.5 V
Gear position (GP) sensor voltage	min. 0.6 V
Injector voltage	Battery voltage

Fuel pump

Discharge rate	
GSX-R600 and GSX-R750T and V models	min. 1.0 litre per minute
GSX-R750W and X models	26 to 30 cc per 3 secs.

Torque settings

Carburettor heaters (UK models)	3 Nm
Throttle position sensor screws	3.5 Nm
Fuel pressure check bolt	10 Nm
Fuel pump mounting plate bolts	3 Nm
Fuel pressure regulator bolts	5 Nm
Fuel rail bolts	13 Nm
Silencer to downpipe assembly nuts	26 Nm
Silencer mounting nut/bolt	23 Nm
Downpipe assembly bolts	23 Nm

1 General information and precautions

General information

The fuel system consists of the fuel tank, the fuel pump and its relay, the strainer and/or filter, the fuel valve (carburettor models), the fuel hoses and control cables. All GSX-R600 models and GSX-R750T and V models have carburettors, while GSX-R750W and X models have a fuel injection system controlled by various sensors which feed information to the electronic management system.

The fuel pump is housed inside the tank. On models with carburettors, the pump incorporates a strainer. On fuel injected models, the pump incorporates a strainer and a filter, and fuel pressure is controlled by a regulator.

The fuel valve is opened by a vacuum sourced from the inlet manifold and created when the engine is turned over.

The carburettors used are CV types, and there is a carburettor for each cylinder. A throttle position sensor mounted on the carburettors feeds information to the electronic ignition system.

Fuel injected models have an injector for each cylinder, housed in the throttle body.

For cold starting, a choke lever is incorporated in the left-handlebar switch housing and is connected by a cable.

The fuel warning circuit is operated by a level sensor inside the tank.

Air is drawn into the carburettors or throttle bodies via an air filter which is housed under the fuel tank.

The exhaust system is a two piece four-into-one design.

Many of the fuel system service procedures are considered routine maintenance items and for that reason are included in Chapter 1.

Precautions

 Warning: Petrol (gasoline) is extremely flammable, so take extra precautions when you work on any part of the fuel system. Don't smoke or allow open flames or bare light bulbs near the work area, and don't work in a garage where a natural gas-type appliance is present. If you spill any fuel on your skin, rinse it off immediately with soap and water. When you perform any kind of work on the fuel system, wear safety glasses and have a fire extinguisher suitable for a class B type fire (flammable liquids) on hand.

Always perform service procedures in a well-ventilated area to prevent a build-up of fumes.

Never work in a building containing a gas appliance with a pilot light, or any other form of naked flame. Ensure that there are no naked light bulbs or any sources of flame or sparks nearby.

Do not smoke (or allow anyone else to smoke) while in the vicinity of petrol (gasoline) or of components containing it. Remember the possible presence of vapour from these sources and move well clear before smoking.

Check all electrical equipment belonging to the house, garage or workshop where work is being undertaken (see the Safety first! section of this manual). Remember that certain electrical appliances such as drills, cutters etc. create sparks in the normal course of operation and must not be used near petrol (gasoline) or any component containing it. Again, remember the possible presence of fumes before using electrical equipment.

Always mop up any spilt fuel and safely dispose of the rag used.

Any stored fuel that is drained off during servicing work must be kept in sealed containers that are suitable for holding petrol (gasoline), and clearly marked as such; the containers themselves should be kept in a safe place. Note that this last point applies equally to the fuel tank if it is removed from the machine; also remember to keep its filler cap closed at all times.

Read the Safety first! section of this manual carefully before starting work.

Owners of machines used in the US, particularly California, should note that their machines must comply at all times with Federal or State legislation governing the permissible levels of noise and of pollutants such as unburnt hydrocarbons, carbon monoxide etc. that can be emitted by those machines. All vehicles offered for sale must comply with legislation in force at the date of manufacture and must not subsequently be altered in any way which will affect their emission of noise or of pollutants.

In practice, this means that adjustments may not be made to any part of the fuel, ignition or exhaust systems by anyone who is not authorised or mechanically qualified to do so, or who does not have the tools, equipment and data necessary to properly carry out the task. Also if any part of these systems is to be renewed it must be renewed with only genuine Suzuki components or by components which are approved under the relevant legislation. The machine must never be used with any part of these systems removed, modified or damaged.

2 Fuel tank – removal and installation

 Warning: Refer to the precautions given in Section 1 before starting work.

Raise

1 Make sure the fuel cap is secure.
2 Remove the rider's and passenger seats (see Chapter 8). Remove the fuel tank support bar from the storage space.
3 Unscrew the two bolts securing the front of the fuel tank to the frame **(see illustration)**. Lift up the front of the tank and place the support between it and the steering head nut, locating the very angled end of the support through the hole in the nut and the straighter

2.3a Unscrew the bolts (arrowed) . . .

2.3b . . . then raise the tank and position the support bar as described

2.8a Detach the fuel hose (A) and the vacuum hose (B) . . .

2.8b . . . and disconnect the wiring connector

2.9a Attach a clamp to the return hose . . .

2.9b . . . and detach it from the regulator

2.9c Press in the clip ears . . .

end through one of the fuel tank mounting bolt holes **(see illustration)**.

Removal

4 Make sure the fuel cap is secure.

5 Remove the rider's and passenger seats (see Chapter 8). Remove the fuel tank support bar from the storage space.

6 Remove the seat cowling (see Chapter 8).

7 Unscrew the two bolts securing the front of the fuel tank to the frame **(see illustration 2.3a)**. Lift up the front of the tank and place the support between it and the steering head nut, locating the very angled end of the support through the hole in the nut and the straighter end through one of the fuel tank mounting bolt holes **(see illustration 2.3b)**.

8 On GSX-R600 and GSX-R750T and V models, release the clamps securing the fuel hose and vacuum hose to the fuel valve and detach the hoses, noting which fits where **(see illustration)**. Disconnect the fuel pump wiring connector **(see illustration)**.

9 On GSX-R750W and X models, attach a hose clamp (see *Tools and Workshop Tips)* to the fuel return hose which runs from the pressure regulator to the fuel tank **(see illustration)**. Have a rag handy to catch any residue fuel, then detach the hose from the regulator **(see illustration)**. Fit a suitable plug into the end of the hose as a back-up to the clamp. Press in the clip ears on the fuel supply hose from the outlet on the fuel tank and detach the hose **(see illustrations)**. Disconnect the fuel pump wiring connector **(see illustration)**.

2.9d . . . and detach the fuel supply hose from the tank

10 Unscrew the bolts securing the fuel tank bracket to the frame **(see illustration)**. Remove the tank support, then carefully lift the tank off the bike, drawing the drain and breather hoses with it, noting their routing and

2.9e Disconnect the wiring connector

making sure they do not snag **(see illustration)**. Take care not to lose the mounting rubbers from between the sides of the tank and the frame, noting how they fit.

11 Inspect the tank mounting rubbers for

2.10a Unscrew the tank bracket bolts . . .

2.10b . . . and remove the tank

2.14 Route the hoses as described and through the guide (arrowed)

signs of damage or deterioration and renew them if necessary. Also inspect the rubbers on the fuel tank mounting brackets. Renew the rubbers if necessary.

Installation

12 Check that the front and side tank rubbers are fitted, then carefully lower the fuel tank into position, making sure the rubbers remain in place.

13 Install the tank rear bracket bolts to locate the bracket, but leave the bolts loose **(see illustration 2.10a)**. Raise the tank up onto its support bar **(see illustration 2.3b)**.

14 Route the drain and breather hoses down the right-hand side of the shock absorber, between the frame and the swingarm and the frame and the engine, and through the hose guide at the bottom **(see illustration)**. Make sure the breather hose does not become kinked or pinched as this could prevent a full flow of fuel.

15 On GSX-R600 and GSX-R750T and V models, attach the fuel hose to the union on the side of the fuel valve, and the vacuum hose to the union on the bottom of the valve, and secure them with their clamps **(see illustration 2.8a)**. Connect the fuel pump wiring connector **(see illustration 2.8b)**.

16 On GSX-R750W and X models, make sure the hose clamp on the fuel return hose is secure. Remove the plug from the end of the hose and attach the hose to the union on the fuel pressure regulator **(see illustration 2.9b)**. Also attach the fuel supply hose to the outlet on the fuel tank, making sure the clip ears lock into the cutouts **(see illustration 2.9d)**.

4.7 Fuel valve bolts (arrowed)

Connect the fuel pump wiring connector **(see illustration 2.9e)**.

17 Remove the support from the front of the tank, then lower the tank. Install the front tank bolts and tighten them securely **(see illustration 2.3a)**. Now tighten the tank bracket bolts.

18 Start the engine and check that there is no sign of fuel leakage, then shut if off.

19 Install the seat cowling (if the tank was removed) and the seats (see Chapter 8).

---

3 Fuel tank – cleaning and repair

1 All repairs to the fuel tank should be carried out by a professional who has experience in this critical and potentially dangerous work. Even after cleaning and flushing of the fuel system, explosive fumes can remain and ignite during repair of the tank.

2 If the fuel tank is removed from the bike, it should not be placed in an area where sparks or open flames could ignite the fumes coming out of the tank. Be especially careful inside garages where a natural gas-type appliance is located, because the pilot light could cause an explosion.

---

4 Fuel valve (GSX-R600 and GSX-R750T and V models) – check, removal and installation

⚠ **Warning: Refer to the precautions given in Section 1 before starting work.**

Check

1 Raise the fuel tank (see Section 2).

2 Release the clamp securing the fuel hose to the outlet union on the fuel valve and detach the hose **(see illustration 2.8a)**. Obtain an auxiliary length of hose and attach one end to the outlet union on the valve. Place the open end of the hose in a container suitable for holding fuel.

3 Switch the ignition ON and turn the engine over on the starter motor. Fuel should flow into the container as soon as the engine is turned. If it doesn't (and there is fuel in the tank), first

5.4a Fuel pump relay (arrowed)

check that the vacuum hose from the inlet manifold is secure at both ends and is not split or cracked. Fit a new hose if in doubt.

4 If there is still no flow, remove the valve (see below) and apply a vacuum (negative pressure) of -1.89 psi to the vacuum union using a vacuum pump and gauge. With the vacuum applied and held, blow through the fuel outlet union. If air flows through the valve when you blow into the outlet, the valve is good. If no air flows, a new valve must be fitted – no internal parts are available.

5 If the valve is good, check the fuel pump, strainer and filter.

Removal

6 Remove the fuel tank (see Section 2). Connect a drain hose to the fuel outlet union and insert its end in a container suitable for holding fuel. Also connect a hose to the vacuum union. Apply a vacuum to the hose and allow the fuel to drain from the tank.

7 Turn the tank upside down and rest it on some rags. Unscrew the two bolts securing the valve to the tank and remove the valve **(see illustration)**. Discard the O-ring and the bolt sealing washers as new ones must be used.

Installation

8 Fit the valve onto the tank, using a new O-ring. Fit new sealing washers onto the bolts and tighten the bolts securely.

9 Install the fuel tank (see Section 2).

---

5 Fuel pump, relay and fuel level sensor – check, removal and installation

⚠ **Warning: Refer to the precautions given in Section 1 before starting work.**

Check

Fuel pump and relay

1 The fuel pump is located inside the fuel tank.

2 On GSX-R600 and GSX-R750T and V models, it should be possible to hear the fuel pump running whenever the engine is turning over – remove the rider's seat (see Chapter 8) and place your ear close to the rear of the tank. If you can't hear anything, check the relay (see Step 4).

3 On GSX-R750W and X models, the fuel pump runs for three seconds when the ignition is switched ON, then cuts out when the system is up to operating pressure, until the engine is started. If you can't hear anything, first check the fuse (see Chapter 9), then check the relay (see Step 4). If they are good, renew the pump.

4 To access the relay, remove the seat cowling (see Chapter 8). The relay is on the left-hand side of the rear sub-frame **(see illustration)**. Disconnect the relay wiring connector. Using a continuity tester, check for continuity between terminals 1 and 2 on the relay side of the

5.4b Fuel pump relay terminal identification (see text)

connector (**see illustration**). There should be no continuity. If there is, renew the relay. Using a fully charged 12 volt battery and two insulated jumper wires, connect the battery positive (+ve) terminal to terminal 3 on the connector, and the battery negative (-ve) terminal to terminal 4 on the connector. Now check again for continuity between terminals 1 and 2 on the connector. There should be continuity with the battery connected. If not, renew the relay. If the fuse and relay are good, check the wiring and terminals for physical damage or loose or corroded connections and rectify as necessary (see the *Wiring Diagrams* at the end of Chapter 9).

5 On GSX-R600 and GSX-R750T and V models, if the pump still does not work, raise the fuel tank (see Section 2) and disconnect the fuel pump wiring connector (**see illustration 2.8b**). Using a fully charged 12 volt battery and two insulated jumper wires, connect the battery positive (+ve) terminal to the pump's yellow/red wire terminal, and the battery negative (-ve) terminal to the pump's black/white wire terminal. The pump should operate. If the pump does not operate, renew it.

6 If the pump operates but is thought to be delivering an insufficient amount of fuel, first check that the fuel tank breather hose is unobstructed, that all fuel hoses are in good condition and not pinched or trapped. Check that the fuel strainer or filter is not blocked. On GSX-R600 and GSX-R750T and V models, check the fuel valve (see Section 4). On GSX-R750W and X models, check the fuel injection system (see Section 16).

7 The fuel pump's output can be checked as follows: make sure there is at least 5 litres of

5.12 Unscrew the nuts (A) and detach the wires, then remove the screws (B) and remove the sensor

fuel in the tank, the battery is fully charged and the ignition switch is OFF. Raise the fuel tank (see Section 2).

8 On GSX-R600 and GSX-R750T and V models, release the clamp securing the fuel hose to the outlet union on the fuel valve and detach the hose (**see illustration 2.8a**). Obtain an auxiliary length of hose and attach one end to the outlet union on the valve. Place the other end into a graduated beaker. Also detach the vacuum hose from the fuel valve and apply a vacuum (negative pressure) of -1.89 psi to the union using a vacuum pump and gauge. Disconnect the fuel pump wiring connector (**see illustration 2.8b**). Using a fully charged 12 volt battery and two insulated jumper wires, connect the battery positive (+ve) terminal to the pump's yellow/red wire terminal, and the battery negative (-ve) terminal to the pump's black/white wire terminal. Let fuel flow from the pump into the beaker for 1 minute, then disconnect the battery.

9 On GSX-R750W and X models, attach a hose clamp (see *Tools and Workshop Tips*) to the fuel return hose which runs from the pressure regulator to the fuel tank (**see illustration 2.9a**). Have a rag handy to catch

any residue fuel, then detach the hose from the regulator (**see illustration 2.9b**). Fit a suitable plug into the end of the hose as a back-up to the clamp. Obtain an auxiliary length of hose and attach one end to the outlet union on the regulator. Place the other end into a graduated beaker. Turn the ignition switch ON and let fuel flow from the pump into the beaker for 3 seconds, then switch the ignition OFF.

10 Measure the amount of fuel that has flowed into the beaker, then compare it to the amount specified at the beginning of the Chapter. If the flow rate recorded is below the minimum required, the fuel pump must be renewed. On GSX-R750W and X models, if the pump is good but the system is still suspect, perform a fuel pressure check (see Section 17).

Fuel level sensor

11 Remove the fuel pump/level sensor assembly (see below).

12 Unscrew the nuts securing the sensor wires to their terminals on the mounting plate and detach the wires (**see illustration**). Remove the screws securing the fuel level sensor to the fuel pump and remove the sensor, noting how it fits.

13 Connect a test light as shown in the four separate tests (**see illustration**). Give the light

5.13 Fuel level sensor test set-ups

5.15a Unscrew the bolts (arrowed) – numbers indicate tightening sequence . . .

5.15b . . . and remove the pump assembly

5.15c Discard the gasket and fit a new one

a few seconds to react in each case, and stir the sensor around in the water when submerged. If the test results are as shown, the level sensor is good, which means there is a fault elsewhere in the circuit, or in the display in the instrument cluster (see Chapter 9). If the test results are not as described, a new fuel pump and level sensor assembly must be installed – the level sensor is not available separately. Take care to wipe all

water off the sensor before installing it in the fuel tank.

Removal

14 Make sure the ignition is switched OFF. Remove the fuel tank and drain it (see Section 2). Turn the tank upside down and rest it on some clean rag.

15 Unscrew the bolts securing the fuel pump mounting plate to the tank, then withdraw the pump assembly **(see illustrations)**. Discard the gasket as a new one must be used. If a new fuel pump/level sensor is being installed it comes as an assembly with the mounting plate, so there is no need to dismantle the old assembly. It is wise to order the new pump along with a new strainer and/or filter (according to model).

Installation

16 Installation is the reverse of removal, noting the following:

a) *Check the condition of the strainer and/or filter on the fuel pump and clean or renew as required (see Chapter 1).*
b) *Make sure the wires are correctly and securely fitted to the pump and sensor.*

c) *Install the pump assembly using a new gasket and tighten the cover bolts evenly and a little at a time in the numerical sequence shown to the torque setting specified at the beginning of the Chapter* **(see illustrations 5.15c and a)**.
d) *On completion, start the engine and look carefully for any signs of leaks around the pump mounting plate and at the hose connections.*

6 Air filter housing – removal and installation

Removal

1 Raise the fuel tank (see Section 2). If required for improved access, remove the tank completely.

2 Unscrew the bolt securing the front of the airbox to the frame **(see illustration)**.

3 Release the clamp securing the crankcase breather hose to the back of the housing and detach the hose from its union **(see illustration)**.

6.2 Unscrew the bolt (arrowed)

6.3 Detach the breather hose

6.4a Detach the IAT sensor wiring connector (arrowed) . . .

6.4b . . . and remove the screw (arrowed) securing the IAP sensor

6.5a On carburettor models, slacken the screw on each clamp (arrowed)

6.5b On injection models, slacken the double-clamp screw (arrowed) on each side

6.5c On carburettor models, detach the vent hose

6.5d On injection models detach the vacuum hose

4 On GSX-R750W and X models, disconnect the IAT sensor wiring connector from the right-hand side of the housing, and remove the screw securing the IAP sensor to the back of the housing (see illustrations).

5 Slacken the clamp screws securing the housing to the carburettors or throttle bodies; on carburettor models, there is a clamp screw for each clamp, while on injection models double-clamps are used, whereby one screw acts on two clamps (see illustrations). Carefully lift the housing up, on GSX-R600 and GSX-R750T and V models, detaching the carburettor vent hose from the front of the housing (see illustration), and on GSX-R750W and X models detaching the vacuum hose from the inlet air control system diaphragm on the underside of the housing (see illustration), and remove the housing.

Installation

6 Installation is the reverse of removal. Make sure the inlets in the housing locate correctly against the ducts in the frame – there should be no gaps between them.

7 Idle fuel/air mixture adjustment (carburettor models) – general information

1 Due to the increased emphasis on controlling motorcycle exhaust emissions, certain governmental regulations have been

formulated which directly affect the carburation of this machine. In order to comply with the regulations, the carburettors on US models are sealed so they can't be tampered with. The pilot screws on other models are accessible, but the use of an exhaust gas analyser is the only accurate way to adjust the idle fuel/air mixture and be sure the machine doesn't exceed the emissions regulations.

2 The pilot screws are set to their correct position by the manufacturer and should not be adjusted unless it is necessary to do so for a carburettor overhaul. If the screws are adjusted they should be reset to the settings specified at the beginning of the Chapter.

3 If the engine runs extremely rough at idle or continually stalls, and if a carburettor overhaul does not cure the problem, take the motorcycle to a Suzuki dealer equipped with an exhaust gas analyser. They will be able to properly adjust the idle fuel/air mixture to achieve a smooth idle and restore low speed performance.

8 Carburettor overhaul – general information

1 Poor engine performance, hesitation, hard starting, stalling, flooding and backfiring are all signs that major carburettor maintenance may be required.

2 Keep in mind that many so-called carburettor problems are really not carburettor problems at all, but mechanical problems within the engine or ignition system malfunctions. Try to establish for certain that the carburettors are in need of maintenance before beginning a major overhaul.

3 Check the fuel filter, the fuel hoses, the inlet manifold joint clamps, the air filter, the ignition system, the spark plugs and carburettor synchronisation before assuming that a carburettor overhaul is required.

4 Most carburettor problems are caused by dirt particles, varnish and other deposits which build up in and block the fuel and air passages. Also, in time, gaskets and O-rings shrink or deteriorate and cause fuel and air leaks which lead to poor performance.

5 When overhauling the carburettors, disassemble them completely and clean the parts thoroughly with a carburettor cleaning solvent and dry them with filtered, unlubricated compressed air. Blow through the fuel and air passages with compressed air to force out any dirt that may have been loosened but not removed by the solvent. Once the cleaning process is complete, reassemble the carburettor using new gaskets and O-rings.

6 Before disassembling the carburettors, make sure you have all necessary O-rings and other parts, some carburettor cleaner, a supply of clean rags, some means of blowing out the carburettor passages and a clean

9.3 Remove the screw (arrowed) and detach the idle speed adjuster

9.4 Disconnect the TPS wiring connector (arrowed)

9.5 Disconnect the carburettor heater wiring connectors (A), and where fitted the solenoid valve wiring connector(s) (B)

place to work. It is recommended that only one carburettor be overhauled at a time to avoid mixing up parts.

9 Carburettors – removal and installation

> **Warning: Refer to the precautions given in Section 1 before starting work.**

Removal

1 Remove the air filter housing (see Section 6).
2 If the fuel tank was raised rather than removed, release the clamp securing the fuel hose to the fuel valve and detach the hose **(see illustration 2.8a)**.
3 Remove the left-hand fairing side panel. Remove the coolant reservoir screw which retains the idle speed adjuster and release the adjuster **(see illustration)**. Feed it through to the carburettors.
4 Disconnect the throttle position sensor wiring connector **(see illustration)**.
5 On UK models, disconnect the carburettor heater wiring connectors from the carburettors **(see illustration)**. On GSX-R600W, X and Y models, disconnect the two solenoid valve wiring connectors, and on GSX-R750T and V models disconnect the single solenoid valve wiring connector.
6 On California models disconnect the two

EVAP system purge hoses from their T-piece unions under the carburettors.
7 Detach the throttle cables and the choke cable from the carburettors (see Sections 22 and 23). If access is too restricted with the carburettors in situ, detach them after the carburettors have been displaced and lifted.
8 Remove the blanking plug from the access hole in each side of the frame. Using a long screwdriver inserted through the hole, slacken the clamp screws securing the carburettors to the inlets – one screw on each side secures both carburettors for that side **(see illustration)**. Ease the carburettors up off the inlets and remove them, noting the routing of the various hoses **(see illustration)**.
9 Place a suitable container below the float chambers then slacken the drain screw on the bottom of each carburettor and drain all the fuel from them **(see illustration)**. Once all the fuel has been drained, tighten the drain screws securely.
10 If required, remove the screws securing the inlet adapters to the cylinder head and remove the adapters and O-rings, noting how they fit. Discard the O-rings as new ones must be used. Also note the UP mark which must be at the top.

Installation

11 Installation is the reverse of removal, noting the following.
  a) *Check for cracks or splits in the cylinder head inlet adapters and the air filter*

housing rubbers, and renew them if necessary.
  b) *If removed, make sure the inlet adapters are installed correctly using new O-rings (see Step 10).*
  c) *Make sure the air filter housing and the cylinder head inlet adapters are fully engaged with the carburettors and their retaining clamps are securely tightened.*
  d) *Make sure all hoses are correctly routed and secured and not trapped or kinked.*
  e) *Do not forget to connect the throttle position sensor wiring connector, the carburettor heater wiring connectors, and the solenoid valve wiring connector (s), as appropriate to your model.*
  f) *Check the operation of the choke and throttle cables and adjust them as necessary (see Chapter 1).*
  g) *Check idle speed and carburettor synchronisation and adjust as necessary (see Chapter 1).*

10 Carburettors – disassembly, cleaning and inspection

> **Warning: Refer to the precautions given in Section 1 before starting work.**

Disassembly

1 Remove the carburettors from the machine as described in the previous Section. **Note:**

9.8a Slacken the clamp screws using a long screwdriver as shown . . .

9.8b . . . then remove the carburettors

9.9 Carburettor drain screws (arrowed)

10.2a Remove the screws (arrowed) and lift off the cover . . .

10.2b . . . then remove the spring . . .

10.2c . . . and the O-ring

Do not separate the carburettors unless absolutely necessary; each carburettor can be dismantled sufficiently for all normal cleaning and adjustments while in place on the mounting brackets. Dismantle the carburettors separately to avoid interchanging parts.

2 On GSX-R750 models, disconnect the air hose from the top cover. Unscrew and remove the top cover retaining screws **(see illustration)**. Lift off the cover and remove the spring from inside the piston **(see illustration)**. Also remove the small O-ring from around the air passage **(see illustration)**.

3 Carefully peel the diaphragm away from its sealing groove in the carburettor and withdraw the diaphragm and piston assembly, noting which way round it fits **(see illustration)**.

Caution: Do not use a sharp instrument to

displace the diaphragm as it is easily damaged.

4 Grasp the needle holder using a pair of pliers and carefully draw it out of the piston **(see illustration)**. Push the jet needle up from the bottom of the piston and withdraw it from the top **(see illustration)**. Take care not to lose the washer on the top of the needle and the spring in the holder **(see illustrations 12.10a and c)**.

5 On UK models, if required, remove the carburettor heater (see Section 13). On GSX-R750 models, disconnect the solenoid valve system air hoses from the float chamber, noting which fits where **(see illustration 14.10)**.

6 Remove the screws securing the float chamber to the base of the carburettor and remove the float chamber, noting how it fits **(see illustration)**. Remove the rubber gasket

and discard it as a new one must be used. Depending on your model and which carburettor is being worked on, it may be necessary to displace the solenoid valve from its bracket to access the screws.

7 Using a pair of thin-nose pliers, carefully withdraw the float pivot pin **(see illustration)**. If necessary, carefully displace the pin using a small punch or a nail. Remove the float assembly, noting how it fits **(see illustration 12.6d)**. Unhook the needle valve from the tab on the float, noting how it fits **(see illustration 12.6c)**. If required, remove the screw securing the needle valve seat and draw out the seat **(see illustrations 12.6b and a)**. Discard its O-ring as a new one must be used.

8 Unscrew and remove the main jet from the base of the needle jet **(see illustration)**.

10.3 Carefully remove the diaphragm and piston assembly

10.4a Grasp the needle holder and pull it out . . .

10.4b . . . then push the needle up from the bottom and remove it

10.6 Remove the float chamber screws (arrowed)

10.7 Withdraw the float pivot pin (arrowed) and remove the float assembly

10.8 Unscrew and remove the main jet (arrowed)

10.9 Unscrew and remove the needle jet (arrowed)

10.10 Unscrew and remove the pilot jet (arrowed)

10.11 Unscrew and remove the pilot screw (arrowed)

10.12a Remove the screws (arrowed) securing the linkage bar and remove the bar

10.12b Unscrew the choke plunger nut using thin-nosed pliers

9 Unscrew and remove the needle jet **(see illustration)**.

10 Unscrew and remove the pilot jet **(see illustration)**.

11 The pilot screw can be removed if required, but note that its setting will be disturbed (see **Haynes Hint**). On UK models unscrew and remove the pilot screw along with its spring, washer and O-ring **(see illustration)**. Discard the O-ring as a new one must be used. Pilot screw removal is the same for US models, except that the screw head is sealed off with a blanking plug. Carefully drill or punch a hole in the plug and prise it out using a hooked tool, or by threading in a self-tapping screw and grasping that with a pair of pliers. If drilling

through, do not drill further than a depth of 6 mm.

 To record the pilot screw's current setting, turn the screw in until it seats lightly, counting the number of turns necessary to achieve this, then fully unscrew it. On installation, the screw is simply backed out the number of turns you've recorded.

12 Remove the screws securing the choke linkage bar to the carburettors, noting the plastic washers **(see illustration)**. Lift off the bar, noting how it fits **(see illustration 12.1b)**. Unscrew the choke plunger nut, using a pair

of thin nosed pliers as access is too restricted for a spanner, and withdraw the plunger and spring from the carburettor body, noting how they fit **(see illustration)**. Take care not to lose the spring when removing the nut.

13 If required, remove the bolts securing the inlet funnel and remove the funnel, noting how it fits **(see illustration)**. Discard the O-ring as a new one must be used.

14 If required, remove the throttle position sensor from the right-hand (no. 4) carburettor (see Section 15).

Caution: Suzuki advise against removing the sensor from the carburettors unless absolutely necessary.

Cleaning

Caution: Use only a petroleum based solvent or dedicated carburettor cleaner for carburettor cleaning. Don't use caustic cleaners.

15 Submerge the metal components in the solvent for approximately thirty minutes (or longer, if the directions recommend it).

16 After the carburettor has soaked long enough for the cleaner to loosen and dissolve most of the varnish and other deposits, use a nylon-bristled brush to remove the stubborn deposits. Rinse it again, then dry it with compressed air.

17 Use a jet of compressed air to blow out all of the fuel and air passages in the main and upper body, not forgetting the air jets in the carburettor inlet **(see illustration)**.

10.13 Inlet funnel bolts (arrowed)

10.17 Do not forget the small air passages (arrowed) in the inlet

10.18 Check the choke plunger as described

10.19 Check the tapered portion of the pilot screw (arrowed) for wear

10.24 Check the valve's spring loaded rod (A) and tip (B) for wear or damage

Caution: Never clean the jets or passages with a piece of wire or a drill bit, as they will be enlarged, causing the fuel and air metering rates to be upset.

Inspection

18 Check the operation of each choke plunger. If the plunger doesn't move smoothly, inspect the needle and seat on the end of the choke plunger, the spring and the plunger linkage bar **(see illustration)**. Renew any component that is worn, damaged or bent.

19 If removed from the carburettor, check the tapered portion of the pilot screw and the spring and O-ring for wear or damage **(see illustration)**. Renew them if necessary.

20 Check the carburettor body, float chamber and top cover for cracks, distorted sealing surfaces and other damage. If any defects are found, renew the faulty component, although renewal of the entire carburettor will probably be necessary (check with a Suzuki dealer on the availability of separate components).

21 Check the piston diaphragm for splits, holes and general deterioration. Holding it up to a light will help to reveal problems of this nature.

22 Insert the piston guide and piston in the carburettor body and check that the piston moves up-and-down smoothly. Check the surface of the piston for wear. If it's worn excessively or doesn't move smoothly in the guide, renew the components as necessary.

23 Check the jet needle for straightness by

rolling it on a flat surface such as a piece of glass (having first removed the E-clip and spacer, noting which notch the E-clip fits into) **(see illustration 12.10a)**. Renew it if it's bent or if the tip is worn.

24 Check the tip of the float needle valve and the valve seat **(see illustration)**. If either has grooves or scratches in it, or is in any way worn, they must be renewed as a set.

25 Operate the throttle shaft to make sure the throttle butterfly valves open and close smoothly. If they do not, cleaning the throttle linkage may help. Otherwise, renew the carburettors.

26 Check the float for damage. This will usually be apparent by the presence of fuel inside one of the floats. If the float is damaged, it must be renewed.

11 Carburettors – separation and joining

> **Warning: Refer to the precautions given in Section 1 before proceeding**

Separation

1 The carburettors do not need to be separated for normal overhaul. If you need to separate them (to renew a carburettor body, for example), refer to the following procedure.

2 Remove the carburettors from the machine (see Section 9). Mark the body of each

carburettor with its cylinder location to ensure that it is positioned correctly on reassembly.

3 Remove the screws securing the choke linkage bar to the carburettors, noting the plastic washers **(see illustrations 10.12a)**. Lift off the bar, noting how it fits **(see illustration 12.1b)**.

4 Make a note of how the throttle return springs, linkage assembly and carburettor synchronisation springs are arranged to ensure that they are fitted correctly on reassembly **(see illustration)**. Also note carefully the arrangement of the various hoses and their unions, and make drawings as an aid if required **(see illustrations)**. Refer to Section 14 and remove the solenoid valve system components if required.

5 Unscrew and withdraw the two long bolts which hold the carburettors together **(see illustration)**.

11.4a Note carefully how the linkage assembly . . .

11.4b . . . the synchronisation springs . . .

11.4c . . . and the hoses and unions fit

11.5 Unscrew the bolts (arrowed) and carefully separate the carburettors

12.1a Fit the plunger into the carburettor and tighten the nut . . .

12.1b . . . then locate the linkage bar onto the plungers . . .

12.1c . . . and install the screws with their plastic washers

6 Carefully separate the carburettors. Retrieve the synchronisation springs and note the fitting of the various fuel hose T-pieces and O-rings or seals, and the vent hose T-pieces, and the solenoid valve system hoses connections (see Section 14) as they are separated. Discard the O-rings or seals as new ones must be used.

Joining

7 Assembly is the reverse of the disassembly procedure, noting the following.

a) Make sure the fuel hose T-pieces and O-rings or seals and the air vent hose T-pieces are correctly and securely inserted into the carburettors (see illustration 11.4c).

b) Install the synchronisation springs after the carburettors are joined together. Make sure they are correctly and squarely seated (see illustration 11.4b).

c) Check the operation of both the choke and throttle linkages ensuring that both operate smoothly and return quickly under spring pressure before installing the carburettors on the machine (see illustration 11.4a).

d) Install the carburettors (see Section 9) and check carburettor synchronisation and idle speed (see Chapter 1).

12 Carburettors – reassembly and float height check

Warning: Refer to the precautions given in Section 1 before proceeding.

Note: When reassembling the carburettors, be sure to use new O-rings and seals. Do not overtighten the carburettor jets and screws as they are easily damaged.

1 Install the choke plunger and spring into the carburettor body and tighten the nut to secure it (see illustration). Fit the choke linkage bar onto the plungers, making sure the slots locate correctly behind the nipple on the end of each choke plunger (see illustration). Fit the plastic washers and secure the linkage bar in place with the screws (see illustration).

2 Install the pilot screw (if removed) along with its spring, washer and O-ring, turning it in until it seats lightly (see illustration 10.11). Now, turn the screw out the number of turns previously recorded, or as specified at the beginning of the Chapter. If the pilot screw was disturbed on US models, read the notes in Sections 1 and 7 concerning maladjustment and emissions; the pilot screw housing should be sealed by fitting a new blanking plug.

3 Install the pilot jet (see illustration).

4 Install the needle jet (see illustration).

5 Install the main jet into the needle jet (see illustration).

6 If removed, fit a new O-ring onto the needle valve seat, then press it into place and secure it with the screw (see illustrations). Hook the float needle valve onto the tab on the float assembly, then position the float assembly in the carburettor, making sure the needle valve

12.3 Install the pilot jet . . .

12.4 . . . the needle jet . . .

12.5 . . . and the main jet

12.6a Press the needle valve seat in . . .

12.6b . . . and secure it with the screw

12.6c Fit the needle valve onto the float tab . . .

12.6d . . . then install the float assembly . . .

12.6e . . . and slide in the pin

locates in the seat, and install the pin, making sure it is secure (see illustrations).

7 To check the float height, hold the carburettor so the float hangs down, then tilt it back until the needle valve is just seated, but not so far that the needle's spring-loaded tip is compressed (the float chamber mating surface will be at approx. 45°). Measure the height from the top of the float to the mating surface with an accurate ruler (see illustration). The correct setting should be as given in the Specifications at the beginning of the Chapter. If it is incorrect, adjust the float height by carefully bending the float tab a little at a time until the correct height is obtained.

8 With the float height checked, fit a new sealing ring into the float chamber, making sure it is seated properly in its groove, then install the chamber and tighten its screws securely (see illustration). Where appropriate, locate the solenoid valve onto its bracket. On GSX-R750 models, connect the solenoid valve system air hoses to the chamber, referring to Section 14 for the system diagram (see illustration 14.10).

9 If removed, install the carburettor heater (see Section 13).

10 Fit the washer onto the jet needle, then fit the needle into the piston (see illustrations). Fit a new O-ring onto the retainer and check that the spring is correctly fitted, then locate the holder onto the top of the needle and press it down until the O-ring is felt to locate (see illustrations).

11 Insert the piston/diaphragm assembly into

12.7 Check the float height as described

12.8 Install the float chamber using a new gasket

12.10a Make sure the washer, E-clip and seat are fitted on the needle . . .

12.10b . . . then insert it in the piston

the carburettor (see illustration). Lightly push the piston down, ensuring the needle is correctly aligned with the needle jet. Press the

diaphragm outer edge into its groove, making sure it is correctly seated (see illustration 10.3). Check the diaphragm is not

12.10c Fit the O-ring and spring onto the holder . . .

12.10d . . . then press it into position

12.11a Fit the piston into the carburettor and seat the diaphragm

12.11b Fit the O-ring around the air passage

12.12a Install the spring and fit the top cover lug into it . . .

12.12b . . . then fit the cover screws

creased, and that the piston moves smoothly up and down in the guide. Fit a new O-ring around the air passage (see illustration).

12 Install the spring into the piston assembly, making sure it locates correctly, then fit the top cover, making sure the top of the spring fits over the lug in the middle of the cover, and that the protrusion in the cover locates over the O-ring and air passage, and tighten its screws securely (see illustrations). On GSX-R750 models, connect the air hose from the diaphragm assembly on the float chamber to the top cover.

13 If removed, install the inlet funnel using a new O-ring and apply a suitable non-permanent thread locking compound to the bolts (see illustration 10.13). Do not overtighten them.

14 If removed, install the throttle position sensor (see Section 15).

15 Install the carburettors (see Section 9).

13 Carburettor heater system (UK models) – check

> ⚠️ **Warning: Refer to the precautions given in Section 1 before starting work.**

1 On all GSX-R600 models and on GSX-R750T and V models, each carburettor has a heater unit threaded into its float chamber. The heaters are controlled by a thermo-switch, housed in the fairing.

2 Raise the fuel tank (see Section 2), and disconnect the wiring connectors from the heaters (see illustration 9.5).

3 Using an ohmmeter or multimeter set to the ohms x 1 scale, connect the positive (+ve) probe to the tip of the heater and the negative (-ve) probe to the spade terminal on No. 1 carburettor or to the hex on the base of each heater on the other carburettors (see illustration). The resistance of each heater should be as specified at the beginning of the Chapter.

4 If a meter is not available, connect a fully charged 12 volt battery to each heater in turn, using the terminals as described above. After about five minutes, the float chamber should be felt to be warm.

5 If any heater does not perform as described, unscrew it from the carburettor. Apply a smear of thermo-grease to the new heater, then thread it into the carburettor and tighten it to the torque setting specified at the beginning of the Chapter.

6 To check the thermo switch, remove the inner panel from the left-hand fairing side panel (see Chapter 8). Locate the thermo-switch and unplug it from the wiring loom (see illustration). Using a continuity tester or multimeter, insert the probes into the switch wiring connector and check for continuity. In normal or warm conditions, there should be no continuity. Now immerse the switch into a bowl of ice. After a few minutes the switch should close and continuity should be shown. If not, the switch is faulty.

7 If the heaters and the switch are all good, turn the ignition switch ON and check for battery voltage at each heater wiring connector, and at the switch wiring connector in the loom. If there is none, refer to the wiring diagrams at the end of Chapter 9 and check the circuits for damaged or broken wiring.

14 Carburettor solenoid valve system – check

> ⚠️ **Warning: Refer to the precautions given in Section 1 before starting work.**

GSX-R600W, X and Y models

1 The solenoid valves are controlled electronically by the ignition control unit, and when open allow an extra amount of air via an air jet in the hose into the carburettor to weaken the mixture. Information fed to the ECU concerning engine speed determines when it is necessary for the valve to open and close. There is one valve for carburettors 1 and 4, and one for carburettors 2 and 3.

2 Raise the fuel tank (see Section 2), and disconnect the wiring connector from each solenoid valve (see illustration 9.5). Release the clip and slip the valve off its mounting bracket, then disconnect the hoses, noting which fits where (see illustration).

3 Using jumper wires, connect the positive (+ve) lead from a fully charged 12 volt battery

13.3 Measure the resistance between the tip (A) and the base (B)

13.6 Carburettor heater thermo switch (A) and its wiring connector (B)

14.2 Release the clip, detach the hoses and remove the solenoid

to the orange/white wire terminal of the solenoid valve. Now connect the negative (-ve) lead to the other terminal on the valve. At the moment of contact of the negative lead, the valve should be heard to click. Now disconnect the negative lead – the valve should again be heard to click. If the valve does not click when it is connected and disconnected, it is faulty, and a new one must be installed. If the valve is good, reconnect the hoses, then fit the valve onto its bracket and connect the wiring connector. The valve for carburettors 1 and 4 is mounted on the bracket on No. 3 carburettor, and has the white wiring connector. The valve for carburettors 2 and 3 is mounted on the bracket on No. 1 carburettor, and has the black wiring connector.

4 To check that each valve is switching ON (open) and OFF (closed) at the correct time, insert the positive (+ve) probe of a voltmeter into the orange/white socket of the wiring connector, which must remain connected to the valve, and the negative (-ve) probe into the light green socket (when testing the valve with the white connector for Nos. 1 and 4 carburettors) or the dark green socket (when testing the valve with the black connector for Nos. 2 and 3 carburettors). Start the engine and slowly increase its speed. Referring to the tables, check that each valve switches at the specified engine speed. When the valve is closed, the meter should read zero volts. When the valve is open, the meter should read battery voltage (a little over 12 volts).

GSX-R600W (all markets) and GSX-R600X and Y (UK)

Valve for Nos. 1 and 4 carburettors	Engine speed/rpm (approx.)
OPEN	2700
CLOSED	4200
OPEN	5700
CLOSED	8800

Valve for Nos. 2 and 3 carburettors	Engine speed/rpm (approx.)
OPEN	2700
CLOSED	5000
OPEN	7300
CLOSED	10,000

GSX-R600X and Y – US and California

Valve for Nos. 1 and 4 carburettors	Engine speed/rpm (approx.)
OPEN	2700
CLOSED	4050
OPEN	5800
CLOSED	9100

Valve for Nos. 2 and 3 carburettors	Engine speed/rpm (approx.)
OPEN	2700
CLOSED	4950
OPEN	7650
CLOSED	10,550

5 If either valve does not operate at all (but is heard to click when tested in Step 3), or opens and closes at the wrong engine speeds, refer to the wiring diagrams at the end of Chapter 9 and check the circuit for faulty wiring and connectors. If the wiring is good, it is possible that the ignition control unit is faulty (see Chapter 5).

GSX-R750T and V

6 The solenoid valve is controlled electronically by the ignition control unit, and is activated when the throttle is opened quickly from the closed position. Information on engine speed, throttle position and gear position is fed to the ECU, which determines when it is necessary for the valve to open and close. When open, the valve allows a vacuum from the inlet manifold of No. 4 carburettor to act on a diaphragm mounted on the float chamber of each carburettor, which opens an airway from the air filter housing to the top cover of the carburettor. This affects the rate at which the piston lifts, thereby compensating the fuel/air mixture, so that the sudden opening of the throttle does not upset carburation.

7 Raise the fuel tank (see Section 2), and disconnect the wiring connector from the solenoid valve. Slip the valve off its mounting bracket and disconnect the hoses, noting which fits where.

8 Using jumper wires, connect the positive (+ve) lead from a fully charged 12 volt battery to the orange/white terminal of the solenoid valve. Now connect the negative (-ve) lead to the other terminal on the valve. At the moment of contact of the negative lead, the valve should be heard to click. Now disconnect the negative lead – the valve should again be heard to click. If the valve does not click when it is connected and disconnected, it is faulty and a new one must be installed. If the valve is good, reconnect the hoses, then fit the valve onto its bracket and connect the wiring connector.

9 To check that the valve is switching ON (open) at the correct time, insert the positive (+ve) probe of a voltmeter into the orange/white socket of the wiring connector, which must remain connected to the valve, and the negative (-ve) probe into the light green socket. Start the engine and allow it to idle. When the engine is idling, the valve is closed and the meter should read zero volts. Now open the throttle quickly and suddenly, then shut it off again. The meter should deflect to read battery voltage (a little over 12 volts) as the valve opens, then drop back to zero as the throttle is closed.

10 If the solenoid is good, but the system is thought to be malfunctioning, for example if the engine stalls when the throttle is snapped open from the fully closed position, then it is likely that the vacuum side of the system is faulty. First check that all the hoses, including the larger bore ones from the air filter housing, are securely connected, that they are in good condition without any signs of cracks or splits, and are not kinked or trapped (see illustration). Next disconnect the hoses from the vacuum valve, fitted in the hose between the vacuum take-off point and the solenoid valve. Note which way round the valve fits – its brown side should face away from the solenoid valve, and its black side should face towards it. Apply a vacuum to the union on the brown side – the valve should be open and allow air to be sucked through it. Now apply a vacuum to the union on the black side – the valve should close and no air should pass. If either of the conditions are not as described, the valve is faulty and a new one must be installed. Make sure it is fitted with the coloured sides facing as described.

11 If the valve is good, remove the carburettors (see Section 9) and check the diaphragm in the base of each float chamber. Remove the screws securing the diaphragm cover, then carefully lift off the cover, noting that it is under spring pressure. Remove the spring, spring seat, spacer and diaphragm, noting how they fit. Hold the diaphragm up to the light and check for splits and holes. Also check the rim for evidence of wear or damage that will not allow it to seat properly. If the diaphragm is damaged, the whole float chamber must be renewed as individual components are not available.

14.10 Solenoid valve system – GSX-R750T and V

15 Throttle position sensor – check, removal and installation

Warning: Refer to the precautions given in Section 1 before starting work.

Check

GSX-R600 and GSX-R750T and V models

1 The throttle position sensor is mounted on the outside of the right-hand (No. 4) carburettor. Raise the fuel tank for access (see Section 2).

2 Disconnect the wiring connector from the top of the sensor **(see illustration 9.4)**. Using a multimeter set to the K-ohm scale, connect the probes to the two outer terminals on the sensor. If the resistance reading obtained is not within the range specified at the beginning of the Chapter, take the sensor to a Suzuki dealer for testing. If it is confirmed to be faulty, a new one must be installed; the sensor is a sealed unit and cannot therefore be repaired.

3 Check the sensor visually for cracks and other damage.

4 Using a multimeter set to resistance or a continuity tester, check for continuity between the terminals of the sensor wiring connector and the corresponding terminals on the ignition control module connector. There should be continuity between each terminal. If not, this is probably due to a damaged or broken wire between the connectors; pinched or broken wires can usually be repaired.

GSX-R750W and X models

5 Refer to Section 16.

Removal

Caution: Suzuki advise against removing the sensor from the carburettors or throttle bodies unless absolutely necessary.

6 The throttle position sensor is mounted on the outside of the right-hand (No. 4) carburettor or throttle body. Raise the fuel tank for access (see Section 2). Disconnect

15.7 Throttle position sensor screws (arrowed) – mark their position relative to the switch before removing them

the wiring connector from the top of the sensor **(see illustration 9.4)**.

7 Before removing the mounting screws, mark or scribe lines on the sensor to indicate the exact position of the screws in relation to it **(see illustration)**. Remove the screws and remove the sensor, noting how it fits.

Installation

8 If the original sensor is being installed, and its set-up is not suspected of being incorrect, fit the sensor onto the carburettor or throttle body and install the screws, aligning them exactly with the marks made on removal. On GSX-R750W and X models smear some grease around the throttle shaft end before installing the sensor. Tighten the screws to the torque setting specified at the beginning of the Chapter, making sure the position of the sensor is not disturbed.

9 On GSX-R600 and GSX-R750T and V models, if a new sensor is being installed, or if you want to check the set-up is correct, fit the sensor onto the carburettor and install screws, but do not tighten them, so that the sensor can be turned. Using two ohmmeters set to the K-ohm scale, and set up as shown, and with the throttle held open, check the reading on meter 1, then adjust the sensor until the reading on meter 2 is 76% of the reading on meter 1 **(see illustration)**. For example (see graph), if meter 1 reads 5 K-ohms, meter 2 must read 3.8 K-ohms. When it is correctly adjusted, tighten the screws to the torque setting specified at the beginning of

15.9 Throttle position sensor test set-up – carburettor models

the Chapter, making sure the position of the sensor is not disturbed.

10 On GSX-R750W and X models, if a new sensor is being installed, or if you want to check the set-up is correct, smear some grease onto the seal around the throttle shaft end before installing the sensor, then fit the sensor onto the carburettor and install the screws, but do not tighten them, so that the sensor can be turned. Using an ohmmeter or multimeter set to the K-ohms scale, measure the resistance between the blue and black/brown wire terminals on the sensor itself, first with the throttle closed, then with it fully open. Adjust the position until the readings are as specified at the beginning of the Chapter. When it is correctly adjusted, tighten the screws to the torque setting specified at the beginning of the Chapter, making sure the position of the sensor is not disturbed. If the sensor cannot be set-up properly, take the motorcycle to a dealer with the special fault code reader – it has a specific function on it for setting up the sensor.

11 Connect the wiring connector to the top of the sensor and lower the fuel tank.

16 Fuel injection system – general description and fault diagnosis

Warning: Refer to the precautions given in Section 1 before starting work.

General description

1 The electronic fuel injection system consists of two main component groups, namely the fuel circuit and the electronic control circuit.

2 The fuel circuit consists of the tank, pump, filter, pressure regulator and injectors. Fuel is supplied from the tank and pumped by an electric pump through a filter to the fuel distributor rail, from which the individual injectors are fed. Operating pressure is generated by the pump and is maintained and controlled by the pressure regulator. Excess fuel released by the regulator flows back to the tank.

3 The electronic control circuit consists of the electronic control unit which assesses information which it receives form various sensors in the engine. These sensors provide information on engine load (air flow into the engine), engine speed, crankshaft position, air temperature, engine temperature, throttle position and air density. The control unit uses this information to calculate the required opening time of the fuel injectors and thus the quantity of fuel required, and sends the equivalent electrical pulse to each injector. As the injector opens, pressurised fuel is sprayed around the inlet valve, where it mixes with air and vaporises, before entering the cylinder where it is compressed and ignited.

4 The system incorporates two safety

circuits. When the ignition is switched ON, the fuel pump runs for three seconds and pressurises the system. Thereafter the pump automatically switches off until the engine is started. The second circuit incorporates a tip-over sensor, which automatically switches off the fuel pump and cuts the ignition and injection circuits if the motorcycle falls over.

Fault diagnosis

5 The system incorporates a self-diagnostic function, whereby any faults are detected by the electronic control unit. In the event of a sensor failing, the unit will determine whether the engine can still be run. If it can, the fail-safe set-up means that the bike can be ridden home or to a dealer. When this occurs, the LCD display in the instrument cluster will indicate the letters FI every two seconds (alternating with the coolant temperature reading), and the LED lamp will come on. If the unit decides that the fault is too serious, it will be impossible to start the engine. When this occurs, the LCD display in the instrument cluster will indicate the letters FI continuously, and the LED lamp will flash.

6 To diagnose the exact cause of a failure in the system, a fault code reader, specifically designed for this system, is essential. Special meters are also required to test the individual sensors. Hence if a problem occurs, the motorcycle should be taken to a Suzuki dealer.

7 However the system is not completely untouchable, and the components that can be checked or worked on at home are covered in this and the next few sections. Also, if a fault is indicated, first check the wiring and connectors from the electronic control unit to the various sensors – it may well be that a connector has come loose or a wire has become pinched and is shorting out. A continuity test of all wires will locate such a problem – refer to the Wiring Diagrams at the end of Chapter 9. Where appropriate, also check that any air hoses attached to the sensors are secure, and are not cracked or split, blocked, kinked or trapped.

8 It is also possible to check all of the sensors individually using a multimeter and referring to the tests below and the specifications given at the beginning of the Chapter, but note that different meters could well give slightly different results to those specified even though the sensor being tested is not faulty – so do not consign a sensor to the bin before having it double-checked. Also, the tests given are those which can be carried out at home using only a multimeter and may only cover one aspect of a sensor's function. Therefore a correct resistance reading does not necessarily mean that the sensor will perform correctly in all circumstances. Peak voltage adapters and other testing equipment are needed to make a full check. This is why it is best to leave it to a dealer. Also, the problem may lie in the ignition control unit rather than any of the other components in the system (see Chapter 5).

Camshaft position (CMP) sensor

9 Make sure the ignition is switched OFF. Remove the air filter housing (see Section 6). The CMP sensor is on the left-hand end of valve cover **(see illustration)**. Disconnect the wiring connector and check the resistance between the terminals is as specified. Also check that there is no continuity between each terminal and earth.

Crankshaft position (CKP) sensor (pulse generator coil)

10 Make sure the ignition is switched OFF. The CKP sensor is on the right-hand end of the crankshaft. Remove the seat cowling (see Chapter 8). Trace the wiring from the end cover and disconnect it at the wiring connector with the green and black wires **(see illustration)**. Check the resistance between the terminals is as specified. Also check that there is no continuity between each terminal and earth.

Inlet air pressure (IAP) sensor

11 Make sure the ignition is switched OFF. Raise the fuel tank (see Section 2). The IAP sensor is on the back of the air filter housing **(see illustration)**. Disconnect the wiring connector from the sensor and turn the ignition switch ON. Connect the positive (+ve) probe of a voltmeter to the red wire terminal on the loom side of the wiring connector and the negative (-ve) probe first to ground, then to the black/brown wire terminal – in each case the input voltage should be as specified. If not, check the connector and the wiring.

12 Connect the wiring to the sensor, then start the engine and allow it idle. Check the output voltage by inserting the positive (+ve) probe of a voltmeter into the dark brown wire terminal and the negative (-ve) probe to the black/brown wire – it may be necessary to insert short pieces of wire into the connector to make contact, and attach crocodile clips to these, if your meter probes are too thick. If the reading is not as specified, and the wiring and vacuum hose are good, the sensor is faulty. If the reading is good, and the wiring and vacuum hose are good, take the sensor to a dealer for further testing.

Throttle position (TP) sensor

13 Make sure the ignition is switched OFF. Raise the fuel tank (see Section 2). The TP sensor is on the right-hand end of the throttle bodies. Disconnect the wiring connector from the sensor and turn the ignition switch ON **(see illustration 19.4b)**. Connect the positive (+ve) probe of a voltmeter to the red wire terminal on the loom side of the wiring connector and the negative (-ve) probe first to ground, then to the black/brown wire terminal – in each case the input voltage should be as specified. If not, check the connector and the wiring.

14 Now check for continuity between the blue wire terminal in the connector and ground – there should be no continuity.

15 Using an ohmmeter or multimeter set to the K-ohms scale, measure the resistance between the blue and black/brown wire terminals on the sensor itself, first with the throttle closed, then with it fully open. If the readings are not as specified, but are close to them, slacken the sensor mounting screws and adjust its position until the readings are as specified. If the sensor cannot be adjusted to the range, or if no readings are obtained, the sensor is faulty.

16 Connect the wiring to the sensor, then switch the ignition ON. Check the output voltage by inserting the positive (+ve) probe of a voltmeter into the blue wire terminal and the negative (-ve) probe to the black/brown wire –

16.9 Camshaft position (CMP) sensor

16.10 Crankshaft position (CKP) sensor wiring connector (arrowed)

16.11 Inlet air pressure (IAP) sensor (arrowed)

16.17 Engine coolant temperature (ECT) sensor (arrowed)

16.19 Disconnect the inlet air temperature (IAT) sensor wiring connector

16.21 Atmospheric pressure (AP) sensor (arrowed)

it may be necessary to insert short pieces of wire into the connector to make contact, and attach crocodile clips to these, if your meter probes are too thick. Measure the voltage first with the throttle closed, then with it fully open. If the readings are not as specified, the sensor is faulty.

Engine coolant temperature (ECT) sensor

17 Make sure the ignition is switched OFF. Remove the air filter housing (see Section 6). The ECT sensor is in the thermostat housing on the right-hand side of the engine **(see illustration)**. Disconnect the wiring connector from the sensor and turn the ignition switch ON. Connect the positive (+ve) probe of a voltmeter to the black/green wire terminal on the loom side of the wiring connector and the negative (-ve) probe first to ground, then to the black/brown wire terminal – in each case the input voltage should be as specified. If not, check the connector and the wiring.

18 Using an ohmmeter or multimeter set to the K-ohms scale, measure the resistance between the terminals on the sensor itself. If the reading is not as specified, the sensor is faulty.

Inlet air temperature (IAT) sensor

19 Make sure the ignition is switched OFF. Raise the fuel tank (see Section 2). The IAT sensor is on the right-hand side of the air filter housing. Disconnect the wiring connector from the sensor and turn the ignition switch ON **(see illustration)**. Connect the positive

(+ve) probe of a voltmeter to the light blue wire terminal on the loom side of the wiring connector and the negative (-ve) probe first to ground, then to the black/brown wire terminal – in each case the input voltage should be as specified. If not, check the connector and the wiring.

20 Using an ohmmeter or multimeter set to the K-ohms scale, measure the resistance between the terminals on the sensor itself. If the reading is not as specified, the sensor is faulty.

Atmospheric pressure (AP) sensor

21 Make sure the ignition is switched OFF. Raise the fuel tank (see Section 2). The AP sensor is on the inside of the right-hand frame spar **(see illustration)**. Disconnect the wiring connector from the sensor and turn the ignition switch ON. Connect the positive (+ve) probe of a voltmeter to the red wire terminal on the loom side of the wiring connector and the negative (-ve) probe first to ground, then to the black/brown wire terminal – in each case the input voltage should be as specified. If not, check the connector and the wiring.

22 Connect the wiring to the sensor, then turn the ignition switch ON. Check the output voltage by inserting the positive (+ve) probe of a voltmeter into the blue/black wire terminal and the negative (-ve) probe to the black/brown wire – it may be necessary to insert short pieces of wire into the connector to make contact, and attach crocodile clips to these, if your meter probes are too thick. If the reading is not as specified, and the wiring and

vacuum hose are good, the sensor is faulty. If the reading is good, and the wiring and vacuum hose are good, take the sensor to a dealer for further testing.

Tip-over (TO) sensor

23 Make sure the ignition is switched OFF. The TO sensor is behind the seat cowling on the left-hand side – remove the cowling for access (see Chapter 8). Disconnect the sensor wiring connector **(see illustration)**. Using an ohmmeter or multimeter set to the K-ohms scale, measure the resistance between the terminals on the sensor side of the connector. If the reading is not as specified, the sensor is faulty.

24 Reconnect the wiring connector and turn the ignition switch ON. Connect the positive (+ve) probe of a voltmeter into the black wire terminal on the loom side of the wiring connector and the negative (-ve) probe into the black/brown wire terminal – it may be necessary to insert short pieces of wire into the connector to make contact, and attach crocodile clips to these, if your meter probes are too thick. If the reading is not as specified, and the wiring and connector are good, the sensor is faulty. If the reading is good, with the aid of an assistant carefully lean the motorcycle to an angle of 43°, first on one side and then on the other – at each point the reading should drop to zero. If not the sensor is faulty.

Gear position (GP) switch

25 Place the motorcycle on an auxiliary stand and raise the sidestand. Remove the seat cowling (see Chapter 8). Trace the gear position switch wiring from the left-hand side of the engine to the white connector with the blue, pink and black/white wires, and leave it connected **(see illustration)**. Turn the ignition switch ON and make sure the engine kill switch is in the RUN position.

26 Connect the positive (+ve) probe of a voltmeter into the pink wire terminal on the loom side of the wiring connector and the negative (-ve) probe to ground – it may be necessary to insert a short piece of wire into the connector to make contact, and attach a crocodile clip to it, if your meter probe is too thick. Select each gear in turn and check that

16.23 Tip-over (TO) sensor (A) and its wiring connector (B)

16.25 Gear position (GP) sensor wiring connector (arrowed)

the voltage in each gear is as specified (the voltage will be different for each gear selected, but they must all be above the specified minimum). If not, and the wiring and connector are good, the switch is faulty.

17 Fuel pressure and pressure regulator (GSX-R750W and X models) – check

⚠️ **Warning: Refer to the precautions given in Section 1 before starting work.**

1 To check the fuel pressure, a suitable gauge and adapter piece (which screws into the end of the fuel rail) will be needed. Suzuki provide a kit (Pt. Nos. 09915-74520, 09915-77330 and 09940-40210) for this purpose.

2 Raise the fuel tank (see Section 2).

3 Place a container suitable for holding petrol (gasoline) under the right-hand end of the fuel rail, then slacken the pressure check bolt and allow the residual fuel to drain **(see illustration)**. Unscrew the bolt and thread the adapter in its place. Connect the gauge to the adapter.

4 Turn the ignition switch ON and check the pressure reading on the gauge. The pressure should as specified at the start of this Chapter.

5 Turn the ignition OFF and unscrew the gauge and adapter from the fuel rail, being prepared to catch the residual fuel as before.

6 Install the pressure check bolt using a new sealing washer, and tighten it to the torque setting specified at the beginning of this Chapter.

7 If the pressure is too low, either the pressure regulator is stuck open, the fuel pump is faulty, the strainer or filter is blocked, or there is a leak in the system, probably from a hose joint.

8 If the pressure is too high, either the return hose is pinched or clogged, the regulator is stuck closed or the fuel pump check valve is faulty.

9 Refer to the relevant Sections of this Chapter and Chapter 1 and check the possible problems according to whether the pressure was too low or too high. Suzuki provide no test procedure for the pressure regulator. However, if it is stuck open, it will be possible to blow through it with a low pressure air source. If it is stuck closed, then a high pressure air source with a gauge can be used to check the pressure at which it does open, if at all. Alternatively, substitute the suspect one with a known good one and repeat the fuel pressure check.

10 To remove the pressure regulator, unscrew the two bolts securing it to the fuel rail and pull it out of its socket **(see illustration)**. Discard the O-ring as a new one must be used. Fit a new O-ring, then press the regulator into the rail and tighten the bolts to the specified torque setting.

17.3 Fuel pressure check bolt (arrowed)

17.10 Fuel pressure regulator bolts (arrowed)

18 Inlet air control valve system (GSX-R750W and X models) – check

1 The system operates a flap in the air filter housing which regulates the air flow into it according to engine speed. At low to medium engine speeds, the flap is closed. At medium to high engine speeds, the flap is open. The flap is activated by a rod connected to a diaphragm, which itself is activated by a vacuum taken from the inlet manifold. The vacuum to the diaphragm is controlled by a solenoid valve, which is controlled by the ECU. At low to medium engine speeds, the solenoid valve is open so the vacuum acts on the diaphragm and closes the flap. At medium to high engine speeds, the solenoid valve is closed so the vacuum is cut off and the flap opens. A one-way valve and a damper are incorporated in the vacuum hose between the manifold and the solenoid valve.

2 To check that the system is operating correctly, remove the air filter (see Chapter 1). Start the engine and slowly open the throttle while looking inside the filter housing at the flap in its base. The flap should open at 5400 rpm and stay open at engine speeds above that. Slowly close the throttle – the flap should close at 5200 rpm and remain closed at engine speeds below that. If the flap does not open and close as described,

check the system components as described below.

3 First check that all the hoses are securely connected, that they are in good condition without any signs of cracks or splits, and are not kinked or trapped. It will be necessary to displace the air filter housing to check the hose from the solenoid valve to the diaphragm on the underside of the housing (see Section 6).

4 To check the solenoid valve, located on the inside of the right-hand frame spar, first disconnect the wiring connector from the solenoid **(see illustration)**. Using an ohmmeter or multimeter set to the ohms x 10 scale, measure the resistance between the terminals on the solenoid and compare the reading to that specified at the beginning of the Chapter. If the reading obtained is not within the specified range, a new solenoid valve must be installed.

5 To check the one-way valve, located at the right-hand end of the throttle bodies, disconnect the valve hoses **(see illustration)**. Blow through the valve from the orange side – the valve should be open and allow air to pass through. Now reverse the valve and blow through from the other side – the valve should be closed and not allow air to pass through. If either of the conditions are not as described, the valve is faulty and a new one must be installed. Make sure it is fitted with the orange side facing back towards the solenoid valve.

18.4 Disconnect the solenoid valve wiring connector (arrowed)

18.5 Disconnect the valve hoses (arrowed)

18.6 Damper (arrowed)

19.4a Disconnect the fuel injector loom wiring connector . . .

19.4b . . . the throttle position sensor wiring connector . . .

6 Visually check the damper, located on the inside of the right-hand frame spar, for cracks, dents or any other damage and renew it if any are found (see illustration).

7 To check the diaphragm, remove the air filter and first check that the connecting rod between it and the flap has not come away. Now trace the vacuum hose from the diaphragm on the underside of the filter housing and disconnect it from the solenoid. Using a hand-operated vacuum pump, apply a vacuum through the hose and check whether the flap closes when the vacuum is applied and opens when it is released. Do not apply more than -180 mmHg of vacuum (negative pressure) to avoid damaging the diaphragm. If the flap does not open and close, a new diaphragm must be installed.

19 Throttle bodies (GSX-R750W and X models) – removal and installation

⚠️ **Warning: Refer to the precautions given in Section 1 before starting work.**

Removal

1 Remove the air filter housing (see Section 6).
2 Place a container suitable for holding petrol (gasoline) under the right-hand end of the fuel rail, then slacken the pressure check bolt and allow the residual fuel to drain (see illustration 17.3). When the fuel has drained, tighten the bolt to the torque setting specified at the beginning of the Chapter, using a new sealing washer if necessary.

3 If the fuel tank was raised rather than removed, attach a hose clamp (see Tools and Workshop Tips) to the fuel return hose which runs from the pressure regulator to the fuel tank (see illustration 2.9a). Have a rag handy to catch any residue fuel, then detach the hose from the regulator (see illustration 2.9b). Fit a suitable plug into the end of the hose as a back-up to the clamp. Also detach the fuel supply hose from either the fuel tank or the inlet union on the fuel rail (see illustrations 2.9c and d).
4 Disconnect the common wiring connector for all the fuel injectors (as opposed to the connector on each individual injector) (see illustration). Also disconnect the throttle position sensor wiring connector (see illustration), and the inlet air pressure sensor wiring connector (see illustration).
5 Remove the left-hand fairing side panel. Remove the coolant reservoir screw which retains the idle speed adjuster and release the adjuster (see illustration 9.3). Feed it through to the carburettors.
6 Detach the throttle cables and the choke cable from the throttle bodies (see Sections 22 and 23). Also disconnect the vacuum hose from its union on the No. 4 throttle body (see illustration).
7 Remove the blanking plug from the access hole in each side of the frame (see illustration). Using a long screwdriver inserted through the hole, slacken the clamp screws securing the throttle bodies to the inlets – one screw on each side secures both bodies for that side (see illustration). Ease the bodies up off the inlets and remove them (see illustration).

19.4c . . . and the IAP wiring connector

19.6 Pull the vacuum hose off its union (arrowed)

19.7a Remove the blanking caps . . .

19.7b . . . then slacken the clamp screws . . .

19.7c . . . and remove the throttle bodies

Installation

8 Installation is the reverse of removal, noting the following.

 a) *Make sure the throttle bodies are fully engaged with the inlet manifolds on the cylinder heads.*

 b) *Make sure the throttle body retaining clamps are secure, but take care not to overtighten them.*

 c) *Make sure all the wiring connectors are reconnected.*

 d) *Make sure the hose clamp on the fuel return hose is secure, then remove the plug from the end of the hose and attach the hose to the union on the bottom of the fuel pressure regulator. Also make sure the fuel supply hose clicks properly onto its union and is secure.*

 e) *Check the operation of the choke and throttle cables and adjust them as necessary (see Chapter 1).*

 f) *Check idle speed and throttle synchronisation and adjust as necessary (see Chapter 1).*

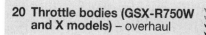

20 Throttle bodies (GSX-R750W and X models) – overhaul

Warning: Refer to the precautions given in Section 1 before starting work.

Disassembly

1 Remove the fuel injectors (see section 21).

2 If required, remove the throttle position sensor, but only do so if absolutely necessary (see Section 15).

3 If required, disconnect the vacuum hoses from the throttle bodies and the pressure regulator and release them from the clip, but leave the hoses connected to each other (unless they need renewing) **(see illustration)**.

4 The pilot air screws, located just ahead of the vacuum hose unions, can be removed if required, but note that their setting will be disturbed (see *Haynes Hint*). On UK models unscrew and remove the pilot screw along with its spring, washer and O-ring. Discard the O-ring as a new one must be used. Pilot screw removal is the same for US models, except that the screw head is sealed off with a blanking plug. Carefully drill or punch a hole in the plug and prise it out using a hooked tool, or by threading in a self-tapping screw and grasping that with a pair of pliers. If drilling, do not drill further than a depth of 6 mm.

HAYNES HiNT *To record the air screw's current setting, turn the screw in until it seats lightly, counting the number of turns necessary to achieve this, then fully unscrew it. On installation, the screw is simply backed out the number of turns you've recorded.*

20.3 Pull the hoses off the unions on the throttle bodies (A) and the pressure regulator (B)

Cleaning

Caution: Use only a petroleum based solvent or dedicated carburettor cleaner for throttle body cleaning. Don't use caustic cleaners.

5 Submerge the metal components in the solvent for approximately thirty minutes (or longer, if the directions recommend it). If a spray cleaner is used, direct the spray into all passages.

6 After the components have soaked long enough for the cleaner to loosen and dissolve most of the varnish and other deposits, use a nylon-bristled brush to remove the stubborn deposits. Rinse them again, then dry them with compressed air.

7 Use a jet of compressed air to blow out all of the fuel and air passages.

Caution: Never clean the jets or passages with a piece of wire or a drill bit, as they will be enlarged, causing the fuel and air metering rates to be upset.

Inspection

8 Check the throttle bodies for cracks or any other damage which may result in air getting in.

9 Check that the throttle butterflies move smoothly and freely in the bodies, and make sure that the inside of each body is completely clean.

10 Check that the throttle and choke cable cams move smoothly and freely, taking into

20.14 Carefully note the arrangement of the linkage assembly and synchronisation springs (arrowed)

20.13 Joining bracket screws (arrowed)

account spring pressure. Clean any grit and dirt from around the cams.

Separation and joining

11 The throttle bodies do not need to be separated for normal overhaul. If you need to separate them (to renew a body, for example), refer to the following procedure:

12 Mark each body with its cylinder location to ensure that it is positioned correctly on reassembly.

13 Remove the screws securing the joining bracket and remove the bracket, noting how it fits **(see illustration)**.

14 Make a note of how the throttle return springs, linkage assembly and synchronisation springs are arranged to ensure that they are fitted correctly on reassembly **(see illustration)**. Also note carefully the arrangement of the various hoses and their unions, and make drawings as an aid if required.

15 Unscrew and withdraw the long bolt which holds the bodies together **(see illustration)**.

16 Carefully separate the bodies. Retrieve the synchronisation springs and note the fitting of the joining spacers.

17 Joining is the reverse of the separation procedure. Install the synchronisation springs after the carburettors are joined together. Make sure they are correctly and squarely seated. Check the operation of the throttle linkage ensuring it operates smoothly and

20.15 Unscrew and withdraw the bolt (arrowed)

21.2 Disconnect the injector wiring connector

21.6 Pull the vacuum hose off the pressure regulator

21.8a Unscrew the bolts (arrowed) . . .

returns quickly under spring pressure. Check carburettor synchronisation and idle speed (see Chapter 1) after installation.

Reassembly

18 Install the pilot air screw (if removed) along with its spring, washer and using a new O-ring, turning it in until it seats lightly. Now, turn the screw out the number of turns previously recorded, or as specified at the beginning of the Chapter. If the pilot screw was disturbed on US models, read the notes in Sections 1 and 7 concerning maladjustment and emissions; the pilot screw housing should be sealed by fitting a new blanking plug.
19 If disconnected, attach the vacuum hoses to the throttle bodies **(see illustration 20.3)**.
20 If removed, install the throttle position sensor (see Section 15).
21 Install the fuel injectors (see section 21).

21 Fuel injectors (GSX-R750W and X models) – check, removal and installation

> ⚠ **Warning: Refer to the precautions given in Section 1 before proceeding.**

Check

1 Raise the fuel tank (see Section 2).
2 Make sure the ignition is switched OFF. Disconnect the wiring connector from the

injector being tested **(see illustration)**. Using an ohmmeter or multimeter, check that the resistance between the terminals on the injector is as specified. Also check that there is no continuity between each terminal and ground. If the readings are not as specified, install a new injector.
3 If the readings are good, set the meter to read dc volts and check that battery voltage exists between the yellow/red wire terminal on the injector wiring connector and ground, with the ignition switched ON, noting that after it is switched ON you only have 3 seconds to take the reading before the ECU automatically cuts the voltage. If no voltage exists, check the connector and the wiring for faults. If voltage exists, it is likely that there is a fault elsewhere in the system or in the ECU itself (see Section 16).

Removal

4 Remove the air filter housing (see Section 6). The fuel injectors can be removed with the throttle bodies in situ. If the bodies have been removed, ignore the Steps which do not apply.
5 Place a container suitable for holding petrol (gasoline) under the right-hand end of the fuel rail, then slacken the pressure check bolt and allow the residual fuel to drain **(see illustration 17.3)**. When the fuel has drained, tighten the bolt to the torque setting specified at the beginning of the Chapter, using a new sealing washer if necessary.

6 If the fuel tank was raised rather than removed, attach a hose clamp (see *Tools and Workshop Tips*) to the fuel return hose which runs from the pressure regulator to the fuel tank **(see illustration 2.9a)**. Have a rag handy to catch any residue fuel, then detach the hose from the regulator **(see illustration 2.9b)**. Fit a suitable plug into the end of the hose as a back-up to the clamp. Also detach the fuel supply hose from either the fuel tank or the inlet union on the fuel rail **(see illustrations 2.9c and d)**. Pull the vacuum hose off its union on the pressure regulator **(see illustration)**.
7 Disconnect the common wiring connector for all the fuel injectors (as opposed to the connector on each individual injector) **(see illustration 19.4a)**.
8 Unscrew the bolts securing the fuel rail and lift the rail off the throttle bodies – the injectors will come away with the rail **(see illustrations)**.
9 To separate the injectors from the fuel rail, release the clip on the injector wiring connector and detach the connector **(see illustration 21.2)**. Carefully pull the injector out of the fuel rail, noting how it fits **(see illustration)**. Discard the injector seals and O-ring as new ones must be used **(see illustration)**.
10 If required, unscrew the bolts or screws securing the pressure regulator and/or the fuel inlet union to the fuel rail and detach them

21.8b . . . and remove the fuel rail and injectors

21.9a Carefully pull the injector out of the rail

21.9b Discard the seals (A) and O-ring (B)

21.10 Remove the pressure regulator (A) and inlet union (B) if required

21.13a Fit a new bottom seal . . .

21.13b . . . top seal . . .

21.13c . . . and O-ring

21.14a Install the bolts . . .

21.14b . . . and tighten them to the specified torque

(see illustration). Discard the O-rings as new ones must be used.

11 Modern fuels contain detergents which should keep the injectors clean and free of gum or varnish from residue fuel. If the injector is suspected of being blocked, clean it through with injector cleaner. If the injector is clean but its performance is suspect, take it to a Suzuki dealer for assessment.

Installation

12 If removed, fit a new O-ring onto the fuel supply union and the pressure regulator and smear them with clean engine oil. Press each component into the fuel rail and tighten its screws or bolts to the torque settings specified at the beginning of the Chapter.

13 Fit new seals and O-ring onto each injector (see illustrations). Push the injector into the fuel rail, making sure you do not turn it whilst doing so, and that it is properly seated (see illustration 21.9a).

14 Fit the fuel rail and injectors onto the throttle bodies, making sure each injector seats correctly (see illustration 21.8b). Install the fuel rail bolts and tighten them to the specified torque setting (see illustrations). Connect the individual injector wiring connectors (see illustration 21.2), and the common connector into the wiring loom (see illustration 19.4a).

15 If the fuel tank was raised rather than removed, make sure the hose clamp on the fuel return hose is secure, then remove the

plug from the end of the hose and attach the hose to the union on the bottom of the fuel pressure regulator (see illustration 2.9b). Also connect the fuel supply hose to either the tank or the inlet union according to your removal procedure, making sure it clicks properly onto its union and is secure (see illustration 2.9d). Attach the vacuum hose to its union on the pressure regulator (see illustration 21.6).

16 Install the air filter housing (see Section 6).

22 Throttle cables – removal and installation

> ⚠ **Warning: Refer to the precautions given in Section 1 before proceeding.**

Removal

1 Raise the fuel tank (see Section 2).

2 Slacken the top locknut on one of the cables, then unscrew the adjuster until the bottom locknut is clear of the bracket (see illustration). Free the adjuster from its mounting bracket, then rotate the cam using your finger and detach the inner cable from the throttle cam (see illustrations). Repeat for the other cable.

3 Remove the screw securing the front (accelerator) cable retaining plate to the

22.2a Slacken the top locknut (A) and unscrew the adjuster (B) . . .

22.2b . . . then free it from the bracket . . .

22.2c ... and detach the cable end (arrowed) from the throttle cam

22.3a Remove the retainer plate screw (A) and unscrew the ring (B)

22.3b Remove the housing screws (arrowed) and separate the halves

handlebar switch/throttle pulley housing, and unscrew the rear (decelerator) cable retaining ring **(see illustration)**. Remove the handlebar switch/throttle pulley housing screws and separate the halves **(see illustration)**. Hook the cable ends out of the pulley and remove the cable elbows from the housing **(see illustrations)**. Mark each cable to ensure it is connected correctly on installation.

4 Slacken the bolt securing the cable guide to the frame **(see illustration)**. Remove the cables from the machine noting the correct routing of each cable.

Installation

5 Install the cables making sure they are correctly routed – tighten the guide bolt after fitting the cables into it **(see illustration 22.4)**.

The cables must not interfere with any other component and should not be kinked or bent sharply. Note that on carburettor models, the top cable is the accelerator (throttle opening cable) and the bottom cable is the decelerator (throttle closing) cable. On fuel injected models, it is the other way around (not counting the choke cable).

6 Install the cables into the throttle pulley housing, making sure the accelerator cable is at the front and the decelerator is at the back. Secure the accelerator cable elbow with the retainer plate **(see illustration)**, and thread the decelerator cable retaining ring into the housing. Lubricate the end of each inner cable with multi-purpose grease, then locate the lower half of the housing and attach them to the pulley **(see illustration 22.3c)**.

7 Assemble the housing, aligning its locating pin with the hole in the top of the handlebar **(see illustration)**. Install the retaining screws, and tighten them securely **(see illustration 22.3b)**.

8 Lubricate the lower end of each inner cable with multi-purpose grease and attach them to the carburettor throttle cam **(see illustration 22.2c)**.

9 Make sure the cables are correctly connected and locate the outer cable adjusters in the mounting brackets **(see illustration 22.2b)**. Set the adjuster locknuts so that the slack in the inner cable is taken up, but not so that it is tight **(see illustration 22.2a)**. Tighten the top locknut securely.

10 Lower the fuel tank (see Section 2).

11 Adjust the cables as described in Chapter 1. Turn the handlebars back and forth to make sure the cables don't cause the steering to bind.

12 Install the fuel tank (see Section 2).

13 Start the engine and check that the idle speed does not rise as the handlebars are turned. If it does, correct the problem before riding the motorcycle.

23 Choke cable –
removal and installation

Removal

1 Raise the fuel tank (see Section 2).
2 On GSX-R600 and GSX-R750T and V

22.3c Detach the cable ends from the pulley ...

22.3d ... and draw them out of the housing

22.4 Slacken the bolt (arrowed) and free the cables from the guide

22.6 Fit the cable elbows into the housing

22.7 Locate the pin (A) into the hole (B)

23.2a Pull the outer cable out of its bracket . . .

23.2b . . . and detach the inner cable from the bar

23.3a Slacken the top locknut (A) and unscrew the adjuster (B) . . .

models, free the choke outer cable from its bracket on the carburettor by pulling it out, then free the inner cable from the choke linkage bar **(see illustrations)**.

3 On GSX-R750W and X models, slacken the top locknut on the cable, then unscrew the adjuster until the bottom locknut is clear of the bracket **(see illustration)**. Free the adjuster from its mounting bracket and detach the inner cable from the choke cam **(see illustrations)**.

4 Slacken the choke lever clamp screw, then unscrew the two handlebar switch/choke lever housing screws, one of which secures the choke cable elbow via a retainer plate, and separate the two halves; open the choke lever fully as you separate the halves, noting how it fits into the housing **(see illustrations)**. Detach the cable nipple from the choke lever,

23.3b . . . then free it from the bracket . . .

23.3c . . . and detach the cable end from the throttle cam

23.4a Slacken the clamp screw (A) then remove the housing screws (B)

23.4b Push the lever fully open as you separate the housing

then withdraw the cable and elbow from the housing **(see illustrations)**.

5 Slacken the bolt securing the cable guide to

the frame **(see illustration 22.4)**. Remove the cable from the machine noting its correct routing.

Installation

6 Install the cable making sure it is correctly routed – tighten the guide bolt after fitting the cable into it **(see illustration 22.4)**. The cable must not interfere with any other component and should not be kinked or bent sharply.

7 Lubricate the upper cable nipple with multi-purpose grease. Install the cable in the switch/choke lever housing and attach the nipple to the choke lever **(see illustrations 23.4d and c)**. Fit the two halves of the housing onto the handlebar, again with the choke lever in the fully open position, making sure the lever fits correctly, and make sure the pin in the upper half locates in the hole in the top of the handlebar **(see illustration and 23.4b)**. Install

23.4c Detach the cable end from the lever . . .

23.4d . . . and draw it out of the housing

23.7 Locate the pin (A) into the hole (B)

24.1 Silencer-to-downpipe nuts (arrowed)

24.2 Silencer mounting (A), downpipe rear mounting (B)

24.10 Downpipe clamp bolts (arrowed)

the screws, making sure the elbow retainer is correctly positioned, and tighten them securely, then tighten the spring clamp screw **(see illustration 23.4a)**.

8 On GSX-R600 and GSX-R750T and V models, lubricate the lower cable nipple with multi-purpose grease and attach it to the choke linkage bar on the carburettor **(see illustration 23.2b)**. Fit the outer cable into its bracket **(see illustration 23.2a)**.

9 On GSX-R750W and X models, lubricate the lower cable nipple with multi-purpose grease and attach it to the choke cam **(see illustration 23.3c)**. Locate the outer cable adjuster in the mounting bracket **(see illustration 23.3b)**. Set the adjuster locknuts so that the slack in the inner cable is taken up, but not so that it is tight **(see illustration 23.3a)**. Tighten the top locknut securely.

10 Check the operation of the choke cable (see Chapter 1).

11 Lower the fuel tank (see Section 2).

---

24 Exhaust system – removal and installation

 Warning: If the engine has been running the exhaust system will be very hot. Allow the system to cool before carrying out any work.

Silencer
Removal
1 Unscrew the nuts and remove the washers securing the silencer to the downpipe assembly **(see illustration)**.

2 Unscrew and remove the silencer mounting nut and bolt, then release the silencer from the exhaust downpipe assembly **(see illustration)**.

3 Remove the sealing ring from the end of the downpipe assembly and discard it as a new one should be used.

Installation
4 Fit the new sealing ring onto the end of the downpipe assembly.

5 Fit the silencer onto the downpipe assembly, making sure it is pushed fully home. Align the silencer mounting bracket at the rear and install the bolt, but do not yet tighten the nut.

6 Install the silencer nuts with their washers and tighten them to the torque setting specified at the beginning of the Chapter, then tighten the silencer mounting bolt to the specified torque.

7 Run the engine and check the system for leaks.

Complete system
Removal
8 Remove the fairing side panels and the lower fairing (see Chapter 8).

9 Unscrew the silencer mounting nut but do not yet remove the bolt **(see illustration 24.2)**. Unscrew the bolt securing the rear of the downpipe assembly to the frame **(see illustration 24.2)**.

10 Unscrew the eight downpipe clamp retaining bolts from the cylinder head **(see illustration)**.

11 Supporting the system, remove the silencer mounting bolt, then lower the system from the machine **(see illustration 24.14)**.

12 Remove the gasket from each port in the cylinder head and discard them as new ones must be fitted.

Installation
13 Fit a new gasket into each of the cylinder head ports with the tabs on each gasket facing inwards **(see illustration)**. Apply a smear of grease to the gaskets to keep them in place whilst fitting the downpipe if necessary.

14 Manoeuvre the assembly into position so that the head of each downpipe is located in its port in the cylinder head, then install the silencer mounting bolt and the rear bolt for the downpipe assembly, but do not yet tighten them **(see illustration)**.

15 Install the downpipe clamp bolts and tighten them to the torque setting specified at the beginning of the Chapter **(see illustration)**. Now tighten the other bolts to the specified torque.

16 Run the engine and check that there are no air leaks from the exhaust system.

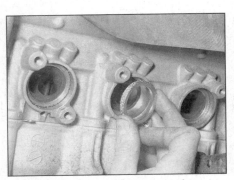

24.13 Fit a new gasket into each port

24.14 Manoeuvre the system into position and locate the rear bolts to support it

24.15 Install the downpipe clamp bolts and tighten them to the specified torque

25 EVAP and PAIR systems
(California models)

Evaporative emission control system (EVAP)

General information

1 This system prevents the escape of fuel vapour into the atmosphere by storing it in a charcoal-filled canister located on the frame right-hand side at the rear **(see illustration)**.
2 When the engine is stopped, fuel vapour from the tank is directed into the canister where it is absorbed and stored whilst the motorcycle is standing. When the engine is started, inlet manifold depression opens the purge control valves, thus drawing vapours which are stored in the canister into the carburettors to be burned during the normal combustion process.
3 The tank vent pipe also incorporates a rollover valve which closes and prevents any fuel from escaping through it in the event of the bike falling over. The tank filler cap has a one way valve which allows air into the tank as the

volume of fuel decreases, but prevents any fuel vapour from escaping.
4 The system is not adjustable and can be properly tested only by a Suzuki dealer. However the owner can check that all the hoses are in good condition and are securely connected at each end. Renew any hoses that are cracked, split or generally deteriorated.
5 The purge control valves can be checked by disconnecting their hoses (noting which way round they fit) and blowing through them. If the valve is working correctly, air should pass through when blowing into the union on the narrower side of the valve, but should not pass through when blowing into the union on the fatter side. When installing the valves, make sure the union on the narrower side is connected to the hose that goes to the canister, and the union on the fatter side is connected to the hose that comes from the carburettor or throttle body.

Removal and installation

6 To access the canister remove the seat cowling (see Chapter 8). Label and disconnect the hoses, remove the clamp screw and take the canister out. Make sure the hoses are correctly reconnected on installation.

7 The two purge control valves and the rollover valve are mounted under the fuel tank.

Pulse secondary air injection system (PAIR)

General information

8 When the engine is running, the depression present in the inlet manifold of No. 2 or No. 3 cylinder (whichever cylinder the hose connects to) acts on a diaphragm in the PAIR control valve, opening the valve. With the control valve open, whenever there is a negative pulse in the exhaust system, filtered fresh air is drawn from the PAIR air cleaner, through the reed valves and into the exhaust ports in the front of the cylinder head.
9 This fresh air promotes the burning of any excess fuel present in the exhaust gases, so reducing the amount of harmful hydrocarbons emitted into the atmosphere via the exhaust gases. Exhaust gases are prevented from passing back into the PAIR system by the reed valves.
10 The system is not adjustable and requires no maintenance, except to ensure that the hoses are in good condition and are securely connected at each end. Renew any hoses that

25.1 EVAP system

are cracked, split or generally deteriorated. Also check the other components for evidence of physical damage. The reed valves can be checked for any build-up of carbon – if any is found, install new reed valves. The control valve should allow air to pass through it only when a vacuum is applied to the vacuum union. As a specific vacuum range is required (270 to 450 mmHg), it is best to have the valve tested by a dealer. On later models, the reed valves and control valve are incorporated into one unit.

Removal and installation

11 Remove the fuel tank for access to the PAIR air cleaner. The control valve and reed valves are located between the radiator and the oil filter on the front of the engine.

12 Before disconnecting any of the components from their mountings, label the hoses to ensure correct reconnection. It is not possible to dismantle or repair any of the PAIR components. If the metal pipes from the reed valve hoses to the cylinder head are removed, always use new gaskets at the cylinder joint on installation.

Chapter 5
Ignition system

Contents

Degrees of difficulty

Easy, suitable for novice with little experience	**Fairly easy,** suitable for beginner with some experience	**Fairly difficult,** suitable for competent DIY mechanic	**Difficult,** suitable for experienced DIY mechanic	**Very difficult,** suitable for expert DIY or professional

Specifications

General information

Firing order	1–2–4–3
Cylinder identification	1–2–3–4, from left to right
Spark plugs	see Chapter 1

Ignition timing

At idle

All GSX-R600 except US and California GSX-R600X/Y	5° BTDC
All GSX-R750 and US and California GSX-R600X/Y	4° BTDC

Ignition rev limiter

GSX-R600	13,400 rpm
GSX-R750	13,200 rpm

Pulse generator coil*

Resistance	50 to 200 ohms

Crankshaft position (CKP) sensor on GSX-R750 W and X models

Ignition HT coils

GSX-R750T and V

Primary winding resistance	2.3 to 3.3 ohms
Secondary winding resistance (with plug lead and cap)	30 to 40 K-ohms

GSX-R600 and GSX-R750W and X

Primary winding resistance	0.07 to 0.11 ohms
Secondary winding resistance	4.5 to 6.9 K-ohms

1 General information

All models are fitted with a fully transistorised electronic ignition system, which due to its lack of mechanical parts is totally maintenance free. The system comprises a rotor, pulse generator coil (crankshaft position sensor on GSX-R750W and X models), electronic control unit and ignition HT coils (refer to the wiring diagrams at the end of Chapter 9 for details).

The triggers on the rotor, which is fitted to the right-hand end of the crankshaft, magnetically operate the pulse generator coil as the crankshaft rotates. The pulse generator coil sends a signal to the ECU (electronic control unit) which then supplies the HT coils with the power necessary to produce a spark at the plugs.

On GSX-R750T and V models, the system uses two coils mounted on the inside of the right-hand frame spar. The top coil supplies Nos. 1 and 4 cylinder spark plugs and the bottom coil supplies Nos. 2 and 3 cylinder plugs.

On all GSX-R600 and GSX-R750W and X models, the coil for each spark plug is incorporated in the spark plug cap.

The ECU incorporates an electronic advance system controlled by signals generated by the pulse generator coil, and a limiter to prevent the engine exceeding its maximum rpm. On all models, the ECU is also supplied with throttle position information from a sensor mounted on No. 4 carburettor or throttle body. On GSX-R750W and X (fuel injected) models, the crankshaft position sensor, gear position sensor and engine coolant temperature sensor also provide information which helps the ECU determine the optimum ignition timing for any situation.

The system incorporates a safety interlock circuit which will cut the ignition if the sidestand is put down whilst the engine is running and in gear, or if a gear is selected whilst the engine is running and the sidestand is down.

Because of their nature, the individual ignition system components can be checked but not repaired. If ignition system troubles occur, and the faulty component can be isolated, the only cure for the problem is to renew the part. Keep in mind that most electrical parts, once purchased, cannot be returned. To avoid unnecessary expense, make very sure the faulty component has been positively identified before buying a renewal part.

Note that there is no provision for checking or adjusting the ignition timing on these models.

2 Ignition system – check

 Warning: The energy levels in electronic systems can be very high. On no account should the ignition be switched on whilst the plugs or plug caps are being held. Shocks from the HT circuit can be most unpleasant. Secondly, it is vital that the engine is not turned over or run with any of the plug caps removed, and that the plugs are soundly earthed (grounded) when the system is checked for sparking. The ignition system components can be seriously damaged if the HT circuit becomes isolated.

1 As no means of adjustment is available, any failure of the system can be traced to failure of a system component or a simple wiring fault. Of the two possibilities, the latter is by far the most likely. In the event of failure, check the system in a logical fashion, as described below.

2 Remove the air filter housing (see Chapter 4). On GSX-R750T and V models, pull the spark plug caps off the spark plugs. On GSX-R600 and GSX-R750W and X models, disconnect the ignition coil/plug cap wiring connectors, then pull the coil/ cap off each spark plug **(see illustrations)**. Connect each cap to a spare spark plug and lay each plug on the engine with the threads contacting the engine **(see illustration)**. If necessary, hold each spark plug with an insulated tool. Do not hold the plug against the valve cover or any other engine cover that is magnesium coated as the coating could be damaged.

 Warning: Do not remove any of the spark plugs from the engine to perform this check – atomised fuel being pumped out of the open spark plug hole could ignite, causing severe injury!

3 Having observed the above precautions, check that the kill switch is in the RUN position and the transmission is in neutral, then turn the ignition switch ON and turn the engine over on the starter motor. If the system is in good condition a regular, fat blue spark should be evident at each plug electrode. If the spark appears thin or yellowish, or is non-existent, further investigation will be necessary. Before proceeding further, turn the ignition off and remove the key as a safety measure.

4 The ignition system must be able to produce a spark which is capable of jumping a particular size gap. Suzuki specify that a healthy system should produce a spark capable of jumping 8 mm. A simple testing tool can be made to test the minimum gap across which the spark will jump (see **Tool Tip**) or alternatively it is possible to buy an ignition spark gap tester tool and some of these tools are adjustable to alter the spark gap.

5 Connect one of the spark plug caps to the protruding electrode on the test tool, and clip the tool to a good earth (ground) on the

2.2a Disconnect the wiring connector ...

2.2b ... then pull the coil/plug cap off the spark plug

2.2c Ground (earth) the spark plug and operate the starter – bright blue sparks should be visible

TOOL TiP

A simple spark gap testing tool can be made from a block of wood, a large alligator clip and two nails, one of which is fashioned so that a spark plug cap or bare HT lead end can be connected to its end. Make sure the gap between the two nail ends is the same as specified

2.5 Connect the tester as shown – when the engine is cranked sparks should jump the gap between the nails

engine or frame (see illustration). Check that the kill switch is in the RUN position, turn the ignition switch ON and turn the engine over on the starter motor. If the system is in good condition a regular, fat blue spark should be seen to jump the gap between the nail ends. Repeat the test for the other coil or coil/caps, as applicable. If the test results are good the entire ignition system can be considered good. If the spark appears thin or yellowish, or is non-existent, further investigation will be necessary.

6 Ignition faults can be divided into two categories, namely those where the ignition system has failed completely, and those which are due to a partial failure. The likely faults are listed below, starting with the most probable source of failure. Work through the list systematically, referring to the subsequent sections for full details of the necessary checks and tests. **Note:** *Before checking the following items ensure that the battery is fully charged and that all fuses are in good condition.*

a) *Loose, corroded or damaged wiring connections, broken or shorted wiring between any of the component parts of the ignition system (see Chapter 9).*

b) *Faulty HT lead or spark plug cap (GSX-R750T and V only), faulty spark plug, dirty, worn or corroded plug electrodes, or incorrect gap between electrodes.*

c) *Faulty ignition (main) switch or engine kill switch (see Chapter 9).*

d) *Faulty clutch, neutral or sidestand switch (see Chapter 9).*

e) *Faulty pulse generator coil or damaged rotor.*

f) *Faulty ignition HT coil(s) - GSX-R750T and V only.*

g) *Faulty electronic control unit.*

7 If the above checks don't reveal the cause of the problem, have the ignition system tested by a Suzuki dealer.

3 Ignition HT coils – check, removal and installation

Check

1 In order to determine conclusively that the ignition coils are defective, they should be tested by a Suzuki dealer.

2 However, the coils can be checked visually (for cracks and other damage) and the primary and secondary coil resistances can be measured with a multimeter. If the coils are undamaged, and if the resistance readings are as specified at the beginning of the Chapter, they are probably capable of proper operation.

3 Remove the rider's seat (see Chapter 8) and disconnect the battery negative (-ve) lead. To gain access to the coils, remove the air filter housing (see Chapter 4). On GSX-R750T and V models, the coils are mounted on the inside of the right-hand frame spar. The top coil supplies Nos. 1 and 4 cylinder spark plugs and the bottom coil supplies Nos. 2 and 3 cylinder plugs. On all GSX-R600 and GSX-R750W and X models, the coil for each spark plug is incorporated in the spark plug cap.

GSX-R750T and V models

4 Disconnect the primary circuit electrical connectors from the coil being tested and the pull the spark plug caps off the spark plugs. Mark the locations of all wires and leads before disconnecting them.

5 Set the meter to the ohms x 1 scale and measure the resistance between the primary circuit terminals (see illustration). This will give a resistance reading of the primary windings and should be consistent with the value given in the Specifications at the beginning of the Chapter.

6 To check the condition of the secondary windings, set the meter to the K-ohm scale. Connect one meter probe to one spark plug cap

and the other probe to the other spark plug cap (see illustration 3.5). If the reading obtained is not within the range shown in the Specifications, it is possible that the coil is defective, though it could be a spark plug cap or HT lead. The caps are available separately, but the leads are integral with the coil. Suzuki provide no test specifications for the caps, but it is worth substituting a known good one from another cylinder before consigning the coil to the bin.

7 Should any of the above checks not produce the expected result, have your findings confirmed by a Suzuki dealer. If the coil is confirmed to be faulty, it must be renewed; the coil is a sealed unit and cannot therefore be repaired.

GSX-R600 and GSX-R750W and X models

8 Disconnect the ignition coil/plug cap wiring connectors (see illustration 2.2a). Pull the coil/cap off each spark plug (see illustration 2.2b).

9 Set the meter to the ohms x 1 scale and measure the resistance between the primary circuit terminals on the coil/cap (see illustration). This will give a resistance reading of the primary windings and should be consistent with the value given in the Specifications at the beginning of the Chapter.

10 To check the condition of the secondary windings, set the meter to the K-ohm scale. Connect one meter probe to the negative primary circuit terminal and the other probe to the spark plug cap (see illustration). If the reading obtained is not within the range shown in the Specifications, it is possible that the coil is defective.

11 Should any of the above checks not produce the expected result, have your findings confirmed by a Suzuki dealer. If the coil is confirmed to be faulty, it must be renewed; the coil is a sealed unit and cannot therefore be repaired.

Removal

12 Remove the rider's seat (see Chapter 8) and disconnect the battery negative (-ve) lead, then remove the air filter housing (see Chapter 4).

13 On GSX-R750T and V models, disconnect the primary circuit electrical connectors from the coils and pull the spark plug caps off the spark plugs. Mark the locations of all wires and leads before disconnecting them.

3.5 Ignition HT coil test connections
A Primary winding test
B Secondary winding test

3.9 To test the primary circuit resistance, connect the multimeter as shown

3.10 To test the secondary circuit resistance, connect the multimeter as shown

4.2 Disconnect the pulse generator coil wiring connector (arrowed)

4.8 Remove the mounting plate screws (A) and the clamp screw (B), and free the grommet (C) from its cutout

4.10 Install the pulse generator coil . . .

Unscrew the two bolts securing each coil, noting the position of the spacers, and remove the coils. Note the routing of the HT leads.

14 On all GSX-R600 and GSX-R750W and X models, disconnect the ignition coil/plug cap wiring connectors **(see illustration 2.2a)**. Pull the coil/cap off each spark plug **(see illustration 2.2b)**.

Installation

15 Installation is the reverse of removal. Make sure the wiring connectors and HT leads are securely connected.

4 Pulse generator coil assembly – check, removal and installation

Note: *The pulse generator coil is termed the crankshaft position (CKP) sensor on the GSX-R750W and X models.*

Check

1 Remove the seat cowling (see Chapter 8) and disconnect the battery negative (-ve) lead.
2 Trace the pulse generator coil wiring back from the top of the right-hand side crankcase cover and disconnect it at the 2-pin connector with the black and green wires **(see illustration)**. Using a multimeter set to the ohms x 100 scale, measure the resistance between the terminals on the pulse generator coil side of the connector.
3 Compare the reading obtained with that given in the Specifications at the beginning of this Chapter. The pulse generator coil must be renewed if the reading obtained differs greatly

from that given, particularly if the meter indicates a short circuit (no measurable resistance) or an open circuit (infinite, or very high resistance).
4 If the pulse generator coil is thought to be faulty, first check that this is not due to a damaged or broken wire from the coil to the connector; pinched or broken wires can usually be repaired. Note that the coil is not available individually but comes as an assembly with the mounting plate and wiring.

Removal

5 Remove the seat cowling (see Chapter 8) and disconnect the battery negative (-ve) lead.
6 Trace the pulse generator coil switch wiring back from the top of the right-hand side crankcase cover and disconnect it at the 2-pin connector with the black and green wires **(see illustration 4.2)**. Free the wiring from any clips or ties and feed it through to its exit hole.
7 Remove the starter clutch (see Chapter 2).
8 Remove the screws securing the pulse generator coil assembly mounting plate to the crankcase cover and the screw securing the wiring clamp **(see illustration)**. Remove the rubber wiring grommet from its recess, then remove the coil assembly, noting how it fits.
9 Examine the rotor for signs of damage and install a new one if necessary (see Chapter 2, Section 9).

Installation

10 Install the pulse generator coil assembly onto the crankcase and tighten its screws securely **(see illustration)**.
11 Apply a smear of sealant to the rubber

wiring seal and fit the grommet in its recess in the crankcase **(see illustration)**. Locate the wiring under its clamp and tighten the clamp screw **(see illustration 4.8)**.
12 Install the starter clutch (see Chapter 2).
13 Route the wiring up to the connector and reconnect it **(see illustration 4.2)**. Secure the wiring in its clips or ties.
14 Reconnect the battery negative (-ve) lead and install the seat cowling (see Chapter 8).

5 Electronic control unit (ECU) – check, removal and installation

Check

1 If the tests shown in the preceding Sections have failed to isolate the cause of an ignition fault, it is likely that the electronic control unit itself is faulty. No test details are available with which the unit can be tested on home workshop equipment. Take the machine to a Suzuki dealer for testing.

Removal

2 Remove the rider's seat (see Chapter 8) and disconnect the battery negative (-ve) lead.
3 Disconnect the wiring connectors from the electronic control unit **(see illustrations)**.
4 Free the control unit from its mounting and remove it.

Installation

5 Installation is the reverse of removal. Make sure the wiring connectors are correctly and securely connected.

4.11 . . . and fit the grommet into its cutout

5.3a Electronic control unit – GSX-R600 and GSX-R750T and V

5.3b Electronic control unit – GSX-R750W and X

Chapter 6
Frame, suspension and final drive

Contents

Degrees of difficulty

Easy, suitable for novice with little experience	**Fairly easy,** suitable for beginner with some experience	**Fairly difficult,** suitable for competent DIY mechanic 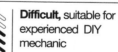	**Difficult,** suitable for experienced DIY mechanic	**Very difficult,** suitable for expert DIY or professional

Specifications

Front forks

Fork oil type	SAE 10W fork oil
Fork oil capacity	
GSX-R600	533 cc
GSX-R750T and V	480 cc
GSX-R750W and X	490 cc
Fork oil level*	
GSX-R600	110 mm
GSX-R750T and V	105 mm
GSX-R750W and X	99 mm
Fork spring free length (min)	
GSX-R600V	251 mm
GSX-R600W, X and Y	261 mm
GSX-R750	250 mm
Fork tube runout limit	0.2 mm
Fork tube protrusion above top yoke (not inc. top bolt)	
GSX-R600	3.2 mm
GSX-R750	2.0 mm

*Oil level is measured from the top of the tube with the fork spring removed and the leg fully compressed.

Rear suspension

Swingarm pivot bolt runout (max) . . . .   0.3 mm

Final drive

Chain type
  GSX-R600 . . . .   RK525SMOZ2 (108 links, endless)
  GSX-R750T and V . . . .   RK50MFOZ1 (108 links, soft-link)
  GSX-R750W and X . . . .   RK525ROZ2 (108 links, soft-link)
Distance between outside of joining link and side plate (unstaked)
  (RK chain) – 750 models . . . .   21.85 to 22.15 mm
Joining link staked ends diameter (RK chain) – 750 models . . . .   5.45 to 5.85 mm

Torque settings

Front footrest bracket bolts	39 Nm
Steering stem nut	90 Nm
Fork clamp bolts (top and bottom yoke)	23 Nm
Handlebar set bolts	10 Nm
Handlebar clamp bolts	23 Nm
Front master cylinder clamp bolts	10 Nm
Fork top bolt	35 Nm
Damper rod Allen bolt	35 Nm
Damper rod locknut	20 Nm
Steering head bearing adjuster nut (see text)	45 Nm
Steering head bearing locknut	80 Nm
Steering stem nut	90 Nm
Shock absorber upper mounting bracket nut	
GSX-R750T	85 Nm
All other models	115 Nm
Rear shock absorber nut/bolt	50 Nm
Rear suspension linkage arm and linkage rod nuts	78 Nm
Swingarm pivot boss nuts (750 models)	65 Nm
Swingarm pivot bolt	15 Nm
Swingarm pivot nut	100 Nm
Swingarm pivot bolt locknut	90 Nm
Front sprocket nut	120 Nm
Speedometer rotor bolt	13 Nm
Rear sprocket nuts	60 Nm

---

1 General information

All models use a twin spar box-section aluminium frame which uses the engine as a stressed member.

Front suspension is by a pair of oil-damped telescopic forks. On GSX-R600 models, the forks have a cartridge damper and are adjustable for spring pre-load and rebound damping on all models, and also for compression damping on W, X and Y models. On GSX-R750 models, the forks are upside-down with a cartridge damper and are adjustable for spring pre-load, rebound and compression damping on all models.

At the rear, an alloy swingarm acts on a single shock absorber via a three-way linkage. The shock absorber is adjustable for spring pre-load, rebound and compression damping on all models.

The drive to the rear wheel is by chain. GSX-R600 models use an endless chain, while 750 models use a soft-link type due to the construction of the swingarm.

2 Frame – inspection and repair

1 The frame should not require attention unless accident damage has occurred. In most cases, frame renewal is the only satisfactory remedy for such damage. A few frame specialists have the jigs and other equipment necessary for straightening the frame to the required standard of accuracy, but even then there is no simple way of assessing to what extent the frame may have been over stressed.

2 After the machine has accumulated a lot of miles, the frame should be examined closely for signs of cracking or splitting at the welded joints. Loose engine mount bolts can cause ovaling or fracturing of the mounting tabs. Minor damage can often be repaired by welding, depending on the extent and nature of the damage.

3 Remember that a frame which is out of alignment will cause handling problems. If misalignment is suspected as the result of an accident, it will be necessary to strip the machine completely so the frame can be thoroughly checked.

3 Footrests, brake pedal and gearchange lever – removal and installation

Rider's footrests
Removal
1 Remove the split pin from the bottom of the footrest pivot pin, then withdraw the pivot pin and remove the footrest, noting the fitting of the return spring and spacer **(see illustration)**.

3.1 Remove the split pin (A) and withdraw the pin from the top. Note how the return spring ends (B) locate

3.3 Remove the E-clip (A) and withdraw the pin from the top. Note how the detent plate, ball and spring (B) locate

3.5 Unscrew the bolts (arrowed) and displace the bracket

3.6 Free the return spring end (A), remove the split pin and washer (B), and the clevis pin (C), then unscrew the bolt (D)

Installation

2 Installation is the reverse of removal.

Passenger footrests

Removal

3 Remove the E-clip from the bottom of the footrest pivot pin, then withdraw the pivot pin and remove the footrest, noting the fitting of the detent plate, ball and spring, and take care that they do not spring out when removing the footrest **(see illustration)**.

Installation

4 Installation is the reverse of removal.

Brake pedal

Removal

5 The pedal pivots on the footrest holder. Unscrew the two bolts securing the footrest bracket to the frame, then lift the bracket to dislodge the brake light switch spring and turn it round to access the inside **(see illustration)**.
6 Unhook the brake pedal return spring **(see illustration)**.
7 Remove the split pin and washer from the clevis pin securing the brake pedal to the master cylinder pushrod **(see illustration 3.6)**. Remove the clevis pin and separate the pedal from the pushrod.
8 Remove the bolt on the inside of the footrest bracket and remove the footrest, its

holder and the brake pedal, then slide the pedal off the holder **(see illustration 3.6)**.

Installation

9 Installation is the reverse of removal, noting the following:
a) *Apply molybdenum disulphide grease to the brake pedal pivot.*
b) *Align the flat on the footrest holder with that in the bracket.*
c) *Apply a suitable non-permanent thread locking compound to the footrest holder bolt and tighten it securely.*
d) *Use a new split pin on the clevis pin securing the brake pedal to the master cylinder pushrod.*
e) *Tighten the footrest bracket bolts to the torque setting specified at the beginning of the Chapter.*
f) *Check the operation of the rear brake light switch (see Chapter 1).*

Gearchange lever

Removal

10 Slacken the gearchange lever linkage rod locknuts, then unscrew the rod and separate it from the lever and the arm (the rod is reverse-threaded on one end and so will simultaneously unscrew from both lever and arm when turned in the one direction) **(see illustration)**. Note the how far the rod is threaded into the lever and arm as this determines the height of the lever relative to the footrest.

11 The lever pivots on the footrest holder. Unscrew the two bolts securing the footrest bracket to the frame and turn it round to access the holder bolt **(see illustrations)**. Unscrew the bolt and remove the footrest, its holder and the lever, then slide the lever off the holder.

Installation

12 Installation is the reverse of removal, noting the following:
a) *Apply molybdenum disulphide grease to the gear lever pivot.*
b) *Align the flat on the footrest holder with that in the bracket.*
c) *Apply a suitable non-permanent thread locking compound to the footrest holder bolt and tighten it securely.*
d) *Tighten the footrest bracket bolts to the torque setting specified at the beginning of the Chapter.*
e) *Adjust the gear lever height as required by screwing the rod in or out of the lever and arm. Tighten the locknuts securely.*

4 Sidestand – removal and installation

1 The sidestand is attached to a bracket on the frame. Springs between the bracket and the stand ensure that it is held in the retracted or extended position.

3.10 Slacken the locknuts (arrowed) and unscrew the rod

3.11a Unscrew the bolts (arrowed) and displace the bracket . . .

3.11b . . . to access the bolt (arrowed) on the inside

4.3a Unscrew the nut (arrowed) and remove the pivot bolt . . .

4.3b . . . and free the spring ends

5.1 Disconnect the brake light switch wiring connectors (arrowed)

2 Support the bike using an auxiliary stand. If required, remove the sidestand switch (see Chapter 9).

3 Unscrew the pivot bolt nut, then remove the pivot bolt from the inside of the bracket and remove the stand, releasing the springs as you do **(see illustrations)**.

4 If required, unscrew the bolts securing the sidestand bracket to the frame and remove the bracket, noting that the top bolt is also the engine lower rear mounting bolt **(see illustration 4.4a)**. This must be tightened to the torque setting specified at the beginning of Chapter 2 on installation.

5 On installation apply grease to the pivot bolt shank and tighten the nut securely. Check that the sidestand springs hold the stand securely up when not in use – an

accident is almost certain to occur if the stand extends while the machine is in motion.

6 Check the operation of the sidestand switch (see Chapter 1).

5 Handlebars and levers – removal and installation

Right handlebar removal

1 Disconnect the brake light switch wires from the switch on the underside of the master cylinder assembly **(see illustration)**. Free the handlebar switch wiring from its guide under the top yoke **(see illustration 8.2)**. Release the throttle cables from

the throttle pulley (see Chapter 4). Position the switch housing away from the handlebar.

2 Unscrew the two front brake master cylinder assembly clamp bolts and the bolt securing the reservoir to the handlebar and position the assembly clear, making sure no strain is placed on the hydraulic hose **(see illustration)**. Keep the master cylinder reservoir upright to prevent possible fluid leakage.

3 Slacken both the fork clamp bolts in the top yoke **(see illustration)**. Unscrew the set bolt securing the handlebar clamp to the top yoke **(see illustration)**. Unscrew and remove the steering stem nut and remove the washer **(see illustration)**.

4 Raise the fuel tank and remove the air filter housing (see Chapter 4). Disconnect the ignition switch wiring connector to provide some slack and free the wiring from any clips or ties **(see illustration)**. Gently ease the top yoke upwards off the fork tubes and position it clear, using a rag to protect other components.

5 Slacken the handlebar clamp bolt, then ease the handlebar up and off the fork **(see illustration 5.3a)**. If necessary, unscrew the handlebar end-weight retaining screw, then remove the weight from the end of the handlebar and slide off the throttle twistgrip.

Left handlebar removal

6 Disconnect the clutch switch wiring connector from the switch on the clutch lever

5.2 Unscrew the clamp bolts (A) and the reservoir bolt (B)

5.3a Fork clamp bolt (A). Handlebar clamp bolt (B)

5.3b Handlebar set bolt (arrowed)

5.3c Steering stem nut (arrowed)

5.4 Ignition switch wiring connector (arrowed)

5.6 Clutch switch wiring connector (A), clutch cable adjuster (B)

5.7 Slacken the bracket bolt (arrowed)

5.11 Align the clamp mating surfaces with the punchmark (arrowed)

bracket **(see illustration)**. Free the handlebar switch wiring from its guide under the top yoke **(see illustration 8.2)**. Release the choke cable from the lever (see Chapter 4). Position the switch housing away from the handlebar.

7 Screw the clutch cable adjuster fully into the lever bracket **(see illustration 5.6)**. Align the slot in the adjuster with that in the bracket, then pull the outer cable end from the socket in the adjuster and release the inner cable from the lever. If there is not enough slack in the cable to free it from the adjuster, remove the clutch lever (see below). Slacken the clutch lever bracket bolt **(see illustration)**.

8 Slacken the fork clamp bolts in the top yoke **(see illustration 5.3a)**. Unscrew the set bolt securing the handlebar clamp to the top yoke **(see illustration 5.3b)**. Unscrew and remove the steering stem nut and remove the washer **(see illustration 5.3c)**.

9 Raise the fuel tank and remove the air filter housing (see Chapter 4). Disconnect the ignition switch wiring connector to provide some slack and free the wiring from any clips or ties **(see illustration 5.4)**. Gently ease the top yoke upwards off the fork tubes and position it clear, using a rag to protect other components.

10 Slacken the handlebar clamp bolt **(see illustration 5.3a)**, then ease the handlebar up and off the fork. If necessary, unscrew the handlebar end-weight retaining screw, then remove the weight from the end of the handlebar and remove the grip. It may be necessary to slit the grip open using a sharp

blade in order to remove it as they are usually stuck in place. This will mean using a new grip on assembly. The clutch lever bracket can now be slid off the handlebar.

Handlebar installation

11 Installation is the reverse of removal, noting the following.

a) *Do not tighten the handlebar clamp bolt until the top yoke has been installed, and tighten the set bolt securing the handlebar to the yoke before the handlebar clamp bolt.*

b) *Refer to the Specifications at the beginning of the Chapter and tighten the steering stem nut, the fork clamp bolts, the handlebar set bolt and the handlebar clamp bolt to the specified torque settings, in that order.*

c) *Make sure the front brake lever assembly clamp is installed with the UP mark facing up, and align the clamp mating surface with the punchmark on the top of the handlebar (see illustration and 5.2). Tighten the brake master cylinder clamp bolts to the torque setting specified at the beginning of the Chapter.*

d) *Refer to Chapter 4 for installation of the throttle and choke cables. Make sure the pin in the upper half of each switch housing locates in the hole in the top of the handlebar.*

e) *If removed, apply a suitable non-permanent locking compound to the*

handlebar end-weight retaining screws. If new grips are being fitted, secure them using a suitable adhesive.

f) *Do not forget to reconnect the front brake light switch and clutch switch wiring connectors.*

Clutch lever removal

12 Screw the clutch cable adjuster fully into the lever bracket to provide maximum freeplay in the cable **(see illustration)**. Unscrew the lever pivot bolt locknut, then unscrew the pivot bolt and remove the lever, detaching the cable nipple as you do.

Front brake lever removal

13 Unscrew the lever pivot bolt locknut, then unscrew the pivot bolt and remove the lever **(see illustrations)**.

Lever installation

14 Installation is the reverse of removal. Apply grease to the pivot bolt shafts and the contact areas between the lever and its bracket, and to the clutch cable nipple. Adjust the clutch cable freeplay (see Chapter 1).

| 6 | Forks –
removal and installation |

Removal

1 Remove the fairing and the fairing side panels (see Chapter 4).

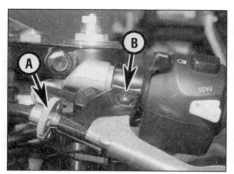

5.12 Clutch cable adjuster (A), lever pivot bolt (B)

5.13a Unscrew the locknut (arrowed) . . .

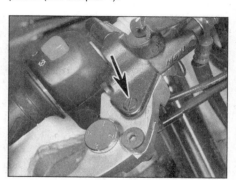

5.13b . . . then unscrew the pivot bolt (arrowed)

6.4 Slacken the fork top bolt if required

6.5a Slacken the fork clamp bolts (arrowed) in the bottom yoke . . .

6.5b . . . and remove the fork

2 Remove the front wheel (see Chapter 7) and the mudguard (see Chapter 8). Work on each fork individually.

3 Slacken the handlebar clamp bolt, the handlebar set bolt and the fork clamp bolt in the top yoke **(see illustrations 5.3a and b)**. Depending on the tools available, access to the right-hand fork clamp bolt may be restricted by the front brake reservoir bracket. If this is the case, unscrew the bracket bolt and displace the reservoir from the handlebar, making sure it stays upright and no strain is placed on the hose.

4 If the forks are to be disassembled, or if the fork oil is being changed, it is advisable at this stage to slacken the fork top bolt **(see illustration)**.

5 Slacken but do not remove the fork clamp bolts in the bottom yoke, and remove the fork by twisting it and pulling it downwards **(see illustrations)**. Make sure the handlebar clamp does not get cocked in the fork as it is withdrawn as the lug for the set bolt could shear.

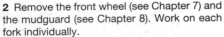

HAYNES HINT *If the fork legs are seized in the yokes, spray the area with penetrating oil and allow time for it to soak in before trying again.*

Installation

6 Remove all traces of corrosion from the fork tubes and the yokes. Install each fork individually. Slide the fork up through the bottom yoke and the handlebar and up into the top yoke, and set the fork in the yoke so that the amount of protrusion of the fork tube

above the top yoke is as specified at the beginning of the Chapter, and equal on both sides **(see illustrations)**.

7 Tighten the fork clamp bolts in the bottom yoke to the torque setting specified at the beginning of the Chapter **(see illustration)**. If the fork has been dismantled or if the fork oil has been changed, the fork top bolt should now be tightened to the specified torque setting **(see illustration)**. Now tighten the fork clamp bolt in the top yoke, the handlebar set bolt and the handlebar clamp bolt to the specified torque setting **(see illustration)**.

8 If displaced, position the front brake reservoir on the handlebar and tighten the bracket bolt securely.

9 Install the front mudguard (see Chapter 8), and the front wheel (see Chapter 7).

10 Install the fairing and fairing side panels (see Chapter 8).

11 Check the operation of the front forks and brakes before taking the machine out on the road.

---

7 Forks – disassembly, inspection and reassembly

GSX-R600 models
Disassembly

1 Always dismantle the fork legs separately to avoid interchanging parts and thus causing an accelerated rate of wear. Store all

6.6a Slide the fork up through the yokes and handlebar . . .

6.6b . . . and set it to the correct height

6.7a Tighten the bottom yoke clamp bolts . . .

6.7b . . . the fork top bolt (if necessary) . . .

6.7c . . . the top yoke clamp bolt and handlebar bolts to the specified torque settings

1 Top bolt
2 O-ring
3 Pre-load adjuster
4 O-ring
5 Slotted collar
6 Washer
7 Spacer
8 Spring seat
9 Spring
10 O-ring
11 Damping adjuster
12 Locknut
13 Damper rod/cartridge
14 Fork tube
15 Bottom bush
16 Dust seal
17 Retaining clip
18 Oil seal
19 Washer
20 Top bush
21 Damper rod/cartridge seat
22 Fork slider
23 Damper rod bolt and sealing
    washer

H31258

7.1 Front fork components – GSX-R600

components in separate, clearly marked containers **(see illustration)**.

2 Before dismantling the fork, it is advised that the damper rod bolt be slackened at this stage. Compress the fork tube in the slider so that the spring exerts maximum pressure on the damper rod head, then have an assistant slacken the damper rod bolt in the base of the fork slider **(see illustration)**. If an assistant is not available, clamp the brake caliper lugs on the fork slider between the padded jaws of a vice.

3 If the fork top bolt was not slackened with the fork in situ, carefully clamp the fork tube between the padded jaws of a vice, taking care not to overtighten or score its surface, and slacken the top bolt **(see illustration 7.4)**.

4 Unscrew the fork top bolt from the top of the fork tube **(see illustration)**. The pre-load adjuster will remain threaded on the damper rod.

5 Carefully clamp the brake caliper lugs on the fork slider between the padded jaws of a vice and slide the fork tube down into the slider a little way (wrap a rag around the top of the tube to minimise oil spillage). Now grasp the spacer while, with the aid of an assistant if necessary, keep the damper rod fully extended and press down on the spacer, thereby compressing the spring, to expose the locknut, and slip a spanner onto it **(see illustration)**. Counter-hold the pre-load adjuster, then slacken the locknut and thread it to the base of its threads **(see illustration)**. Now counter-hold the locknut and

7.2 Slacken the damper rod bolt

7.4 Unscrew the fork top bolt

7.5a Push the spacer down to expose the locknut (arrowed)

7.5b Counter-hold the pre-load adjuster and slacken the locknut

7.5c Draw the top bolt assembly out of the fork

7.8 Unscrew and remove the damper rod bolt

7.10 Prise out the dust seal using a flat-bladed screwdriver

thread the pre-load adjuster with the top bolt off the damper rod. Lift the top bolt assembly out of the fork **(see illustration)**. If you want to disassemble the damping adjuster/pre-load adjuster/top bolt assembly, thread the top bolt off the top of the pre-load adjuster, then counter-hold the pre-load adjuster and screw the damping adjuster into and out of the bottom of the pre-load adjuster. If this is done, discard the O-rings as new ones should be used.

6 Remove the slotted collar by slipping it out to the side **(see illustration 7.28)**, then remove the washer, the spacer and the spring seat **(see illustrations 7.27d, c and b)**. Withdraw the spring from the tube, noting which way up it fits **(see illustration 7.27a)**.

7.11 Prise out the retaining clip using a flat-bladed screwdriver

7 Invert the fork leg over a suitable container and pump the fork and damper rod vigorously to expel as much fork oil as possible.

8 Remove the previously slackened damper rod bolt and its sealing washer from the bottom of the slider **(see illustration)**. Discard the washer as a new one must be used on reassembly.

9 Invert the fork and withdraw the damper rod from inside the fork tube **(see illustration 7.25a)**. The damper rod seat may come away with the rod, otherwise remove it later.

10 Carefully prise out the dust seal from the top of the slider to gain access to the oil seal retaining clip **(see illustration)**. Discard the dust seal as a new one must be used.

11 Carefully remove the retaining clip, taking care not to scratch the surface of the tube **(see illustration)**.

12 To separate the tube from the slider it is necessary to displace the top bush and oil seal. The bottom bush should not pass through the top bush, and this can be used to good effect. Push the tube gently inwards until it stops against the damper rod seat. Take care not to do this forcibly or the seat may be damaged. Then pull the tube sharply outwards until the bottom bush strikes the top bush **(see illustration)**. Repeat this operation until the top bush and seal are tapped out of the slider.

13 With the tube removed, slide off the oil seal, washer and top bush, noting which way

up they fit **(see illustration)**. Discard the oil seal as a new one must be used.

Caution: Do not remove the bottom bush from the tube unless it is to be renewed.

14 If the damper rod seat did not come out with the rod, tip it out of the slider, noting which way up it fits. On W, X and Y models, discard the O-ring as a new one should be used.

Inspection

15 Clean all parts in solvent and blow them dry with compressed air, if available. Check the fork tube for score marks, scratches, flaking of the chrome finish and excessive or abnormal wear. Look for dents in the tube and renew the tube in both forks if any are found. Check the fork seal seat for nicks, gouges and scratches. If damage is evident, leaks will occur. Also check the oil seal washer for damage or distortion and renew it if necessary.

16 Check the fork tube for runout using V-blocks and a dial gauge, or have it done by a Suzuki dealer or suspension specialist **(see illustration)**. If the amount of runout exceeds the service limit specified, the tube should be renewed.

⚠️ *Warning: If the tube is bent or exceeds the runout limit, it should not be straightened; renew it with a new one.*

7.12 To separate the fork tube and slider, pull them apart firmly several times – the slide-hammer action will pull them apart

7.13 The oil seal (1), washer (2), top bush (3) and bottom bush (4) will come out with the fork tube

7.16 Check the fork tube for runout using V-blocks and a dial gauge

7.18 Prise the bottom bush apart at its split using a flat-bladed screwdriver

7.20 Slide the fork tube into the slider

7.21a Install the top bush . . .

17 Check the spring for cracks and other damage. Measure the spring free length and compare the measurement to the specifications at the beginning of the Chapter. If it is defective or sagged below the service limit, renew the springs in both forks with new ones. Never renew only one spring.

18 Examine the working surfaces of the two bushes; if worn or scuffed they must be renewed. Suzuki recommend new ones are fitted as a matter of course. To remove the bottom bush from the fork tube, prise it apart at the slit using a flat-bladed screwdriver and slide it off **(see illustration)**. Make sure the new one seats properly.

19 Check the damper rod cartridge assembly for damage and wear, and renew it if necessary. Holding the outside of the cartridge, gently pump the rod in and out of the damper. If the rod does not move smoothly in the damper it must be renewed.

Reassembly

20 Oil the fork tube and bottom bush with the specified fork oil and insert the assembly into the slider **(see illustration)**.

21 Push the fork tube fully into the slider, then oil the top bush and slide it down over the tube **(see illustration)**. Press the bush squarely into its recess in the slider as far as possible, then install the oil seal washer with its flat side facing up **(see illustration)**. Either use the service tool (Pt. No. 09940-52861) or a suitable piece of tubing to tap the bush fully

7.21b . . . followed by the washer

into place; the tubing must be slightly larger in diameter than the fork tube and slightly smaller in diameter than the bush recess in the slider. Take care not to scratch the fork tube during this operation; it is best to make sure that the fork tube is pushed fully into the slider so that any accidental scratching is confined to the area above the oil seal.

22 When the bush is seated fully and squarely in its recess in the slider, (remove the washer to check, wipe the recess clean, then reinstall the washer), install the new oil seal. Smear the seal's lips with fork oil and slide it over the tube so that its markings face upwards and drive the seal into place as described in Step 21 until the retaining clip groove is visible above the seal **(see illustration)**.

23 Once the seal is correctly seated, fit the

7.22 Make sure the oil seal is the correct way up

> **HAYNES HiNT** *Place the old oil seal on top of the new one to protect it when driving the seal into place.*

retaining clip, making sure it is correctly located in its groove **(see illustration)**.

24 Lubricate the lips of the new dust seal then slide it down the fork tube and press it into position **(see illustration)**.

25 On W, X and Y models, fit a new O-ring onto the bottom of the damper rod seat. On all models, fit the damper rod seat onto the bottom of the rod. Keeping the assembly vertical to prevent the damper rod seat dropping out, insert the damper rod cartridge into the fork tube and slide it fully down **(see illustration)**. Fit

7.23 Install the retaining clip . . .

7.24 . . . followed by the dust seal

7.25a Slide the damper rod cartridge into the fork tube

7.25b Apply a thread locking compound to the damper rod bolt and use a new sealing washer

7.25c Use wire as shown to keep the damper rod extended

7.26a Pour the oil into the top of the tube

a new copper sealing washer to the damper rod bolt and apply a few drops of a suitable non-permanent thread locking compound, then install the bolt into the bottom of the slider **(see illustration)**. Tighten the bolt to the specified torque setting. If the damper rod cartridge rotates inside the tube, temporarily install the spring, spacer and fork top bolt and compress the fork leg to hold the assembly in place, then remove them when the bolt has been tightened. As the damper rod will have to be kept extended out of the slider later on, it is worth at this stage securing a piece of wire around the base of the locknut on the top of the rod to use as a holder **(see illustration)**.

26 Slowly pour in the specified quantity of specified grade of fork oil and pump the fork and

damper rod at least ten times each to distribute it evenly and expel all the air **(see illustration)**. It may be necessary to pump the fork and rod even more, or to hold the fork upright for several minutes, before all the air bleeds out. The oil level should also be measured – fully compress the fork tube and damper rod into the slider and measure the fork oil level from the top of the tube **(see illustration)**. Add or subtract fork oil until it is at the level specified at the beginning of the Chapter.

27 Clamp the brake caliper lugs on the slider between the padded jaws of a vice, taking care not to overtighten and damage them. Pull the fork tube and damper rod out of the slider as far as possible then install the spring with its tapered end downwards **(see illustration)**.

Install the spring seat, the spacer and the washer **(see illustrations)**.

28 Keeping the damper rod fully extended, slide the slotted collar into position between the washer and the nut on the damper rod – it may be necessary to compress the spring slightly by pushing down on the spacer to provide the clearance **(see illustration)**. You can now remove the piece of wire, if used.

29 If the damping adjuster/pre-load adjuster/top bolt assembly was disassembled, fit a new O-ring onto the damping adjuster rod and thread it into the pre-load adjuster so that it protrudes approximately 1.5 mm from the top. Fit a new O-ring onto the pre-load adjuster and thread the fork top bolt onto it.

30 Fit a new O-ring onto the fork top bolt,

7.26b Measure the oil level with the fork held vertical

7.27a Install the spring . . .

7.27b . . . followed by the spring seat . . .

7.27c . . . the spacer . . .

7.27d . . . and the washer

7.28 Slip the slotted collar under the locknut

7.30 Slide the damping adjuster into the damper rod

then insert the damping adjuster/pre-load adjuster/top bolt assembly into the top of the damper rod and slide it fully down **(see illustration)**. Thread the pre-load adjuster onto the damper rod, holding the rod to prevent it from turning, until the wider section of the damping adjuster just seats on the top of the damper rod. Counter-hold the pre-load adjuster and tighten the locknut securely against it, to the specified torque if the correct tools are available **(see illustration 7.5b)**.

31 Withdraw the tube fully from the slider and carefully screw the top bolt into the fork tube making sure it is not cross-threaded **(see illustration 7.3)**. Note: *The top bolt can be tightened to the specified torque setting at this stage if the tube is held between the padded jaws of a vice, but do not risk distorting the tube by doing so. A better method is to tighten the top bolt when the fork leg has been installed and is securely held in the yokes.*

TOOL TiP

Use a ratchet-type tool when installing the fork top bolt. This makes it unnecessary to remove the tool from the bolt whilst threading it in making it easier to maintain a downward pressure on the spring.

If the damper rod Allen bolt requires tightening (see Step 25), clamp the brake caliper lugs on the fork slider between the padded jaws of a vice and have an assistant compress the tube into the slider so that maximum spring pressure is placed on the damper rod head – tighten the damper Allen bolt to the specified torque setting.

7.33 Front fork components – GSX-R750

1 Snap-ring	10 Spacer seat	19 Bottom bush
2 Pre-load adjuster	11 Spacer	20 Washer
3 O-ring	12 Spring seat	21 Oil seal
4 Adjuster tripod	13 Spring	22 Retaining clip
5 Top bolt	14 Damping adjuster rod	23 Dust seal
6 O-ring	15 Locknut	24 Top bush
7 Damping adjuster	16 Damper rod/cartridge	25 Fork slider
8 Washer	17 Damper rod/cartridge seat	26 Damper rod bolt and
9 Top bolt rubber seat	18 Fork tube	sealing washer

32 Install the forks (see Section 6). Adjust the fork settings as required (see Section 12).

GSX-R750 models

Disassembly

33 Always dismantle the fork legs separately to avoid interchanging parts and thus causing an accelerated rate of wear. Store all components in separate, clearly marked containers **(see illustration)**.

34 Before dismantling the fork, it is advised that the damper rod bolt be slackened at this stage. Compress the fork tube in the slider so that the spring exerts maximum pressure on the damper rod head, then have an assistant slacken the damper rod bolt in the base of the fork slider **(see illustration 7.2)**. If an assistant is not available, clamp the brake caliper lugs on the fork slider between the padded jaws of a vice.

35 If the fork top bolt was not slackened with the fork in situ, carefully clamp the fork tube in a vice equipped with soft jaws, taking care not to overtighten or score its surface, and slacken the top bolt **(see illustration 7.4)**.

36 Unscrew the fork top bolt from the top of the fork tube. The bolt will remain threaded on the damper rod.

37 Carefully clamp the brake caliper lugs on the fork slider between the padded jaws of a vice and slide the fork tube fully down onto the slider (wrap a rag around the top of the tube to minimise oil spillage) while, with the aid of an assistant if necessary, keeping the damper rod fully extended. Push down on the spacer and insert a suitably sized washer with a slot cut into it between the washer on the top of the spacer and the base of the locknut on the damper rod **(see illustration 7.28)**. This will keep the spacer and spring compressed while removing the top bolt assembly.

38 Using two spanners, one on the locknut and one on the flats on the base of the damping adjuster housing, counter-hold the

7.43 Prise off the dust seal . . .

7.44 . . . then lever out the retaining clip using a flat-bladed screwdriver

7.46a Carefully lever apart the ends of the top bush and remove it from the slider

7.46b Bottom bush (A), oil seal washer (B), oil seal (C), retaining clip (D), dust seal (E)

housing and slacken the locknut, and thread it to the base of its threads. Now counter-hold the locknut and thread the damping adjuster/pre-load adjuster/top bolt assembly off the damper rod. Withdraw the damping adjuster rod from inside the damper rod. If you want to disassemble the damping adjuster/pre-load adjuster/top bolt assembly, remove the snap-ring from the top of the damping adjuster housing, then unscrew and remove the pre-load adjuster and withdraw the adjuster tripod. You may need either a magnet, or a piece of wire or welding rod, flattened at the end and hooked over slightly, to remove it. Again, if required, thread the top bolt off the top of the damping adjuster housing. Note the rubber seat on the base of the top bolt.

39 Remove the fabricated slotted washer used to hold the spacer down, then remove the washer, the spacer seat if loose (it fits into the top of the spacer and will probable stay with it), the spacer and the spring seat (which fits into the bottom of the spacer and will probably stay with it). Withdraw the spring from the tube, noting which way up it fits.

40 Invert the fork leg over a suitable container and gently pump the fork and damper rod to expel as much fork oil as possible.

41 Remove the previously slackened damper rod bolt and its sealing washer from the bottom of the slider **(see illustration 7.8)**. Discard the sealing washer as a new one must be used on reassembly.

42 Invert the fork and withdraw the damper rod cartridge from inside the fork tube. The damper rod seat may come away with the cartridge, otherwise remove it later.

43 Carefully prise out the dust seal from the bottom of the tube to gain access to the oil seal retaining clip **(see illustration)**. Discard the dust seal as a new one must be used.

44 Carefully remove the retaining clip, taking care not to scratch the surface of the tube **(see illustration)**.

45 To separate the slider from the tube it is necessary to displace the bottom bush and oil seal. The top bush should not pass through the bottom bush, and this can be used to good effect. Push the slider gently inwards until it stops. Take care not to do this forcibly.

7.53a Slide the dust seal, the retaining clip, the oil seal, the oil seal washer and the bottom bush onto the slider as shown

Then pull the slider sharply outwards until the top bush strikes the bottom bush **(see illustration 7.12)**. Repeat this operation until the bottom bush and seal are tapped out of the tube.

46 With the tube and slider separated, remove the top bush from the slider by carefully levering its ends apart using a screwdriver **(see illustration)**. Slide the bottom bush, the oil seal washer, the oil seal, the retaining clip and the dust seal off the slider, noting which way up they fit **(see illustration)**. Discard the oil seal and the dust seal as new ones must be used.

47 If the damper rod seat did not come out with the rod, tip it out of the slider, noting which way up it fits.

Inspection

48 Clean all parts in solvent and blow them dry with compressed air, if available. Check the fork tube for score marks, scratches, flaking of the chrome finish and excessive or abnormal wear. Look for dents in the tube and renew the tube in both forks if any are found. Check the fork seal seat for nicks, gouges and scratches. If damage is evident, leaks will occur. Also check the oil seal washer for damage or distortion and renew it if necessary.

49 Check the fork slider for runout using V-blocks and a dial gauge, or have it done by a Suzuki dealer or suspension specialist **(see illustration 7.16)**. If the amount of runout exceeds the service limit specified, the slider should be renewed.

 Warning: If the slider is bent or exceeds the runout limit, it should not be straightened; renew it with a new one.

50 Check the spring for cracks and other damage. Measure the spring free length and compare the measurement to the specifications at the beginning of the Chapter. If it is defective or sagged below the service limit, renew the springs in both forks with new ones. Never renew only one spring.

51 Examine the working surfaces of the two bushes; if worn or scuffed they must be renewed. Suzuki recommend new ones are fitted as a matter of course.

52 Check the damper rod cartridge assembly for damage and wear, and renew it if necessary. Holding the outside of the cartridge, pump the rod in and out of the damper. If the rod does not move smoothly in the damper it must be renewed.

Reassembly

53 Wrap some insulating tape over the ridges on the end of the fork slider to protect the lips of the new oil seal as it is installed. Apply a smear of the specified clean fork oil to the lips of the oil seal and the inner surface of each bush, then slide the new dust seal, the retaining clip, the oil seal, the oil seal washer and the bottom bush onto the fork slider, making sure that the marked side of the oil seal faces the dust seal **(see illustration)**.

7.53b Make sure the top bush seats properly in its recess

7.54 Fit the slider into the bottom of the fork tube

7.55 Make sure the bottom bush enters the fork tube squarely

Remove the insulating tape and fit the top bush into its recess in the slider **(see illustration)**.

54 Apply a smear of the specified clean fork oil to the outer surface of each bush, then carefully insert the slider fully into the fork tube **(see illustration)**.

55 Support the fork upside down, then press the bottom bush squarely into its recess in the fork tube as far as possible **(see illustration)**. Slide the oil seal washer on top of the bush, and keep the oil seal, the retaining clip and the dust seal out of the way by sliding them up the slider. If necessary, tape them to the slider to prevent them from falling down and interfering as the bush is drifted into place.

56 Using either the special service tool (Pt. No. 09940-52861) or a suitable drift, carefully drive the bottom bush fully into its recess using the oil seal washer to prevent damaging the edges of the bush. Make sure the bush enters the recess squarely, and take care not to scratch or gouge the slider (it is best to make sure that the fork slider is pushed fully into the tube so that any accidental scratching is confined to the area that does not come into contact with the oil seal).

57 When the bush is seated fully and squarely in its recess in the tube, (remove the washer to check, wipe the recess clean, then reinstall the washer), drive the oil seal into place as described in Step 56 until the retaining clip groove is visible above the seal **(see illustration)**.

58 Once the oil seal is correctly seated, fit the

retaining clip, making sure it is correctly located in its groove, then press the dust seal into position **(see illustrations)**.

59 Lay the fork flat and slide the slider fully into the tube. Fit the damper rod/cartridge seat onto the bottom of the damper rod/cartridge, then insert the damper rod/cartridge into the top of the fork tube and into the slider until it seats on the bottom of the slider **(see illustration)**. Fit a new sealing washer onto the damper rod bolt and apply a few drops of a suitable non-permanent thread locking compound, then install the bolt into the bottom of the slider and tighten it to the torque setting specified at the beginning of the Chapter **(see illustration 7.25b)**. If the damper rod cartridge rotates inside the tube, temporarily install the spring, spacer and fork top bolt and compress the fork leg to hold the assembly in place, then remove them when the bolt has been tightened. As the damper rod will have to be kept extended out of the tube later on, it is worth at this stage securing a piece of wire around the base of the locknut on the top of the rod to use as a holder **(see illustration 7.25c)**.

60 Stand the fork upright. Slowly pour in the specified quantity of the specified grade of fork oil and pump the fork and damper rod at least ten times each to distribute it evenly and expel all the air **(see illustration 7.26a)**. It may be necessary to pump the fork and rod even more, or to hold the fork upright for several minutes, before all the air bleeds out. The oil level should also be measured – fully

compress the fork tube and damper rod onto the slider and measure the fork oil level from the top of the tube **(see illustration 7.26b)**. Add or subtract fork oil until it is at the level specified at the beginning of the Chapter.

61 If removed, fit the spring seat into the bottom of the spacer and the spacer seat into the top. Withdraw the damper rod as far as possible out of the fork tube, and keep it extended using the aid of an assistant. Install the spring, with its tapered end upwards, into the fork tube, then fit the damping adjuster rod into the centre of the damper rod. Install the spacer, making sure the lip on the bottom of the spring seat fits into the top of the spring. Fit the washer onto the top of the spacer. Push down on the spacer and insert a suitably sized washer with a slot cut into it (as

7.57 Drive the oil seal into the bottom of the tube . . .

7.58a . . . and fit its retaining clip, making sure it is properly seated . . .

7.58b . . . then press the dust seal into place

7.59 Fit the seat onto the end of the end of the damper rod/cartridge

8.2 Free the wiring from the guide (arrowed)

8.3a Unscrew the bolt (arrowed) and detach the brake hose

8.3b Unscrew the bolt (arrowed) and detach the steering damper

used on removal) between the washer on the top of the spacer and the base of the locknut on the damper rod. This will keep the spacer and spring compressed while installing the top bolt assembly. You can now remove the piece of wire.

62 If the damping adjuster/pre-load adjuster/top bolt assembly was disassembled, set the damping adjuster so that it protrudes approximately 1.5 mm from the top of the adjuster housing. Fit a new O-ring onto the top bolt and thread it down onto the damping adjuster housing. Fit the pre-load adjuster tripod into the top bolt, making sure its legs locate into the three holes in the bottom. Fit a new O-ring onto the pre-load adjuster and thread it into the top bolt. Fit the snap-ring into its groove in the top of the damping adjuster housing.

63 If removed, fit the rubber seat onto the base of the top bolt. Thread the damping adjuster/pre-load adjuster/top bolt assembly onto the damper rod, holding the rod to prevent it from turning, until the damper rod is felt to just seat on the inside of the housing. Counter-hold the flats on the base of the housing and tighten the locknut securely against it, to the specified torque if the correct tools are available.

64 Apply a smear of the specified clean oil to the top bolt O-ring. Fully extend the fork tube and screw the bolt securely into the tube (see *Tool Tip on page 6•11*).

65 Install the forks as described in Section 6. Adjust the fork settings as required (see Section 12).

8 Steering stem – removal and installation

Removal

1 Remove the front forks (see Section 6).
2 Free the handlebar switch wiring from its guide under the top yoke **(see illustration)**. Remove the set bolt securing each handlebar to the top yoke and support the handlebars so they are out of the way **(see illustration 5.3b)**. Try to keep the master cylinder and reservoir

upright and make sure no strain is placed on the brake hose.
3 Unscrew the bolt securing the front brake hose clamp to the bottom yoke **(see illustration)**. Where fitted, remove the bolt securing the steering damper to the bottom yoke and swing it aside **(see illustration)**.
4 Raise the fuel tank (unless already removed) and remove the air filter housing (see Chapter 4). Disconnect the ignition switch wiring connector to provide some slack and free the wiring from its guide **(see illustration 5.4)**.
5 Unscrew and remove the steering stem nut and remove the washer **(see illustration 5.3c)**. Gently ease the top yoke upwards and position it clear, using a rag to protect other components, or remove it completely.

6 Unscrew the locknut using either a C-spanner, a peg spanner or a suitable drift located in one of the notches **(see illustration)**. Remove the lockwasher, noting how it fits.
7 Supporting the bottom yoke, unscrew the adjuster nut using either a C-spanner, a peg-spanner or a suitable drift located in one of the notches, then remove the adjuster nut from the steering stem.
8 Gently lower the bottom yoke and steering stem out of the steering head.
9 Remove the bearing cover and the upper bearing from the top of the steering head. Remove all traces of old grease from the bearings and races and check them for wear or damage as described in Section 9. **Note:** *Do not attempt to remove the outer races*

1 Steering stem nut and washer
2 Top yoke
3 Locknut
4 Lockwasher
5 Adjuster nut
6 Bearing cover
7 Upper bearing
8 Lower bearing
9 Dust seal
10 Bottom yoke and steering stem

H31260

8.6 Steering stem components

from the frame or the lower bearing from the steering stem unless new ones are being installed.

Installation

10 Smear a liberal quantity of grease on the bearing outer races in the frame. Work the grease well into both the upper and lower bearings.

11 Carefully lift the steering stem/bottom yoke up through the steering head. Install the upper bearing in the top of the steering head, then install the bearing cover.

12 Thread the adjuster nut onto the steering stem. If the correct tools are available, tighten the nut to the torque setting specified at the beginning of the Chapter, then turn the steering stem from lock to lock five or six times to settle the bearings, then slacken the adjuster nut by 1/4 to 1/2 a turn, until steering is able to move freely but without any freeplay. If the tools are not available, tighten the nut a little at a time until all freeplay is removed but also so that the steering is able to move freely, then tighten 1/2 a turn further. Now turn the steering stem from lock to lock five or six times to settle the bearings, then slacken the adjuster nut by 1/4 to 1/2 a turn, until steering is able to move freely but without any freeplay.

Caution: Take great care not to apply excessive pressure because this will cause premature failure of the bearings. The object is to set the adjuster nut so that the bearings are under a very light loading, just enough to remove any freeplay.

13 Fit the washer onto the steering stem, aligning the tab on its inside with the groove in the stem. Fit the locknut and tighten it to the specified torque setting.

14 Fit the top yoke onto the steering stem. Raise the fuel tank onto its support and reconnect the ignition switch wiring connector, making sure it is correctly routed, and secure it in its guide **(see illustration 5.4)**. Install the air filter housing (see Chapter 4).

15 Install the steering stem nut and its washer and tighten it finger-tight at this stage. Temporarily install one of the forks to align the top and bottom yokes, and secure it by

tightening the bottom yoke clamp bolts only. Tighten the steering stem nut to the specified torque setting.

16 Attach the front brake hose clamp to the bottom yoke **(see illustration 8.3a)**. Where fitted, also attach the steering damper to the bottom yoke **(see illustration 8.3b)**.

17 Locate each handlebar onto the underside of the top yoke and secure them with the set bolts, but leave them slack. Feed the handlebar switch wiring into its guide under the top yoke **(see illustration 8.2)**.

18 Where fitted, reconnect the steering damper. Install the front forks (see Section 6).

19 Carry out a check of the steering head bearing freeplay as described in Chapter 1, and if necessary re-adjust.

9 Steering head bearings – inspection and renewal

Inspection

1 Remove the steering stem (see Section 8).

2 Remove all traces of old grease from the bearings and races and check them for wear or damage.

3 The outer races should be polished and free from indentations. Inspect the bearing balls for signs of wear, damage or discoloration, and examine their retainer cage for signs of cracks or splits. Spin the bearings by hand. They should spin freely and smoothly. If there are any signs of wear on any of the above components both upper and

lower bearing assemblies must be renewed as a set. Only remove the outer races from the frame if they need to be renewed – do not re-use them once they have been removed.

Renewal

4 The outer races are an interference fit in the frame steering head and can be tapped from position with a suitable drift **(see illustration)**. Tap firmly and evenly around each race to ensure that it is driven out squarely. It may prove advantageous to curve the end of the drift slightly to improve access.

5 Alternatively, the outer races can be removed using a slide-hammer type bearing extractor – these can often be hired from tool shops.

6 The new outer races can be pressed into the steering head using a drawbolt arrangement **(see illustration)**, or by using a large diameter tubular drift which bears only on the outer edge of the race. Ensure that the drawbolt washer or drift (as applicable) bears only on the outer edge of the race and does not contact the working surface. Alternatively, have the races installed by a Suzuki dealer equipped with the bearing race installing tools.

> **HAYNES HiNT** *Installation of new bearing outer races is made much easier if the races are left overnight in the freezer. This causes them to contract slightly making them a looser fit.*

7 To remove the lower bearing from the steering stem, use two screwdrivers or cold chisels placed on opposite sides of the race to work it free. If the bearing is firmly in place it will be necessary to use a bearing puller, or in extreme circumstances to split the bearing's inner section **(see illustration)**. Take the steering stem to a Suzuki dealer if required. Check the condition of the dust seal and fit a new one if necessary.

9.4 Drive the bearing outer races out with a brass drift as shown

9.6 Drawbolt arrangement for fitting steering head bearing outer races

1   Long bolt or threaded bar
2   Thick washer
3   Guide for lower outer race

9.7 It is best to remove the lower bearing using a puller

9.8 Drive the new bearing on using a suitable bearing driver or a length of pipe that bears only against the inner edge and not against the rollers or cage

8 Fit the new lower bearing onto the steering stem. A length of tubing with an internal diameter slightly larger than the steering stem will be needed to tap it into position (see illustration). Ensure that the drift bears only on the inner edge of the bearing and does not contact the balls or cage.

9 Install the steering stem (see Section 8).

10 Rear shock absorber – removal, inspection and installation

Removal

1 Place the machine on an auxiliary stand. Position a support under the rear wheel so that it does not drop when the shock absorber is removed, but also making sure that the weight of the machine is off the rear suspension so that the shock is not compressed.

2 Remove the seat cowling and the lower fairing (see Chapter 8).

3 Unscrew the two bolts securing the front of the rear mudguard to the frame (see illustration).

4 Unscrew the bolt securing the bottom of the shock absorber to the suspension linkage arm (see illustration).

5 Access to the shock absorber upper mounting bolt and nut is best achieved using a socket extension via the hole in each side of the frame. Counter-hold the bolt and unscrew the nut (see illustration). Support the shock absorber and withdraw the bolt, then manoeuvre the shock absorber out through the top of the frame, pulling the front of the rear mudguard off its lugs on the frame and down to provide clearance (see illustration).

Inspection

6 Inspect the shock absorber for obvious physical damage and the coil spring for looseness, cracks or signs of fatigue.

7 Inspect the damper rod for signs of bending, pitting and oil leakage (see illustration).

10.3 Unscrew the bolt (arrowed) on each side of the mudguard

10.5a ... followed by the upper mounting bolt nut ...

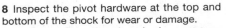

8 Inspect the pivot hardware at the top and bottom of the shock for wear or damage.

9 If the shock absorber is in any way damaged or worn a new one must be installed. Individual components are not available from Suzuki although it is worth checking whether the shock can be rebuilt by a suspension specialist.

10 Check the tightness of the shock absorber upper mounting bracket secured in the frame. If the bracket is loose, tighten the nut to the torque setting specified at the beginning of the Chapter. On 600 models if the bracket is disturbed for any reason, note that the white mark on the bracket should face the frame. On 750 models, don't remove the bracket from the frame unless you need to renew it; on GSX-R750T models there is a

10.7 Check the damper rod for oil leakage and corrosion

10.4 Unscrew the lower mounting bolt ...

10.5b ... then withdraw the upper bolt, pull the mudguard back and remove the shock

spacer between the adjuster bracket and frame.

Installation

11 Installation is the reverse of removal, noting the following.

a) Apply general purpose grease to the pivot points and to the bearings in the linkage arm.

b) Install the upper mounting bolt first, but do not tighten the nut until the lower mounting bolt is installed.

c) Tighten the upper nut and lower bolt to the torque setting specified at the beginning of the Chapter (see illustration).

d) Adjust the suspension as required (see Section 12).

10.11 Tighten the upper nut and lower bolt to the specified torque

11.3 Linkage arm to shock absorber bolt (A), linkage arm to linkage rods bolt (B), linkage arm to frame bolt (C)

11.6 Linkage rods to swingarm nut (arrowed)

11.7a Withdraw the spacers from the bearings

11 Rear suspension linkage – removal, inspection and installation

Removal

1 Place the machine on an auxiliary stand. Position a support under the rear wheel so that it does not drop when the linkage is removed, but also making sure that the weight of the machine is off the rear suspension so that the shock is not compressed.

2 Remove the lower fairing (see Chapter 8).

3 Unscrew the bolt securing the linkage arm to the bottom of the shock absorber **(see illustration)**.

4 Unscrew the nut and withdraw the bolt securing the linkage arm to the linkage rods **(see illustration 11.3)**.

5 Unscrew the nut and withdraw the bolt securing the linkage arm to the frame, then remove the arm, noting the washers fitted between the arm and the frame **(see illustration 11.3)**.

6 Unscrew the nut and withdraw the bolt securing the linkage rods to the swingarm and remove the rods **(see illustration)**.

Inspection

7 Withdraw the spacers from the linkage arm, noting their different sizes **(see illustration)**. Thoroughly clean all components, removing all traces of dirt, corrosion and grease **(see illustration)**.

8 Inspect all components closely, looking for obvious signs of wear such as heavy scoring, or for damage such as cracks or distortion. Slip each spacer back into its bearing and check that there is not an excessive amount of freeplay between the two components. Renew any components as required.

9 Check the condition of the needle roller bearings in the linkage arm and in the bottom of the swingarm. Refer to *Tools and Workshop Tips* (Section 5) in the Reference section for more information on bearings. If the linkage rod bearings in the swingarm need to be

renewed, remove the swingarm (see Section 13).

10 Worn bearings can be drifted out of their bores, but note that removal will destroy them; new bearings should be obtained before work commences. The new bearings should be pressed or drawn into their bores rather than driven into position. In the absence of a press, a suitable drawbolt tool can be made up as described in *Tools and Workshop Tips* in the Reference section.

11 Lubricate the needle roller bearings and the pivot bolts with general purpose grease and install the spacers.

Installation

12 Installation is the reverse of removal, noting the following.

a) *Apply general purpose grease to the bearings, spacers, pivot points and pivot bolts.*

1 Shock absorber
2 Linkage rods
3 Linkage arm
4 Bearing spacers
5 Needle roller bearings
6 Washers

11.7b Suspension linkage components

11.12a Fit the washers between each side of the linkage arm and the frame

b) *Do not forget to fit the washers between the linkage arm and the frame* **(see illustration)**.

c) *Do not fully tighten any of the bolts until they have all been installed.*

d) *Tighten the nuts and bolt to the torque setting specified at the beginning of the Chapter* **(see illustration)**.

e) *Check the operation of the rear suspension before taking the machine on the road.*

12 Suspension – adjustments

Note: *The owners manual supplied with your bike contains full details of the standard*

11.12b Tighten the nuts and bolt to the specified torque settings

suspension settings and recommended settings to suit the load carried and riding style.

Front forks

1 On GSX-R600V models, the forks are adjustable for spring pre-load and rebound damping. On all other 600 models and all 750 models the forks are adjustable for spring pre-load, rebound damping and compression damping.

2 Spring pre-load is adjusted using a suitable spanner on the adjuster flats **(see illustrations)**. Turn it clockwise to increase pre-load and anti-clockwise to decrease it. The amount of pre-load is indicated by lines on the adjuster. Always make sure both adjusters are set equally.

3 Rebound damping is adjusted using a screwdriver in the slot in the damping adjuster

rod protruding from the pre-load adjuster **(see illustration 12.2a or b)**. Turn it clockwise to increase damping and anti-clockwise to decrease it.

4 Compression damping is adjusted using a screwdriver in the slot in the damping adjuster in the base of each fork **(see illustration)**. Turn it clockwise to increase damping and anti-clockwise to decrease it.

Rear shock absorber

5 On all models the rear shock absorber is adjustable for spring pre-load, rebound damping and compression damping.

6 Spring pre-load is adjusted by turning the adjuster nut on the threads on the shock absorber body. Slacken the locknut, then turn the adjuster nut clockwise to increase pre-load and anti-clockwise to decrease it **(see illustration)**. Tighten the locknut securely after adjustment. Do not set the spring length to anything less than 190 mm, the hardest setting.

7 Rebound damping is adjusted using a screwdriver in the slot in the adjuster at the bottom of the shock absorber **(see illustration)**. To increase the damping, turn the adjuster clockwise. To decrease the damping, turn the adjuster anti-clockwise.

8 Compression damping is adjusted using a screwdriver in the slot in the adjuster at the top of the shock absorber **(see illustration)**. To increase the damping, turn the adjuster clockwise. To decrease the damping, turn the adjuster anti-clockwise.

12.2a Spring pre-load adjuster (A), rebound damping adjuster (B) – GSX-R600

12.2b Spring pre-load adjuster (A), rebound damping adjuster (B) – GSX-R750

12.4 Compression damping adjuster (arrowed)

12.6 Slacken the locknut (A) and turn the adjuster (B) as required to adjust pre-load

12.7 Rebound damping adjuster (arrowed)

12.8 Compression damping adjuster (arrowed)

13.3a Detach the torque arm at either the caliper (A) or the swingarm (B)

13.3b Feed the brake hose through the closed guide (arrowed) . . .

13.3c . . . and out of the open guides (arrowed)

13 Swingarm – removal and installation

Removal

Note 1: *Before removing the swingarm, it is advisable to perform the rear suspension checks described in Chapter 1 to assess the extent of any wear.*

Note 2: *The swingarm can be removed with the shock absorber and linkage assembly attached if required. Otherwise, the shock absorber must be removed, and the linkage assembly must either be removed completely, or it can remain attached either to the swingarm and removed with it after detaching it from the frame, or it can remain attached to the frame after detaching it from the swingarm. If the rear suspension is being removed as an assembly, but is later to be disassembled, it is advisable to slacken all the bolts before removing the assembly.*

Note 3: *The rear brake hose is fitted through a closed guide on the inside of the swingarm. The only way to separate the hose from the swingarm is to disconnect it from either the brake caliper or the master cylinder and feed it through. This will mean bleeding the brake system after installation. To prevent opening the system, it can be removed complete along with the swingarm – this is*

better, unless a new swingarm is being installed, or extensive work is being carried out on the old one.

Note 4: *On 600 models, the chain can remain on the front sprocket. On 750 models, due to the construction of the swingarm, the chain must either be split (see Section 15) or must be slipped off the front sprocket and removed along with the swingarm. If a new swingarm is being installed , or extensive work is being carried out on it, split the chain and remove it (see Section 15).*

Removal

1 Remove the seat cowling and the lower fairing (see Chapter 8).

2 Remove the rear wheel (see Chapter 7).

3 If the brake system is being removed along with the swingarm, secure the caliper bracket to the swingarm to prevent it dropping off, then refer to Chapter 7 and displace the master cylinder and reservoir and position them so they will come away with the swingarm. Otherwise, refer to Chapter 7 and separate the hydraulic hose from the caliper (following all precautions), then unscrew the nut and remove the bolt securing the brake torque arm to either the bracket or the swingarm and remove the caliper along with the bracket **(see illustration)**. Feed the hose through the closed guide, free it from the

other guides and secure it clear **(see illustrations)**.

4 On GSX-R750 models, either remove the front sprocket cover and slip the chain off the sprocket (if the chain is being left intact and removed with the swingarm) (see Section 16), or split the chain and free it from the swingarm (see Section 15).

5 Either remove the shock absorber (see Section 10), or if it is to be removed with the swingarm and suspension linkage, remove the shock absorber upper mounting bolt (see **Note 2** above) **(see illustration 10.5a)**.

6 Either remove the suspension linkage completely (see Section 11), or separate it from either the swingarm (if it is to remain in place) or the frame (if it is being removed with the swingarm) as required (see **Note 2** above) **(see illustration 11.6 or 11.3)**.

7 Before removing the swingarm it is advisable to re-check for play in the bearings (see Chapter 1). Any problems which may have been overlooked with the other suspension components attached to the frame are highlighted with them loose.

8 Unscrew the locknut on the right-hand end of the swingarm pivot bolt **(see illustration)**. This requires the use of a Suzuki service tool (Pt. No. 09940-14970) or a suitable peg spanner, which can be fabricated using an old socket or an old nut (see **Tool Tip**).

13.8 Unscrew and remove the locknut (arrowed)

TOOL TiP

A peg 'socket' can be made by cutting an old 32 mm socket as shown – measure the width and depth of the slots in the locknut to determine the size of the castellations on the socket (left). If an old socket is not available, a nut can be used and suitable pegs can be brazed or welded onto it (right).

13.9 Unscrew and remove the nut (arrowed)

13.10 Support the swingarm and withdraw the pivot bolt

13.11a The chain slider is secured by two bolts (arrowed) . . .

13.11b . . . and the chainguard by two screws (arrowed)

13.17a Loop the chain around the front of the swingarm . . .

13.17b . . . then slide the pivot bolt through . . .

9 Counter-hold the pivot bolt using a 27 mm socket or spanner and unscrew the nut on the left-hand end of the bolt using a 36 mm socket or spanner **(see illustration)**. Remove the washer.

10 Support the swingarm, then withdraw the pivot bolt and remove the swingarm **(see illustration)**. On 750 models, check that the pivot bosses in the frame are not worn or damaged and that they are tight in the frame. If they are loose, tighten the nuts on the inside of the frame to the torque setting specified at the beginning of the Chapter. Do not remove the bosses unless new ones are being fitted. If they are worn or damaged, new ones must be fitted.

11 Remove the chain slider, and if necessary the chainguard from the swingarm, noting how they fit **(see illustrations)**. If the chain

slider is badly worn or damaged, a new one should be fitted.

12 If attached, and if required, separate the suspension linkage from the swingarm (see Section 11).

13 Clean inspect and lubricate all components as described in Section 14.

Installation

14 On 750 models, check that the pivot bosses in the frame are not worn or damaged and that they are tight in the frame. If they are loose, tighten the nuts on the inside of the frame to the torque setting specified at the beginning of the Chapter. Do not remove the bosses unless new ones are being fitted. If they are worn or damaged, new ones must be fitted.

15 If not already done, remove the dust

seals, washers and bearing spacers, then clean them and lubricate the bearings, spacers and the pivot bolt with grease **(see illustrations 14.2b and c)**. Install the bearing spacers, then fit the washers and dust seals.

16 Install the chain slider, and if removed the chainguard **(see illustrations 13.11a and b)**.

17 Offer up the swingarm, making sure the chain is correctly looped around it (unless removed on 750 models), and have an assistant hold it in place **(see illustration)**. Slide the pivot bolt through the swingarm from the right-hand side and tighten it to the torque setting specified at the beginning of the Chapter using a 27 mm socket **(see illustrations)**.

18 Thread the swingarm pivot nut with its washer finger-tight onto the left-hand end of the bolt **(see illustration)**. Counter-hold the

13.17c . . . and tighten it to the specified torque

13.18a Fit the washer and nut . . .

13.18b . . . and tighten it while counter-holding the bolt

13.19a Fit the locknut . . .

13.19b . . . and tighten it to the specified torque setting

14.1 Clean off all accumulated chain lube and road dirt using a suitable degreaser

pivot bolt using a 27 mm socket or spanner and tighten the nut to the specified torque setting using a 36 mm socket **(see illustration)**.

19 Thread the locknut finger-tight onto the right-hand end of the pivot bolt **(see illustration)**. Make a reference mark between the head of the pivot bolt and the frame as a check against the bolt turning when the locknut is tightened. Using the same tool as on removal, tighten the locknut to the specified torque setting **(see illustration)**. Check that the reference marks still align – if not remove the locknut and nut and slacken the pivot bolt, then repeat the tightening procedure.

20 Install the rear shock absorber and linkage assembly as required by your removal procedure (see Sections 10 and 11).

21 On 750 models, either fit the drive chain around the front sprocket, then install the sprocket cover (see Section 16), or fit the split chain and stake it using a new soft link as described in Section 15.

22 Install the rear brake components as required by your removal procedure (see Chapter 7).

23 Install the rear wheel (see Chapter 7), and the lower fairing and the seat cowling (see Chapter 8).

24 Check and adjust the drive chain slack (see Chapter 1). Check the operation of the rear suspension and brake before taking the machine on the road.

14.2a Swingarm components

1 Pivot bolt	5 Bearing spacer	8 Linkage rod bearings
2 Locknut	6 Swingarm bearings	9 Washer
3 Dust seal	7 Bearing spacer	10 Pivot bolt nut
4 Washer		

14 Swingarm – inspection and bearing renewal

Inspection

1 Thoroughly clean the swingarm, removing all traces of dirt, corrosion and grease **(see illustration)**.

2 Remove the dust seals, washers and bearing spacers **(see illustrations)**.

3 Inspect all components closely, looking for obvious signs of wear such as heavy scoring, and cracks or distortion due to accident damage. Check the bearings for roughness,

14.2b Remove the dust seal and washer . . .

14.2c . . . and withdraw the spacer

looseness and any other damage, referring to *Tools and Workshop Tips* (Section 5) in the Reference section **(see illustration)**. Any damaged or worn component must be renewed.

4 Check the swingarm pivot bolt for straightness by rolling it on a flat surface such as a piece of plate glass (first wipe off all old grease and remove any corrosion using fine emery cloth). If the equipment is available, place the axle in V-blocks and measure the runout using a dial gauge. If the axle is bent or the runout exceeds the limit specified, fit a new one.

Bearing renewal

5 Remove the dust seals, washers and bearing spacers **(see illustrations 14.2b and c)**. Refer to *Tools and Workshop Tips* (Section 5) in the Reference section for more information on bearing checks and renewal methods.

6 Needle bearings can be drawn or driven out of their bores, but note that removal will destroy them; new bearings should be obtained before work commences. It may be possible to pass a long drift with a hooked end through the swingarm and locate it between the central spacer and the inner edge of the bearing. Tap the drift around the bearing's inner edge to ensure that it leaves its bore squarely. Once removed, withdraw the centre spacer and use the same method to extract the other bearing. If available, a slide-hammer with knife-edged bearing puller can be used, and is better than using a drift, to extract the bearings.

7 The new bearings should be pressed or drawn into their bores rather than driven into position. In the absence of a press, a suitable drawbolt arrangement can be made up as described in *Tools and Workshop Tips* (Section 5) in the Reference section. Do not forget to install the centre spacer between the two bearings, and fit the bearings with their marked side facing out.

15 Drive chain – removal, cleaning and installation

Removal

GSX-R600 models

Note: *The original equipment drive chain fitted to all 600 models is an endless chain. Removal requires the removal of the swingarm as detailed below.*

> **Warning: NEVER install a drive chain which uses a clip-type master (split) link.**

1 Remove the swingarm (see Section 13).
2 Remove the front sprocket cover (see Section 16).
3 Slip the chain off the front sprocket and remove it from the bike. If there is not enough clearance between the sprocket and the

14.3 Check the bearings as described

frame to remove the chain, remove the sprocket (see Section 16), then remove the chain.

GSX-R750 models

Note: *The original equipment drive chain fitted to these models has a staked -type master (soft) link which can be disassembled using either Suzuki service tool, Pt. No. 09922-22711, or one of several commercially-available drive chain cutting/staking tools. Such chains can be recognised by the soft link side plate's identification marks (and usually its different colour), as well as by the staked ends of the link's two pins which look as if they have been deeply centre-punched, instead of peened over as with all the other pins.*

> **Warning: Use ONLY the correct service tools to disassemble the staked-type of soft link – if you do not have access to such tools or do not have the skill to operate them correctly, have the chain removed by a motorcycle dealer.**

4 Remove the front sprocket cover (see Section 16).
5 Locate the soft link in a suitable position to work on by rotating the back wheel.
6 Slacken the drive chain as described in Chapter 1.
7 Split the chain at the soft link using the chain cutter, following carefully the manufacturer's operating instructions (see also Section 8 in *Tools and Workshop Tips* in the Reference Section). Remove the chain from the bike, noting its routing through the swingarm.

Cleaning

8 Soak the chain in paraffin (kerosene) for approximately five or six minutes.
Caution: Don't use gasoline (petrol), solvent or other cleaning fluids. Don't use high-pressure water. Remove the chain, wipe it off, then blow dry it with compressed air immediately. The entire process shouldn't take longer than ten minutes – if it does, the O-rings in the chain rollers could be damaged.

Installation

GSX-R600 models

9 Installation is the reverse of removal. On completion adjust and lubricate the chain following the procedures described in Chapter 1.

GSX-R750 models

> **Warning: NEVER install a drive chain which uses a clip-type master (split) link. Use ONLY the correct service tools to secure the staked-type of soft link – if you do not have access to such tools or do not have the skill to operate them correctly, have the chain installed by a motorcycle dealer.**

10 Slip the drive chain through the swingarm sections and around the front sprocket, leaving the two ends in a convenient position to work on.
11 Refer to Section 8 in *Tools and Workshop Tips* in the Reference Section. Install the new soft link from the inside. Fit an O-ring onto each pin, then slide the link through and fit the other two O-rings. Install the new side plate with its identification marks facing out and press it into position. If fitting the original equipment type RK chain, measure the distance between the outer edges of the soft link and side plate and check they are within the measurements specified at the beginning of the Chapter **(see illustration)**.
12 Stake the new link using the drive chain cutting/staking tool, following carefully the instructions of both the chain manufacturer and the tool manufacturer. DO NOT re-use old soft link components. After staking, check the soft link and staking for any signs of cracking. If there is any evidence of cracking,

15.11 Press sideplate on to specified distance (arrowed) on RK chain – 750 models
Soft link left-hand pin shown in cross-section

16.1 Unscrew the bolt (arrowed) and slide the arm off the shaft

16.2 Disconnect the speedometer sensor wiring connector

16.3 Sprocket cover bolts (arrowed)

the soft link, O-rings and side plate must be renewed. If fitting the original equipment type RK chain, measure the diameter of the staked ends in two directions and check that it is evenly staked and within the measurements specified at the beginning of the Chapter.

13 Install the sprocket cover (see Section 16).

14 On completion, adjust and lubricate the chain following the procedures described in Chapter 1.

16 Sprockets –
check and renewal

Check

1 Unscrew the gearchange linkage arm pinch bolt and remove the arm from the shaft, noting any alignment marks **(see illustration)**. If no marks are visible, make your own before removing the arm so that it can be correctly aligned with the shaft on installation.

2 Trace the wiring from the speedometer sensor on the front sprocket cover and disconnect it at the connector **(see illustration)**.

3 Unscrew the bolts securing the sprocket cover to the crankcase and move the cover aside **(see illustration)**. There is no need to detach the clutch cable from the cover. On W, X and Y models, note the rubber bushing for the gearchange shaft and remove it from the cover if required.

4 Check the wear pattern on both sprockets (see Chapter 1). If the sprocket teeth are worn excessively, renew the chain and both sprockets as a set. Whenever the sprockets are inspected, the drive chain should be inspected also (see Chapter 1). If you are fitting a new chain, fit new sprockets as well.

5 Adjust and lubricate the chain following the procedures described in Chapter 1.

Renewal

Front sprocket

6 Unscrew the gearchange linkage arm pinch bolt and remove the arm from the shaft, noting any alignment marks **(see illustration 16.1)**. If no marks are visible, make your own before removing the arm so that it can be correctly aligned with the shaft on installation.

7 Trace the wiring from the speedometer sensor on the front sprocket cover and disconnect it at the connector **(see illustration 16.2)**.

8 Unscrew the bolts securing the sprocket cover to the crankcase and move the cover aside **(see illustration 16.3)**. There is no need to detach the clutch cable from the cover. On W, X and Y models, note the rubber bushing for the gearchange shaft and remove it from the cover if required.

9 Counter-hold the sprocket nut and unscrew the bolt securing the speedometer rotor **(see illustration)**. Remove the rotor, and on GSX-R750T models the washer.

10 Have an assistant apply the rear brake hard. This will lock the sprocket and enable you to slacken and remove the nut. Unscrew the sprocket nut and remove it with the washer **(see illustration)**.

11 Slide the sprocket and chain off the shaft, then slip the sprocket out of the chain **(see illustration)**. If the chain is too tight to allow the sprocket to be slid off the shaft, slacken the chain adjusters to provide some freeplay (see Chapter 1), or, if the rear sprocket is being renewed as well, remove the rear wheel (see Chapter 7).

12 Engage the new sprocket with the chain and slide it on the shaft **(see illustration)**.

13 Install the sprocket nut with its washer and tighten it to the torque setting specified at

16.9 Unscrew the bolt (A) and remove the rotor (B)

16.10 Unscrew the nut (arrowed) . . .

16.11 . . . then slide the sprocket off the shaft and out of the chain

16.12 Fit the sprocket into the chain and onto the shaft . . .

16.13a . . . then fit the washer and nut . . .

16.13b . . . and tighten the nut to the specified torque

16.14 Fit the rotor and tighten its bolt to the specified torque

16.16a Locate the rotor (A) into the sensor (B)

16.16b Where fitted, and if removed, slide the rubber bush onto the shaft

16.21 The sprocket is secured by six nuts (arrowed)

the beginning of the Chapter, applying the rear brake as before to prevent the sprocket turning (see illustrations).

14 Now install the speedometer rotor, on GSX-R750T models with its washer, and tighten the bolt to the specified torque setting while counter-holding the sprocket nut (see illustration).

15 If detached, fit the clutch cable into the release mechanism in the sprocket cover (see Chapter 2).

16 Make sure the dowels are either in the crankcase or the sprocket cover. Install the cover, making sure the speedometer rotor fits properly into the sensor and the dowels locate correctly, and tighten its bolts (see illustration). On W, X and Y models, if removed, fit the rubber bushing for the gear-change shaft into the cover (see illustration).

17 Slide the gearchange linkage arm onto the shaft, aligning the marks, and tighten the pinch bolt (see illustration 16.1).

18 Reconnect the speedometer sensor wiring connector (see illustration 16.2).

19 Adjust and lubricate the chain following the procedures described in Chapter 1.

Rear sprocket

20 Remove the rear wheel (see Chapter 7). Caution: Do not lay the wheel down on the disc as it could become warped. Lay the wheel on wooden blocks so that the disc is off the ground.

21 Unscrew the nuts securing the sprocket to the wheel coupling, then remove the sprocket, noting which way round it fits (see illustration).

22 Before installing the new rear sprocket, check the wheel coupling and damper assembly components (see Section 17).

23 Install the sprocket onto the coupling with the stamped mark facing out, then tighten the sprocket nuts to the torque setting specified at the beginning of the Chapter.

24 Install the rear wheel (see Chapter 7).

25 Adjust and lubricate the chain following the procedures described in Chapter 1.

17 Rear wheel coupling/rubber dampers – check and renewal

1 Remove the rear wheel (see Chapter 7). Caution: Do not lay the wheel down on the disc as it could become warped. Lay the wheel on wooden blocks so that the disc is off the ground.

17.2 Lift the coupling out of the wheel . . .

2 Lift the sprocket coupling out of the wheel leaving the rubber dampers in position in the wheel (see illustration). Note the spacer inside the coupling. Check the coupling for cracks or any obvious signs of damage. Also check the sprocket studs for wear or damage, and that they are secure.

3 Lift the rubber damper segments from the wheel and check them for cracks, hardening and general deterioration (see illustration). Renew the rubber dampers as a set if necessary.

4 Checking and renewal procedures for the sprocket coupling bearing are described in Chapter 7.

5 Check that the coupling spacer is correctly located in the bearing in the coupling. Fit the coupling into the wheel, making sure the spacer also locates into the bearing in the wheel.

6 Install the rear wheel (see Chapter 7).

17.3 . . . and check the damper segments

Chapter 7
Brakes, wheels and tyres

Contents

Degrees of difficulty

| **Easy,** suitable for novice with little experience | | **Fairly easy,** suitable for beginner with some experience | | **Fairly difficult,** suitable for competent DIY mechanic | 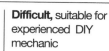 | **Difficult,** suitable for experienced DIY mechanic | | **Very difficult,** suitable for expert DIY or professional | |

Specifications

Brakes

Brake fluid type . . . . DOT 4
Disc minimum thickness
  Front
    GSX-R600V and GSX-R750T and V models
      Standard . . . . 4.3 to 4.7 mm
      Service limit . . . . 4.0 mm
    GSX-R600W, X and Y and GSX-R750W and X models
      Standard . . . . 4.8 to 5.2 mm
      Service limit . . . . 4.5 mm
  Rear
    Standard . . . . 4.8 to 5.2 mm
    Service limit . . . . 4.5 mm

Brakes (continued)

Disc maximum runout (front and rear, all models)	0.3 mm

Caliper bore ID
  Front
    GSX-R600

Lower	27.000 to 27.076 mm
Upper	30.230 to 30.306 mm

    GSX-R750

Lower	24.000 to 24.076 mm
Middle and upper	27.000 to 27.076 mm
Rear	38.180 to 38.256 mm

Caliper piston OD
  Front
    GSX-R600

Lower	26.920 to 26.970 mm
Upper	30.150 to 30.200 mm

    GSX-R750

Lower	23.925 to 23.975 mm
Middle and upper	26.920 to 26.970 mm
Rear	38.098 to 38.148 mm

Master cylinder bore ID
  Front

GSX-R600	14.000 to 14.043 mm
GSX-R750	15.870 to 15.913 mm
Rear	12.700 to 12.743 mm

Master cylinder piston OD
  Front

GSX-R600	13.957 to 13.984 mm
GSX-R750	15.827 to 15.854 mm
Rear	12.657 to 12.684 mm

Wheels

Maximum wheel runout (front and rear)

Axial (side-to-side)	2.0 mm
Radial (out-of-round)	2.0 mm
Maximum axle runout (front and rear)	0.25 mm

Tyres

Tyre pressures	see *Daily (pre-ride) checks*

Tyre sizes*
  GSX-R600

Front	120/70-ZR17 (58W)
Rear	180/55-ZR17 (73W)

  GSX-R750

Front	120/70-ZR17 (58W)
Rear	190/50-ZR17 (73W)

Refer to the owners handbook or the tyre information label on the swingarm for approved tyre brands.

Torque settings

Front brake caliper joining bolts	23 Nm
Front brake caliper mounting bolts	39 Nm
Brake hose banjo bolts	23 Nm
Front brake disc bolts	23 Nm
Front brake master cylinder clamp bolts	10 Nm
Rear brake caliper joining bolts	33 Nm
Rear brake caliper mounting bolts	26 Nm
Rear brake torque arm nut	35 Nm
Rear brake disc bolts	35 Nm
Rear brake master cylinder mounting bolts	10 Nm
Brake system bleed valves	8 Nm
Front axle clamp bolts and axle holder clamp bolts	23 Nm
Front axle	100 Nm
Rear axle nut	100 Nm

2.1 Unscrew the bolts (arrowed) and remove the pad spring

2.2a Remove the R-pin (arrowed) . . .

2.2b . . . then withdraw the pad pin . . .

1 General information

All models covered in this manual are fitted with cast alloy wheels designed for tubeless tyres only.

Both front and rear brakes are hydraulically operated disc brakes. On GSX-R600 models, the front has twin calipers with twin opposed pistons, the rear has a single caliper with single opposed pistons. On GSX-R750, the front has twin calipers with triple opposed pistons, the rear has a single caliper with single opposed pistons.

Caution: Disc brake components rarely require disassembly. Do not disassemble components unless absolutely necessary. If a hydraulic brake line is loosened, the entire system must be disassembled, drained, cleaned and then properly filled and bled upon reassembly. Do not use solvents on internal brake components. Solvents will cause the seals to swell and distort. Use only clean brake fluid of the correct type for cleaning. Use care when working with brake fluid as it can injure your eyes and it will damage painted surfaces and plastic parts.

2 Front brake pads – renewal

Warning: The dust created by the brake system may contain asbestos, which is harmful to your health. Never blow it out with compressed air and don't inhale any of it. An approved filtering mask should be worn when working on the brakes.

1 Unscrew the two bolts securing the pad spring and remove the spring **(see illustration)**.
2 Remove the R-pin from the end of the pad retaining pin, then withdraw the pad pin **(see illustrations)**. Remove the pads from the caliper, noting how they fit **(see illustration)**.
3 Inspect the surface of each pad for contamination and check that the friction material has not worn beyond its service limit (see Chapter 1, Section 11). If either pad is worn down to, or beyond, the service limit wear indicator (ie the wear indicator is no longer visible), fouled with oil or grease, or heavily scored or damaged by dirt and debris, both sets of pads must be renewed as a set.

Note that it is not possible to degrease the friction material; if the pads are contaminated in any way new ones must be fitted.
4 If the pads are in good condition clean them carefully, using a fine wire brush which is completely free of oil and grease to remove all traces of road dirt and corrosion. Using a pointed instrument, clean out the grooves in the friction material and dig out any embedded particles of foreign matter. Any areas of glazing may be removed using emery cloth. Spray with a dedicated brake cleaner to remove any dust.
5 Check the condition of the brake disc (see Section 4).
6 Remove all traces of corrosion from the pad pin. Inspect the pin for signs of damage and renew it if necessary.
7 Push the pistons as far back into the caliper as possible using hand pressure or a piece of wood as leverage **(see illustration)**. Due to the increased friction material thickness of new pads, it may be necessary to remove the master cylinder reservoir cover and diaphragm and siphon out some fluid.
8 Smear the backs of the pads and the shank of the pad pin with copper-based grease, making sure that none gets on the front or sides of the pads.
9 Insert the pads into the caliper so that the

2.2c . . . and lift the pads out

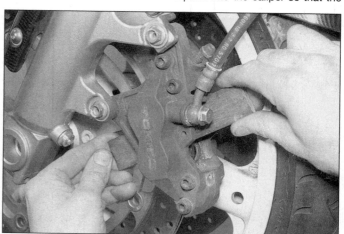

2.7 Use a block of wood to press the pistons back

2.9a Insert the pads . . .

2.9b . . . then slide in the pad pin . . .

2.9c . . . and fit the R-pin

2.10 Fit the pad spring

friction material of each pad faces the disc **(see illustration)**. Install the pad retaining pin, making sure it passes through the hole in each pad, and secure it with the R-pin, using a new one if necessary **(see illustrations)**.

10 Fit the pad spring and secure it with the bolts **(see illustration)**.

11 Top up the master cylinder reservoir if necessary (see *Daily (pre-ride) checks*), and renew the reservoir cover and diaphragm.

12 Operate the brake lever several times to bring the pads into contact with the disc. Check the operation of the brake before riding the motorcycle.

3 Front brake calipers – removal, overhaul and installation

⚠ **Warning: If a caliper indicates the need for an overhaul (usually due to leaking fluid or sticky operation), all old brake fluid should be flushed from the system. Also, the dust created by the brake system may contain asbestos, which is harmful to your health. Never blow it out with compressed air and don't inhale any of it. An approved filtering mask should be worn when working on the brakes. Do not, under any circumstances, use petroleum-based solvents to clean brake parts. Use the specified clean brake fluid, dedicated brake cleaner or denatured alcohol only, as described.**

Removal

1 If the calipers are being overhauled, remove the brake pads (see Section 2). If the calipers are just being displaced or removed, the pads can be left in place **(see illustration)**.

2 If the calipers are just being displaced and not completely removed or overhauled, do not disconnect the brake hose. If the calipers are being overhauled, remove the brake hose banjo bolt and detach the hose, noting its alignment with the caliper **(see illustration)**. When working on the right-hand caliper, note the double hose arrangement **(see**

1 Pad spring
2 R-pin
3 Pad pin
4 Brake pads
5 Caliper seal
6 Dust seal
7 Piston
8 Piston seal
9 Bleed valve

H31264

3.1 Front brake caliper components. GSX-R600 shown – GSX-R750 models have an extra piston

3.2a Left-hand caliper banjo bolt (arrowed)

3.2b Right-hand caliper banjo bolt (arrowed) – note the double hose arrangement

3.3 Caliper body joining bolts (arrowed)

3.4a Unscrew the mounting bolts (arrowed) . . .

illustration). Plug the hose end(s) or wrap a plastic bag tightly around to minimise fluid loss and prevent dirt entering the system. Discard the sealing washers as new ones must be used on installation. **Note:** *If you are planning to overhaul the caliper and don't have a source of compressed air to blow out the pistons, just loosen the banjo bolt at this stage and retighten it lightly. The bike's hydraulic system can then be used to force the pistons out of the caliper once the pads have been removed. Disconnect the hose once the pistons have been sufficiently displaced.*

3 If the caliper body is to be split into its halves for overhaul, slacken the caliper body joining bolts at this stage and retighten them lightly **(see illustration)**.

4 Unscrew the caliper mounting bolts and slide the caliper off the disc **(see illustrations)**.

Overhaul

5 Clean the exterior of the caliper with denatured alcohol or brake system cleaner.

6 Displace the pistons as far as possible from the caliper body, either by pumping them out by operating the front brake lever, or by forcing them out using compressed air – do not allow the piston heads to touch. If the compressed air method is used, place a wad of rag between the pistons and the caliper to act as a cushion, then use compressed air

directed into the fluid inlet to force the pistons out of the body. Use only low pressure to ease the pistons out and make sure all pistons are displaced at the same time. If the air pressure is too high and the pistons are forced out, the caliper and/or pistons may be damaged.

 Warning: Never place your fingers in front of the pistons in an attempt to catch or protect them when applying compressed air, as serious injury could result.

7 Unscrew the caliper body joining bolts and separate the body halves. Remove the pistons from each half. Mark each piston head and caliper body with a felt marker to ensure that the pistons can be matched to their original bores on reassembly. Note that two sizes of piston are used (see Specifications). Extract the caliper seal from whichever body half it is in and discard it as a new one must be used.

8 Using a wooden or plastic tool, remove the dust seals from the caliper bores **(see illustration)**. Discard them as new ones must be used on installation. If a metal tool is being used, take great care not to damage the caliper bores.

9 Remove and discard the piston seals in the same way.

10 Clean the pistons and bores with clean brake fluid of the specified type. If compressed air is available, use it to dry the

parts thoroughly (make sure it's filtered and unlubricated).

Caution: Do not, under any circumstances, use a petroleum-based solvent to clean brake parts.

11 Inspect the caliper bores and pistons for signs of corrosion, nicks and burrs and loss of plating. If surface defects are present, the caliper assembly must be renewed. If the necessary measuring equipment is available, compare the dimensions of the pistons and bores to those given in the Specifications Section of this Chapter, renewing any component that is worn beyond the service limit. If the caliper is in bad shape the master cylinder should also be checked.

12 Lubricate the new piston seals with clean brake fluid and install them in their grooves in the caliper bores, making sure the thicker side of the seal is facing the disc **(see illustration)**. Note that two sizes of bore and piston are used (see Specifications), and care must therefore be taken to ensure that the correct size seals are fitted to the correct bores. The same applies when fitting the new dust seals and pistons.

13 Lubricate the new dust seals with clean brake fluid and install them in their grooves in the caliper bores.

14 Lubricate the pistons with clean brake fluid and install them closed-end first into the

3.4b . . . and slide the caliper off the disc

3.8 Use a plastic or wooden tool (a pencil works well) to remove the seals

3.12 Ensure that the piston fluid seal is fitted correctly

3.16 Slide the caliper onto the disc . . .

3.17 . . . and tighten the mounting bolts to the specified torque setting

4.2 Set up a dial gauge to contact the brake disc, then rotate the wheel to check for runout

caliper bores. Using your thumbs, push the pistons all the way in, making sure they enter the bore squarely.

15 Lubricate the new caliper seals with clean brake fluid and install them into one half of the caliper body. Join the two halves of the caliper body together, making sure that the caliper seals stay correctly seated in their recesses. Install the joining bolts and tighten them to the torque setting specified at the beginning of the Chapter. If it is not possible to tighten the bolts fully at this stage, tighten them as much as possible, then tighten them fully once the caliper has been installed on the machine.

Installation

16 Push the pistons a little way back into the caliper using hand pressure or a piece of wood as leverage. Slide the caliper onto the brake disc, making sure the pads sit squarely either side of the disc if they weren't removed **(see illustration)**.

17 Install the caliper mounting bolts, and tighten them to the torque setting specified at the beginning of the Chapter **(see illustration)**.

18 If the calipers were overhauled and if not already done, tighten the caliper body joining bolts to the specified torque setting **(see illustration 3.3)**.

19 If removed, connect the brake hose(s) to the caliper, using new sealing washers on each side of the fitting(s). Align the hose(s) as

noted on removal **(see illustration 3.2a and b)**. Tighten the banjo bolt to the torque setting specified at the beginning of the Chapter. If removed, install the brake pads (see Section 2).

20 Top up the master cylinder reservoir with DOT 4 brake fluid (see *Daily (pre-ride) checks*) and bleed the hydraulic system as described in Section 11.

21 Check for leaks and thoroughly test the operation of the brake before riding the motorcycle.

---

4 Front brake disc – inspection, removal and installation

Inspection

1 Visually inspect the surface of the disc for score marks and other damage. Light scratches are normal after use and won't affect brake operation, but deep grooves and heavy score marks will reduce braking efficiency and accelerate pad wear. If a disc is badly grooved it must be machined or a new one fitted.

2 To check disc runout, position the bike on an auxiliary stand and support it so that the front wheel is raised off the ground. Mount a dial gauge to a fork leg, with the plunger on the gauge touching the surface of the disc about 10 mm (1/2 in) from the outer edge **(see**

illustration). Rotate the wheel and watch the gauge needle, comparing the reading with the limit listed in the Specifications at the beginning of the Chapter. If the runout is greater than the service limit, check the wheel bearings for play (see Chapter 1). If the bearings are worn, install new ones (see Section 16) and repeat this check. If the disc runout is still excessive, a new one will have to be fitted, although machining by an engineer may be possible.

3 The disc must not be machined or allowed to wear down to a thickness less than the service limit as listed in this Chapter's Specifications and as marked on the disc itself **(see illustration)**. The thickness of the disc can be checked with a micrometer **(see illustration)**. If the thickness of the disc is less than the service limit, a new one must be fitted.

Removal

4 Remove the wheel (see Section 14).
Caution: Do not lay the wheel down and allow it to rest on the disc – the disc could become warped. Set the wheel on wood blocks so the disc doesn't support the weight of the wheel.

5 Mark the relationship of the disc to the wheel, so it can be installed in the same position. Unscrew the disc retaining bolts, loosening them evenly and a little at a time in a criss-cross pattern to avoid distorting the disc, then remove the disc from the wheel **(see illustration)**.

4.3a The minimum disc thickness is marked on the disc

4.3b Using a micrometer to measure disc thickness

4.5 The disc is secured by five bolts (arrowed)

Installation

6 Install the disc on the wheel with its marked side facing out, aligning the previously applied matchmarks (if you're reinstalling the original disc).

7 Clean the threads of the disc mounting bolts, then apply a suitable non-permanent thread locking compound. Install the bolts and tighten them evenly and a little at a time in a criss-cross pattern to the torque setting specified at the beginning of the Chapter. Clean off all grease from the brake disc using acetone or brake system cleaner. If a new brake disc has been installed, remove any protective coating from its working surfaces.

8 Install the front wheel (see Section 14).

9 Operate the brake lever several times to bring the pads into contact with the disc. Check the operation of the brakes carefully before riding the bike.

5 Front brake master cylinder – removal, overhaul and installation

1 If the master cylinder is leaking fluid, or if the lever does not produce a firm feel when the brake is applied, and bleeding the brakes does not help (see Section 11), and the hydraulic hoses are all in good condition, then master cylinder overhaul is recommended **(see illustration)**.

2 Before disassembling the master cylinder, read through the entire procedure and make sure that you have the correct rebuild kit. Also, you will need some new DOT 4 brake fluid, some clean rags and internal circlip pliers. **Note:** *To prevent damage to the paint from spilled brake fluid, always cover the fuel tank when working on the master cylinder.*

Caution: Disassembly, overhaul and reassembly of the brake master cylinder must be done in a spotlessly clean work area to avoid contamination and possible failure of the brake hydraulic system components.

Removal

3 Remove the reservoir cap clamp screw, then slacken the cap but do not fully unscrew it **(see illustration)**.

4 Disconnect the electrical connectors from the brake light switch **(see illustration)**.

5 Remove the front brake lever (see Chapter 6).

6 Unscrew the brake hose banjo bolt and separate the hose from the master cylinder, noting its alignment **(see illustration)**. Discard the sealing washers as new ones must be used. Wrap the end of the hose in a clean rag and suspend it in an upright position or bend it down carefully and place the open end in a clean container. The objective is to prevent excessive loss of brake fluid, fluid spills and system contamination.

7 Unscrew the bolt securing the reservoir

H31266

5.1 Front brake master cylinder components

1	Rubber dust boot	4	Cup	7	Circlip
2	Circlip	5	Spring	8	Union
3	Piston assembly	6	Rubber cap	9	O-ring

bracket to the handlebar **(see illustration 5.3)**. Unscrew the master cylinder clamp bolts, then lift the master cylinder and reservoir away from the handlebar **(see illustration)**.

8 Unscrew the reservoir cap and remove the diaphragm plate and the diaphragm. Drain the brake fluid from the master cylinder and reservoir into a suitable container. Release the clamp securing the reservoir hose to the union on the master cylinder and detach the hose **(see illustration 5.3)**. Wipe any remaining fluid out of the reservoir with a clean rag.

5.3 Reservoir cap clamp screw (A), reservoir bracket bolt (B), hose union (C)

5.4 Brake light switch wiring connectors (A) and mounting screw (B)

5.6 Brake hose banjo bolt (arrowed)

5.7 Master cylinder clamp bolts (arrowed)

5.10 Remove the rubber boot from the end of the master cylinder piston . . .

5.11a . . . then depress the piston and remove the circlip using a pair of internal circlip pliers

5.11b Lay out the internal parts as shown, even if new parts are being used, to avoid confusion on reassembly

9 If required, remove the screw securing the brake light switch to the bottom of the master cylinder and remove the switch **(see illustration 5.4)**.

Caution: Do not tip the master cylinder upside down or brake fluid will run out.

Overhaul

10 Carefully remove the dust boot from the end of the piston **(see illustration)**.

11 Using circlip pliers, remove the circlip and slide out the piston assembly and the spring, noting how they fit **(see illustration)**. Lay the parts out in the proper order to prevent confusion during reassembly **(see illustration)**.

12 Remove the fluid reservoir hose union rubber cap, then remove the circlip and detach the union from the master cylinder. Discard the O-ring as a new one must be used. Inspect the reservoir hose for cracks or splits and renew it if necessary.

13 Clean all parts with the correct type of clean brake fluid. If compressed air is available, use it to dry the parts thoroughly (make sure it's filtered and unlubricated).

Caution: Do not, under any circumstances, use a petroleum-based solvent to clean brake parts.

14 Check the master cylinder bore for corrosion, scratches, nicks and score marks. If the necessary measuring equipment is available, compare the dimensions of the piston and bore to those given in the Specifications Section of this Chapter. If damage or wear is evident, the master cylinder must be renewed. If the master cylinder is in poor condition, then the calipers should be checked as well. Check that the fluid inlet and outlet ports in the master cylinder are clear.

15 The dust boot, circlip, piston, seal, primary cup and spring are included in the rebuild kit. Use all of the new parts, regardless of the apparent condition of the old ones. If the seal and cup are not already on the piston, fit them according to the layout of the old piston assembly.

16 Install the spring in the master cylinder so that its tapered end faces out towards the piston.

17 Lubricate the piston, seal and cup with clean brake fluid. Install the assembly into the master cylinder, making sure it is the correct way round **(see illustration 5.11b)**. Make sure the lips on the cup do not turn inside out when they are slipped into the bore. Depress the piston and install the new circlip, making sure that it locates in the master cylinder groove **(see illustration 5.11a)**.

18 Install the rubber dust boot, making sure the lip is seated correctly in the piston groove **(see illustration 5.10)**.

19 Fit a new O-ring onto the reservoir hose union, then press the union into the master cylinder and secure it with the circlip. Fit the rubber cap over the circlip.

20 Inspect the reservoir cap rubber diaphragm and fit a new one it if it is damaged or deteriorated.

Installation

21 If removed, fit the brake light switch onto the bottom of the master cylinder **(see illustration 5.4)**.

22 Attach the master cylinder to the handlebar and fit the clamp with its UP mark facing up **(see illustration 5.7)**. Align the clamp top mating surface with the punchmark in the handlebar, then tighten the upper bolt to the torque setting specified at the beginning of the Chapter, followed by the lower bolt **(see illustration)**.

23 Connect the brake hose to the master cylinder, using new sealing washers on each side of the union, and aligning the hose as noted on removal **(see illustration 5.6)**.

Tighten the banjo bolt to the torque setting specified at the beginning of this Chapter.

24 Install the brake lever (see Chapter 6).

25 Mount the reservoir onto the handlebar and tighten its bracket bolt securely **(see illustration 5.3)**. Connect the reservoir hose to the union and secure it with the clamp.

26 Connect the brake light switch wiring **(see illustration 5.4)**.

27 Fill the fluid reservoir with new DOT 4 brake fluid as described in *Daily (pre-ride) checks*. Refer to Section 11 of this Chapter and bleed the air from the system.

28 Fit the rubber diaphragm, making sure it is correctly seated, the diaphragm plate and the cap onto the master cylinder reservoir. Tighten the cap and secure it with the clamp **(see illustration 5.3)**.

29 Check the operation of the front brake before riding the motorcycle.

6 Rear brake pads – renewal

> ⚠ *Warning: The dust created by the brake system may contain asbestos, which is harmful to your health. Never blow it out*
> *with compressed air and don't inhale any of it. An approved filtering mask should be worn when working on the brakes.*

1 Prise off the brake pad cover using a flat-bladed screwdriver **(see illustration)**.

5.22 Align the mating surfaces of the clamp with the punchmark (arrowed)

6.1 Prise off the cover . . .

6.2 . . . then remove the pad pin retaining clip

6.3 Withdraw the pins (arrowed) and remove the springs . . .

6.4 . . . then remove the pads and shims

2 Remove the pad pin retaining clip, noting how its ends fit through the holes in the pad pins **(see illustration)**.

3 Withdraw the pad pins from the caliper using a suitable pair of pliers and remove the pad springs, noting how they fit **(see illustration)**.

4 Withdraw the pads from the caliper body and remove the anti-chatter shim from the back of each pad, noting how it fits **(see illustration)**.

5 Inspect the surface of each pad for contamination and check that the friction material has not worn beyond its service limit (see Chapter 1, Section 11). If either pad is worn down to, or beyond, the service limit wear indicator (ie the wear indicator is no longer visible), fouled with oil or grease, or heavily scored or damaged by dirt and debris, both pads must be renewed as a set. Note that it is not possible to degrease the friction material; if the pads are contaminated in any way new ones must be fitted.

6 If the pads are in good condition clean them carefully, using a fine wire brush which is completely free of oil and grease to remove all traces of road dirt and corrosion. Using a pointed instrument, clean out the grooves in the friction material and dig out any embedded particles of foreign matter. Any areas of glazing may be removed using emery cloth. Spray with a dedicated brake cleaner to remove any dust.

7 Check the condition of the brake disc (see Section 8).

8 Remove all traces of corrosion from the pad

pins. Inspect them for signs of damage, and renew them if necessary.

9 Push the pistons as far back into the caliper as possible using hand pressure or a piece of wood as leverage **(see illustration 2.7)**. Due to the increased friction material thickness of new pads, it may be necessary to remove the master cylinder reservoir cover and diaphragm and siphon out some fluid. Remove the seat cowling to access the reservoir (see Chapter 8).

10 Smear the backs of the pads and the shank of each pad pin with copper-based grease, making sure that none gets on the front or sides of the pads.

11 Fit the anti-chatter shim onto the back of each pad with its open end facing forward **(see illustration)**. Insert the pads up into the caliper so that the friction material of each

pad is facing the disc, then slide one pad pin, with its holed end on the outside, through the caliper and the holes in the pads **(see illustration)**. Slide the other pin into the outer pad only, then fit the pad springs, locating one end under the installed pad pin and onto the edge of the friction material, and fitting the central hooked section onto the bottom edge of the pad backing **(see illustration)**. Press up on the free end of the outer pad spring and slide the other pad pin over the spring end **(see illustration)**. Now press up on the inner spring end and slide the pin the rest of the way through. Secure the pins with the retaining clip, making sure that its ends fit through the holes in the pad pins – if necessary rotate the pad pins to align their holes correctly **(see illustration)**. Do not forget to install the pad cover.

6.11a Make sure the anti-chatter shims are the right way round

6.11b Install one pin through both pads . . .

6.11c . . . and the other pin through one pad only, then install the springs . . .

6.11d . . . and push up on the spring end to locate it under the second pin as you slide it through

6.11e Do not forget the cover

7.1 Rear brake caliper components

1 Bleed valve cap
2 Bleed valve
3 Caliper body half
4 Caliper seal

5 Piston seal
6 Dust seal
7 Piston
8 Anti-chatter shim

9 Pad pin
10 Pad spring
11 Pad pin clip
12 Brake pad cover

13 Caliper body half
14 Caliper joining bolt
15 Caliper mounting bolt
16 Brake pads

12 Top up the master cylinder reservoir if necessary (see *Daily (pre-ride) checks*).
13 Operate the brake pedal several times to bring the pads into contact with the disc. Check the operation of the brake before riding the motorcycle.

7 Rear brake caliper – removal, overhaul and installation

 Warning: If a caliper indicates the need for an overhaul (usually due to leaking fluid or sticky operation), all old brake fluid should be flushed from the system. Also, the dust created by the brake system may contain asbestos, which is harmful to your health. Never blow it out with compressed air and don't inhale any of it. An approved filtering mask should be worn when working on the brakes. Do not, under any circumstances, use petroleum-based solvents to clean brake parts. Use the specified clean brake fluid, dedicated brake cleaner or denatured alcohol only, as described.

Removal

1 If the caliper is being overhauled, remove the brake pads (see Section 6). If the caliper is just being displaced or removed, the pads can be left in place **(see illustration)**.
2 If the calipers are just being displaced and not completely removed or overhauled, do not disconnect the brake hose. If the calipers are being overhauled, note the alignment of the brake hose on the caliper then unscrew the

brake hose banjo bolt and separate the hose from the caliper **(see illustration)**. Plug the hose end or wrap a plastic bag tightly around it to minimise fluid loss and prevent dirt entering the system. Discard the sealing washers as new ones must be used on installation. **Note:** *If you are planning to overhaul the caliper and don't have a source of compressed air to blow out the pistons, just loosen the banjo bolt at this stage and retighten it lightly. The bike's hydraulic system can then be used to force the pistons out of the body once the pads have been removed. Disconnect the hose once the pistons have been sufficiently displaced.*
3 If the caliper body is to be split into its halves for overhaul, slacken the caliper body joining bolts at this stage and retighten them lightly **(see illustration 7.2)**.
4 Slacken the caliper mounting bolts, but do not yet remove them **(see illustration 7.2)**.

Unscrew the nut securing the brake torque arm to the caliper, but do not yet remove the bolt. **(see illustration 7.2)**.
5 Unscrew the caliper mounting bolts, then support the caliper and withdraw the bolt from the torque arm. Drop the arm off the caliper and slide the caliper down off the disc **(see illustration)**.

Overhaul

6 Clean the exterior of the caliper with denatured alcohol or brake system cleaner.
7 Displace the pistons as far as possible from the caliper body, either by pumping them out by operating the rear brake pedal, or by forcing them out using compressed air – do not allow the piston heads to touch. If the compressed air method is used, place a wad of rag between the pistons to act as a cushion, then use compressed air directed into the fluid inlet to force the pistons out of

7.2 Brake hose banjo bolt (A), caliper body joining bolts (B), caliper mounting bolts (C), torque arm nut (D)

7.5 Slide the caliper down off the disc

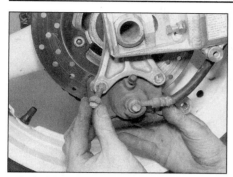

7.18 Slide the caliper onto the disc and install the bolts

7.19a Locate the torque arm onto the caliper . . .

7.19b . . . then fit the nut . . .

7.19c . . . and tighten it to the specified torque

7.19d Now tighten the caliper mounting bolts to the specified torque

the body. Use only low pressure to ease the pistons out. If the air pressure is too high and the pistons are forced out, the caliper and/or pistons may be damaged.

 Warning: Never place your fingers in front of the piston in an attempt to catch or protect it when applying compressed air, as serious injury could result.

8 Unscrew the caliper body joining bolts and separate the body halves. Remove the piston from each half. Mark each piston head and caliper body with a felt marker to ensure that the pistons can be matched to their original bores on reassembly. Extract the caliper seal from whichever body half it is in and discard it as a new one must be used.

9 Using a wooden or plastic tool, remove the dust seal from each caliper bore and discard them **(see illustration 3.8)**. New seals must be used on installation. If a metal tool is being used, take great care not to damage the caliper bore.

10 Remove and discard the piston seals in the same way.

11 Clean the pistons and bores with the correct type of clean brake fluid. If compressed air is available, use it to dry the parts thoroughly (make sure it's filtered and unlubricated).

Caution: Do not, under any circumstances, use a petroleum-based solvent to clean brake parts.

12 Inspect the caliper bores and pistons for signs of corrosion, nicks and burrs and loss of plating. If surface defects are present, the caliper assembly must be renewed. If the necessary measuring equipment is available, compare the dimensions of the pistons and bores to those given in the Specifications Section of this Chapter, renewing any component that is worn beyond the service limit. If the caliper is in bad shape the master cylinder should also be checked.

13 Lubricate the new piston seals with clean brake fluid and install them in their grooves in the caliper bores, making sure the thicker side of the seal is facing the disc **(see illustration 3.12)**.

14 Lubricate the new dust seals with clean brake fluid and install each one in its groove in the caliper bore.

15 Lubricate the pistons with clean brake fluid and install each one closed-end first into

its caliper bore. Using your thumbs, push the pistons all the way in, making sure they enter the bores squarely.

16 Lubricate the new caliper seal and install it into one half of the caliper body. Join the two halves of the caliper body together, making sure that the seal stays correctly seated in its recess. Install the caliper body joining bolts and tighten them to the torque setting specified at the beginning of the Chapter. If it is not possible to tighten the bolts fully at this stage, tighten them as much as possible, then tighten them fully once the caliper has been installed on the machine.

Installation

17 Push the pistons a little way back into the caliper using hand pressure or a piece of wood as leverage.

18 Slide the caliper onto the brake disc, making

7.21a Locate the hose in its open guides (arrowed) . . .

sure the pads sit squarely either side of the disc if they weren't removed **(see illustration 7.5)**. Install the caliper mounting bolts, and tighten them finger-tight **(see illustration)**.

19 Fit the brake torque arm onto the caliper and secure it with its bolt **(see illustration)**. Tighten the nut to the torque setting specified at the beginning of the Chapter **(see illustrations)**. Now tighten the caliper mounting bolts to the specified torque setting **(see illustration)**.

20 If the calipers were overhauled and if not already done, tighten the caliper body joining bolts to the specified torque setting **(see illustration 7.2)**.

21 If removed, connect the brake hose to the caliper, making sure it is routed through its guides on the swingarm, using new sealing washers on each side of the fitting **(see illustrations)**. Align the hose as noted on

7.21b . . . and make sure it passes through the closed guide on the inside of the swingarm (arrowed)

8.3 The disc is secured by five bolts (arrowed)

removal **(see illustration 7.2)**. Tighten the banjo bolt to the torque setting specified at the beginning of the Chapter. If removed, install the brake pads (see Section 6).

22 Top up the master cylinder reservoir with DOT 4 brake fluid (see *Daily (pre-ride) checks*) and bleed the hydraulic system as described in Section 11.

23 Check for leaks and thoroughly test the operation of the brake before riding the motorcycle.

8 Rear brake disc – inspection, removal and installation

Inspection

1 Refer to Section 4 of this Chapter, noting that the dial gauge should be attached to the swingarm.

Removal

2 Remove the rear wheel (see Section 15).
3 Mark the relationship of the disc to the wheel so it can be installed in the same position. Unscrew the disc retaining bolts, loosening them evenly and a little at a time in a criss-cross pattern to avoid distorting the disc, and remove the disc **(see illustration)**.

Installation

4 Install the disc on the wheel with its marked side facing out, aligning the previously applied matchmarks (if you're reinstalling the original disc).
5 Clean the threads of the disc mounting bolts, then apply a suitable non-permanent thread locking compound. Install the bolts and tighten them evenly and a little at a time in a criss-cross pattern to the torque setting specified at the beginning of the Chapter. Clean off all grease from the brake disc using acetone or brake system cleaner. If a new brake disc has been installed, remove any protective coating from its working surfaces.
6 Install the rear wheel (see Section 15).
7 Operate the brake pedal several times to

1 Reservoir cover
2 Rubber diaphragm
3 Reservoir
4 Reservoir hose
5 Brake hose
6 Banjo bolt
7 Sealing washer
8 Reservoir hose elbow
9 O-ring
10 Master cylinder
11 Spring
12 Piston assembly
13 Pushrod
14 Circlip
15 Rubber dust boot
16 Clevis
17 Clevis pin
18 Split pin
19 Locknut
20 Clevis nut

H29138

9.1 Rear brake master cylinder components

bring the pads into contact with the disc. Check the operation of the brake carefully before riding the motorcycle.

9 Rear brake master cylinder – removal, overhaul and installation

1 If the master cylinder is leaking fluid, or if the lever does not produce a firm feel when the brake is applied, and bleeding the brakes does not help (see Section 11), and the hydraulic hoses are all in good condition, then master cylinder overhaul is recommended **(see illustration)**.
2 Before disassembling the master cylinder, read through the entire procedure and make

sure that you have the correct rebuild kit. Also, you will need some new DOT 4 brake fluid, some clean rags and internal circlip pliers. **Note:** *To prevent damage to the paint from spilled brake fluid, always cover the surrounding components when working on the master cylinder.*
Caution: Disassembly, overhaul and reassembly of the brake master cylinder must be done in a spotlessly clean work area to avoid contamination and possible failure of the brake hydraulic system components.

Removal

3 Remove the seat cowling (see Chapter 8).
4 Remove the master cylinder fluid reservoir cover screws, but leave the cover in place

9.4a Reservoir cover screws (A), reservoir mounting bolt (B)

9.4b Reservoir hose clamp (A), brake hose banjo bolt (B)

9.6 Remove the split pin and washer (A) and withdraw the clevis pin (B)

(see illustration). Unscrew the bolt securing the reservoir to the frame, then remove the reservoir cover and diaphragm and pour the fluid into a container. Release the clamp securing the reservoir hose to the union on the master cylinder and detach the hose – have a rag handy to catch any drips **(see illustration)**.

5 Unscrew the brake hose banjo bolt and separate the brake hose from the master cylinder, noting its alignment **(see illustration 9.4b)**. Discard the two sealing washers as they must be renewed. Wrap the end of the hose in a clean rag and suspend the hose in an upright position or bend it down carefully and place the open end in a clean container. The objective is to prevent excessive loss of brake fluid, fluid spills and system contamination.

6 Remove the split pin and washer from the clevis pin securing the master cylinder pushrod to the brake pedal **(see illustration)**. Withdraw the clevis pin and separate the pushrod from the pedal. Discard the split pin as a new one must be used.

7 Unscrew the two bolts securing the heel plate and master cylinder to the bracket **(see illustration)**.

Overhaul

8 If required, mark the position of the clevis locknut on the pushrod, then slacken the locknut and thread the clevis and its base nut off the pushrod **(see illustration)**.

9 Dislodge the rubber dust boot from the base of the master cylinder to reveal the pushrod retaining circlip **(see illustration)**.

10 Depress the pushrod and, using circlip pliers, remove the circlip **(see illustration)**. Slide out the piston assembly and spring. If they are difficult to remove, apply low pressure compressed air to the fluid outlet. Lay the parts out in the proper order to prevent confusion during reassembly.

11 Clean all of the parts with DOT 4 brake fluid.

Caution: Do not, under any circumstances, use a petroleum-based solvent to clean brake parts. If compressed air is available, use it to dry the parts thoroughly (make sure it's filtered and unlubricated).

12 Check the master cylinder bore for corrosion, scratches, nicks and score marks. If the necessary measuring equipment is available, compare the dimensions of the piston and bore to those given in the Specifications Section of this Chapter. If damage is evident, the master cylinder must be renewed. If the master cylinder is in poor condition, then the caliper should be checked as well.

13 Unscrew the fluid reservoir hose union screw and detach the union from the master cylinder. Discard the O-ring as a new one must be used. Inspect the reservoir hose for cracks or splits and renew it if necessary.

14 The dust boot, circlip, piston, seal, primary cup and spring are included in the

rebuild kit. Use all of the new parts, regardless of the apparent condition of the old ones. If the seal and cup are not already on the piston, fit them according to the layout of the old piston assembly.

15 Install the spring in the master cylinder so that its tapered end faces out towards the piston.

16 Lubricate the piston, seal and cup with clean brake fluid. Install the assembly into the master cylinder, making sure it is the correct way round **(see illustration 9.1)**. Make sure the lips on the cup do not turn inside out when they are slipped into the bore.

17 Install and depress the pushrod, then fit a new circlip, making sure it is properly seated in the groove **(see illustration 9.10)**.

18 Fit the rubber dust boot, making sure the

9.7 Unscrew the bolts (arrowed) and remove the heel plate and master cylinder

9.8 Hold the clevis and slacken the locknut

9.9 Remove the dust boot from the pushrod . . .

9.10 . . . then depress the piston and remove the circlip

9.21 Locate the master cylinder and install the heel plate and bolts

9.24 Locate the pin (A) in the hole (B)

10.2 Flex the brake hoses and check for cracks, bulges and leaking fluid

lip is seated properly in its groove (see illustration 9.9).

19 Fit a new O-ring onto the fluid reservoir hose union, then install the union onto the master cylinder and secure it with its screw.

Installation

20 If removed, install the clevis locknut, the clevis and its base nut onto the master cylinder pushrod end. Position the clevis as noted on removal, but do not yet tighten the locknut.

21 Locate the master cylinder on the inside of the footrest bracket, then install the heel plate and tighten the mounting bolts to the torque setting specified at the beginning of the Chapter (see illustration).

22 Align the brake pedal with the master cylinder pushrod clevis, then slide in the clevis pin, fit the washer and secure it using a new

split pin (see illustration 9.6). If the clevis position on the pushrod was disturbed during overhaul, reset the brake pedal to its specified height (see Chapter 1, Section 12). Tighten the clevis locknut securely.

23 Connect the brake hose banjo bolt to the master cylinder, using a new sealing washer on each side of the banjo union (see illustration 9.4b). Ensure that the hose is positioned so that it butts against the lugs and tighten the banjo bolt to the specified torque setting.

24 Secure the fluid reservoir to the frame with its retaining bolt, making sure the pin on the reservoir locates in the lower hole (see illustration). Ensure that the hose is correctly routed behind the frame tube, then connect it to the union on the master cylinder and secure it with the clamp (see illustration 9.4b). Check that the hose is secure

and clamped at the reservoir end as well. If the clamps have weakened, use new ones.

25 Fill the fluid reservoir with new DOT 4 brake fluid (see *Daily (pre-ride) checks*) and bleed the system following the procedure in Section 11.

26 Fit the rubber diaphragm, making sure it is correctly seated, and the cover onto the master cylinder reservoir. Tighten the cover screws.

27 Install the seat cowling (see Chapter 8). Check the operation of the brake carefully before riding the motorcycle.

---

10 Brake hoses and unions – inspection and renewal

Inspection

1 Brake hose condition should be checked regularly and the hoses renewed at the specified interval (see Chapter 1).

2 Twist and flex the rubber hoses while looking for cracks, bulges and seeping fluid (see illustration). Check extra carefully around the areas where the hoses connect with the banjo fittings, as these are common areas for hose failure.

3 Inspect the metal banjo union fittings connected to the brake hoses. If the fittings are rusted, scratched or cracked, fit new hoses.

Renewal

4 The brake hoses have banjo union fittings on each end (see illustration). Cover the surrounding area with plenty of rags and unscrew the banjo bolt at each end of the hose, noting its alignment. Free the hose from any clips or guides and remove the hose. Discard the sealing washers.

5 Position the new hose, making sure it isn't twisted or otherwise strained, and abut the tab on the hose union with the lug on the component casting, where present. Otherwise align the hose as noted on removal. Install the banjo bolts, using new sealing washers on both sides of the unions, and tighten them to the torque setting specified at the beginning

10.4 Front brake hose arrangement

H31267

10.5 Use a new sealing washer on each side of the union

11.6a Remove the dust cap from the caliper bleed valve

11.6b To bleed the brakes you need a spanner to fit on the bleed valve, a short section of clear tubing, and a clear container part-filled with brake fluid so that the end of the tubing is submerged

of this Chapter **(see illustration)**. Make sure they are correctly aligned and routed clear of all moving components.

6 Flush the old brake fluid from the system, refill with new DOT 4 brake fluid (see *Daily (pre-ride) checks*) and bleed the air from the system (see Section 11). Check the operation of the brakes carefully before riding the motorcycle.

11 Brake system – bleeding

1 Bleeding the brakes is simply the process of removing all the air bubbles from the brake fluid reservoirs, the hoses and the brake calipers. Bleeding is necessary whenever a brake system hydraulic connection is loosened, when a component or hose is renewed, or when the master cylinder or caliper is overhauled. Leaks in the system may also allow air to enter, but leaking brake fluid will reveal their presence and warn you of the need for repair.

2 To bleed the brakes, you will need some new DOT 4 brake fluid, a length of clear vinyl or plastic tubing, a small container partially filled with clean brake fluid, some rags and a spanner to fit the brake caliper bleed valves.

3 Cover the fuel tank and other painted components to prevent damage in the event that brake fluid is spilled.

4 If bleeding the rear brake, remove the seat cowling (see Chapter 8) for access to the fluid reservoir.

5 Remove the reservoir cap or cover, diaphragm plate (front reservoir) and diaphragm and slowly pump the brake lever or pedal a few times, until no air bubbles can be seen floating up from the holes in the bottom of the reservoir. Doing this bleeds the air from the master cylinder end of the line. Loosely refit the reservoir cap or cover.

6 Pull the dust cap off the bleed valve **(see illustration)**. Attach one end of the clear vinyl or plastic tubing to the bleed valve and submerge the other end in the brake fluid in the container **(see illustration)**.

7 Remove the reservoir cap or cover and

check the fluid level. Do not allow the fluid level to drop below the lower mark during the bleeding process.

8 Carefully pump the brake lever or pedal three or four times and hold it in (front) or down (rear) while opening the caliper bleed valve. When the valve is opened, brake fluid will flow out of the caliper into the clear tubing and the lever will move toward the handlebar or the pedal will move down.

9 Retighten the bleed valve, then release the brake lever or pedal gradually. Repeat the process until no air bubbles are visible in the brake fluid leaving the caliper, or if the fluid is being changed until new fluid is coming out, and the lever or pedal is firm when applied. On completion, disconnect the bleeding equipment, then tighten the bleed valve to the torque setting specified at the beginning of the chapter and install the dust cap.

> **HAYNES HiNT**
> *Old brake fluid is invariably much darker in colour than new fluid, making it easy to see when all old fluid has been expelled from the system.*

10 Install the diaphragm, diaphragm plate (front reservoir) and cap or cover, not forgetting the cap clamp on the front reservoir. Wipe up any spilled brake fluid and check the entire system for leaks.

12.2 Check the wheel for radial (out-of-round) runout (A) and axial (side-to-side) runout (B)

> **HAYNES HiNT**
> *If it's not possible to produce a firm feel to the lever or pedal the fluid my be aerated. Let the brake fluid in the system stabilise for a few hours and then repeat the procedure when the tiny bubbles in the system have settled out.*

12 Wheels – inspection and repair

1 In order to carry out a proper inspection of the wheels, it is necessary to support the bike upright so that the wheel being inspected is raised off the ground. Position the motorcycle on an auxiliary stand. Clean the wheels thoroughly to remove mud and dirt that may interfere with the inspection procedure or mask defects. Make a general check of the wheels (see Chapter 1) and tyres (see *Daily (pre-ride) checks*).

2 Attach a dial gauge to the fork or the swingarm and position its stem against the side of the rim **(see illustration)**. Spin the wheel slowly and check the axial (side-to-side) runout of the rim. In order to accurately check radial (out of round) runout with the dial gauge, the wheel would have to be removed from the machine, and the tyre from the wheel. With the axle clamped in a vice and the dial gauge positioned on the top of the rim, the wheel can be rotated to check the runout.

3 An easier, though slightly less accurate, method is to attach a stiff wire pointer to the fork or the swingarm and position the end a fraction of an inch from the wheel (where the wheel and tyre join). If the wheel is true, the distance from the pointer to the rim will be constant as the wheel is rotated. **Note:** *If wheel runout is excessive, check the wheel or hub bearings very carefully before renewing the wheel.*

13.5 Wheel alignment check using string

Fix string here

String held taut

H29679

Check for contact here

Hold string so that these distances are equal

4 The wheels should also be visually inspected for cracks, flat spots on the rim and other damage. Look very closely for dents in the area where the tyre bead contacts the rim. Dents in this area may prevent complete

sealing of the tyre against the rim, which leads to deflation of the tyre over a period of time. If damage is evident, or if runout in either direction is excessive, the wheel will have to be renewed. Never attempt to repair a damaged cast alloy wheel.

13 Wheels – alignment check

1 Misalignment of the wheels, which may be due to a cocked rear wheel or a bent frame or fork yokes, can cause strange and possibly serious handling problems. If the frame or yokes are at fault, repair by a frame specialist or renewal with new parts are the only alternatives.

2 To check the alignment you will need an assistant, a length of string or a perfectly straight piece of wood and a ruler. A plumb bob or other suitable weight will also be required.

3 In order to make a proper check of the wheels it is necessary to support the bike in an upright position, using an auxiliary stand. Measure the width of both tyres at their widest points. Subtract the smaller measurement from the larger measurement, then divide the difference by two. The result is the amount of offset that should exist between the front and rear tyres on both sides.

4 If a string is used, have your assistant hold one end of it about halfway between the floor and the rear axle, touching the rear sidewall of the tyre.

5 Run the other end of the string forward and pull it tight so that it is roughly parallel to the floor **(see illustration)**. Slowly bring the string into contact with the front sidewall of the rear tyre, then turn the front wheel until it is parallel with the string. Measure the distance from the front tyre sidewall to the string.

6 Repeat the procedure on the other side of the motorcycle. The distance from the front tyre sidewall to the string should be equal on both sides.

7 As was previously pointed out, a perfectly straight length of wood or metal bar may be substituted for the string **(see illustration)**. The procedure is the same.

8 If the distance between the string and tyre is greater on one side, or if the rear wheel appears to be cocked, refer to Chapter 1, Section 1 and check that the chain adjuster markings coincide on each side of the swingarm.

9 If the front-to-back alignment is correct, the wheels still may be out of alignment vertically.

10 Using the plumb bob, or other suitable weight, and a length of string, check the rear wheel to make sure it is vertical. To do this, hold the string against the tyre upper sidewall and allow the weight to settle just off the floor. When the string touches both the upper and lower tyre sidewalls and is perfectly straight, the wheel is vertical. If it is not, place thin spacers under one leg of the stand.

11 Once the rear wheel is vertical, check the front wheel in the same manner. If both wheels are not perfectly vertical, the frame and/or major suspension components are bent.

14 Front wheel – removal and installation

Removal

1 Remove the fairing side panels (see Chapter 8). Position the motorcycle on an auxiliary stand and support it under the crankcase so that the front wheel is off the ground. Always make sure the motorcycle is properly supported.

2 Remove the brake caliper mounting bolts and slide the calipers off the disc **(see illustration 3.4a and b)**. Support the calipers with pieces of wire, string or bungee cords so that no strain is placed on the hydraulic hoses. There is no need to disconnect the hoses from the calipers. **Note:** *Do not operate the front brake lever with the calipers removed.*

3 Slacken the axle clamp bolts on the bottom of the right-hand fork, then unscrew the axle **(see illustration)**. Support the wheel (a good way to do this is to slide your foot part way under it), then withdraw the axle from the right-hand side, drawing the wheel to the right as you do so that it comes off the axle holder

14.3a Slacken the axle clamp bolts (A), then unscrew the axle (B)

Distance between gauge and tyre must be equal each side and front and back

Perfectly straight lengths of wood or metal bar

Rear tyre must be parallel to gauge at front and back

H29680

13.7 Wheel alignment check using a straight-edge

14.3b Withdraw the axle and remove the wheel

14.4 Remove the axle holder if required

14.9 Tighten the axle to the specified torque

in the bottom of the left-hand fork, and carefully lower the wheel **(see illustration)**.

4 If required (ie if the forks are being disassembled), slacken the axle holder clamp bolts on the bottom of the left-hand fork and withdraw the holder **(see illustration)**. *Caution: Don't lay the wheel down and allow it to rest on the disc – the disc could become warped. Set the wheel on wood blocks so the disc doesn't support the weight of the wheel.*

5 Check the axle for straightness by rolling it on a flat surface such as a piece of plate glass (first wipe off all old grease and remove any corrosion using fine emery cloth). If the equipment is available, place the axle in V-blocks and measure the runout using a dial gauge. If the axle is bent or the runout exceeds the limit specified, fit a new one.

6 Check the condition of the wheel bearings (see Section 16).

Installation

7 Manoeuvre the wheel into position, making sure the directional arrow is pointing in the normal direction of rotation. Apply a thin coat of grease to the axle and to the lips of the bearing seals.

8 If removed, locate the axle holder into the bottom of the left-hand fork and push it in so that its flanged rim is pressed against the fork, then tighten the holder clamp bolts to the

torque setting specified at the beginning of the Chapter, making sure the holder remains pressed against the fork **(see illustration 14.4)**.

9 Lift the wheel between the forks and slide the axle through from the right-hand side, and thread it into the holder **(see illustration 14.3b)**. Now slide the wheel to the left so that the inner end of the holder locates into the bearing seal, then tighten the axle to the torque setting specified at the beginning of the Chapter **(see illustration)**.

10 Push the pistons a little way back into the caliper using hand pressure or a piece of wood on the pads as leverage. Slide the brake calipers onto the discs, making sure the pads sit squarely on each side of the discs **(see illustration 3.16)**. Tighten the caliper mounting bolts to the torque setting specified at the beginning of the Chapter **(see illustrations 3.17)**.

11 Apply the front brake a few times to bring the pads back into contact with the discs. Move the motorcycle off its stand, apply the front brake and pump the front forks a few times to settle all components in position.

12 Tighten the axle clamp bolts on the right-hand fork to the specified torque setting.

13 Install the fairing side panels (see Chapter 8).

14 Check for correct operation of the front brake before riding the motorcycle.

15 Rear wheel – removal and installation

Removal

1 Position the motorcycle on an auxiliary stand so that the wheel is just off the ground. If required, remove the lower fairing and/or fairing side panels so that the stand can be fitted (see Chapter 8).

2 On US models, remove the split pin from the axle nut.

3 Unscrew the axle nut, and on UK models remove the washer **(see illustration)**. Remove the chain adjuster block, noting how it fits **(see illustration)**.

4 Support the wheel (a good way to do this is to slide your foot part way under it) then withdraw the axle along with the adjuster block from the right-hand side **(see illustration)**. Gently lower the wheel to the ground, making sure no strain is placed on the brake hose as the caliper lowers with it, then disengage the chain from the sprocket and draw the wheel back so the disc is clear of the caliper and remove the wheel. Note how the axle passes through the caliper mounting bracket.

5 Remove the spacers from both sides of the

15.3a Unscrew the axle nut and washer (UK models) . . .

15.3b . . . and remove the chain adjuster block

15.4 Withdraw the axle from the right and lower the wheel

15.5 Remove the spacers from the wheel

15.9 Fit the spacer into each side of the wheel

15.10 Locate the caliper onto the disc . . .

wheel, noting which fits on which side **(see illustration)**.
Caution: Do not lay the wheel down and allow it to rest on the disc or the sprocket – they could become warped. Set the wheel on wood blocks so the disc or the sprocket doesn't support the weight of the wheel. Do not operate the brake pedal with the wheel removed.

6 Check the axle for straightness by rolling it on a flat surface such as a piece of plate glass (if the axle is corroded, first remove the corrosion with fine emery cloth). If the equipment is available, place the axle in V-blocks and measure the runout using a dial gauge. If the axle is bent or the runout exceeds the limit specified at the beginning of the Chapter, fit a new one.

7 Check the condition of the wheel bearings (see Section 16).

Installation

8 Push the pistons a little way back into the brake caliper using hand pressure or a piece of wood on the pads as leverage.

9 Apply a thin coat of grease to the lips of each bearing seal, to the inside and the inner faces of the spacers where they contact the seals, and to the axle. Install the spacers into the wheel **(see illustration and 15.5)**. Slide the right-hand side adjuster block onto the axle, making sure it is the right way round.

10 Manoeuvre the wheel so that it is in between the ends of the swingarm and move

it forward so that the brake disc slides into the caliper, making sure the pads sit squarely on each side of the disc **(see illustration)**.

11 Engage the drive chain with the sprocket, then lift the wheel into position, making sure the caliper stays on the disc and the caliper bracket is correctly aligned with the wheel and the swingarm, and the spacers remain correctly in place in the wheel **(see illustration)**.

12 Install the axle from the right, making sure it passes through the caliper mounting bracket **(see illustration)**. Push it all the way through, locating the chain adjuster block in the swingarm and the flats on the axle head in the adjuster block. Check that everything is correctly aligned, then fit the left-hand side adjuster block, the washer (UK models) and the axle nut, but do not tighten it yet **(see illustrations 15.3b and a)**. If it is difficult to insert the axle due to the tension of the drive chain, back off the chain adjusters (see Chapter 1).

13 Adjust the chain slack as described in Chapter 1.

14 Tighten the axle nut to the torque setting specified at the beginning of the Chapter. On US models, fit a new split pin into the nut.

15 Operate the brake pedal several times to bring the pads into contact with the disc. Check the operation of the rear brake carefully before riding the bike.

16 Wheel bearings – removal, inspection and installation

Front wheel bearings

Note: *Always renew the wheel bearings in pairs. Never renew the bearings individually. Avoid using a high pressure cleaner on the wheel bearing area.*

1 Remove the wheel (see Section 14).

2 Set the wheel on blocks so as not to allow the weight of the wheel to rest on the brake disc.

3 Lever out the bearing seal on each side of the wheel using a flat-bladed screwdriver, taking care not to damage the rim of the hub **(see illustration)**. Discard the seals as new ones should be used.

HAYNES HiNT

A small block of wood placed between the screwdriver and the rim will negate the possibility of damage and will improve leverage.

4 Using a metal rod (preferably a brass drift punch) inserted through the centre of one bearing, tap evenly around the inner race of the other bearing to drive it from the hub **(see**

15.11 . . . and fit the chain around the sprocket . . .

15.12 . . . then lift the wheel and slide in the axle

16.3 Lever out the bearing seals . . .

16.4a . . . then drive out the bearings . . .

16.4b . . . locating the drift as shown

16.9 Drive the new bearings into place . . .

illustrations). The bearing spacer will also come out.

5 Lay the wheel on its other side so that the remaining bearing faces down. Drive the bearing out of the wheel using the same technique as above.

6 If the bearings are of the unsealed type or are only sealed on one side, clean them with a high flash-point solvent (one which won't leave any residue) and blow them dry with compressed air (don't let the bearings spin as you dry them). Apply a few drops of oil to the bearing. **Note:** *If the bearing is sealed on both sides don't attempt to clean it.*

 HAYNES HiNT *Refer to Tools and Workshop Tips (Section 5) for more information about bearings.*

7 Hold the outer race of the bearing and rotate the inner race – if the bearing doesn't turn smoothly, has rough spots or is noisy, renew it.

8 If the bearing is good and can be re-used, wash it in solvent once again and dry it, then pack the bearing with grease.

9 Thoroughly clean the hub area of the wheel. First install the left-hand side bearing into its recess in the hub, with the marked or sealed side facing outwards. Using the old bearing (if new ones are being fitted), a bearing driver or a socket large enough to contact the outer race of the bearing, drive it

in until it's completely seated **(see illustration)**.

10 Turn the wheel over and install the bearing spacer. Drive the right-hand side bearing into place as described above.

11 Apply a smear of grease to the lips of the seals, then press them into the wheel, using a seal or bearing driver, a suitable socket or a flat piece of wood to drive it into place if necessary **(see illustration)**.

12 Clean off all grease from the brake discs using acetone or brake system cleaner, then install the wheel (see Section 14).

Rear wheel bearings

13 Remove the rear wheel (see Section 15). Lift the sprocket coupling out of the wheel, noting how it fits **(see illustration)**. If not already done, remove the spacer from the right-hand side of the wheel **(see illustration 15.5)**.

14 Set the wheel on blocks so as not to allow the weight of the wheel to rest on the brake disc.

15 Lever out the bearing seal on the right-hand side of the wheel using a flat-bladed screwdriver, taking care not to damage the rim of the hub (see *Haynes Hint* after step 3) **(see illustration 16.3)**. Discard the seal as a new one should be used.

16 Using a suitable socket located onto the rim of the bearing spacer, which fits inside the bearing, drive out the bearing on the other side **(see illustration)**. The bearing spacer will also come out.

17 Lay the wheel on its other side so that the remaining bearing faces down. Drive the bearing out of the wheel using the same technique as above.

18 Refer to Steps 6 to 8 above and check the bearings.

19 Thoroughly clean the hub area of the wheel. First install the right-hand bearing into its recess in the hub, with the marked or sealed side facing outwards. Using the old bearing (if new ones are being fitted), a bearing driver or a socket large enough to contact the outer race of the bearing, drive it in squarely until it's completely seated **(see illustration 16.9)**.

20 Turn the wheel over and install the bearing spacer. Drive the left-hand side bearing into place as described above **(see illustration)**.

16.11 . . . then fit new bearing seals

16.13 Lift the sprocket coupling out of the wheel

16.16 Locate the socket inside the bearing and onto the rim of the spacer and drive out the opposite bearing

16.20 Drive in the new bearings using a suitable socket

16.27 Drive the bearing out from the inside . . .

16.29 . . . and drive the new bearing in from the outside

16.30 Fit the spacer into the bearing

21 Apply a smear of grease to the lips of the new grease seal, then press it into the right-hand side of the wheel, using a seal or bearing driver, a suitable socket or a flat piece of wood to drive it into place if necessary **(see illustration 16.11)**.

22 Clean off all grease from the brake disc using acetone or brake system cleaner. Fit the sprocket coupling into the wheel, making sure the coupling spacer locates into the bearing **(see illustration 16.13)**.

23 Install the wheel (see Section 15).

Sprocket coupling bearing

24 Remove the rear wheel (see Section 15). Lift the sprocket coupling out of the wheel, noting how it fits **(see illustration 16.13)**.

25 If not already done, remove the spacer from the outside of the sprocket coupling **(see illustration 15.9)**. Also remove the spacer from the inside of the coupling, noting which way round it fits **(see illustration 16.30)**.

26 Lever out the bearing seal on the outside of the coupling using a flat-bladed screwdriver, taking care not to damage the rim

of the hub (see **Haynes Hint** after step 3). Discard the seal as a new one should be used.

27 Support the coupling on blocks of wood and drive the bearing out from the inside using a bearing driver or socket **(see illustration)**.

28 Refer to Steps 6 to 8 above and check the bearings.

29 Thoroughly clean the bearing recess then install the bearing into the outside of the coupling, with the marked or sealed side facing out. Using the old bearing (if new ones are being fitted), a bearing driver or a socket large enough to contact the outer race of the bearing, drive it in until it is completely seated.

30 Fit the spacer into the inside of the coupling, making sure it locates into the bearing **(see illustration)**.

31 Apply a smear of grease to the lips of the new seal, then press it into the coupling, using a seal or bearing driver, a suitable socket or a flat piece of wood to drive it into place if necessary.

32 Check the sprocket coupling/rubber damper (see Chapter 6).

33 Clean off all grease from the brake disc using acetone or brake system cleaner. Fit the sprocket coupling into the wheel, making sure the coupling spacer locates into the bearing **(see illustration 16.13)**.

34 Install the wheel (see Section 15).

17 Tyres – general information and fitting

General information

1 The wheels fitted to all models are designed to take tubeless tyres only. Tyre sizes are given in the Specifications at the beginning of this chapter.

2 Refer to the *Daily (pre-ride) checks* listed at the beginning of this manual for tyre maintenance.

Fitting new tyres

3 When selecting new tyres, refer to the tyre information label on the swingarm and the tyre options listed in the owners handbook. Ensure that front and rear tyre types are compatible, the correct size and correct speed rating; if necessary seek advice from a Suzuki dealer or tyre fitting specialist **(see illustration)**.

4 It is recommended that tyres are fitted by a motorcycle tyre specialist rather than attempted in the home workshop. This is particularly relevant in the case of tubeless tyres because the force required to break the seal between the wheel rim and tyre bead is substantial, and is usually beyond the capabilities of an individual working with normal tyre levers. Additionally, the specialist will be able to balance the wheels after tyre fitting.

5 Note that punctured tubeless tyres can in some cases be repaired. Repairs must be carried out by a motorcycle tyre fitting specialist. Suzuki advise that a repaired tyre should not be used at speeds above 50 mph (80 kmh) for the first 24 hours, and not above 80 mph (130 kmh) thereafter.

17.3 Common tyre sidewall markings

Chapter 8
Bodywork

Contents

Degrees of difficulty

Easy, suitable for novice with little experience	**Fairly easy,** suitable for beginner with some experience	**Fairly difficult,** suitable for competent DIY mechanic	**Difficult,** suitable for experienced DIY mechanic	**Very difficult,** suitable for expert DIY or professional

---

1 General information

This Chapter covers the procedures necessary to remove and install the body parts. Since many service and repair operations on these motorcycles require the removal of the body parts, the procedures are grouped here and referred to from other Chapters.

In the case of damage to the body parts, it is usually necessary to remove the broken component and replace it with a new (or used) one. The material that the body panels are composed of doesn't lend itself to conventional repair techniques. Note that there are however some companies that specialise in 'plastic welding' and there are a number of bodywork repair kits now available for motorcycles.

When attempting to remove any body panel, first study it closely, noting any fasteners and associated fittings, to be sure of returning everything to its correct place on installation. In some cases the aid of an assistant will be required when removing panels, to help avoid the risk of damage to paintwork. Once the evident fasteners have been removed, try to withdraw the panel as described but DO NOT FORCE IT – if it will not release, check that all fasteners have been removed and try again. Where a panel engages another by means of tabs, be careful not to break the tab or its mating slot or to damage the paintwork. Remember that a few moments of patience at this stage will save you a lot of money in replacing broken fairing panels!

When installing a body panel, first study it closely, noting any fasteners and associated fittings removed with it, to be sure of returning everything to its correct place.

Check that all fasteners are in good condition, including all trim nuts or clips and damping/rubber mounts; any of these must be renewed if faulty before the panel is reassembled. Check also that all mounting brackets are straight and repair or renew them if necessary before attempting to install the panel.

Tighten the fasteners securely, but be careful not to overtighten any of them or the panel may break (not always immediately) due to the uneven stress.

> **HAYNES HiNT**
>
> *Note that a small amount of lubricant (liquid soap or similar) applied to the mounting rubber grommets of the seat cowling will assist the lugs to engage without the need for undue pressure.*

2.1a Lift up each corner and remove the bolt (arrowed) . . .

2.1b . . . then remove the seat, noting how the tab (A) locates in the bracket (B)

2 Seats –
removal and installation

Removal

1 To remove the rider's seat, lift up the rear corner on each side and unscrew the bolt **(see illustration)**. Remove the seat, noting how the tab at the front locates **(see illustration)**.
2 To remove the passenger's seat, insert the ignition key into the seat lock located under the left-hand side of the seat cowling, and turn it clockwise to unlock the seat **(see illustration)**. Lift up the front of the seat and draw it forward, noting how the tab locates in the bracket **(see illustration)**.

Installation

3 Installation is the reverse of removal. Make sure the tab at the front of the rider's seat and the tab at the rear of the passenger's seat locate correctly into the brackets **(see illustrations 2.1b and 2.2b)**. Push down on the passenger's seat to engage the latch.

2.2a Turn the key in the lock and lift the front of the seat . . .

2.2b . . . then draw it forward to release the tab (A) from the bracket (B)

3 Seat cowling –
removal and installation

Removal

1 Remove the seats (see Section 2).
2 Remove the two bolts securing each side of the seat cowling, noting how the seat rubbers and collars fit **(see illustrations)**. Remove the screws securing the two clips joining the halves in the middle, and the two screws securing the underside at the back **(see illustrations)**. Carefully pull each side of the front of the cowling out away from the frame to free the two lugs on each side from their rubber grommets **(see illustration)**. Carefully draw the cowling rearwards and off the bike, taking care not to pull the front sides too far apart as this will stress the fasteners at the back.

Installation

3 Installation is the reverse of removal.

3.2a Remove the two bolts (arrowed) on each side . . .

3.2b . . . noting the collars and rubbers on the rear bolts

3.2c Remove the screws and clips joining the middle . . .

3.2d . . . and the screws at the back (arrowed) . . .

3.2e . . . then pull the sides away to free the lugs (arrowed) from their grommets and remove the cowling

4.1 Unscrew the nuts and remove the mirror

5.1a Remove the screws securing each inner panel (arrowed)

5.1b Disconnect the wiring connectors

4 Rear view mirrors –
removal and installation

Removal

1 Unscrew the two nuts securing each mirror and remove the mirror along with its rubber insulator pad **(see illustration)**.

Installation

2 Installation is the reverse of removal.

5 Fairing panels –
removal and installation

Fairing

Removal

1 Remove the screws securing the inner panels to the inside front of each fairing side panel and remove the inner panels **(see illustration)**. Disconnect the various wiring connectors, including the turn signal connectors **(see illustration)**.
2 Reach behind the instrument cluster, then pull back the rubber cover and disconnect the wiring connector **(see illustration)**.
3 Remove the two screws located below the instrument cluster **(see illustration)**.
4 Remove the screws securing each side of the fairing to the fairing side panels **(see illustration)**.
5 Remove the rear view mirrors (see Section 4).

5.2 Disconnect the instrument cluster wiring connector

6 Carefully draw the fairing forward and off the bike, bringing the left-hand air duct (with the fusebox attached – W, X and Y models) with the fairing **(see illustration)**. The right-hand duct will stay on the bike – note how the fairing locates into it.

Installation

7 Installation is the reverse of removal. Make sure the lugs on the headlight locate correctly into the rubber grommets in the mountings under the instrument cluster **(see**

5.3 Remove the screws (arrowed)

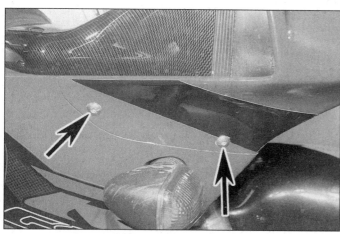

5.4 Remove the screws (arrowed) on each side

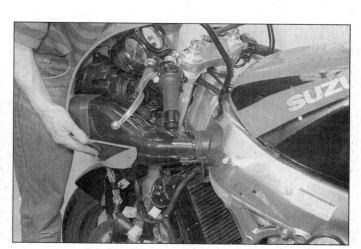

5.6 Carefully draw the fairing forward

5.7 Locate the lugs (A) into the grommets (B)

5.8a Remove the screws (arrowed) . . .

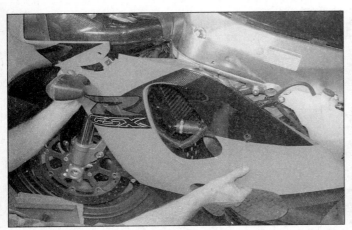

5.8b . . . then displace the panel . . .

5.8c . . . and disconnect the turn signal wiring connector

illustration). Make sure the wiring connectors are correctly and securely connected.

Fairing side panels

Removal

8 To remove the left-hand panel only, remove the nine screws securing the panel, then carefully draw it down and away until the turn signal wiring connector becomes accessible **(see illustrations)**. Disconnect the connector and remove the panel, noting how it engages with the fairing along its top edge and the other side panel along its bottom edge **(see illustrations)**.

9 To remove the right-hand panel only, remove the nine screws securing the panel, then carefully draw it down and away until the turn signal wiring connector becomes accessible **(see illustration and 5.8b)**. Disconnect the connector and remove the panel, noting how it engages with the fairing along its top edge and the other side panel along its bottom edge **(see illustrations 5.8c and d)**.

10 If both panels are being removed, first remove the right-hand panel as described above. Now remove the left-hand panel, but do not remove the two lower front screws which secure the side panel to the centre panel, and bring the centre panel away with the side panel.

Installation

11 Installation is the reverse of removal. Make sure the tabs along the top edge locate correctly with the fairing **(see illustration 5.8b)**, and the tabs on the bottom edge of the right-hand panel locate into the slots in the bottom edge of the left-hand panel **(see illustration 5.8d)**.

5.8d Note how the panels locate together on the underside

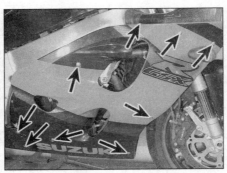

5.9 Remove the screws (arrowed)

5.12a Lower fairing screws – right-hand side

5.12b Lower fairing screws (arrowed) – left-hand side

6.1 Release the brake hoses as described . . .

6.2a . . . then unscrew the bolts (arrowed) on each side . . .

Lower fairing

Removal

12 Remove the screws securing each side, then carefully lower the fairing and manoeuvre it from under the bike **(see illustrations)**.

Installation

13 Installation is the reverse of removal.

6 Front mudguard –
    removal and installation

Removal

1 Release the brake hoses from the mudguard **(see illustration)**. The hoses can either be prised out of the guides on the side, or the bolts securing the guides can be removed and the guides can come away with the hoses. There is a nut on each bolt on the inside of the mudguard – it is likely that after a while these could become corroded and prove difficult to remove, in which case it is best not to disturb them in case the mudguard is damaged. If you do remove them, apply some copper grease to the bolt threads on installation to prevent future problems. Release the central hose clip by pressing together the clip ends on the underside of the mudguard and drawing the clip out of the top.

2 Unscrew the two bolts securing the mudguard to each fork, noting the arrangement of the washers, and remove the mudguard, noting how it fits **(see illustrations)**.

Installation

3 Installation is the reverse of removal.

7 Windshield –
    removal and installation

Removal

1 Remove the screws securing the windshield to the fairing, noting the washers and nut inserts **(see illustration)**. Remove the windshield, noting how it fits.

Installation

2 Installation is the reverse of removal. Do not overtighten the screws.

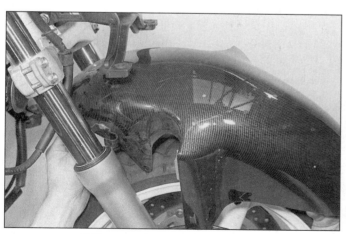

6.2b . . . and remove the mudguard

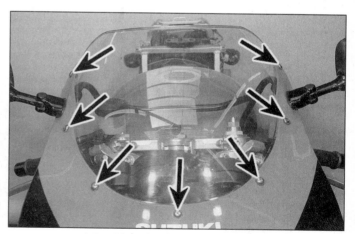

7.1 Windshield screws (arrowed)

Notes

Chapter 9
Electrical system

Contents

Degrees of difficulty

Easy, suitable for novice with little experience	**Fairly easy,** suitable for beginner with some experience	**Fairly difficult,** suitable for competent DIY mechanic	**Difficult,** suitable for experienced DIY mechanic	**Very difficult,** suitable for expert DIY or professional

Specifications

Battery

Capacity	12V, 8Ah
Electrolyte specific gravity	1.320 at 20°C
Current leakage	1 mA (max)

Charging system

Alternator stator coil resistance	
GSX-R600 and GSX-R750T and V models	approx. 0.3 ohms
GSX-R750W and X models	0.24 to 0.36 ohms
Alternator output (max)	
GSX-R600 and GSX-R750T and V models	approx. 378W @ 5000 rpm
GSX-R750W and X models	approx. 406W @ 5000 rpm
Unregulated voltage output (no-load)	
GSX-R600 and GSX-R750T and V models	min. 55V (ac) @ 5000 rpm
GSX-R750W and X models	min. 70V (ac) @ 5000 rpm
Regulated voltage output	13.5 to 15.0V @ 5000 rpm

Starter motor

Brush length (min) . . . .   Not available
Starter relay resistance . . . .   3.0 to 5.0 ohms

Fuses

Main 30A
Headlight (high beam) 15A
Headlight (low beam) 15A
Turn signal 15A
Ignition 10A
Tail light (except GSX-R750W and X) 10A
Fuel system (GSX-R750W and X) 10A

Bulbs

Headlight
  GSX-R600 and GSX-R750T and V . . . .   55/50W H4 halogen x 2
  GSX-R750W and X . . . .   60/55W H4 halogen x 2
Sidelight (UK only) 5.0W
Brake/tail light . . . .   21/5W x 2
Turn signal lights 21W
Meter lights 1.7W
Turn signal indicator light 1.7W
Neutral indicator light 1.7W
High beam indicator light 1.7W
Fuel warning light 1.7W

Torque settings

Oil pressure switch . . . .   14 Nm
Alternator rotor bolt . . . .   120 Nm

---

1 General information

All models have a 12-volt electrical system charged by a three-phase alternator with a separate regulator/rectifier.

The regulator maintains the charging system output within the specified range to prevent overcharging, and the rectifier converts the ac (alternating current) output of the alternator to dc (direct current) to power the lights and other components and to charge the battery. The alternator rotor is mounted on the left-hand end of the crankshaft.

The starter motor is mounted behind the cylinders. The starting system includes the motor, the battery, the relay and the various wires and switches. If the engine kill switch in the RUN position and the ignition (main) switch is ON, the starter relay allows the starter motor to operate only if the transmission is in neutral (neutral switch on) and the clutch lever is pulled in or, if the transmission is in gear, if the sidestand is up and the clutch lever is pulled in.

Note: *Keep in mind that electrical parts, once purchased, cannot be returned. To avoid unnecessary expense, make very sure the faulty component has been positively identified before buying a renewal part.*

2 Electrical system –
   fault finding

Warning: To prevent the risk of short circuits, the ignition (main) switch must always be OFF and the battery negative (-ve) terminal should be disconnected before any of the bike's other electrical components are disturbed. Don't forget to reconnect the terminal securely once work is finished or if battery power is needed for circuit testing.

1 A typical electrical circuit consists of an electrical component, the switches, relays, etc. related to that component and the wiring and connectors that hook the component to both the battery and the frame. To aid in locating a problem in any electrical circuit, refer to the wiring diagrams at the end of this Chapter.

2 Before tackling any troublesome electrical circuit, first study the wiring diagram (see end of Chapter) thoroughly to get a complete picture of what makes up that individual circuit. Trouble spots, for instance, can often be narrowed down by noting if other components related to that circuit are operating properly or not. If several components or circuits fail at one time, chances are the fault lies in the fuse or earth (ground) connection, as several circuits often are routed through the same fuse and earth (ground) connections.

3 Electrical problems often stem from simple causes, such as loose or corroded connections or a blown fuse. Prior to any electrical fault finding, always visually check the condition of the fuse, wires and connections in the problem circuit. Intermittent failures can be especially frustrating, since you can't always duplicate the failure when it's convenient to test. In such situations, a good practice is to clean all connections in the affected circuit, whether or not they appear to be good. All of the connections and wires should also be wiggled to check for looseness which can cause intermittent failure.

4 If testing instruments are going to be utilised, use the wiring diagram to plan where you will make the necessary connections in order to accurately pinpoint the trouble spot.

5 The basic tools needed for electrical fault finding include a battery and bulb test circuit, a continuity tester, a test light, and a jumper wire. A multimeter capable of reading volts, ohms and amps is also very useful as an alternative to the above, and is necessary for performing more extensive tests and checks.

Refer to Fault Finding Equipment in the Reference section for details of how to use electrical test equipment.

3 Battery – removal, installation, inspection and maintenance

Caution: Be extremely careful when handling or working around the battery. The electrolyte is very caustic and an explosive gas (hydrogen) is given off when the battery is charging.

Removal and installation

1 Remove the rider's seat (see Chapter 8).
2 Unscrew the negative (-ve) terminal bolt first and disconnect the lead from the battery **(see illustration)**. Lift up the red insulating cover to access the positive (+ve) terminal, then unscrew the bolt and disconnect the lead. Lift the battery from the bike **(see illustration)**.
3 On installation, clean the battery terminals and lead ends with a wire brush or knife and emery paper. Reconnect the leads, connecting the positive (+ve) terminal first.

 HAYNES HiNT *Battery corrosion can be kept to a minimum by applying a layer of petroleum jelly to the terminals after the cables have been connected.*

4 Install the seat (see Chapter 8).

Inspection and maintenance

5 The battery fitted to the models covered in this manual is of the maintenance free (sealed) type, therefore requiring no regular maintenance. However, the following checks should still be regularly performed.
6 Check the battery terminals and leads for tightness and corrosion. If corrosion is evident, unscrew the terminal screws and disconnect the leads from the battery, disconnecting the negative (-ve) terminal first, and clean the terminals and lead ends with a wire brush or knife and emery paper. Reconnect the leads, connecting the negative (-ve) terminal last, and apply a thin coat of petroleum jelly to the connections to slow further corrosion.
7 The battery case should be kept clean to prevent current leakage, which can discharge the battery over a period of time (especially when it sits unused). Wash the outside of the case with a solution of baking soda and water. Rinse the battery thoroughly, then dry it.
8 Look for cracks in the case and renew the battery if any are found. If acid has been spilled on the frame or battery box, neutralise it with a baking soda and water solution, dry it thoroughly, then touch up any damaged paint.
9 If the motorcycle sits unused for long periods of time, disconnect the cables from the battery terminals, negative (-ve) terminal first. Refer to Section 4 and charge the battery once every month to six weeks.
10 The condition of the battery can be assessed by measuring the voltage present at the battery terminals. Connect the voltmeter

3.2a Disconnect the negative lead (A) first, then the positive lead (B) . . .

positive (+ve) probe to the battery positive (+ve) terminal and the negative (-ve) probe to the battery negative (-ve) terminal. When fully charged there should be more than 12.5 volts present. If the voltage falls below 12.0 volts the battery must be removed, disconnecting the negative (-ve) terminal first, and recharged as described below in Section 4.

4 Battery – charging

Caution: Be extremely careful when handling or working around the battery. The electrolyte is very caustic and an explosive gas (hydrogen) is given off when the battery is charging.

1 Remove the battery (see Section 3). Connect the charger to the battery, making sure that the positive (+ve) lead on the charger is connected to the positive (+ve) terminal on the battery, and the negative (-ve) lead is connected to the negative (-ve) terminal.
2 Suzuki recommend that the battery is charged at a maximum rate of 0.9 amps for 5 hours. Exceeding this figure can cause the battery to overheat, buckling the plates and rendering it useless. Few owners will have access to an expensive current controlled charger, so if a normal domestic charger is used check that after a possible initial peak, the charge rate falls to a safe level **(see**

4.2 If the charger doesn't have ammeter built in, connect one in series as shown. DO NOT connect the ammeter between the battery terminals or it will be ruined

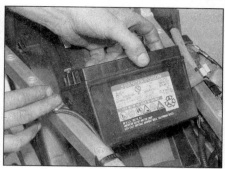

3.2b . . . and lift the battery out

illustration). If the battery becomes hot during charging **stop**. Further charging will cause damage. **Note:** *In emergencies the battery can be charged at a higher rate of around 4.0 amps for a period of 1 hour. However, this is not recommended and the low amp charge is by far the safer method of charging the battery.*
3 After charging, allow the battery to stand undisturbed for about 30 minutes, then check its voltage as described in Section 3. If the battery is still below 12.5 V, charge it some more. If the voltage is still low, the battery is failing and a new one should be installed.
4 If the recharged battery discharges rapidly if left disconnected it is likely that an internal short caused by physical damage or sulphation has occurred. A new battery will be required. A sound item will tend to lose its charge at about 1% per day.
5 Install the battery (see Section 3).
6 If the motorcycle sits unused for long periods of time, charge the battery once every month to six weeks and leave it disconnected.

5 Fuses – check and renewal

1 The electrical system is protected by fuses of different ratings. All except the main fuse are housed in the fusebox, which on T and V models is located below the instrument cluster, and on W, X and Y models is on the inside of the left-hand air duct in the fairing **(see illustration)**. The main fuse is integral

5.1 Fusebox (arrowed) – W, X and Y models shown

5.2a Release the fusebox lid to access the fuses

5.2b Remove the starter relay cover . . .

with the starter relay, which is located behind the left-hand side of the seat cowling **(see illustration 5.2c)**.

2 To access the fusebox fuses, on T and V models remove the screw securing the retainer, then on all models unclip the fusebox lid **(see illustration)**. To access the main fuse, remove the seat cowling (see Chapter 8) and the starter relay cover **(see illustrations)**.

3 The fuses can be removed and checked visually. If you can't pull the fuse out with your fingertips, use a pair of needle-nose pliers. A blown fuse is easily identified by a break in the element **(see illustration)**. Each fuse is clearly marked with its rating and must only be renewed by a fuse of the correct rating. A spare fuse of each rating is housed in the fusebox, and a spare main fuse is housed in the bottom of the starter relay **(see illustration 5.2c)**. If a spare fuse is used, always renew it so that a spare of each rating is carried on the bike at all times.

⚠️ *Warning: Never put in a fuse of a higher rating or bridge the terminals with any other substitute, however temporary it may be. Serious damage may be done to the circuit, or a fire may start.*

4 If a fuse blows, be sure to check the wiring circuit very carefully for evidence of a short-circuit. Look for bare wires and chafed,

melted or burned insulation. If the fuse is renewed before the cause is located, the new fuse will blow immediately.

5 Occasionally a fuse will blow or cause an open-circuit for no obvious reason. Corrosion of the fuse ends and fusebox terminals may occur and cause poor fuse contact. If this happens, remove the corrosion with a wire brush or emery paper, then spray the fuse end and terminals with electrical contact cleaner.

6 Lighting system – check

1 The battery provides power for operation of the headlight, tail light, brake light and instrument cluster lights. If none of the lights operate, always check battery voltage before proceeding. Low battery voltage indicates either a faulty battery or a defective charging system. Refer to Section 3 for battery checks and Section 32 for charging system tests. Also, check the condition of the fuses (see Section 5).

Headlight

2 If the headlight fails to work, check the bulb first (see Section 7), then the fuse and the wiring connector, then check for battery voltage at the black/yellow (HI beam) and/or

black/green (LO beam) wire terminal on the supply side of the headlight wiring connector. If voltage is present, check the earth (ground) circuit for an open or poor connection.

3 If no voltage is indicated, check the wiring between the headlight, the lighting switch (UK only) and the ignition switch, then check the switches themselves.

Tail light

4 If the tail light fails to work, check the bulb and the bulb terminals first, then the fuse and the wiring connector, then check for battery voltage at the brown wire terminal on the supply side of the tail light wiring connector. If voltage is present, check the earth (ground) circuit for an open or poor connection.

5 If no voltage is indicated, check the wiring between the tail light, the lighting switch (UK only) and the ignition switch, then check the switches themselves.

Brake light

6 If the brake light fails to work, check the bulb and the bulb terminals first (see Section 9), then the fuse and the wiring connector, then check for battery voltage at the white/black wire terminal on the supply side of the tail light wiring connector, with the brake lever pulled in or the pedal depressed. If voltage is present, check the earth (ground) circuit for an open or poor connection.

7 If no voltage is indicated, check the brake light switches (see Section 14), then the wiring between the tail light and the switches.

Instrument and warning lights

8 See Section 17 for instrument and warning light bulb renewal.

Turn signal lights

9 If one light fails to work, check the bulb and the bulb terminals first, then the wiring connector. If none of the turn signals work, first check the fuse.

10 If the fuse is good, see Section 13 for the turn signal circuit check.

5.2c . . . to access the main fuse (A). The spare is in the base of the relay (B)

H28946

5.3 A blown fuse can be identified by a break in its element

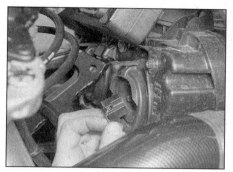

7.1a Disconnect the wiring connector . . .

7.1b . . . and remove the rubber cover

7.2a Release the retaining clip . . .

7.2b . . . and withdraw the bulb

7.6a Unscrew and remove the trim clips (arrowed) . . .

7.6b . . . and remove the panel

7 Headlight bulb and sidelight bulb – renewal

Note: *The headlight bulb is of the quartz-halogen type. Do not touch the bulb glass as skin acids will shorten the bulb's service life. If the bulb is accidentally touched, it should be wiped carefully when cold with a rag soaked in methylated spirit and dried before fitting.*

⚠ **Warning: Allow the bulb time to cool before removing it if the headlight has just been on.**

Headlight

1 Disconnect the relevant wiring connector from the back of the headlight assembly and remove the rubber dust cover, noting how it fits **(see illustrations)**.

2 Release the bulb retaining clip, noting how it fits, then remove the bulb **(see illustrations)**.

3 Fit the new bulb, bearing in mind the information in the **Note** above. Make sure the tabs on the bulb fit correctly in the slots in the bulb housing, and secure it in position with the retaining clip.

4 Install the dust cover, making sure it is

 HAYNES HiNT *Always use a paper towel or dry cloth when handling new bulbs to prevent injury if the bulb should break and to increase bulb life.*

correctly seated and with the 'TOP' mark at the top, and connect the wiring connector.

5 Check the operation of the headlight.

Sidelight

6 Unscrew and remove the trim clips securing the access panel in the base of the fairing and remove the panel **(see illustrations)**.

7 Pull the bulbholder out of its socket in the base of the headlight, then carefully pull the bulb out of the holder **(see illustrations)**.

8 Install the new bulb in the bulbholder, then install the bulbholder by pressing it in. Make sure the rubber cover is correctly seated.

9 Fit the access panel, then install the trim clips and press in their pins **(see illustration)**.

10 Check the operation of the sidelight.

7.7a Pull the bulbholder out of the headlight . . .

7.7b . . . and the bulb out of the holder

7.9 Press the pins back into the clips

8.2 Release the wiring from the clip (arrowed) . . .

8.3 . . . then disconnect the wiring connectors (arrowed)

8.4 Remove the screws (arrowed) and remove the headlight

8 Headlight assembly – removal and installation

Removal

1 Remove the fairing (see Chapter 8).
2 Move the air duct aside. Release the wiring loom from its clip on the lower left-hand side of the headlight **(see illustration)**.
3 Disconnect the headlight and sidelight wiring connectors **(see illustration)**.
4 Remove the screws securing the headlight to the fairing, noting the wiring clip secured by the lower left-hand screw **(see illustration)**. Remove the headlight, noting how it fits.

Installation

5 Installation is the reverse of removal. Make sure all the wiring is correctly connected and secured. Check the operation of the headlight and sidelight. Check the headlight aim (see Chapter 1).

9 Tail/brake light bulbs – renewal

1 Remove the passenger seat (see Chapter 8).
2 Turn the relevant bulbholder anti-clockwise

9.2 Release the bulbholder . . .

and withdraw it from the tail light **(see illustration)**.
3 Push the bulb into the holder and twist it anti-clockwise to remove it **(see illustration)**.
4 Check the socket terminals for corrosion and clean them if necessary. Line up the pins of the new bulb with the slots in the socket, then push the bulb in and turn it clockwise until it locks into place. **Note:** *The pins on the bulb are offset so it can only be installed one way. It is a good idea to use a paper towel or dry cloth when handling the new bulb to prevent injury if the bulb should break and to increase bulb life.*
5 Fit the bulbholder into the tail light and turn it clockwise to secure it.
6 Install the seat (see Chapter 8).

9.3 . . . and remove the bulb

10 Tail light assembly – removal and installation

Removal

1 Remove the seat cowling (see Chapter 8).
2 Either turn the bulbholders anti-clockwise and withdraw them from the tail light **(see illustration 9.2)**, or trace the wiring from the tail light and disconnect it at the connector **(see illustration)**.
3 Remove the screws securing the tail light assembly and carefully remove it **(see illustration)**.

10.2 Tail light wiring connector (arrowed)

10.3 The tail light is secured by three screws (arrowed)

11.1a Remove the screw . . .

11.1b . . . and withdraw the lens

11.2 Release the bulbholder . . .

Installation

4 Installation is the reverse of removal. Check the operation of the tail light and the brake light.

11 Turn signal bulbs – renewal

1 Remove the screw securing the turn signal lens and remove the lens, noting how it fits (see illustrations).
2 Turn the bulbholder anti-clockwise and withdraw it from the lens (see illustration).
3 Push the bulb into the holder and twist it anti-clockwise to remove it (see illustration). Check the socket terminals for corrosion and clean them if necessary. Line up the pins of the new bulb with the slots in the socket, then push the bulb in and turn it clockwise until it locks into place.
4 Fit the bulbholder back into the lens and turn it clockwise, making sure it is securely held.
5 Fit the lens into the holder, locating the tab on the side of the lens behind the plate in the housing, then install the screw (see illustration).

If the socket contacts are dirty or corroded, scrape them clean and spray with electrical contact cleaner before a new bulb is installed.

12 Turn signal assemblies – removal and installation

Front

Removal

1 Remove the screws securing the inner trim panel on the inside of the fairing side panel and remove the trim (see illustration).
2 Disconnect the turn signal wiring connector (see illustration 12.3).
3 Remove the screws securing the stalk to the inside of the fairing and remove the mounting plate, then twist the stalk to free the tabs and withdraw it from the fairing, noting

11.3 . . . and remove the bulb

how it fits (see illustration). Take care not to snag the wiring as you pull it through.

Installation

4 Installation is the reverse of removal. Check the operation of the turn signals.

Rear

Removal

5 Remove the passenger seat (see Chapter 8). Trace the wiring back from the turn signal and disconnect it at the connector, located behind the seat cowling on the left-hand side (see illustration). If the connectors are difficult to access, remove the seat cowling (see Chapter 8).
6 Unscrew the nut securing the turn signal assembly to the inside of the mudguard,

11.5 Locate the tab (A) behind the plate (B)

12.1 Remove the screws (arrowed) to free the trim panel

12.3 Disconnect the turn signal wiring connector (A), then remove the screws (B) and the mounting plate

12.5 Disconnect the relevant wiring connector (arrowed) . . .

12.6 . . . then unscrew the nut (arrowed)
and withdraw the turn signal

13.3a On W, X and Y models the turn signal
relay (arrowed) is next to the fusebox . . .

13.3b . . . and can be pulled off its
connector

noting the washer, and draw the turn signal out of the mudguard **(see illustration)**. Remove the spacer from the mounting hole to allow the wiring connector through. Take care not to snag the connector as you draw it through.

Installation

7 Installation is the reverse of removal. Make sure the wiring is correctly routed and securely connected. Check the operation of the turn signals.

13 Turn signal circuit – check

1 Most turn signal problems are the result of a burned out bulb or corroded socket. This is especially true when the turn signals function properly in one direction, but fail to flash in the other direction. Check the bulbs and the sockets (see Section 11) and the wiring connectors. Also, check the fuse (see Section 5) and the switch (see Section 20).
2 The battery provides power for operation of the turn signal lights, so if they do not operate, also check the battery voltage. Low battery voltage indicates either a faulty battery or a defective charging system. Refer to Section 3 for battery checks and Section 32 for charging system tests.
3 If the all the above are good, check the relay, which on T and V models is located below the instrument cluster, and on W, X and Y models is on the inside of the left-hand air duct in the fairing, next to the fusebox and integral with the sidestand relay and diode **(see illustration)**. On T and V models, disconnect the relay wiring connector and release the relay from its mounting. On W, X and Y models, pull the relay off its connector **(see illustration)**. Check for battery voltage at the dark green wire terminal on the connector with the ignition ON. Connect the positive (+ve) probe of the meter to the terminal and the negative (-ve) probe to the frame or engine. Turn the ignition OFF when the check is complete and plug the relay back in.
4 If no power was present at the relay, check the wiring from the relay to the ignition (main) switch for continuity.

5 If power was present at the relay, trace the wiring from the relay to the connector block, but do not disconnect it. Check for battery voltage at the light blue terminal on the relay side of the connector with the ignition switch ON. Connect the positive (+ve) probe of the meter to the terminal and the negative (-ve) probe to the frame or engine. Turn the ignition OFF when the check is complete. If no power was present, and the wiring between the connector and the relay is good, the relay is probably faulty. As Suzuki provide no test data for the relay, the only way to test it is to substitute it with a known good one. If power was present at the connector, use the appropriate wiring diagram at the end of this Chapter and check the wiring between the relay, turn signal switch and turn signal lights for continuity.

14 Brake light switches – check and renewal

Circuit check

1 Before checking any electrical circuit, check the bulb (see Section 9) and fuse (see Section 5).
2 The front brake light switch is mounted on the underside of the brake master cylinder **(see illustration 14.6)**. The rear brake light switch is mounted on the inside of the frame on the right-hand side, above the brake pedal **(see illustration 14.9)**. Disconnect the wiring connector(s) from the switch.

14.6 Front brake light switch wiring
connectors (A) and mounting screw (B)

3 Using a multimeter or test light connected to a good earth (ground), check for voltage at the black/red (dark green on certain models) – front, or orange/green – rear, wire terminal on the connector with the ignition switch ON – there should be battery voltage. If there's no voltage present, check the wiring between the switch and the ignition switch (see the *wiring diagrams* at the end of this Chapter).
4 If voltage is available, reconnect the connector(s) and touch the probe of the meter or test light to the other terminal of the switch, then pull the brake lever in or depress the brake pedal. If no reading is obtained or the test light doesn't light up, renew the switch.
5 If a reading is obtained or the test light does light up, check the wiring between the switch and the brake light bulb (see the *wiring diagrams* at the end of this Chapter).

Switch renewal

Front brake lever switch

6 The switch is mounted on the underside of the brake master cylinder. Disconnect the wiring connectors from the switch **(see illustration)**.
7 Remove the single screw securing the switch to the bottom of the master cylinder and remove the switch.
8 Installation is the reverse of removal. The switch isn't adjustable.

Rear brake pedal switch

9 The switch is mounted on the inside of the frame on the right-hand side, above the brake pedal **(see illustration)**. Pull up the rubber

14.9 Rear brake light switch (arrowed)

cover and disconnect the wiring connector from the switch.

10 Detach the lower end of the switch spring from the brake pedal, then hold the adjusting nut and unscrew and remove the switch.

11 Installation is the reverse of removal. Make sure the brake light is activated just before the rear brake pedal takes effect. If adjustment is necessary, either hold the switch and turn the adjusting nut on the switch body, or disconnect the wiring connector and turn the switch itself while holding the nut, until the brake light is activated when required.

15.2a Instrument cluster mounting bolts (A). Warning light cover (B)

15.2b Lift the instruments off the bracket, noting how the mounting lugs locate in the grommets

15 Instrument cluster – removal and installation

Removal

1 Remove the fairing (see Chapter 8).
2 Unscrew the bolts securing the instrument cluster to the bracket and lift the cluster away (see illustrations).

Installation

3 Installation is the reverse of removal. Check the condition of the rubber wiring grommets and fit new ones if they are damaged or deteriorated.

16 Instruments – check and renewal

Speedometer and speed sensor

Check

1 Special equipment is needed to check the operation of the speedometer and sensor. If the speedometer doesn't work, take the motorcycle to a Suzuki dealer for assessment.

Renewal

2 Remove the instrument cluster (see Section 15).

3 Remove the screws securing the rear cover and remove the cover (see illustrations).
4 Remove the screw securing the instruments in the front cover and lift them out of the cover (see illustrations). The speedometer is not available individually from the other instruments, so the whole assembly must be renewed.
5 Fit the new instruments into the front cover, then fit the back cover and install the cluster.
6 To renew the sensor, disconnect its wiring connector, which is on the inside of the left-hand fairing side panel (remove the panel for improved access – see Chapter 8), then unscrew the bolt securing the sensor to the front sprocket cover and remove it (see illustrations).

16.3a Remove the screws (arrowed) . . .

16.3b . . . and lift off the cover

16.4a Remove the single screw . . .

16.4b . . . and lift out the instruments

16.6a Disconnect the speed sensor wiring connector . . .

16.6b . . . then unscrew the bolt (arrowed) and remove the sensor

Tachometer

Check

7 No test procedure or data is provided. If the tachometer is not working, take the motorcycle to a Suzuki dealer for assessment.

Renewal

8 Remove the instrument cluster (see Section 15).
9 Remove the screws securing the rear cover and remove the cover **(see illustrations 16.3a and b)**.
10 Remove the screw securing the instruments in the front cover and lift them out of the cover **(see illustrations 16.4a and b)**. The tachometer is not available individually from the other instruments, so the whole assembly must be renewed.
11 Fit the new instruments into the front cover, then fit the back cover and install the cluster.

Coolant temperature display

Check

12 Special equipment is needed to check the operation of this circuit. If it's not working, and the temperature sensor is not faulty (see Chapter 3), take the motorcycle to a Suzuki dealer for assessment.

Renewal

13 See Steps 8 to 11 above.

Oil pressure display

Check

14 Turn the ignition switch ON – the oil warning display should flicker until the engine is started, then it should go out.
15 The oil pressure switch is screwed into the right-hand side of the crankcase – remove the right-hand fairing side panel for access (see Chapter 8). Remove the screw and detach the wiring connector from the switch **(see illustration 18.5)**. With the

ignition switched ON, earth (ground) the wire on the crankcase and check that the display and warning light come on. If they don't, check for voltage at the wire terminal. If there is no voltage present, check the wire between the switch, the instrument cluster and fusebox for continuity (see the *wiring diagrams* at the end of this Chapter). If the wiring is good, then the display is faulty. If the display and light come on, check the oil pressure switch (see Section 18).
16 If the display and warning light come on whilst the engine is running, yet the oil pressure is satisfactory, remove the screw and detach the wire from the oil pressure switch **(see illustration 18.5)**. With the wire detached and the ignition switched ON the display and light should be out. If they are illuminated, the wire between the switch and instrument cluster must be earthed (grounded) at some point. If the wiring is good, the switch must be assumed faulty and a new one must be fitted (see Section 18).

Renewal

17 See Steps 8 to 11 above.

Fuel level warning display

Check

18 First check the bulb (see Section 17). If the bulb is good, raise the fuel tank (see Chapter 4) and disconnect the fuel pump wiring connector.
19 Turn the ignition switch ON – the fuel warning light should come on for three seconds, after which it will go out if there are more than 4 litres of fuel in the tank, or will flicker if there are between 2.5 and 4 litres, or will remain on if there are less than 2.5 litres.
20 Connect a jumper wire between the black/white and red/black terminals on the wiring loom side of the connector. With the ignition switched ON, the light should flicker. Now connect the jumper wire between the black/white and black/light green terminals on the wiring loom side of the connector. With

the ignition switched ON, the light should be on. If not, check the wiring between the connector and the instruments. If the wiring is good, then the display is faulty.

Renewal

21 Remove the instrument cluster (see Section 15).
22 Remove the screws securing the rear cover and remove the cover **(see illustrations 16.3a and b)**.
23 Remove the screw securing the instruments in the front cover and lift them out of the cover **(see illustrations 16.4a and b)**. As individual parts are not available the whole assembly must be renewed.
24 Fit the new instruments into the front cover, then fit the back cover and install the cluster.

17 Instrument and warning light bulbs – renewal

Meter light bulbs

1 Remove the instrument cluster (see Section 15).
2 Remove the screws securing the rear cover and remove the cover **(see illustrations 16.3a and b)**.
3 Twist the relevant bulbholder anticlockwise to release it, then carefully pull out the bulb **(see illustrations)**.
4 Fit the new bulb, then install the holder.
5 Fit the back cover and install the cluster.

Warning light bulbs

6 Remove the fairing (see Chapter 8).
7 Remove the rubber cover from the back of the instrument cluster **(see illustration 15.2a)**.
8 Twist the relevant bulbholder anticlockwise to release it, then carefully pull out the bulb.
9 Fit the new bulb, then install the holder, the rubber cover and the fairing.

17.3a Release the bulbholder . . .

17.3b . . . and remove the bulb

18.5 Remove the screw and detach the wire from the switch

18 Oil pressure switch – check, removal and installation

Check

1 The oil pressure warning display should flicker and the warning light come on when the ignition (main) switch is turned ON, and they extinguish after the engine is started. If they come on as described whilst the engine is running, stop the engine immediately and carry out an oil pressure check as described in Chapter 1.

2 If the oil pressure warning light does not come on when the ignition is turned on, check the display (see Section 16).

3 If the display and wiring are good, the switch must be assumed faulty and a new one must be installed.

Removal

4 Drain the engine oil (see Chapter 1).

5 The oil pressure switch is screwed into the right-hand side of the crankcase – remove the right-hand fairing side panel for access (see Chapter 8). Remove the screw and detach the wiring connector from the switch **(see illustration)**.

6 Unscrew the oil pressure switch and withdraw it from the crankcase.

Installation

7 Apply a suitable sealant (Suzuki-Bond 1207B or equivalent) to the threads near the switch body, then install it in the crankcase and tighten it to the torque setting specified at the beginning of the Chapter.

8 Attach the wiring connector and tighten the screw **(see illustration 18.5)**.

9 Fill the engine with the correct type and quantity of oil as described in Chapter 1. Start the engine and check for leaks around the switch.

10 Install the fairing side panel (see Chapter 8).

19 Ignition (main) switch – check, removal and installation

⚠️ **Warning: To prevent the risk of short circuits, disconnect the battery negative (-ve) lead before making any ignition (main) switch checks.**

Check

1 Raise the fuel tank and remove the air filter housing (see Chapter 4). Disconnect the ignition switch wiring connector **(see illustration)**.

2 Using an ohmmeter or a continuity tester, check the continuity of the connector terminal pairs (see the *wiring diagrams* at the end of this Chapter). Continuity should exist between the terminals connected by a solid line on the diagram when the switch is in the indicated position.

3 If the switch fails any of the tests, renew it.

Removal

4 Remove the fairing (see Chapter 8).

5 Raise the fuel tank and remove the air filter housing (see Chapter 4). Disconnect the ignition switch wiring connector, then free the wiring from its guide and feed it through to the switch **(see illustration 19.1)**.

6 Torx bolts are used to mount the ignition switch to the underside of the top yoke. Remove the two bolts, turning the handlebars as required to provide best access for your tools **(see illustration)**.

Installation

7 Installation is the reverse of removal. Make sure the wiring is correctly routed and securely connected.

20 Handlebar switches – check

1 Generally speaking, the switches are reliable and trouble-free. Most troubles, when they do occur, are caused by dirty or corroded contacts, but wear and breakage of internal parts is a possibility that should not be overlooked. If breakage does occur, the entire switch and related wiring harness will have to be renewed, since individual parts are not available.

2 The switches can be checked for continuity using an ohmmeter or a continuity test light. Always disconnect the battery negative (-ve) lead, which will prevent the possibility of a short circuit, before making the checks.

3 Remove the screws securing the inner trim panel on the inside of the fairing side panel and remove the trim **(see illustration 12.1)**. Trace the wiring harness of the switch in question back to its connector and disconnect it **(see illustration)**. The black connector is for the right-hand switches and the yellow connector is for the left-hand switches.

4 Check for continuity between the terminals of the connector on the switch side, with the switch in the various positions (ie switch off – no continuity, switch on – continuity) – see the *wiring diagrams* at the end of this Chapter.

5 If the continuity check indicates a problem exists, refer to Section 21, remove the switch and spray the switch contacts with electrical contact cleaner. If they are accessible, the contacts can be scraped clean with a knife or polished with crocus cloth. If switch components are damaged or broken, it will be obvious when the switch is disassembled.

21 Handlebar switches – removal and installation

Right-hand switch

Removal

1 If the switch is to be removed from the bike, rather than just displaced from the handlebar, remove the screws securing the inner trim

19.1 Disconnect the ignition switch wiring connector (arrowed)

19.6 Turn the handlebars for best access to each bolt (arrowed)

20.3 Handlebar switch wiring connectors (arrowed)

panel on the inside of the fairing side panel and remove the trim **(see illustration 12.1)**. Trace the wiring harness of the switch in question back to its connector and disconnect it **(see illustration 20.3)**. The black connector is for the right-hand switches. Work back along the harness, freeing it from its guide, noting its correct routing.

2 Disconnect the front brake light switch wiring connectors **(see illustration 14.6)**.

3 Remove the throttle cables from the switch (see Chapter 4 – this procedure incorporates switch removal).

Installation

4 Installation is the reverse of removal. Refer to Chapter 4 for installation of the throttle cables. Make sure the locating pin in the upper half of the switch fits into hole in the top of the handlebar.

Left-hand switch

Removal

5 If the switch is to be removed from the bike, rather than just displaced from the handlebar, remove the screws securing the inner trim panel on the inside of the fairing side panel and remove the trim **(see illustration 12.1)**. Trace the wiring harness of the switch in question back to its connector and disconnect it **(see illustration 20.3)**. The yellow connector is for the left-hand switches. Work back along the harness, freeing it from its guide, noting its correct routing.

6 Disconnect the clutch switch wiring connector **(see illustration 25.2)**.

7 Remove the choke cable from the switch (see Chapter 4 – this procedure incorporates switch removal).

Installation

8 Installation is the reverse of removal. Refer to Chapter 4 for installation of the choke cable. Make sure the locating pin in the upper half of the switch fits into hole in the top of the handlebar.

---

22 Neutral switch (gear position sensor) – check, removal and installation

Check

1 Before checking the electrical circuit, check the bulb (see Section 17) and fuse (see Section 5).

2 Remove the seat cowling (see Chapter 8). Trace the neutral switch wiring from the left-hand side of the engine to the white connector with the blue and pink wires (T and V models) or blue, pink and black/white wires (W, X and Y models), and disconnect it **(see illustration)**.

3 Make sure the transmission is in neutral. With the connector disconnected and the ignition switched ON, the neutral light should be out. If not, the wire between the connector and instrument cluster must be earthed (grounded) at some point.

4 Check for continuity between the blue wire terminal on the switch side of the wiring connector and the crankcase. With the transmission in neutral, there should be

continuity. With the transmission in gear, there should be no continuity. If the tests prove otherwise, then either the switch is faulty or the spring and plunger mechanism in the selector drum is faulty. Remove the switch (see below) and check the condition of the spring and plunger; make sure that the plunger moves freely in its hole. If there is any sign of wear or damage, renew the spring and plunger and check the operation of the switch before buying a new switch.

5 If the continuity tests prove the switch is good, check for voltage at the blue wire terminal using a test light. If there's no voltage present, check the wire and components between the switch, diode, the instrument cluster and fusebox (see the *wiring diagrams* at the end of this Chapter).

Removal

6 Unscrew the gearchange linkage arm pinch bolt and remove the arm from the shaft, noting any alignment marks **(see illustration)**. If no marks are visible, make your own before removing the arm so that it can be correctly aligned with the shaft on installation.

7 Trace the wiring from the speedometer sensor on the front sprocket cover and disconnect it at the connector – you may have to remove the left-hand fairing side panel to access it (see Chapter 8) **(see illustration 16.6a)**.

8 Unscrew the bolts securing the sprocket cover to the crankcase and move the cover aside **(see illustration)**. There is no need to detach the clutch cable from the cover. On W, X and Y models, note the rubber bushing for the gearchange shaft and remove it from the cover if required.

9 Remove the seat cowling (see Chapter 8). Trace the neutral switch (gear position sensor) wiring from the left-hand side of the engine to the white connector with the blue and pink wires (T and V models) or blue, pink and black/white wires (W, X and Y models), and disconnect it **(see illustration 22.2)**. Feed it through to the switch, releasing it from any clips or ties and noting its routing.

10 Remove the two screws securing the switch to the crankcase and carefully remove it, together with the contact plunger(s) and spring(s) if required **(see illustrations)**.

22.2 Neutral switch wiring connector (arrowed)

22.6 Unscrew the bolt (arrowed) and slide the arm off the shaft

22.8 Sprocket cover bolts (arrowed)

22.10a Remove the screws (arrowed) and pull out the switch

22.10b Remove the plungers and springs if required

22.11a Install the springs and plungers . . .

22.11b . . . then fit a new O-ring onto the switch . . .

22.11c . . . and fit it onto the engine

22.15a Locate the rotor (A) into the sensor (B)

22.15b Where fitted and if removed, slide the rubber bush onto the shaft

Discard the O-ring as a new one must be used.

Installation

11 If removed, install the spring(s) and plunger(s) into the hole(s) in the end of the selector drum, then install the switch using a new O-ring and tighten its screws securely **(see illustrations)**.

12 Route the wiring up to its connector and reconnect it **(see illustration 22.2)**. Secure the wiring with any clips or ties.

13 Check the operation of the neutral light.

14 If detached, fit the clutch cable into the release mechanism in the sprocket cover (see Chapter 2).

15 Make sure the dowels are either in the crankcase or the sprocket cover. Install the cover, making sure the speedometer rotor fits properly into the sensor and the dowels locate correctly, and tighten its bolts **(see illustration)**. On W, X and Y models, if removed, fit the rubber bushing for the gearchange shaft into the cover **(see illustration)**.

16 Slide the gearchange linkage arm onto the shaft, aligning the marks, and tighten the pinch bolt **(see illustration 22.6)**.

17 Reconnect the speedometer sensor wiring connector **(see illustration 16.6a)**.

23 Sidestand switch – check and renewal

Check

1 The sidestand switch is mounted on the sidestand bracket. The switch is part of the safety circuit which prevents or stops the engine running if the transmission is in gear whilst the sidestand is down, and prevents the engine from starting if the transmission is in gear unless the sidestand is up and the clutch lever is pulled in.

2 Remove the seat cowling (see Chapter 8). Trace the wiring back from the switch to the connector with the green and black/white wires and disconnect it **(see illustration)**.

3 Check the operation of the switch using an ohmmeter or continuity test light. Connect the meter between the terminals on the switch side of the connector. With the sidestand up there should be continuity (zero resistance) between the terminals, and with the stand down there should be no continuity (infinite resistance).

4 If the switch does not perform as expected, it is defective and must be renewed. Check

first that the fault is not caused by a sticking switch plunger due to the ingress of road dirt; spray the switch with a water dispersant aerosol.

5 If the switch is good, check the sidestand relay and diode as described in the relevant sections of this Chapter. Also check the wiring between the various components (see the *wiring diagrams* at the end of this chapter).

Renewal

6 The sidestand switch is mounted on the sidestand bracket. Remove the seat cowling

23.2 Disconnect the sidestand switch wiring connector (arrowed)

23.8a Unscrew the nuts (where fitted) (arrowed) . . .

23.8b . . . then withdraw the bolts and remove the switch (nut/bolt arrangement differs according to model)

24.2 Sidestand relay terminal identification – T and V models

(see Chapter 8). Trace the wiring back from the switch to its connector and disconnect it **(see illustration 23.2)**.

7 Work back along the switch wiring, freeing it from any relevant retaining clips and ties, noting its correct routing.

8 Unscrew the nuts and/or remove the bolts (according to model) securing the switch to the frame **(see illustrations)**.

9 Fit the new switch onto the bracket, then apply a suitable non-permanent thread locking compound to the bolt threads and tighten the nuts securely.

10 Make sure the wiring is correctly routed up to the connector and retained by all the necessary clips and ties. Reconnect the wiring connector.

11 Install the seat cowling (see Chapter 8).

24 Sidestand relay – check and renewal

Check

1 If the sidestand switch and wiring are good, the sidestand relay may be at fault. The relay is

located behind the seat cowling on the left-hand side on T and V models (just ahead of the starter relay), and on the inside of the left-hand air duct in the fairing, next to the fusebox and integral with the turn signal relay and diode on W, X and Y models **(see illustration 13.3a)**.

2 On T and V models, remove the seat cowling (see Chapter 8) and disconnect the relay wiring connector. Using an ohmmeter or continuity tester, connect the positive (+ve) lead to the No. 1 terminal on the relay and the negative (-ve) lead to the No. 2 terminal **(see illustration)**. There should be no continuity between the terminals. Using an auxiliary 12V battery and a set of leads, connect the battery positive (+ve) lead to the No. 3 terminal on the relay, and the battery negative (-ve) lead to the No. 4 terminal. With the battery connected, there should be continuity (zero resistance) between Nos. 1 and 2 terminals. If either of the above conditions do not exist, install a new relay.

3 On W, X and Y models, unplug the sidestand relay/turn signal relay/diode from its connector **(see illustration 13.3b)**. Using an ohmmeter or continuity tester, connect the positive (+ve) lead to the D terminal on the relay and the negative (-ve) lead to the E terminal **(see illustration)**. There should be no continuity between the terminals. Using an auxiliary 12V battery and a set of leads, connect the battery positive (+ve) lead to the D terminal on the relay, and the battery negative (-ve) lead to the C terminal on the relay. With the battery connected, there

should be continuity (zero resistance) between D and E terminals. If either of the above conditions do not exist, install a new sidestand relay/turn signal relay/diode.

4 If the relay is good, check the other components in the starter circuit as described in the relevant sections of this Chapter. If all components are good, check the wiring between the various components (see the *wiring diagrams* at the end of this book).

Renewal

5 The relay is located behind the seat cowling on the left-hand side on T and V models (just ahead of the starter relay), and on the inside of the left-hand air duct in the fairing, next to the fusebox and integral with the turn signal relay and diode on W, X and Y models **(see illustration 13.3a)**.

6 On T and V models, remove the seat cowling (see Chapter 8) and disconnect the relay wiring connector, then remove the relay. Install the new relay and check the operation of the sidestand switch.

7 On W, X and Y models, unplug the sidestand relay/turn signal relay/diode from its connector **(see illustration 13.3b)**. Install the new sidestand relay/turn signal relay/diode and check the operation of the sidestand switch.

25 Clutch switch – check and renewal

Check

1 The clutch switch is situated on the underside of the clutch lever bracket. The switch is part of the safety circuit which prevents or stops the engine running if the transmission is in gear whilst the sidestand is down, and prevents the engine from starting if the transmission is in gear unless the sidestand is up and the clutch lever is pulled in.

2 To check the switch, disconnect the wiring connector **(see illustration)**. Connect the probes of an ohmmeter or a continuity test light to the two switch terminals. With the

24.3 Sidestand relay/turn signal relay/diode terminal identification – W, X and Y models

25.2 Clutch switch wiring connector (arrowed)

clutch lever pulled in, continuity should be indicated. With the clutch lever out, no continuity (infinite resistance) should be indicated.

3 If the switch is good, check the other components in the starter circuit as described in the relevant sections of this Chapter. If all components are good, check the wiring between the various components (see the *wiring diagrams* at the end of this book).

Renewal

4 Disconnect the wiring connector from the clutch switch **(see illustration 25.2)**. Remove the screw and remove the switch.

5 Installation is the reverse of removal. The switch isn't adjustable.

26 Diode –
check and renewal

Check

1 The diode is part of the safety circuit which prevents or stops the engine running if the transmission is in gear whilst the sidestand is down, and prevents the engine from starting if the transmission is in gear unless the sidestand is up and the clutch lever is pulled in. The diode is located under the fuel tank on T and V models, and on the inside of the left-hand air duct in the fairing, next to the fusebox and integral with the turn signal relay and sidestand relay on W, X and Y models **(see illustration 13.3a)**.

2 On T and V models, raise the fuel tank (see Chapter 4) and unplug the diode from its connector – it will probably have insulating tape wrapped round it securing it in the connector, so remove that and wind fresh tape around it on completion. Using an ohmmeter or continuity tester, connect the positive (+ve) probe to one of the outer terminals of the diode and the negative (-ve) probe to the middle terminal of the diode. The diode should show continuity. Now reverse the probes. The diode should show no continuity. Repeat the tests between the other outer terminal and the middle terminal. The same results should be achieved. If it does not behave as stated, install a new diode.

3 On W, X and Y models, unplug the diode/turn signal relay/sidestand relay from its connector **(see illustration 13.3b)**. Using an ohmmeter or continuity tester, connect the positive (+ve) probe to C terminal of the diode and the negative (-ve) probe to A terminal **(see illustration 24.3)**. The diode should show continuity. Now reverse the probes. The diode should show no continuity. Repeat the tests between B terminal and A terminal. The same results should be achieved. If it doesn't behave as stated, install a new diode/turn signal relay/sidestand relay.

27.1a On 600 and 750T and V models, the horn is behind the bottom yoke

4 If the diode is good, check the other components in the starter circuit as described in the relevant sections of this Chapter. If all components are good, check the wiring between the various components (see the *wiring diagrams* at the end of this book).

Renewal

5 On T and V models, raise the fuel tank (see Chapter 4) and unplug the diode from its connector – it will probably have insulating tape wrapped round it securing it in the connector, so remove that and wind fresh tape around it on completion. Plug in the new diode and check the circuit.

6 On W, X and Y models, unplug the diode/turn signal relay/sidestand relay from its connector **(see illustration 13.3b)**. Plug in the new diode/turn signal relay/sidestand relay and check the circuit.

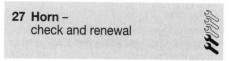

27 Horn –
check and renewal

Check

1 On GSX-R600 models and GSX-R750T and V models, the horn is mounted on the front of the frame below the steering head **(see illustration)**. On GSX-R750W and X models, the horn is mounted on the top left-hand corner of the radiator **(see illustration)**. The horn should be accessible without removing a fairing side panel (right-hand panel on GSX-R600 models and GSX-R750T and V models, left-hand panel on GSX-R750W and X models), but access is improved if you do so (see Chapter 8).

2 Disconnect the wiring connectors from the horn. Using two jumper wires, apply battery voltage directly to the terminals on the horn. If the horn sounds, check the switch (see Section 20) and the wiring between the switch and the horn (see the *wiring diagrams* at the end of this Chapter).

3 If the horn doesn't sound, install a new one.

Renewal

4 On GSX-R600 models and GSX-R750T and

27.1b On 750W and X models, the horn is on the left-hand end of the radiator

V models, the horn is mounted on the front of the frame below the steering head **(see illustration 27.1a)**. On GSX-R750W and X models, the horn is mounted on the top left-hand corner of the radiator **(see illustration 27.1b)**. The horn should be accessible without removing a fairing side panel (right-hand panel on GSX-R600 models and GSX-R750T and V models, left-hand panel on GSX-R750W and X models), but access is improved if you do so (see Chapter 8).

5 Disconnect the wiring connectors from the horn, then remove the screw or bolt securing the horn and remove it from the bike.

6 Install the horn and securely tighten the screw or bolt. Connect the wiring connectors.

28 Starter relay –
check and renewal

Check

1 If the starter circuit is faulty, first check the fuse (see Section 5).

2 Remove the seat cowling (see Chapter 8). The starter relay is located on the rear sub-frame on the left-hand side. Disconnect the battery negative (-ve) lead. Remove the plastic cover on the top of the relay **(see illustration)**. Unscrew the bolt securing the starter motor lead to its terminal and disconnect the lead

28.2a Remove the relay cover

28.2b Starter motor lead terminal (A), battery lead terminal (B)

28.4 Starter relay terminal identification (see text)

28.9 Disconnect the relay wiring connector

(see illustration); position the lead away from the relay terminal. Reconnect the battery negative (-ve) lead. With the ignition switch ON, the engine kill switch in the RUN position, the transmission in neutral and the clutch pulled in, press the starter switch. The relay should be heard to click.

3 If the relay doesn't click, switch off the ignition, then remove the relay as described below and test it as follows.

4 Set a multimeter to the ohms x 1 scale and connect it across the relay's starter motor and battery lead terminals (A and B). Using a fully-charged 12 volt battery and two insulated jumper wires, connect the positive (+ve) battery lead to terminal C of the relay, and its negative (-ve) lead to terminal D (see illustration). At this point the relay should be heard to click and the multimeter should read 0 ohms (continuity). If this is the case the relay

is proved good. If the relay does not click when battery voltage is applied and indicates no continuity (infinite resistance) across its terminals, it is faulty and must be renewed.

5 To check the internal resistance of the relay, use a multimeter set to the ohms x 1 scale and connect its probes to terminals C and D of the relay (see illustration 28.4). The resistance reading obtained should be as specified at the beginning of the Chapter.

6 If the relay is good, check for battery voltage between the yellow/green and the black/white (GSX-R600 and GSX-R750T and V) or yellow/green and yellow/black (GSX-R750W and X) wire terminals on the connector when the starter button is pressed. If voltage is present, check the other components in the starter circuit as described in the relevant sections of this Chapter. If no voltage was present or if all components are good, check the wiring between the various components (see the *wiring diagrams* at the end of this chapter).

Renewal

7 Remove the cowling (see Chapter 8). The starter relay is located on the rear sub-frame on the left-hand side.

8 Disconnect the battery terminals, remembering to disconnect the negative (-ve) terminal first.

9 Remove the plastic cover on the top of the relay (see illustration 28.2a). Unscrew the two bolts securing the starter motor and battery leads to the relay and detach the leads (see illustration 28.2b). Disconnect the relay wiring connector – you will probably need to displace

the relay to access the connector clip at the back (see illustration). Remove the relay.

10 Installation is the reverse of removal, ensuring the terminal bolts are securely tightened. Connect the negative (-ve) lead last when reconnecting the battery.

29 Starter motor – removal and installation

Removal

1 Remove the fuel tank (see Chapter 4). Disconnect the battery negative (-ve) lead.

2 Pull back the rubber cover on the starter motor terminal and remove the screw (600 models) or nut (750 models) securing the lead to the motor (see illustration).

3 Unscrew the two bolts securing the starter motor to the crankcase (see illustration).

4 Slide the starter motor out of the crankcase and remove it from the machine (see illustration 29.7).

5 Remove the O-ring on the end of the starter motor and discard it as a new one must be used (see illustration 29.6).

Installation

6 Install a new O-ring on the end of the starter motor and ensure it is seated in its groove (see illustration). Apply a smear of engine oil or grease to the O-ring to aid installation.

7 Manoeuvre the motor into position and slide it into the crankcase (see illustration).

29.2 Remove the nut (arrowed) or screw and detach the lead

29.3 Unscrew the bolts (arrowed) and remove the starter motor

29.6 Fit a new O-ring (arrowed) . . .

29.7 . . . then install the starter motor

29.8 Install the bolts . . .

29.9 . . . and connect the lead

30.3 Unscrew and remove the two long bolts

Ensure that the starter motor teeth mesh correctly with those of the starter idle/reduction gear.

8 Install the retaining bolts and tighten them securely, but not too tight **(see illustration)**.

9 Connect the starter lead to the motor and secure it with the screw (600 models) or nut (750 models) **(see illustration)**. Make sure the rubber cover is correctly seated over the terminal.

10 Install the fuel tank (see Chapter 4). Connect the battery negative (-ve) lead.

---

30 Starter motor – disassembly, inspection and reassembly

GSX-R600 models

Disassembly

1 Remove the starter motor (see Section 29).
2 Note the alignment marks between the main housing and the front and rear covers, or make your own if they aren't clear.
3 Unscrew the two long bolts and withdraw them from the starter motor **(see illustration)**. Discard their O-rings as new ones must be used.
4 Remove the rear cover from the motor along with its O-ring and the brushplate assembly **(see illustration 30.15)**. The brushes are under spring pressure and will probably pop out when the armature is removed – take care not to lose the springs.

5 Wrap some insulating tape around the teeth on the end of the starter motor shaft – this will protect the oil seal from damage as the front cover is removed. Remove the front cover from the motor along with its O-ring **(see illustration 30.17d)**. Remove the shim from the front end of the armature shaft and the special washer from inside the front cover, noting how it fits **(see illustrations 30.17b and c)**.
6 Withdraw the armature from the main housing, noting that it is held by the attraction of the magnets.

Inspection

7 The parts of the starter motor that are most likely to require attention are the brushes. Suzuki give no specifications for the minimum length of the brushes, however if they are obviously worn down and are close to the wire, cracked, chipped, or otherwise damaged, new

ones should be installed. On GSX-R600Y models, although the brushplate assembly can be removed from the rear cover, Suzuki do not list it as a separate item; if the brushes are worn a new end cover will have to be fitted. On all other models, draw all of the brushes out of their holders and remove the springs **(see illustration)**. Remove the two screws securing the top brushes and remove them, noting how they fit **(see illustration)**. Lift out the brush holder plate, noting how it fits, then lift out the lower brushplate **(see illustrations)**. The top brushes can be renewed individually, the lower brushes come with the lower brushplate. Locate the lower brushplate into the rear cover, then fit the brush holder plate, making sure the lower brushes are correctly located. Install the top brushes, then secure them and the brush holder plate with the two screws **(see illustration)**.

30.7a Remove the springs from behind the brushes . . .

30.7b . . . then remove the screws (arrowed) and the top brushes

30.7c Remove the brush holder plate . . .

30.7d . . . and the lower brush plate

30.7e Install the top brushes and screws

30.9a Continuity should exist between the commutator bars

30.9b There should be no continuity between the commutator bars and the armature shaft

30.13 Check the seal and bearing in the front cover

8 Inspect the commutator bars on the armature for scoring, scratches and discoloration. The commutator can be cleaned and polished with crocus cloth, but do not use sandpaper or emery paper. After cleaning, wipe away any residue with a cloth soaked in electrical system cleaner or denatured alcohol. Also check that the insulation between each bar is not close to the level of the bars. If it is, scrape some away.

9 Using an ohmmeter or a continuity test light, check for continuity between the commutator bars (see illustration). Continuity should exist between each bar and all of the others. Also, check for continuity between the commutator bars and the armature shaft (see illustration). There should be no continuity

(infinite resistance) between the commutator and the shaft. If the checks indicate otherwise, the armature is defective.

10 Check for continuity between each brush and the terminal bolt. There should be continuity (zero resistance). Check for continuity between the terminal bolt and the housing (when assembled). There should be no continuity (infinite resistance).

11 Check the front end of the armature shaft for worn, cracked, chipped and broken teeth. If the shaft is damaged or worn, install a new armature.

12 Check the end covers for signs of cracks or wear. Check the magnets in the main housing and the housing itself for cracks.

13 Check the front cover oil seal and bearing

for signs of wear and damage. On GSX-R600Y models, the oil seal is available as a separate item but if the bearing is worn a new cover will have to be fitted. On all other models, the seal and bearing are integral with the cover – if either component is worn, renew the cover (see illustration).

Reassembly

14 Fit the O-ring onto the rear cover. Slide the springs and brushes back into their holders (see illustration). To make it easy to install the armature, it is necessary to draw the brushes as far back as possible in the holders and secure them there to provide clearance. A good way to do this is to cut up a cable tie into four sections, then use one for each brush, locating them between the brush wire and the wire guide on the holder (see illustrations). This should hold them in place.

15 Apply a smear of molybdenum disulphide grease to the armature shaft rear end. Insert the armature, then remove the cable tie pieces and locate the brushes on the commutator bars (see illustration). Check that each brush is securely pressed against the commutator by its spring and is free to move easily in its holder.

16 Fit the main housing over the armature, aligning the matchmarks on the housing and rear cover (see illustration). Note that the housing will be forcefully drawn onto the armature by the magnets.

17 Apply a smear of grease to the lips of the

30.14a Install the spring . . .

30.14b . . . then hold it back and insert the brush . . .

30.14c . . . and locate a piece of cable-tie between each brush wire and the wire guide to keep the brushes retracted

30.15 Fit the armature into the rear cover, making sure the brushes locate correctly . . .

30.16 . . . then fit the main housing, being ready for the draw of the magnets

30.17a Fit a new O-ring onto the front cover

30.17b Slide the shim onto the shaft . . .

30.17c . . . and fit the special washer into the cover . . .

front cover oil seal and armature shaft and fit a new O-ring onto the cover **(see illustration)**. Fit the shim onto the shaft and the special washer onto the front cover, making sure that its tabs locate correctly in the cover cutouts **(see illustrations)**. Install the cover, aligning the matchmarks **(see illustration)**. Remove the protective tape from the shaft end.

18 Make sure that the O-ring is in place on each of the long bolts, then install them and tighten them securely **(see illustration 30.3)**.

19 Install the starter motor (see Section 29).

GSX-R750 models

Disassembly

20 Remove the starter motor (see Section 29).

21 Note the alignment marks between the main housing and the front and rear covers, or make your own if they aren't clear **(see illustration)**.

22 Unscrew the two long bolts and withdraw them from the starter motor **(see illustration)**. Discard their O-rings as new ones must be used.

23 Wrap some insulating tape around the teeth on the end of the starter motor shaft – this will protect the oil seal from damage as the front cover is removed. Remove the front cover from the motor **(see illustration)**. Remove the cover O-ring from the main housing and discard it as a new one must be used **(see illustration 30.39b)**. Remove the shims from the front end of the armature shaft or the inside of the front cover, noting their correct fitted locations **(see illustration 30.39a)**. Also

remove the special washer from the front cover **(see illustration 30.39c)**.

24 Remove the rear cover and brushplate assembly from the motor **(see illustration)**. Remove the cover O-ring from the main housing and discard it as a new one must be used **(see illustration 30.38)**. Remove the shims from the rear end of the armature shaft or from inside the rear cover after the brushplate assembly has been removed **(see illustration 30.37a)**.

25 Withdraw the armature from the main housing, noting that it is held by the attraction of the magnets.

26 Noting the correct fitted location of each component, unscrew the terminal nut and remove it along with its washer and the insulating washers **(see illustration)**.

30.17d . . . then install the cover

30.21 Note the alignment marks . . .

30.22 . . . then unscrew the bolts (arrowed) . . .

30.23 . . . and remove the front cover . . .

30.24 . . . and the rear cover

30.26 Unscrew the nut (arrowed) and remove the various washers

30.27a Lift the brush springs . . .

30.27b . . . and withdraw the brushes

30.36a Fit the insulator and O-ring . . .

Withdraw the terminal bolt and brushplate assembly from the rear cover **(see illustration 30.36b)**.

27 Lift the brush springs and slide the brushes out from their holders **(see illustrations)**.

Inspection

28 The parts of the starter motor that are most likely to require attention are the brushes. Suzuki give no specifications for the minimum length of the brushes, however if they are obviously worn down and are close to the wire, cracked, chipped, or otherwise damaged, a new brushplate should be installed.

29 Inspect the commutator bars on the armature for scoring, scratches and

30.36b . . . then install the brushplate . . .

discoloration. The commutator can be cleaned and polished with crocus cloth, but do not use sandpaper or emery paper. After cleaning, wipe away any residue with a cloth soaked in electrical system cleaner or denatured alcohol. Also check that the insulation between each bar is not close to the level of the bars. If it is, scrape some away.

30 Using an ohmmeter or a continuity test light, check for continuity between the commutator bars **(see illustration 30.9a)**. Continuity should exist between each bar and all of the others. Also, check for continuity between the commutator bars and the armature shaft **(see illustration 30.9b)**. There should be no continuity (infinite resistance) between the commutator and the shaft. If the checks indicate otherwise, the armature is defective.

31 Check for continuity between each brush and the terminal bolt. There should be continuity (zero resistance). Check for continuity between the terminal bolt and the housing (when assembled). There should be no continuity (infinite resistance).

32 Check the front end of the armature shaft for worn, cracked, chipped and broken teeth. If the shaft is damaged or worn, install a new armature.

33 Check the end covers for signs of cracks or wear. Check the front cover oil seal for signs of wear and damage and renew the front cover if necessary – the seal and bearing

are not available separately. Check the magnets in the main housing and the housing itself for cracks.

34 Check the insulating washers and rubbers for signs of damage and renew them if necessary.

Reassembly

35 Slide the brushes back into position in their holders and place the brush spring ends onto the brushes **(see illustrations 30.27b and a)**. Check that the brushes slide freely in the holders.

36 Ensure that the inner rubber insulator is in place on the terminal bolt, then fit the O-ring if removed **(see illustration)**. Insert the bolt through the rear cover and fit the brushplate assembly in the rear cover, making sure its slot is correctly located around the bolt bore in the cover **(see illustration)**. Fit the insulating washers over the terminal, then fit the standard washer and the nut **(see illustration)**.

37 Slide the shims onto the rear end of the armature shaft, then lubricate the shaft with a molybdenum disulphide grease **(see illustration)**. Insert the armature into the rear cover, locating the brushes on the commutator bars as you do, taking care not to damage them **(see illustration)**. Check that each brush is securely pressed against the commutator by its spring and is free to move easily in its holder.

38 Fit a new O-ring onto the main housing **(see**

30.36c . . . and fit the insulating washers, plain washer and nut

30.37a Slide the shims onto the shaft . . .

30.37b . . . then fit it into the rear cover, making sure the brushes locate correctly

30.38 Fit a new O-ring onto the main housing

30.39a Slide on the shims . . .

30.39b . . . and fit a new O-ring

30.39c Fit the special washer into the front cover . . .

30.39d . . . then install the cover . . .

30.40 . . . and the long bolts

illustration), then fit the housing over the armature and onto the rear cover, aligning the marks made on removal (see illustration 30.24). Note that the housing will be forcefully drawn onto the armature by the magnets.

39 Slide the shims onto the front of the armature shaft, and fit a new O-ring onto the front of the main housing (see illustrations). Apply a smear of grease to the lips of the front cover oil seal. Fit the special washer onto the cover, making sure its tabs locate correctly (see illustration). Install the cover, aligning the marks made on removal (see illustration). Remove the protective tape from the shaft end.

40 Slide a new O-ring onto each of the long bolts. Check the marks made on removal are correctly aligned (see illustration 30.21), then install the long bolts and tighten them securely (see illustration).

41 Install the starter motor (see Section 29).

31 Charging system testing – general information and precautions

1 If the performance of the charging system is suspect, the system as a whole should be checked first, followed by testing of the individual components. **Note:** *Before beginning the checks, make sure the battery is fully charged and that all system connections are clean and tight.*

2 Checking the output of the charging system

and the performance of the various components within the charging system requires the use of a multimeter (with voltage, current and resistance checking facilities).

3 When making the checks, follow the procedures carefully to prevent incorrect connections or short circuits, as irreparable damage to electrical system components may result if short circuits occur.

4 If a multimeter is not available, the job of checking the charging system should be left to a Suzuki dealer.

32 Charging system – leakage and output test

1 If the charging system of the machine is thought to be faulty, remove the rider's seat (see Chapter 8) and perform the following checks.

Leakage test

Caution: Always connect an ammeter in series, never in parallel with the battery, otherwise it will be damaged. Do not turn the ignition ON or operate the starter motor when the ammeter is connected – a sudden surge in current will blow the meter's fuse.

2 Turn the ignition switch OFF and disconnect the lead from the battery negative (-ve) terminal.

3 Set the multimeter to the Amps function

and connect its negative (-ve) probe to the battery negative (-ve) terminal, and positive (+ve) probe to the disconnected negative (-ve) lead (see illustration). Always set the meter to a high amps range initially and then bring it down to the mA (milli Amps) range; if there is a high current flow in the circuit it may blow the meter's fuse.

4 No current flow should be indicated. If current leakage is indicated (generally greater than 0.1 mA), there is a short circuit in the wiring. Disconnect the meter and reconnect the negative (-ve) lead to the battery, tightening it securely,

32.3 Checking the charging system leakage rate. Connect the meter as shown

33.2 Disconnect the alternator wiring connector (arrowed)

5 If leakage is indicated, use the wiring diagrams at the end of this book to systematically disconnect individual electrical components and repeat the test until the source is identified.

Output test

6 Start the engine and warm it up to normal operating temperature.

7 To check the regulated voltage output, allow the engine to idle and connect a multimeter set to the 0-20 volts DC scale (voltmeter) across the terminals of the battery (positive (+ve) meter lead to battery positive (+ve) terminal, negative (-ve) meter lead to battery negative (-ve) terminal **(see illustration 3.2a))**. Slowly increase the engine speed to 5000 rpm and note the reading obtained. At this speed the voltage should be 13.5 to 15.0 volts. If the voltage is outside these limits, check the alternator and the regulator (see Sections 33 and 34).

8 To check the unregulated output, remove the seat cowling (see Chapter 8). Trace the wiring back from the top of the alternator cover on the left-hand side of the engine and disconnect it at the white connector containing the three black wires **(see illustration 33.2)**. Using a multimeter set to 0-250 volts AC range, connect the meter probes to one pair of terminals on the alternator side of the connector. Start the engine and increase its speed to 5000 rpm. Check the voltage output and compare it to the minimum specified at the beginning of the

33.6 Unscrew the bolts (arrowed), noting the ones with the sealing washers (A), and remove the cover

Chapter. Stop the engine, connect the meter to another pair of terminals, and repeat the test. Do this again to the other pair of terminals so that you have taken three readings in all. If any of the readings are below the minimum specified, check the stator coil resistance (see Section 33). If the readings are good, check the regulator/rectifier (see Section 34).

> **HAYNES HINT** *Clues to a faulty regulator are constantly blowing bulbs, with brightness varying considerably with engine speed, and battery overheating.*

33 Alternator – check, removal and installation

Check

1 Remove the seat cowling (see Chapter 8).
2 Trace the wiring back from the top of the alternator cover on the left-hand side of the engine and disconnect it at the white connector containing the three black wires **(see illustration)**.
3 Using a multimeter set to the ohms x 1 (ohmmeter) scale measure the resistance between each of the black wires on the alternator side of the connector, taking a total of three readings, then check for continuity between each terminal and ground (earth). If the

stator coil windings are in good condition the three readings should be within the range shown in the Specifications at the start of this Chapter and there should be no continuity (infinite resistance) between any of the terminals and ground (earth). If not, the alternator stator coil assembly is at fault and should be renewed.
Note: *Before condemning the stator coils, check the fault is not due to damaged wiring between the connector and coils.*

Removal

4 Remove the left-hand fairing side panel and the seat cowling (see Chapter 8). Trace the alternator wiring from the top of the alternator cover and disconnect it at the white connector containing the three black wires **(see illustration 33.2)**. Free the wiring from any clips or ties and feed it through to the alternator cover.
5 Drain the engine oil (see Chapter 1).
6 Unscrew the alternator cover bolts and remove the cover, being prepared to catch any residue oil **(see illustration)**. Discard the gasket as a new one must be used. Remove the dowels from either the cover or the crankcase if they are loose. Note the positions of the two bolts with sealing washers.
7 To remove the rotor bolt it is necessary to stop the rotor from turning. If a rotor holding strap or tool is not available, and the engine is in the frame, place the transmission in gear and have an assistant apply the rear brake, then unscrew the bolt **(see illustration)**. There are also two flats machined into the boss in the rotor which can be used if a suitable holding tool is available **(see illustration)**; a large spanner can be applied to these flats, but note that there is some danger that it might slip due to the awkward angle involved.
8 To remove the rotor from the crankshaft taper it is necessary to use a rotor puller. Thread the rotor puller into the centre of the rotor and turn it until the rotor is displaced from the shaft **(see illustration)**.
9 To remove the stator from the cover, unscrew the bolts securing the stator, and the bolt securing the wiring clamp, then remove the assembly, noting how the rubber wiring grommet fits **(see illustration)**.

Installation

10 Install the stator onto the cover, aligning the rubber wiring grommet with the groove.

33.7a Unscrew the rotor bolt using a holding tool

33.7b The flats (arrowed) can be used to hold the rotor if a suitable tool is available

33.8 Displace the rotor using a puller

33.9 Unscrew the stator bolts (A) and the wiring clamp bolt (B) and free the grommet (C)

33.10 Apply sealant to the grommet

33.11 Slide the rotor onto the shaft . . .

Apply a suitable non-permanent thread locking compound to the stator bolt and wiring clamp bolt threads, then install the bolts and tighten them securely (see illustration 33.9). Apply a suitable sealant to the wiring grommet, then install it into the cut-out in the cover (see illustration).

11 Clean the tapered end of the crankshaft and the corresponding mating surface on the inside of the rotor with a suitable solvent. Make sure that no metal objects have attached themselves to the magnet on the inside of the rotor, then slide the rotor onto the shaft (see illustration).

12 Apply a suitable non-permanent thread locking compound to the rotor bolt threads, then install the bolt with its

washer and tighten it to the torque setting specified at the beginning of the Chapter, using the method employed on removal to prevent the rotor from turning (see illustrations).

13 Apply a suitable sealant to the areas around the crankcase joints (see illustration). If removed, insert the dowels in the cover or crankcase. Install the alternator cover using a new gasket, making sure it locates correctly onto the dowels, then install the cover bolts, using new sealing washers on the two top bolts in front of the wiring grommet (see illustrations). Tighten the bolts evenly in a criss-cross sequence.

14 Feed the alternator wiring back to its connector, making sure it is correctly routed

and secured by any clips or ties, and reconnect it (see illustration 33.2).

15 Refill the engine with oil (see Chapter 1).

16 Install the fairing side panel and the seat cowling (see Chapter 8).

34 Regulator/rectifier – check and renewal

Check

1 Remove the seat cowling (see Chapter 8). The regulator/rectifier is mounted on the left-hand side of the rear sub-frame. Disconnect the wiring connector (see illustration).

2 Using a multimeter or ohmmeter set to the

33.12a . . . then apply a thread-lock to the bolt . . .

33.12b . . . and tighten it to the specified torque

33.13a Apply a sealant to the crankcase joints (arrowed) . . .

33.13b . . . then locate the gasket over the dowels (arrowed) . . .

33.13c . . . and install the cover

34.1 Disconnect the regulator/rectifier wiring connector

Unit: kΩ

		+ Probe of tester to:				
		B/R	B₁	B₂	B₃	B/W
− Probe of tester to:	B/R		∞	∞	∞	∞
	B₁	1 to 10		∞	∞	∞
	B₂	1 to 10	∞		∞	∞
	B₃	1 to 10	∞	∞		∞
	B/W	1 to 20	1 to 10	1 to 10	1 to 10	

∞ = infinity (very high infinite resistance)

H31269

34.2 Regulator/rectifier test data and terminal identification

B Black   B/R Black/red   B/W Black/white

K-ohms scale, check the resistance between the various terminals on the regulator/rectifier as shown in the table **(see illustration)**. If the readings do not compare closely with those shown in the accompanying table the regulator/rectifier unit can be considered faulty. **Note:** *The use of certain multimeters could lead to false readings being obtained, as could a low battery in the meter and contact between the meter probes and your fingers. If the above check shows the regulator/rectifier unit to be faulty, take the unit to a Suzuki dealer for confirmation of its condition before renewing it. Suzuki have a special tester which will perform more detailed tests.*

3 If the regulator appears to be good, check the wiring between the battery, regulator/rectifier and alternator, and the wiring connectors (see the *wiring diagrams* at the end of this book).

Renewal

4 Remove the seat cowling (see Chapter 8).
5 The regulator/rectifier is mounted on the left-hand side of the rear sub-frame. Disconnect the wiring connector **(see illustration 34.1)**.
6 Remove the two screws securing the regulator/rectifier and remove it, noting the spacers behind it **(see illustration)**.
7 Install the new unit and tighten its screws securely, not forgetting the spacers. Connect the wiring connector.
8 Install the seat cowling (see Chapter 8).

34.6 The regulator/rectifier is secured by the two screws (arrowed)

GSX-R600 V

GSX-R600 W, X and Y

GSX-R750 T and V

9

GSX-R750 W and X

H31434
C. J. TURK

Reference

Tools and Workshop Tips

● Building up a tool kit and equipping your workshop ● Using tools ● Understanding bearing, seal, fastener and chain sizes and markings ● Repair techniques

Security

● Locks and chains ● U-locks ● Disc locks ● Alarms and immobilisers ● Security marking systems ● Tips on how to prevent bike theft

Lubricants and fluids

● Engine oils ● Transmission (gear) oils ● Coolant/anti-freeze ● Fork oils and suspension fluids ● Brake/clutch fluids ● Spray lubes, degreasers and solvents

Conversion Factors

● Formulae for conversion of the metric (SI) units used throughout the manual into Imperial measures

MOT Test Checks

● A guide to the UK MOT test ● Which items are tested ● How to prepare your motorcycle for the test and perform a pre-test check

Storage

● How to prepare your motorcycle for going into storage and protect essential systems ● How to get the motorcycle back on the road

Fault Finding

● Common faults and their likely causes ● How to check engine cylinder compression ● How to make electrical tests and use test meters

Technical Terms Explained

● Component names, technical terms and common abbreviations explained

Index

Buying tools

A toolkit is a fundamental requirement for servicing and repairing a motorcycle. Although there will be an initial expense in building up enough tools for servicing, this will soon be offset by the savings made by doing the job yourself. As experience and confidence grow, additional tools can be added to enable the repair and overhaul of the motorcycle. Many of the specialist tools are expensive and not often used so it may be preferable to hire them, or for a group of friends or motorcycle club to join in the purchase.

As a rule, it is better to buy more expensive, good quality tools. Cheaper tools are likely to wear out faster and need to be renewed more often, nullifying the original saving.

> ⚠ **Warning: To avoid the risk of a poor quality tool breaking in use, causing injury or damage to the component being worked on, always aim to purchase tools which meet the relevant national safety standards.**

The following lists of tools do not represent the manufacturer's service tools, but serve as a guide to help the owner decide which tools are needed for this level of work. In addition, items such as an electric drill, hacksaw, files, soldering iron and a workbench equipped with a vice, may be needed. Although not classed as tools, a selection of bolts, screws, nuts, washers and pieces of tubing always come in useful.

For more information about tools, refer to the Haynes *Motorcycle Workshop Practice TechBook* (Bk. No. 3470).

Manufacturer's service tools

Inevitably certain tasks require the use of a service tool. Where possible an alternative tool or method of approach is recommended, but sometimes there is no option if personal injury or damage to the component is to be avoided. Where required, service tools are referred to in the relevant procedure.

Service tools can usually only be purchased from a motorcycle dealer and are identified by a part number. Some of the commonly-used tools, such as rotor pullers, are available in aftermarket form from mail-order motorcycle tool and accessory suppliers.

Maintenance and minor repair tools

1. Set of flat-bladed screwdrivers
2. Set of Phillips head screwdrivers
3. Combination open-end and ring spanners
4. Socket set (3/8 inch or 1/2 inch drive)
5. Set of Allen keys or bits
6. Set of Torx keys or bits
7. Pliers, cutters and self-locking grips (Mole grips)
8. Adjustable spanners
9. C-spanners
10. Tread depth gauge and tyre pressure gauge
11. Cable oiler clamp
12. Feeler gauges
13. Spark plug gap measuring tool
14. Spark plug spanner or deep plug sockets
15. Wire brush and emery paper
16. Calibrated syringe, measuring vessel and funnel
17. Oil filter adapters
18. Oil drainer can or tray
19. Pump type oil can
20. Grease gun
21. Straight-edge and steel rule
22. Continuity tester
23. Battery charger
24. Hydrometer (for battery specific gravity check)
25. Anti-freeze tester (for liquid-cooled engines)

Repair and overhaul tools

1 Torque wrench (small and mid-ranges)
2 Conventional, plastic or soft-faced hammers
3 Impact driver set
4 Vernier gauge
5 Circlip pliers (internal and external, or combination)
6 Set of cold chisels and punches
7 Selection of pullers
8 Breaker bars
9 Chain breaking/ riveting tool set
10 Wire stripper and crimper tool
11 Multimeter (measures amps, volts and ohms)
12 Stroboscope (for dynamic timing checks)
13 Hose clamp (wingnut type shown)
14 Clutch holding tool
15 One-man brake/clutch bleeder kit

Specialist tools

1 Micrometers (external type)
2 Telescoping gauges
3 Dial gauge
4 Cylinder compression gauge
5 Vacuum gauges (left) or manometer (right)
6 Oil pressure gauge
7 Plastigauge kit
8 Valve spring compressor (4-stroke engines)
9 Piston pin drawbolt tool
10 Piston ring removal and installation tool
11 Piston ring clamp
12 Cylinder bore hone (stone type shown)
13 Stud extractor
14 Screw extractor set
15 Bearing driver set

1 Workshop equipment and facilities

The workbench

● Work is made much easier by raising the bike up on a ramp - components are much more accessible if raised to waist level. The hydraulic or pneumatic types seen in the dealer's workshop are a sound investment if you undertake a lot of repairs or overhauls (see illustration 1.1).

1.1 Hydraulic motorcycle ramp

● If raised off ground level, the bike must be supported on the ramp to avoid it falling. Most ramps incorporate a front wheel locating clamp which can be adjusted to suit different diameter wheels. When tightening the clamp, take care not to mark the wheel rim or damage the tyre - use wood blocks on each side to prevent this.

● Secure the bike to the ramp using tie-downs (see illustration 1.2). If the bike has only a sidestand, and hence leans at a dangerous angle when raised, support the bike on an auxiliary stand.

1.2 Tie-downs are used around the passenger footrests to secure the bike

● Auxiliary (paddock) stands are widely available from mail order companies or motorcycle dealers and attach either to the wheel axle or swingarm pivot (see illustration 1.3). If the motorcycle has a centrestand, you can support it under the crankcase to prevent it toppling whilst either wheel is removed (see illustration 1.4).

1.3 This auxiliary stand attaches to the swingarm pivot

1.4 Always use a block of wood between the engine and jack head when supporting the engine in this way

Fumes and fire

● Refer to the Safety first! page at the beginning of the manual for full details. Make sure your workshop is equipped with a fire extinguisher suitable for fuel-related fires (Class B fire - flammable liquids) - it is not sufficient to have a water-filled extinguisher.

● Always ensure adequate ventilation is available. Unless an exhaust gas extraction system is available for use, ensure that the engine is run outside of the workshop.

● If working on the fuel system, make sure the workshop is ventilated to avoid a build-up of fumes. This applies equally to fume build-up when charging a battery. Do not smoke or allow anyone else to smoke in the workshop.

Fluids

● If you need to drain fuel from the tank, store it in an approved container marked as suitable for the storage of petrol (gasoline) (see illustration 1.5). Do not store fuel in glass jars or bottles.

1.5 Use an approved can only for storing petrol (gasoline)

● Use proprietary engine degreasers or solvents which have a high flash-point, such as paraffin (kerosene), for cleaning off oil, grease and dirt - never use petrol (gasoline) for cleaning. Wear rubber gloves when handling solvent and engine degreaser. The fumes from certain solvents can be dangerous - always work in a well-ventilated area.

Dust, eye and hand protection

● Protect your lungs from inhalation of dust particles by wearing a filtering mask over the nose and mouth. Many frictional materials still contain asbestos which is dangerous to your health. Protect your eyes from spouts of liquid and sprung components by wearing a pair of protective goggles (see illustration 1.6).

1.6 A fire extinguisher, goggles, mask and protective gloves should be at hand in the workshop

● Protect your hands from contact with solvents, fuel and oils by wearing rubber gloves. Alternatively apply a barrier cream to your hands before starting work. If handling hot components or fluids, wear suitable gloves to protect your hands from scalding and burns.

What to do with old fluids

● Old cleaning solvent, fuel, coolant and oils should not be poured down domestic drains or onto the ground. Package the fluid up in old oil containers, label it accordingly, and take it to a garage or disposal facility. Contact your local authority for location of such sites or ring the oil care hotline.

OIL CARE
FOLLOW THE CODE

OIL BANK LINE
0800 66 33 66
www.oilbankline.org.uk

Note: It is antisocial and illegal to dump oil down the drain. To find the location of your local oil recycling bank, call this number free.

In the USA, note that any oil supplier must accept used oil for recycling.

2 Fasteners -
screws, bolts and nuts

Fastener types and applications

Bolts and screws

● Fastener head types are either of hexagonal, Torx or splined design, with internal and external versions of each type **(see illustrations 2.1 and 2.2)**; splined head fasteners are not in common use on motorcycles. The conventional slotted or Phillips head design is used for certain screws. Bolt or screw length is always measured from the underside of the head to the end of the item **(see illustration 2.11)**.

2.1 Internal hexagon/Allen (A), Torx (B) and splined (C) fasteners, with corresponding bits

2.2 External Torx (A), splined (B) and hexagon (C) fasteners, with corresponding sockets

● Certain fasteners on the motorcycle have a tensile marking on their heads, the higher the marking the stronger the fastener. High tensile fasteners generally carry a 10 or higher marking. Never replace a high tensile fastener with one of a lower tensile strength.

Washers (see illustration 2.3)

● Plain washers are used between a fastener head and a component to prevent damage to the component or to spread the load when torque is applied. Plain washers can also be used as spacers or shims in certain assemblies. Copper or aluminium plain washers are often used as sealing washers on drain plugs.

2.3 Plain washer (A), penny washer (B), spring washer (C) and serrated washer (D)

● The split-ring spring washer works by applying axial tension between the fastener head and component. If flattened, it is fatigued and must be renewed. If a plain (flat) washer is used on the fastener, position the spring washer between the fastener and the plain washer.

● Serrated star type washers dig into the fastener and component faces, preventing loosening. They are often used on electrical earth (ground) connections to the frame.

● Cone type washers (sometimes called Belleville) are conical and when tightened apply axial tension between the fastener head and component. They must be installed with the dished side against the component and often carry an OUTSIDE marking on their outer face. If flattened, they are fatigued and must be renewed.

● Tab washers are used to lock plain nuts or bolts on a shaft. A portion of the tab washer is bent up hard against one flat of the nut or bolt to prevent it loosening. Due to the tab washer being deformed in use, a new tab washer should be used every time it is disturbed.

● Wave washers are used to take up endfloat on a shaft. They provide light springing and prevent excessive side-to-side play of a component. Can be found on rocker arm shafts.

Nuts and split pins

● Conventional plain nuts are usually six-sided **(see illustration 2.4)**. They are sized by thread diameter and pitch. High tensile nuts carry a number on one end to denote their tensile strength.

2.4 Plain nut (A), shouldered locknut (B), nylon insert nut (C) and castellated nut (D)

● Self-locking nuts either have a nylon insert, or two spring metal tabs, or a shoulder which is staked into a groove in the shaft - their advantage over conventional plain nuts is a resistance to loosening due to vibration. The nylon insert type can be used a number of times, but must be renewed when the friction of the nylon insert is reduced, ie when the nut spins freely on the shaft. The spring tab type can be reused unless the tabs are damaged. The shouldered type must be renewed every time it is disturbed.

● Split pins (cotter pins) are used to lock a castellated nut to a shaft or to prevent slackening of a plain nut. Common applications are wheel axles and brake torque arms. Because the split pin arms are deformed to lock around the nut a new split pin must always be used on installation - always fit the correct size split pin which will fit snugly in the shaft hole. Make sure the split pin arms are correctly located around the nut **(see illustrations 2.5 and 2.6)**.

2.5 Bend split pin (cotter pin) arms as shown (arrows) to secure a castellated nut

2.6 Bend split pin (cotter pin) arms as shown to secure a plain nut

Caution: If the castellated nut slots do not align with the shaft hole after tightening to the torque setting, tighten the nut until the next slot aligns with the hole - never slacken the nut to align its slot.

● R-pins (shaped like the letter R), or slip pins as they are sometimes called, are sprung and can be reused if they are otherwise in good condition. Always install R-pins with their closed end facing forwards **(see illustration 2.7)**.

**2.7 Correct fitting of R-pin.
Arrow indicates forward direction**

Circlips (see illustration 2.8)

● Circlips (sometimes called snap-rings) are used to retain components on a shaft or in a housing and have corresponding external or internal ears to permit removal. Parallel-sided (machined) circlips can be installed either way round in their groove, whereas stamped circlips (which have a chamfered edge on one face) must be installed with the chamfer facing away from the direction of thrust load **(see illustration 2.9)**.

2.8 External stamped circlip (A), internal stamped circlip (B), machined circlip (C) and wire circlip (D)

● Always use circlip pliers to remove and install circlips; expand or compress them just enough to remove them. After installation, rotate the circlip in its groove to ensure it is securely seated. If installing a circlip on a splined shaft, always align its opening with a shaft channel to ensure the circlip ends are well supported and unlikely to catch **(see illustration 2.10)**.

2.9 Correct fitting of a stamped circlip

THRUST LOAD

THRUST WASHER

SHARP EDGE

CHAMFERED EDGE

0650H

**2.10 Align circlip opening
with shaft channel**

● Circlips can wear due to the thrust of components and become loose in their grooves, with the subsequent danger of becoming dislodged in operation. For this reason, renewal is advised every time a circlip is disturbed.

● Wire circlips are commonly used as piston pin retaining clips. If a removal tang is provided, long-nosed pliers can be used to dislodge them, otherwise careful use of a small flat-bladed screwdriver is necessary. Wire circlips should be renewed every time they are disturbed.

Thread diameter and pitch

● Diameter of a male thread (screw, bolt or stud) is the outside diameter of the threaded portion **(see illustration 2.11)**. Most motorcycle manufacturers use the ISO (International Standards Organisation) metric system expressed in millimetres, eg M6 refers to a 6 mm diameter thread. Sizing is the same for nuts, except that the thread diameter is measured across the valleys of the nut.

● Pitch is the distance between the peaks of the thread **(see illustration 2.11)**. It is expressed in millimetres, thus a common bolt size may be expressed as 6.0 x 1.0 mm (6 mm thread diameter and 1 mm pitch). Generally pitch increases in proportion to thread diameter, although there are always exceptions.

● Thread diameter and pitch are related for conventional fastener applications and the accompanying table can be used as a guide. Additionally, the AF (Across Flats), spanner or socket size dimension of the bolt or nut **(see illustration 2.11)** is linked to thread and pitch specification. Thread pitch can be measured with a thread gauge **(see illustration 2.12)**.

2.11 Fastener length (L), thread diameter (D), thread pitch (P) and head size (AF)

AF

L

D

P

**2.12 Using a thread gauge
to measure pitch**

AF size	Thread diameter x pitch (mm)
8 mm	M5 x 0.8
8 mm	M6 x 1.0
10 mm	M6 x 1.0
12 mm	M8 x 1.25
14 mm	M10 x 1.25
17 mm	M12 x 1.25

● The threads of most fasteners are of the right-hand type, ie they are turned clockwise to tighten and anti-clockwise to loosen. The reverse situation applies to left-hand thread fasteners, which are turned anti-clockwise to tighten and clockwise to loosen. Left-hand threads are used where rotation of a component might loosen a conventional right-hand thread fastener.

Seized fasteners

● Corrosion of external fasteners due to water or reaction between two dissimilar metals can occur over a period of time. It will build up sooner in wet conditions or in countries where salt is used on the roads during the winter. If a fastener is severely corroded it is likely that normal methods of removal will fail and result in its head being ruined. When you attempt removal, the fastener thread should be heard to crack free and unscrew easily - if it doesn't, stop there before damaging something.

● A smart tap on the head of the fastener will often succeed in breaking free corrosion which has occurred in the threads **(see illustration 2.13)**.

● An aerosol penetrating fluid (such as WD-40) applied the night beforehand may work its way down into the thread and ease removal. Depending on the location, you may be able to make up a Plasticine well around the fastener head and fill it with penetrating fluid.

2.13 A sharp tap on the head of a fastener will often break free a corroded thread

● If you are working on an engine internal component, corrosion will most likely not be a problem due to the well lubricated environment. However, components can be very tight and an impact driver is a useful tool in freeing them (see illustration 2.14).

2.14 Using an impact driver to free a fastener

● Where corrosion has occurred between dissimilar metals (eg steel and aluminium alloy), the application of heat to the fastener head will create a disproportionate expansion rate between the two metals and break the seizure caused by the corrosion. Whether heat can be applied depends on the location of the fastener - any surrounding components likely to be damaged must first be removed (see illustration 2.15). Heat can be applied using a paint stripper heat gun or clothes iron, or by immersing the component in boiling water - wear protective gloves to prevent scalding or burns to the hands.

2.15 Using heat to free a seized fastener

● As a last resort, it is possible to use a hammer and cold chisel to work the fastener head unscrewed (see illustration 2.16). This will damage the fastener, but more importantly extreme care must be taken not to damage the surrounding component.

Caution: Remember that the component being secured is generally of more value than the bolt, nut or screw - when the fastener is freed, do not unscrew it with force, instead work the fastener back and forth when resistance is felt to prevent thread damage.

2.16 Using a hammer and chisel to free a seized fastener

Broken fasteners and damaged heads

● If the shank of a broken bolt or screw is accessible you can grip it with self-locking grips. The knurled wheel type stud extractor tool or self-gripping stud puller tool is particularly useful for removing the long studs which screw into the cylinder mouth surface of the crankcase or bolts and screws from which the head has broken off (see illustration 2.17). Studs can also be removed by locking two nuts together on the threaded end of the stud and using a spanner on the lower nut (see illustration 2.18).

2.17 Using a stud extractor tool to remove a broken crankcase stud

2.18 Two nuts can be locked together to unscrew a stud from a component

● A bolt or screw which has broken off below or level with the casing must be extracted using a screw extractor set. Centre punch the fastener to centralise the drill bit, then drill a hole in the fastener (see illustration 2.19). Select a drill bit which is approximately half to three-quarters the

2.19 When using a screw extractor, first drill a hole in the fastener . . .

diameter of the fastener and drill to a depth which will accommodate the extractor. Use the largest size extractor possible, but avoid leaving too small a wall thickness otherwise the extractor will merely force the fastener walls outwards wedging it in the casing thread.

● If a spiral type extractor is used, thread it anti-clockwise into the fastener. As it is screwed in, it will grip the fastener and unscrew it from the casing (see illustration 2.20).

2.20 . . . then thread the extractor anti-clockwise into the fastener

● If a taper type extractor is used, tap it into the fastener so that it is firmly wedged in place. Unscrew the extractor (anti-clockwise) to draw the fastener out.

⚠ *Warning: Stud extractors are very hard and may break off in the fastener if care is not taken - ask an engineer about spark erosion if this happens.*

● Alternatively, the broken bolt/screw can be drilled out and the hole retapped for an oversize bolt/screw or a diamond-section thread insert. It is essential that the drilling is carried out squarely and to the correct depth, otherwise the casing may be ruined - if in doubt, entrust the work to an engineer.

● Bolts and nuts with rounded corners cause the correct size spanner or socket to slip when force is applied. Of the types of spanner/socket available always use a six-point type rather than an eight or twelve-point type - better grip

2.21 Comparison of surface drive ring spanner (left) with 12-point type (right)

is obtained. Surface drive spanners grip the middle of the hex flats, rather than the corners, and are thus good in cases of damaged heads **(see illustration 2.21)**.

● Slotted-head or Phillips-head screws are often damaged by the use of the wrong size screwdriver. Allen-head and Torx-head screws are much less likely to sustain damage. If enough of the screw head is exposed you can use a hacksaw to cut a slot in its head and then use a conventional flat-bladed screwdriver to remove it. Alternatively use a hammer and cold chisel to tap the head of the fastener around to slacken it. Always replace damaged fasteners with new ones, preferably Torx or Allen-head type.

HAYNES HINT

A dab of valve grinding compound between the screw head and screwdriver tip will often give a good grip.

Thread repair

● Threads (particularly those in aluminium alloy components) can be damaged by overtightening, being assembled with dirt in the threads, or from a component working loose and vibrating. Eventually the thread will fail completely, and it will be impossible to tighten the fastener.

● If a thread is damaged or clogged with old locking compound it can be renovated with a thread repair tool (thread chaser) **(see illustrations 2.22 and 2.23)**; special thread

2.22 A thread repair tool being used to correct an internal thread

2.23 A thread repair tool being used to correct an external thread

chasers are available for spark plug hole threads. The tool will not cut a new thread, but clean and true the original thread. Make sure that you use the correct diameter and pitch tool. Similarly, external threads can be cleaned up with a die or a thread restorer file **(see illustration 2.24)**.

2.24 Using a thread restorer file

● It is possible to drill out the old thread and retap the component to the next thread size. This will work where there is enough surrounding material and a new bolt or screw can be obtained. Sometimes, however, this is not possible - such as where the bolt/screw passes through another component which must also be suitably modified, also in cases where a spark plug or oil drain plug cannot be obtained in a larger diameter thread size.

● The diamond-section thread insert (often known by its popular trade name of Heli-Coil) is a simple and effective method of renewing the thread and retaining the original size. A kit can be purchased which contains the tap, insert and installing tool **(see illustration 2.25)**. Drill out the damaged thread with the size drill specified **(see illustration 2.26)**. Carefully retap the thread **(see illustration 2.27)**. Install the

2.25 Obtain a thread insert kit to suit the thread diameter and pitch required

2.26 To install a thread insert, first drill out the original thread . . .

2.27 . . . tap a new thread . . .

2.28 . . . fit insert on the installing tool . . .

2.29 . . . and thread into the component . . .

2.30 . . . break off the tang when complete

insert on the installing tool and thread it slowly into place using a light downward pressure **(see illustrations 2.28 and 2.29)**. When positioned between a 1/4 and 1/2 turn below the surface withdraw the installing tool and use the break-off tool to press down on the tang, breaking it off **(see illustration 2.30)**.

● There are epoxy thread repair kits on the market which can rebuild stripped internal threads, although this repair should not be used on high load-bearing components.

Thread locking and sealing compounds

● Locking compounds are used in locations where the fastener is prone to loosening due to vibration or on important safety-related items which might cause loss of control of the motorcycle if they fail. It is also used where important fasteners cannot be secured by other means such as lockwashers or split pins.

● Before applying locking compound, make sure that the threads (internal and external) are clean and dry with all old compound removed. Select a compound to suit the component being secured - a non-permanent general locking and sealing type is suitable for most applications, but a high strength type is needed for permanent fixing of studs in castings. Apply a drop or two of the compound to the first few threads of the fastener, then thread it into place and tighten to the specified torque. Do not apply excessive thread locking compound otherwise the thread may be damaged on subsequent removal.

● Certain fasteners are impregnated with a dry film type coating of locking compound on their threads. Always renew this type of fastener if disturbed.

● Anti-seize compounds, such as copper-based greases, can be applied to protect threads from seizure due to extreme heat and corrosion. A common instance is spark plug threads and exhaust system fasteners.

3 Measuring tools and gauges

Feeler gauges

● Feeler gauges (or blades) are used for measuring small gaps and clearances (see illustration 3.1). They can also be used to measure endfloat (sideplay) of a component on a shaft where access is not possible with a dial gauge.

● Feeler gauge sets should be treated with care and not bent or damaged. They are etched with their size on one face. Keep them clean and very lightly oiled to prevent corrosion build-up.

3.1 Feeler gauges are used for measuring small gaps and clearances - thickness is marked on one face of gauge

● When measuring a clearance, select a gauge which is a light sliding fit between the two components. You may need to use two gauges together to measure the clearance accurately.

Micrometers

● A micrometer is a precision tool capable of measuring to 0.01 or 0.001 of a millimetre. It should always be stored in its case and not in the general toolbox. It must be kept clean and never dropped, otherwise its frame or measuring anvils could be distorted resulting in inaccurate readings.

● External micrometers are used for measuring outside diameters of components and have many more applications than internal micrometers. Micrometers are available in different size ranges, eg 0 to 25 mm, 25 to 50 mm, and upwards in 25 mm steps; some large micrometers have interchangeable anvils to allow a range of measurements to be taken. Generally the largest precision measurement you are likely to take on a motorcycle is the piston diameter.

● Internal micrometers (or bore micrometers) are used for measuring inside diameters, such as valve guides and cylinder bores. Telescoping gauges and small hole gauges are used in conjunction with an external micrometer, whereas the more expensive internal micrometers have their own measuring device.

External micrometer

Note: *The conventional analogue type instrument is described. Although much easier to read, digital micrometers are considerably more expensive.*

● Always check the calibration of the micrometer before use. With the anvils closed (0 to 25 mm type) or set over a test gauge (for

3.2 Check micrometer calibration before use

the larger types) the scale should read zero (see illustration 3.2); make sure that the anvils (and test piece) are clean first. Any discrepancy can be adjusted by referring to the instructions supplied with the tool. Remember that the micrometer is a precision measuring tool - don't force the anvils closed, use the ratchet (4) on the end of the micrometer to close it. In this way, a measured force is always applied.

● To use, first make sure that the item being measured is clean. Place the anvil of the micrometer (1) against the item and use the thimble (2) to bring the spindle (3) lightly into contact with the other side of the item (see illustration 3.3). Don't tighten the thimble down because this will damage the micrometer - instead use the ratchet (4) on the end of the micrometer. The ratchet mechanism applies a measured force preventing damage to the instrument.

● The micrometer is read by referring to the linear scale on the sleeve and the annular scale on the thimble. Read off the sleeve first to obtain the base measurement, then add the fine measurement from the thimble to obtain the overall reading. The linear scale on the sleeve represents the measuring range of the micrometer (eg 0 to 25 mm). The annular scale

3.3 Micrometer component parts

1 Anvil	3 Spindle	5 Frame
2 Thimble	4 Ratchet	6 Locking lever

on the thimble will be in graduations of 0.01 mm (or as marked on the frame) - one full revolution of the thimble will move 0.5 mm on the linear scale. Take the reading where the datum line on the sleeve intersects the thimble's scale. Always position the eye directly above the scale otherwise an inaccurate reading will result.

In the example shown the item measures 2.95 mm (see illustration 3.4):

Linear scale	2.00 mm
Linear scale	0.50 mm
Annular scale	0.45 mm
Total figure	**2.95 mm**

3.5 Micrometer reading of 46.99 mm on linear and annular scales . . .

3.7 Expand the telescoping gauge in the bore, lock its position . . .

3.4 Micrometer reading of 2.95 mm

3.6 . . . and 0.004 mm on vernier scale

3.8 . . . then measure the gauge with a micrometer

Most micrometers have a locking lever (6) on the frame to hold the setting in place, allowing the item to be removed from the micrometer.
● Some micrometers have a vernier scale on their sleeve, providing an even finer measurement to be taken, in 0.001 increments of a millimetre. Take the sleeve and thimble measurement as described above, then check which graduation on the vernier scale aligns with that of the annular scale on the thimble **Note:** *The eye must be perpendicular to the scale when taking the vernier reading - if necessary rotate the body of the micrometer to ensure this.* Multiply the vernier scale figure by 0.001 and add it to the base and fine measurement figures.

In the example shown the item measures 46.994 mm (see illustrations 3.5 and 3.6):

Linear scale (base)	46.000 mm
Linear scale (base)	00.500 mm
Annular scale (fine)	00.490 mm
Vernier scale	00.004 mm
Total figure	**46.994 mm**

Internal micrometer

● Internal micrometers are available for measuring bore diameters, but are expensive and unlikely to be available for home use. It is suggested that a set of telescoping gauges and small hole gauges, both of which must be used with an external micrometer, will suffice for taking internal measurements on a motorcycle.
● Telescoping gauges can be used to measure internal diameters of components. Select a gauge with the correct size range, make sure its ends are clean and insert it into the bore. Expand the gauge, then lock its position and withdraw it from the bore **(see illustration 3.7)**. Measure across the gauge ends with a micrometer **(see illustration 3.8)**.
● Very small diameter bores (such as valve guides) are measured with a small hole gauge. Once adjusted to a slip-fit inside the component, its position is locked and the gauge withdrawn for measurement with a micrometer **(see illustrations 3.9 and 3.10)**.

Vernier caliper

Note: *The conventional linear and dial gauge type instruments are described. Digital types are easier to read, but are far more expensive.*
● The vernier caliper does not provide the precision of a micrometer, but is versatile in being able to measure internal and external diameters. Some types also incorporate a depth gauge. It is ideal for measuring clutch plate friction material and spring free lengths.
● To use the conventional linear scale vernier, slacken off the vernier clamp screws (1) and set its jaws over (2), or inside (3), the item to be measured **(see illustration 3.11)**. Slide the jaw into contact, using the thumb-wheel (4) for fine movement of the sliding scale (5) then tighten the clamp screws (1). Read off the main scale (6) where the zero on the sliding scale (5) intersects it, taking the whole number to the left of the zero; this provides the base measurement. View along the sliding scale and select the division which

3.9 Expand the small hole gauge in the bore, lock its position . . .

3.10 . . . then measure the gauge with a micrometer

lines up exactly with any of the divisions on the main scale, noting that the divisions usually represents 0.02 of a millimetre. Add this fine measurement to the base measurement to obtain the total reading.

3.11 Vernier component parts (linear gauge)

1 Clamp screws	3 Internal jaws	5 Sliding scale	7 Depth gauge
2 External jaws	4 Thumbwheel	6 Main scale	

In the example shown the item measures 55.92 mm **(see illustration 3.12)**:

Base measurement	55.00 mm
Fine measurement	00.92 mm
Total figure	**55.92 mm**

3.12 Vernier gauge reading of 55.92 mm

● Some vernier calipers are equipped with a dial gauge for fine measurement. Before use, check that the jaws are clean, then close them fully and check that the dial gauge reads zero. If necessary adjust the gauge ring accordingly. Slacken the vernier clamp screw (1) and set its jaws over (2), or inside (3), the item to be measured **(see illustration 3.13)**. Slide the jaws into contact, using the thumbwheel (4) for fine movement. Read off the main scale (5) where the edge of the sliding scale (6) intersects it, taking the whole number to the left of the zero; this provides the base measurement. Read off the needle position on the dial gauge (7) scale to provide the fine measurement; each division represents 0.05 of a millimetre. Add this fine measurement to the base measurement to obtain the total reading.

In the example shown the item measures 55.95 mm **(see illustration 3.14)**:

Base measurement	55.00 mm
Fine measurement	00.95 mm
Total figure	**55.95 mm**

3.13 Vernier component parts (dial gauge)

1 Clamp screw	5 Main scale
2 External jaws	6 Sliding scale
3 Internal jaws	7 Dial gauge
4 Thumbwheel	

3.14 Vernier gauge reading of 55.95 mm

Plastigauge

● Plastigauge is a plastic material which can be compressed between two surfaces to measure the oil clearance between them. The width of the compressed Plastigauge is measured against a calibrated scale to determine the clearance.

● Common uses of Plastigauge are for measuring the clearance between crankshaft journal and main bearing inserts, between crankshaft journal and big-end bearing inserts, and between camshaft and bearing surfaces. The following example describes big-end oil clearance measurement.

● Handle the Plastigauge material carefully to prevent distortion. Using a sharp knife, cut a length which corresponds with the width of the bearing being measured and place it carefully across the journal so that it is parallel with the shaft **(see illustration 3.15)**. Carefully install both bearing shells and the connecting rod. Without rotating the rod on the journal tighten its bolts or nuts (as applicable) to the specified torque. The connecting rod and bearings are then disassembled and the crushed Plastigauge examined.

3.15 Plastigauge placed across shaft journal

● Using the scale provided in the Plastigauge kit, measure the width of the material to determine the oil clearance **(see illustration 3.16)**. Always remove all traces of Plastigauge after use using your fingernails.

Caution: Arriving at the correct clearance demands that the assembly is torqued correctly, according to the settings and sequence (where applicable) provided by the motorcycle manufacturer.

3.16 Measuring the width of the crushed Plastigauge

Dial gauge or DTI (Dial Test Indicator)

● A dial gauge can be used to accurately measure small amounts of movement. Typical uses are measuring shaft runout or shaft endfloat (sideplay) and setting piston position for ignition timing on two-strokes. A dial gauge set usually comes with a range of different probes and adapters and mounting equipment.

● The gauge needle must point to zero when at rest. Rotate the ring around its periphery to zero the gauge.

● Check that the gauge is capable of reading the extent of movement in the work. Most gauges have a small dial set in the face which records whole millimetres of movement as well as the fine scale around the face periphery which is calibrated in 0.01 mm divisions. Read off the small dial first to obtain the base measurement, then add the measurement from the fine scale to obtain the total reading.

In the example shown the gauge reads 1.48 mm (see illustration 3.17):

Base measurement	1.00 mm
Fine measurement	0.48 mm
Total figure	**1.48 mm**

3.17 Dial gauge reading of 1.48 mm

● If measuring shaft runout, the shaft must be supported in vee-blocks and the gauge mounted on a stand perpendicular to the shaft. Rest the tip of the gauge against the centre of the shaft and rotate the shaft slowly whilst watching the gauge reading (see illustration 3.18). Take several measurements along the length of the shaft and record the

3.18 Using a dial gauge to measure shaft runout

maximum gauge reading as the amount of runout in the shaft. **Note:** *The reading obtained will be total runout at that point - some manufacturers specify that the runout figure is halved to compare with their specified runout limit.*

● Endfloat (sideplay) measurement requires that the gauge is mounted securely to the surrounding component with its probe touching the end of the shaft. Using hand pressure, push and pull on the shaft noting the maximum endfloat recorded on the gauge (see illustration 3.19).

3.19 Using a dial gauge to measure shaft endfloat

● A dial gauge with suitable adapters can be used to determine piston position BTDC on two-stroke engines for the purposes of ignition timing. The gauge, adapter and suitable length probe are installed in the place of the spark plug and the gauge zeroed at TDC. If the piston position is specified as 1.14 mm BTDC, rotate the engine back to 2.00 mm BTDC, then slowly forwards to 1.14 mm BTDC.

Cylinder compression gauges

● A compression gauge is used for measuring cylinder compression. Either the rubber-cone type or the threaded adapter type can be used. The latter is preferred to ensure a perfect seal against the cylinder head. A 0 to 300 psi (0 to 20 Bar) type gauge (for petrol/gasoline engines) will be suitable for motorcycles.

● The spark plug is removed and the gauge either held hard against the cylinder head (cone type) or the gauge adapter screwed into the cylinder head (threaded type) (see illustration 3.20). Cylinder compression is measured with the engine turning over, but not running - carry out the compression test as described in

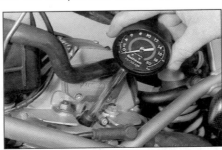

3.20 Using a rubber-cone type cylinder compression gauge

Fault Finding Equipment. The gauge will hold the reading until manually released.

Oil pressure gauge

● An oil pressure gauge is used for measuring engine oil pressure. Most gauges come with a set of adapters to fit the thread of the take-off point (see illustration 3.21). If the take-off point specified by the motorcycle manufacturer is an external oil pipe union, make sure that the specified replacement union is used to prevent oil starvation.

3.21 Oil pressure gauge and take-off point adapter (arrow)

● Oil pressure is measured with the engine running (at a specific rpm) and often the manufacturer will specify pressure limits for a cold and hot engine.

Straight-edge and surface plate

● If checking the gasket face of a component for warpage, place a steel rule or precision straight-edge across the gasket face and measure any gap between the straight-edge and component with feeler gauges (see illustration 3.22). Check diagonally across the component and between mounting holes (see illustration 3.23).

3.22 Use a straight-edge and feeler gauges to check for warpage

3.23 Check for warpage in these directions

● Checking individual components for warpage, such as clutch plain (metal) plates, requires a perfectly flat plate or piece or plate glass and feeler gauges.

4 Torque and leverage

What is torque?

● Torque describes the twisting force about a shaft. The amount of torque applied is determined by the distance from the centre of the shaft to the end of the lever and the amount of force being applied to the end of the lever; distance multiplied by force equals torque.

● The manufacturer applies a measured torque to a bolt or nut to ensure that it will not slacken in use and to hold two components securely together without movement in the joint. The actual torque setting depends on the thread size, bolt or nut material and the composition of the components being held.

● Too little torque may cause the fastener to loosen due to vibration, whereas too much torque will distort the joint faces of the component or cause the fastener to shear off. Always stick to the specified torque setting.

Using a torque wrench

● Check the calibration of the torque wrench and make sure it has a suitable range for the job. Torque wrenches are available in Nm (Newton-metres), kgf m (kilograms-force metre), lbf ft (pounds-feet), lbf in (inch-pounds). Do not confuse lbf ft with lbf in.

● Adjust the tool to the desired torque on the scale (see illustration 4.1). If your torque wrench is not calibrated in the units specified, carefully convert the figure (see Conversion Factors). A manufacturer sometimes gives a torque setting as a range (8 to 10 Nm) rather than a single figure - in this case set the tool midway between the two settings. The same torque may be expressed as 9 Nm ± 1 Nm. Some torque wrenches have a method of locking the setting so that it isn't inadvertently altered during use.

4.1 Set the torque wrench index mark to the setting required, in this case 12 Nm

● Install the bolts/nuts in their correct location and secure them lightly. Their threads must be clean and free of any old locking compound. Unless specified the threads and flange should be dry - oiled threads are necessary in certain circumstances and the manufacturer will take this into account in the specified torque figure. Similarly, the manufacturer may also specify the application of thread-locking compound.

● Tighten the fasteners in the specified sequence until the torque wrench clicks, indicating that the torque setting has been reached. Apply the torque again to double-check the setting. Where different thread diameter fasteners secure the component, as a rule tighten the larger diameter ones first.

● When the torque wrench has been finished with, release the lock (where applicable) and fully back off its setting to zero - do not leave the torque wrench tensioned. Also, do not use a torque wrench for slackening a fastener.

Angle-tightening

● Manufacturers often specify a figure in degrees for final tightening of a fastener. This usually follows tightening to a specific torque setting.

● A degree disc can be set and attached to the socket (see illustration 4.2) or a protractor can be used to mark the angle of movement on the bolt/nut head and the surrounding casting (see illustration 4.3).

4.2 Angle tightening can be accomplished with a torque-angle gauge . . .

4.3 . . . or by marking the angle on the surrounding component

Loosening sequences

● Where more than one bolt/nut secures a component, loosen each fastener evenly a little at a time. In this way, not all the stress of the joint is held by one fastener and the components are not likely to distort.

● If a tightening sequence is provided, work in the REVERSE of this, but if not, work from the outside in, in a criss-cross sequence (see illustration 4.4).

4.4 When slackening, work from the outside inwards

Tightening sequences

● If a component is held by more than one fastener it is important that the retaining bolts/nuts are tightened evenly to prevent uneven stress build-up and distortion of sealing faces. This is especially important on high-compression joints such as the cylinder head.

● A sequence is usually provided by the manufacturer, either in a diagram or actually marked in the casting. If not, always start in the centre and work outwards in a criss-cross pattern (see illustration 4.5). Start off by securing all bolts/nuts finger-tight, then set the torque wrench and tighten each fastener by a small amount in sequence until the final torque is reached. By following this practice,

4.5 When tightening, work from the inside outwards

the joint will be held evenly and will not be distorted. Important joints, such as the cylinder head and big-end fasteners often have two- or three-stage torque settings.

Applying leverage

● Use tools at the correct angle. Position a socket wrench or spanner on the bolt/nut so that you pull it towards you when loosening. If this can't be done, push the spanner without curling your fingers around it **(see illustration 4.6)** - the spanner may slip or the fastener loosen suddenly, resulting in your fingers being crushed against a component.

4.6 If you can't pull on the spanner to loosen a fastener, push with your hand open

● Additional leverage is gained by extending the length of the lever. The best way to do this is to use a breaker bar instead of the regular length tool, or to slip a length of tubing over the end of the spanner or socket wrench.
● If additional leverage will not work, the fastener head is either damaged or firmly corroded in place (see *Fasteners*).

5 Bearings

Bearing removal and installation

Drivers and sockets

● Before removing a bearing, always inspect the casing to see which way it must be driven out - some casings will have retaining plates or a cast step. Also check for any identifying markings on the bearing and if installed to a certain depth, measure this at this stage. Some roller bearings are sealed on one side - take note of the original fitted position.
● Bearings can be driven out of a casing using a bearing driver tool (with the correct size head) or a socket of the correct diameter. Select the driver head or socket so that it contacts the outer race of the bearing, not the balls/rollers or inner race. Always support the casing around the bearing housing with wood blocks, otherwise there is a risk of fracture. The bearing is driven out with a few blows on the driver or socket from a heavy mallet. Unless access is severely restricted (as with wheel bearings), a pin-punch is not recommended unless it is moved around the bearing to keep it square in its housing.

● The same equipment can be used to install bearings. Make sure the bearing housing is supported on wood blocks and line up the bearing in its housing. Fit the bearing as noted on removal - generally they are installed with their marked side facing outwards. Tap the bearing squarely into its housing using a driver or socket which bears only on the bearing's outer race - contact with the bearing balls/rollers or inner race will destroy it **(see illustrations 5.1 and 5.2)**.
● Check that the bearing inner race and balls/rollers rotate freely.

5.1 Using a bearing driver against the bearing's outer race

5.2 Using a large socket against the bearing's outer race

Pullers and slide-hammers

● Where a bearing is pressed on a shaft a puller will be required to extract it **(see illustration 5.3)**. Make sure that the puller clamp or legs fit securely behind the bearing and are unlikely to slip out. If pulling a bearing

5.3 This bearing puller clamps behind the bearing and pressure is applied to the shaft end to draw the bearing off

off a gear shaft for example, you may have to locate the puller behind a gear pinion if there is no access to the race and draw the gear pinion off the shaft as well **(see illustration 5.4)**.

> *Caution: Ensure that the puller's centre bolt locates securely against the end of the shaft and will not slip when pressure is applied. Also ensure that puller does not damage the shaft end.*

5.4 Where no access is available to the rear of the bearing, it is sometimes possible to draw off the adjacent component

● Operate the puller so that its centre bolt exerts pressure on the shaft end and draws the bearing off the shaft.
● When installing the bearing on the shaft, tap only on the bearing's inner race - contact with the balls/rollers or outer race with destroy the bearing. Use a socket or length of tubing as a drift which fits over the shaft end **(see illustration 5.5)**.

5.5 When installing a bearing on a shaft use a piece of tubing which bears only on the bearing's inner race

● Where a bearing locates in a blind hole in a casing, it cannot be driven or pulled out as described above. A slide-hammer with knife-edged bearing puller attachment will be required. The puller attachment passes through the bearing and when tightened expands to fit firmly behind the bearing **(see illustration 5.6)**. By operating the slide-hammer part of the tool the bearing is jarred out of its housing **(see illustration 5.7)**.
● It is possible, if the bearing is of reasonable weight, for it to drop out of its housing if the casing is heated as described opposite. If this

5.6 Expand the bearing puller so that it locks behind the bearing . . .

5.7 . . . attach the slide hammer to the bearing puller

method is attempted, first prepare a work surface which will enable the casing to be tapped face down to help dislodge the bearing - a wood surface is ideal since it will not damage the casing's gasket surface. Wearing protective gloves, tap the heated casing several times against the work surface to dislodge the bearing under its own weight **(see illustration 5.8)**.

5.8 Tapping a casing face down on wood blocks can often dislodge a bearing

● Bearings can be installed in blind holes using the driver or socket method described above.

Drawbolts

● Where a bearing or bush is set in the eye of a component, such as a suspension linkage arm or connecting rod small-end, removal by drift may damage the component. Furthermore, a rubber bushing in a shock absorber eye cannot successfully be driven out of position. If access is available to a engineering press, the task is straightforward. If not, a drawbolt can be fabricated to extract the bearing or bush.

5.9 Drawbolt component parts assembled on a suspension arm

1 Bolt or length of threaded bar
2 Nuts
3 Washer (external diameter greater than tubing internal diameter)
4 Tubing (internal diameter sufficient to accommodate bearing)
5 Suspension arm with bearing
6 Tubing (external diameter slightly smaller than bearing)
7 Washer (external diameter slightly smaller than bearing)

5.10 Drawing the bearing out of the suspension arm

● To extract the bearing/bush you will need a long bolt with nut (or piece of threaded bar with two nuts), a piece of tubing which has an internal diameter larger than the bearing/bush, another piece of tubing which has an external diameter slightly smaller than the bearing/bush, and a selection of washers **(see illustrations 5.9 and 5.10)**. Note that the pieces of tubing must be of the same length, or longer, than the bearing/bush.

● The same kit (without the pieces of tubing) can be used to draw the new bearing/bush back into place **(see illustration 5.11)**.

5.11 Installing a new bearing (1) in the suspension arm

Temperature change

● If the bearing's outer race is a tight fit in the casing, the aluminium casing can be heated to release its grip on the bearing. Aluminium will expand at a greater rate than the steel bearing outer race. There are several ways to do this, but avoid any localised extreme heat (such as a blow torch) - aluminium alloy has a low melting point.

● Approved methods of heating a casing are using a domestic oven (heated to 100°C) or immersing the casing in boiling water **(see illustration 5.12)**. Low temperature range localised heat sources such as a paint stripper heat gun or clothes iron can also be used **(see illustration 5.13)**. Alternatively, soak a rag in boiling water, wring it out and wrap it around the bearing housing.

> ⚠ **Warning: All of these methods require care in use to prevent scalding and burns to the hands. Wear protective gloves when handling hot components.**

5.12 A casing can be immersed in a sink of boiling water to aid bearing removal

5.13 Using a localised heat source to aid bearing removal

● If heating the whole casing note that plastic components, such as the neutral switch, may suffer - remove them beforehand.

● After heating, remove the bearing as described above. You may find that the expansion is sufficient for the bearing to fall out of the casing under its own weight or with a light tap on the driver or socket.

● If necessary, the casing can be heated to aid bearing installation, and this is sometimes the recommended procedure if the motorcycle manufacturer has designed the housing and bearing fit with this intention.

● Installation of bearings can be eased by placing them in a freezer the night before installation. The steel bearing will contract slightly, allowing easy insertion in its housing. This is often useful when installing steering head outer races in the frame.

Bearing types and markings

● Plain shell bearings, ball bearings, needle roller bearings and tapered roller bearings will all be found on motorcycles **(see illustrations 5.14 and 5.15)**. The ball and roller types are usually caged between an inner and outer race, but uncaged variations may be found.

5.14 Shell bearings are either plain or grooved. They are usually identified by colour code (arrow)

5.15 Tapered roller bearing (A), needle roller bearing (B) and ball journal bearing (C)

● Shell bearings (often called inserts) are usually found at the crankshaft main and connecting rod big-end where they are good at coping with high loads. They are made of a phosphor-bronze material and are impregnated with self-lubricating properties.

● Ball bearings and needle roller bearings consist of a steel inner and outer race with the balls or rollers between the races. They require constant lubrication by oil or grease and are good at coping with axial loads. Taper roller bearings consist of rollers set in a tapered cage set on the inner race; the outer race is separate. They are good at coping with axial loads and prevent movement along the shaft - a typical application is in the steering head.

● Bearing manufacturers produce bearings to ISO size standards and stamp one face of the bearing to indicate its internal and external diameter, load capacity and type **(see illustration 5.16)**.

● Metal bushes are usually of phosphor-bronze material. Rubber bushes are used in suspension mounting eyes. Fibre bushes have also been used in suspension pivots.

5.16 Typical bearing marking

Bearing fault finding

● If a bearing outer race has spun in its housing, the housing material will be damaged. You can use a bearing locking compound to bond the outer race in place if damage is not too severe.

● Shell bearings will fail due to damage of their working surface, as a result of lack of lubrication, corrosion or abrasive particles in the oil **(see illustration 5.17)**. Small particles of dirt in the oil may embed in the bearing material whereas larger particles will score the bearing and shaft journal. If a number of short journeys are made, insufficient heat will be generated to drive off condensation which has built up on the bearings.

5.17 Typical bearing failures

● Ball and roller bearings will fail due to lack of lubrication or damage to the balls or rollers. Tapered-roller bearings can be damaged by overloading them. Unless the bearing is sealed on both sides, wash it in paraffin (kerosene) to remove all old grease then allow it to dry. Make a visual inspection looking to dented balls or rollers, damaged cages and worn or pitted races **(see illustration 5.18)**.

● A ball bearing can be checked for wear by listening to it when spun. Apply a film of light oil to the bearing and hold it close to the ear - hold the outer race with one hand and spin the inner

5.18 Example of ball journal bearing with damaged balls and cages

5.19 Hold outer race and listen to inner race when spun

race with the other hand **(see illustration 5.19)**. The bearing should be almost silent when spun; if it grates or rattles it is worn.

6 Oil seals

Oil seal removal and installation

● Oil seals should be renewed every time a component is dismantled. This is because the seal lips will become set to the sealing surface and will not necessarily reseal.

● Oil seals can be prised out of position using a large flat-bladed screwdriver **(see illustration 6.1)**. In the case of crankcase seals, check first that the seal is not lipped on the inside, preventing its removal with the crankcases joined.

6.1 Prise out oil seals with a large flat-bladed screwdriver

● New seals are usually installed with their marked face (containing the seal reference code) outwards and the spring side towards the fluid being retained. In certain cases, such as a two-stroke engine crankshaft seal, a double lipped seal may be used due to there being fluid or gas on each side of the joint.

● Use a bearing driver or socket which bears only on the outer hard edge of the seal to install it in the casing - tapping on the inner edge will damage the sealing lip.

Oil seal types and markings

● Oil seals are usually of the single-lipped type. Double-lipped seals are found where a liquid or gas is on both sides of the joint.

● Oil seals can harden and lose their sealing ability if the motorcycle has been in storage for a long period - renewal is the only solution.

● Oil seal manufacturers also conform to the ISO markings for seal size - these are moulded into the outer face of the seal **(see illustration 6.2)**.

6.2 These oil seal markings indicate inside diameter, outside diameter and seal thickness

7 Gaskets and sealants

Types of gasket and sealant

● Gaskets are used to seal the mating surfaces between components and keep lubricants, fluids, vacuum or pressure contained within the assembly. Aluminium gaskets are sometimes found at the cylinder joints, but most gaskets are paper-based. If the mating surfaces of the components being joined are undamaged the gasket can be installed dry, although a dab of sealant or grease will be useful to hold it in place during assembly.

● RTV (Room Temperature Vulcanising) silicone rubber sealants cure when exposed to moisture in the atmosphere. These sealants are good at filling pits or irregular gasket faces, but will tend to be forced out of the joint under very high torque. They can be used to replace a paper gasket, but first make sure that the width of the paper gasket is not essential to the shimming of internal components. RTV sealants should not be used on components containing petrol (gasoline).

● Non-hardening, semi-hardening and hard setting liquid gasket compounds can be used with a gasket or between a metal-to-metal joint. Select the sealant to suit the application: universal non-hardening sealant can be used on virtually all joints; semi-hardening on joint faces which are rough or damaged; hard setting sealant on joints which require a permanent bond and are subjected to high temperature and pressure. **Note:** *Check first if the paper gasket has a bead of sealant*

impregnated in its surface before applying additional sealant.

● When choosing a sealant, make sure it is suitable for the application, particularly if being applied in a high-temperature area or in the vicinity of fuel. Certain manufacturers produce sealants in either clear, silver or black colours to match the finish of the engine. This has a particular application on motorcycles where much of the engine is exposed.

● Do not over-apply sealant. That which is squeezed out on the outside of the joint can be wiped off, whereas an excess of sealant on the inside can break off and clog oilways.

Breaking a sealed joint

● Age, heat, pressure and the use of hard setting sealant can cause two components to stick together so tightly that they are difficult to separate using finger pressure alone. Do not resort to using levers unless there is a pry point provided for this purpose **(see illustration 7.1)** or else the gasket surfaces will be damaged.

● Use a soft-faced hammer **(see illustration 7.2)** or a wood block and conventional hammer to strike the component near the mating surface. Avoid hammering against cast extremities since they may break off. If this method fails, try using a wood wedge between the two components.

Caution: If the joint will not separate, double-check that you have removed all the fasteners.

7.1 If a pry point is provided, apply gently pressure with a flat-bladed screwdriver

7.2 Tap around the joint with a soft-faced mallet if necessary - don't strike cooling fins

Removal of old gasket and sealant

● Paper gaskets will most likely come away complete, leaving only a few traces stuck on

Most components have one or two hollow locating dowels between the two gasket faces. If a dowel cannot be removed, do not resort to gripping it with pliers - it will almost certainly be distorted. Install a close-fitting socket or Phillips screwdriver into the dowel and then grip the outer edge of the dowel to free it.

the sealing faces of the components. It is imperative that all traces are removed to ensure correct sealing of the new gasket.

● Very carefully scrape all traces of gasket away making sure that the sealing surfaces are not gouged or scored by the scraper **(see illustrations 7.3, 7.4 and 7.5)**. Stubborn deposits can be removed by spraying with an aerosol gasket remover. Final preparation of

7.3 Paper gaskets can be scraped off with a gasket scraper tool . . .

7.4 . . . a knife blade . . .

7.5 . . . or a household scraper

7.6 Fine abrasive paper is wrapped around a flat file to clean up the gasket face

7.7 A kitchen scourer can be used on stubborn deposits

the gasket surface can be made with very fine abrasive paper or a plastic kitchen scourer **(see illustrations 7.6 and 7.7)**.

● Old sealant can be scraped or peeled off components, depending on the type originally used. Note that gasket removal compounds are available to avoid scraping the components clean; make sure the gasket remover suits the type of sealant used.

8 Chains

Breaking and joining final drive chains

● Drive chains for all but small bikes are continuous and do not have a clip-type connecting link. The chain must be broken using a chain breaker tool and the new chain securely riveted together using a new soft rivet-type link. Never use a clip-type connecting link instead of a rivet-type link, except in an emergency. Various chain breaking and riveting tools are available, either as separate tools or combined as illustrated in the accompanying photographs - read the instructions supplied with the tool carefully.

> ⚠ **Warning: The need to rivet the new link pins correctly cannot be overstressed - loss of control of the motorcycle is very likely to result if the chain breaks in use.**

● Rotate the chain and look for the soft link. The soft link pins look like they have been

8.1 Tighten the chain breaker to push the pin out of the link . . .

8.2 . . . withdraw the pin, remove the tool . . .

8.3 . . . and separate the chain link

deeply centre-punched instead of peened over like all the other pins **(see illustration 8.9)** and its sideplate may be a different colour. Position the soft link midway between the sprockets and assemble the chain breaker tool over one of the soft link pins **(see illustration 8.1)**. Operate the tool to push the pin out through the chain **(see illustration 8.2)**. On an O-ring chain, remove the O-rings **(see illustration 8.3)**. Carry out the same procedure on the other soft link pin.

> **Caution: Certain soft link pins (particularly on the larger chains) may require their ends to be filed or ground off before they can be pressed out using the tool.**

● Check that you have the correct size and strength (standard or heavy duty) new soft link - do not reuse the old link. Look for the size marking on the chain sideplates **(see illustration 8.10)**.

● Position the chain ends so that they are engaged over the rear sprocket. On an O-ring

8.4 Insert the new soft link, with O-rings, through the chain ends . . .

8.5 . . . install the O-rings over the pin ends . . .

8.6 . . . followed by the sideplate

chain, install a new O-ring over each pin of the link and insert the link through the two chain ends **(see illustration 8.4)**. Install a new O-ring over the end of each pin, followed by the sideplate (with the chain manufacturer's marking facing outwards) **(see illustrations 8.5 and 8.6)**. On an unsealed chain, insert the link through the two chain ends, then install the sideplate with the chain manufacturer's marking facing outwards.

● Note that it may not be possible to install the sideplate using finger pressure alone. If using a joining tool, assemble it so that the plates of the tool clamp the link and press the sideplate over the pins **(see illustration 8.7)**. Otherwise, use two small sockets placed over

8.7 Push the sideplate into position using a clamp

8.8 Assemble the chain riveting tool over one pin at a time and tighten it fully

8.9 Pin end correctly riveted (A), pin end unriveted (B)

the rivet ends and two pieces of the wood between a G-clamp. Operate the clamp to press the sideplate over the pins.

● Assemble the joining tool over one pin (following the maker's instructions) and tighten the tool down to spread the pin end securely **(see illustrations 8.8 and 8.9)**. Do the same on the other pin.

> ⚠ **Warning: Check that the pin ends are secure and that there is no danger of the sideplate coming loose. If the pin ends are cracked the soft link must be renewed.**

Final drive chain sizing

● Chains are sized using a three digit number, followed by a suffix to denote the chain type **(see illustration 8.10)**. Chain type is either standard or heavy duty (thicker sideplates), and also unsealed or O-ring/X-ring type.

● The first digit of the number relates to the pitch of the chain, ie the distance from the centre of one pin to the centre of the next pin **(see illustration 8.11)**. Pitch is expressed in eighths of an inch, as follows:

8.10 Typical chain size and type marking

8.11 Chain dimensions

Sizes commencing with a 4 (eg 428) have a pitch of 1/2 inch (12.7 mm)
Sizes commencing with a 5 (eg 520) have a pitch of 5/8 inch (15.9 mm)
Sizes commencing with a 6 (eg 630) have a pitch of 3/4 inch (19.1 mm)

● The second and third digits of the chain size relate to the width of the rollers, again in imperial units, eg the 525 shown has 5/16 inch (7.94 mm) rollers **(see illustration 8.11)**.

9 Hoses

Clamping to prevent flow

● Small-bore flexible hoses can be clamped to prevent fluid flow whilst a component is worked on. Whichever method is used, ensure that the hose material is not permanently distorted or damaged by the clamp.

a) A brake hose clamp available from auto accessory shops **(see illustration 9.1)**.
b) A wingnut type hose clamp **(see illustration 9.2)**.

9.1 Hoses can be clamped with an automotive brake hose clamp . . .

9.2 . . . a wingnut type hose clamp . . .

c) Two sockets placed each side of the hose and held with straight-jawed self-locking grips **(see illustration 9.3)**.
d) Thick card each side of the hose held between straight-jawed self-locking grips **(see illustration 9.4)**.

9.3 . . . two sockets and a pair of self-locking grips . . .

9.4 . . . or thick card and self-locking grips

Freeing and fitting hoses

● Always make sure the hose clamp is moved well clear of the hose end. Grip the hose with your hand and rotate it whilst pulling it off the union. If the hose has hardened due to age and will not move, slit it with a sharp knife and peel its ends off the union **(see illustration 9.5)**.

● Resist the temptation to use grease or soap on the unions to aid installation; although it helps the hose slip over the union it will equally aid the escape of fluid from the joint. It is preferable to soften the hose ends in hot water and wet the inside surface of the hose with water or a fluid which will evaporate.

9.5 Cutting a coolant hose free with a sharp knife

Introduction

In less time than it takes to read this introduction, a thief could steal your motorcycle. Returning only to find your bike has gone is one of the worst feelings in the world. Even if the motorcycle is insured against theft, once you've got over the initial shock, you will have the inconvenience of dealing with the police and your insurance company.

The motorcycle is an easy target for the professional thief and the joyrider alike and the official figures on motorcycle theft make for depressing reading; on average a motorcycle is stolen every 16 minutes in the UK!

Motorcycle thefts fall into two categories, those stolen 'to order' and those taken by opportunists. The thief stealing to order will be on the look out for a specific make and model and will go to extraordinary lengths to obtain that motorcycle. The opportunist thief on the other hand will look for easy targets which can be stolen with the minimum of effort and risk.

Whilst it is never going to be possible to make your machine 100% secure, it is estimated that around half of all stolen motorcycles are taken by opportunist thieves. Remember that the opportunist thief is always on the look out for the easy option: if there are two similar motorcycles parked side-by-side, they will target the one with the lowest level of security. By taking a few precautions, you can reduce the chances of your motorcycle being stolen.

Security equipment

There are many specialised motorcycle security devices available and the following text summarises their applications and their good and bad points.

Once you have decided on the type of security equipment which best suits your needs, we recommended that you read one of the many equipment tests regularly carried out by the motorcycle press. These tests compare the products from all the major manufacturers and give impartial ratings on their effectiveness, value-for-money and ease of use.

No one item of security equipment can provide complete protection. It is highly recommended that two or more of the items described below are combined to increase the security of your motorcycle (a lock and chain plus an alarm system is just about ideal). The more security measures fitted to the bike, the less likely it is to be stolen.

Lock and chain

Pros: *Very flexible to use; can be used to secure the motorcycle to almost any immovable object. On some locks and chains, the lock can be used on its own as a disc lock (see below).*

Cons: *Can be very heavy and awkward to carry on the motorcycle, although some types will be supplied with a carry bag which can be strapped to the pillion seat.*

● Heavy-duty chains and locks are an excellent security measure **(see illustration 1)**. Whenever the motorcycle is parked, use the lock and chain to secure the machine to a solid, immovable object such as a post or railings. This will prevent the machine from being ridden away or being lifted into the back of a van.

● When fitting the chain, always ensure the chain is routed around the motorcycle frame or swingarm **(see illustrations 2 and 3)**. Never merely pass the chain around one of the wheel rims; a thief may unbolt the wheel and lift the rest of the machine into a van, leaving you with just the wheel! Try to avoid having excess chain free, thus making it difficult to use cutting tools, and keep the chain and lock off the ground to prevent thieves attacking it with a cold chisel. Position the lock so that its lock barrel is facing downwards; this will make it harder for the thief to attack the lock mechanism.

Ensure the lock and chain you buy is of good quality and long enough to shackle your bike to a solid object

Pass the chain through the bike's frame, rather than just through a wheel . . .

. . . and loop it around a solid object

U-locks

Pros: *Highly effective deterrent which can be used to secure the bike to a post or railings. Most U-locks come with a carrier which allows the lock to be easily carried on the bike.*

Cons: *Not as flexible to use as a lock and chain.*

● These are solid locks which are similar in use to a lock and chain. U-locks are lighter than a lock and chain but not so flexible to use. The length and shape of the lock shackle limit the objects to which the bike can be secured **(see illustration 4)**.

Disc locks

Pros: *Small, light and very easy to carry; most can be stored underneath the seat.*

Cons: *Does not prevent the motorcycle being lifted into a van. Can be very embarrassing if you*

U-locks can be used to secure the bike to a solid object – ensure you purchase one which is long enough

forget to remove the lock before attempting to ride off!

● Disc locks are designed to be attached to the front brake disc. The lock passes through one of the holes in the disc and prevents the wheel rotating by jamming against the fork/brake caliper **(see illustration 5)**. Some are equipped with an alarm siren which sounds if the disc lock is moved; this not only acts as a theft deterrent but also as a handy reminder if you try to move the bike with the lock still fitted.

● Combining the disc lock with a length of cable which can be looped around a post or railings provides an additional measure of security **(see illustration 6)**.

Alarms and immobilisers

Pros: *Once installed it is completely hassle-free to use. If the system is 'Thatcham' or 'Sold Secure-approved', insurance companies may give you a discount.*

Cons: *Can be expensive to buy and complex to install. No system will prevent the motorcycle from being lifted into a van and taken away.*

● Electronic alarms and immobilisers are available to suit a variety of budgets. There are three different types of system available: pure alarms, pure immobilisers, and the more expensive systems which are combined alarm/immobilisers **(see illustration 7)**.

● An alarm system is designed to emit an audible warning if the motorcycle is being tampered with.

● An immobiliser prevents the motorcycle being started and ridden away by disabling its electrical systems.

● When purchasing an alarm/immobiliser system, check the cost of installing the system unless you are able to do it yourself. If the motorcycle is not used regularly, another consideration is the current drain of the system. All alarm/immobiliser systems are powered by the motorcycle's battery; purchasing a system with a very low current drain could prevent the battery losing its charge whilst the motorcycle is not being used.

A typical disc lock attached through one of the holes in the disc

A disc lock combined with a security cable provides additional protection

A typical alarm/immobiliser system

Indelible markings can be applied to most areas of the bike – always apply the manufacturer's sticker to warn off thieves

Chemically-etched code numbers can be applied to main body panels . . .

. . . again, always ensure that the kit manufacturer's sticker is applied in a prominent position

Security marking kits

Pros: *Very cheap and effective deterrent. Many insurance companies will give you a discount on your insurance premium if a recognised security marking kit is used on your motorcycle.*

Cons: *Does not prevent the motorcycle being stolen by joyriders.*

● There are many different types of security marking kits available. The idea is to mark as many parts of the motorcycle as possible with a unique security number **(see illustrations 8, 9 and 10)**. A form will be included with the kit to register your personal details and those of the motorcycle with the kit manufacturer. This register is made available to the police to help them trace the rightful owner of any motorcycle or components which they recover should all other forms of identification have been removed. Always apply the warning stickers provided with the kit to deter thieves.

Ground anchors, wheel clamps and security posts

Pros: *An excellent form of security which will deter all but the most determined of thieves.*

Cons: *Awkward to install and can be expensive.*

● Whilst the motorcycle is at home, it is a good idea to attach it securely to the floor or a solid wall, even if it is kept in a securely locked garage. Various types of ground anchors, security posts and wheel clamps are available for this purpose **(see illustration 11)**. These security devices are either bolted to a solid concrete or brick structure or can be cemented into the ground.

Permanent ground anchors provide an excellent level of security when the bike is at home

Security at home

A high percentage of motorcycle thefts are from the owner's home. Here are some things to consider whenever your motorcycle is at home:

✔ Where possible, always keep the motorcycle in a securely locked garage. Never rely solely on the standard lock on the garage door, these are usual hopelessly inadequate. Fit an additional locking mechanism to the door and consider having the garage alarmed. A security light, activated by a movement sensor, is also a good investment.

✔ Always secure the motorcycle to the ground or a wall, even if it is inside a securely locked garage.
✔ Do not regularly leave the motorcycle outside your home, try to keep it out of sight wherever possible. If a garage is not available, fit a motorcycle cover over the bike to disguise its true identity.
✔ It is not uncommon for thieves to follow a motorcyclist home to find out where the bike is kept. They will then return at a later date. Be aware of this whenever you are returning

home on your motorcycle. If you suspect you are being followed, do not return home, instead ride to a garage or shop and stop as a precaution.
✔ When selling a motorcycle, do not provide your home address or the location where the bike is normally kept. Arrange to meet the buyer at a location away from your home. Thieves have been known to pose as potential buyers to find out where motorcycles are kept and then return later to steal them.

Security away from the home

As well as fitting security equipment to your motorcycle here are a few general rules to follow whenever you park your motorcycle.
✔ Park in a busy, public place.
✔ Use car parks which incorporate security features, such as CCTV.

✔ At night, park in a well-lit area, preferably directly underneath a street light.
✔ Engage the steering lock.
✔ Secure the motorcycle to a solid, immovable object such as a post or railings with an additional lock. If this is not possible,

secure the bike to a friend's motorcycle. Some public parking places provide security loops for motorcycles.
✔ Never leave your helmet or luggage attached to the motorcycle. Take them with you at all times.

Lubricants and fluids

A wide range of lubricants, fluids and cleaning agents is available for motor-cycles. This is a guide as to what is available, its applications and properties.

Four-stroke engine oil

● Engine oil is without doubt the most important component of any four-stroke engine. Modern motorcycle engines place a lot of demands on their oil and choosing the right type is essential. Using an unsuitable oil will lead to an increased rate of engine wear and could result in serious engine damage. Before purchasing oil, always check the recommended oil specification given by the manufacturer. The manufacturer will state a recommended 'type or classification' and also a specific 'viscosity' range for engine oil.

● The oil 'type or classification' is identified by its API (American Petroleum Institute) rating. The API rating will be in the form of two letters, e.g. SG. The S identifies the oil as being suitable for use in a petrol (gasoline) engine (S stands for spark ignition) and the second letter, ranging from A to J, identifies the oil's performance rating. The later this letter, the higher the specification of the oil; for example API SG oil exceeds the requirements of API SF oil. **Note:** *On some oils there may also be a second rating consisting of another two letters, the first letter being C, e.g. API SF/CD. This rating indicates the oil is also suitable for use in a diesel engines (the C stands for compression ignition) and is thus of no relevance for motorcycle use.*

● The 'viscosity' of the oil is identified by its SAE (Society of Automotive Engineers) rating. All modern engines require multigrade oils and the SAE rating will consist of two numbers, the first followed by a W, e.g. 10W/40. The first number indicates the viscosity rating of the oil at low temperatures (W stands for winter – tested at –20°C) and the second number represents the viscosity of the oil at high temperatures (tested at 100°C). The lower the number, the thinner the oil. For example an oil with an SAE 10W/40 rating will give better cold starting and running than an SAE 15W/40 oil.

● As well as ensuring the 'type' and 'viscosity' of the oil match the recommendations, another consideration to make when buying engine oil is whether to purchase a standard mineral-based oil, a semi-synthetic oil (also known as a synthetic blend or synthetic-based oil) or a fully-synthetic oil. Although all oils will have a similar rating and viscosity, their cost will vary considerably; mineral-based oils are the cheapest, the fully-synthetic oils the most expensive with the semi-synthetic oils falling somewhere in-between. This decision is very much up to the owner, but it should be noted that modern synthetic oils have far better lubricating and cleaning qualities than traditional mineral-based oils and tend to retain these properties for far longer. Bearing in mind the operating conditions inside a modern, high-revving motorcycle engine it is highly recommended that a fully synthetic oil is used. The extra expense at each service could save you money in the long term by preventing premature engine wear.

● As a final note always ensure that the oil is specifically designed for use in motorcycle engines. Engine oils designed primarily for use in car engines sometimes contain additives or friction modifiers which could cause clutch slip on a motorcycle fitted with a wet-clutch.

Two-stroke engine oil

● Modern two-stroke engines, with their high power outputs, place high demands on their oil. If engine seizure is to be avoided it is essential that a high-quality oil is used. Two-stroke oils differ hugely from four-stroke oils. The oil lubricates only the crankshaft and piston(s) (the transmission has its own lubricating oil) and is used on a total-loss basis where it is burnt completely during the combustion process.

● The Japanese have recently introduced a classification system for two-stroke oils, the JASO rating. This rating is in the form of two letters, either FA, FB or FC – FA is the lowest classification and FC the highest. Ensure the oil being used meets or exceeds the recommended rating specified by the manufacturer.

● As well as ensuring the oil rating matches the recommendation, another consideration to make when buying engine oil is whether to purchase a standard mineral-based oil, a semi-synthetic oil (also known as a synthetic blend or synthetic-based oil) or a fully-synthetic oil. The cost of each type of oil varies considerably; mineral-based oils are the cheapest, the fully-synthetic oils the most expensive with the semi-synthetic oils falling somewhere in-between. This decision is very much up to the owner, but it should be noted that modern synthetic oils have far better lubricating properties and burn cleaner than traditional mineral-based oils. It is therefore recommended that a fully synthetic oil is used. The extra expense could save you money in the long term by preventing premature engine wear, engine performance will be improved, carbon deposits and exhaust smoke will be reduced.

● Always ensure that the oil is specifically designed for use in an injector system. Many high quality two-stroke oils are designed for competition use and need to be pre-mixed with fuel. These oils are of a much higher viscosity and are not designed to flow through the injector pumps used on road-going two-stroke motorcycles.

Transmission (gear) oil

● On a two-stroke engine, the transmission and clutch are lubricated by their own separate oil bath which must be changed in accordance with the Maintenance Schedule.
● Although the engine and transmission units of most four-strokes use a common lubrication supply, there are some exceptions where the engine and gearbox have separate oil reservoirs and a dry clutch is used.
● Motorcycle manufacturers will either recommend a monograde transmission oil or a four-stroke multigrade engine oil to lubricate the transmission.
● Transmission oils, or gear oils as they are often called, are designed specifically for use in transmission systems. The viscosity of these oils is represented by an SAE number, but the scale of measurement applied is different to that used to grade engine oils. As a rough guide a SAE90 gear oil will be of the same viscosity as an SAE50 engine oil.

Shaft drive oil

● On models equipped with shaft final drive, the shaft drive gears are will have their own oil supply. The manufacturer will state a recommended 'type or classification' and also a specific 'viscosity' range in the same manner as for four-stroke engine oil.
● Gear oil classification is given by the number which follows the API GL (GL standing for gear lubricant) rating, the higher the number, the higher the specification of the oil, e.g. API GL5 oil is a higher specification than API GL4 oil. Ensure the oil meets or

exceeds the classification specified and is of the correct viscosity. The viscosity of gear oils is also represented by an SAE number but the scale of measurement used is different to that used to grade engine oils. As a rough guide an SAE90 gear oil will be of the same viscosity as an SAE50 engine oil.
● If the use of an EP (Extreme Pressure) gear oil is specified, ensure the oil purchased is suitable.

Fork oil and suspension fluid

● Conventional telescopic front forks are hydraulic and require fork oil to work. To ensure the forks function correctly, the fork oil must be changed in accordance with the Maintenance Schedule.
● Fork oil is available in a variety of viscosities, identified by their SAE rating; fork oil ratings vary from light (SAE 5) to heavy (SAE 30). When purchasing fork oil, ensure the viscosity rating matches that specified by the manufacturer.
● Some lubricant manufacturers also produce a range of high-quality suspension fluids which are very similar to fork oil but are designed mainly for competition use. These fluids may have a different viscosity rating system which is not to be confused with the SAE rating of normal fork oil. Refer to the manufacturer's instructions if in any doubt.

Brake and clutch fluid

● All disc brake systems and some clutch systems are hydraulically operated. To ensure correct operation, the hydraulic fluid must be changed in accordance with the Maintenance Schedule.
● Brake and clutch fluid is classified by its DOT rating with most motorcycle manufacturers specifying DOT 3 or 4 fluid. Both fluid types are glycol-based and can be mixed together without adverse effect; DOT 4 fluid exceeds the requirements of DOT 3

fluid. Although it is safe to use DOT 4 fluid in a system designed for use with DOT 3 fluid, never use DOT 3 fluid in a system which specifies the use of DOT 4 as this will adversely affect the system's performance. The type required for the system will be marked on the fluid reservoir cap.
● Some manufacturers also produce a DOT 5 hydraulic fluid. DOT 5 hydraulic fluid is silicone-based and is not compatible with the glycol-based DOT 3 and 4 fluids. Never mix DOT 5 fluid with DOT 3 or 4 fluid as this will seriously affect the performance of the hydraulic system.

Coolant/antifreeze

● When purchasing coolant/antifreeze, always ensure it is suitable for use in an aluminium engine and contains corrosion inhibitors to prevent possible blockages of the internal coolant passages of the system. As a general rule, most coolants are designed to be used neat and should not be diluted whereas antifreeze can be mixed with distilled water to provide a coolant solution of the required strength. Refer to the manufacturer's instructions on the bottle.
● Ensure the coolant is changed in accordance with the Maintenance Schedule.

Chain lube

● Chain lube is an aerosol-type spray lubricant specifically designed for use on motorcycle final drive chains. Chain lube has two functions, to minimise friction between the final drive chain and sprockets and to prevent corrosion of the chain. Regular use of a good-quality chain lube will extend the life of the drive chain and sprockets and thus maximise the power being transmitted from the transmission to the rear wheel.
● When using chain lube, always allow some time for the solvents in the lube to evaporate before riding the motorcycle. This will minimise the amount of lube which will

'fling' off from the chain when the motorcycle is used. If the motorcycle is equipped with an 'O-ring' chain, ensure the chain lube is labelled as being suitable for use on 'O-ring' chains.

Degreasers and solvents

● There are many different types of solvents and degreasers available to remove the grime and grease which accumulate around the motorcycle during normal use. Degreasers and solvents are usually available as an aerosol-type spray or as a liquid which you apply with a brush. Always closely follow the manufacturer's instructions and wear eye protection during use. Be aware that many solvents are flammable and may give off noxious fumes; take adequate precautions when using them (see Safety First!).

● For general cleaning, use one of the many solvents or degreasers available from most motorcycle accessory shops. These solvents are usually applied then left for a certain time before being washed off with water.

Brake cleaner is a solvent specifically designed to remove all traces of oil, grease and dust from braking system components. Brake cleaner is designed to evaporate quickly and leaves behind no residue.

Carburettor cleaner is an aerosol-type solvent specifically designed to clear carburettor blockages and break down the hard deposits and gum often found inside carburettors during overhaul.

Contact cleaner is an aerosol-type solvent designed for cleaning electrical components. The cleaner will remove all traces of oil and dirt from components such as switch contacts or fouled spark plugs and then dry, leaving behind no residue.

Gasket remover is an aerosol-type solvent designed for removing stubborn gaskets from engine components during overhaul. Gasket remover will minimise the amount of scraping required to remove the gasket and therefore reduce the risk of damage to the mating surface.

Spray lubricants

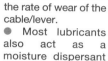

● Aerosol-based spray lubricants are widely available and are excellent for lubricating lever pivots and exposed cables and switches. Try to use a lubricant which is of the dry-film type as the fluid evaporates, leaving behind a dry-film of lubricant. Lubricants which leave behind an oily residue will attract dust and dirt which will increase the rate of wear of the cable/lever.

● Most lubricants also act as a moisture dispersant and a penetrating fluid. This means they can also be used to 'dry out' electrical components such as wiring connectors or switches as well as helping to free seized fasteners.

Greases

● Grease is used to lubricate many of the pivot-points. A good-quality multi-purpose grease is suitable for most applications but some manufacturers will specify the use of specialist greases for use on components such as swingarm and suspension linkage bushes. These specialist greases can be purchased from most motorcycle (or car) accessory shops; commonly specified types include molybdenum disulphide grease, lithium-based grease, graphite-based grease, silicone-based grease and high-temperature copper-based grease.

Gasket sealing compounds

● Gasket sealing compounds can be used in conjunction with gaskets, to improve their sealing capabilities, or on their own to seal metal-to-metal joints. Depending on their type, sealing compounds either set hard or stay relatively soft and pliable.

● When purchasing a gasket sealing compound, ensure that it is designed specifically for use on an internal combustion engine. General multi-purpose sealants available from DIY stores may appear visibly similar but they are not designed to withstand the extreme heat or contact with fuel and oil encountered when used on an engine (see 'Tools and Workshop Tips' for further information).

Thread locking compound

● Thread locking compounds are used to secure certain threaded fasteners in position to prevent them from loosening due to vibration. Thread locking compounds can be purchased from most motorcycle (and car) accessory shops. Ensure the threads of the both components are completely clean and dry before sparingly applying the locking compound (see 'Tools and Workshop Tips' for further information).

Fuel additives

● Fuel additives which protect and clean the fuel system components are widely available. These additives are designed to remove all traces of deposits that build up on the carburettors/injectors and prevent wear, helping the fuel system to operate more efficiently. If a fuel additive is being used, check that it is suitable for use with your motorcycle, especially if your motorcycle is equipped with a catalytic converter.

● Octane boosters are also available. These additives are designed to improve the performance of highly-tuned engines being run on normal pump-fuel and are of no real use on standard motorcycles.

Conversion Factors

Length (distance)

Inches (in)	x 25.4 = Millimetres (mm)	x 0.0394 = Inches (in)
Feet (ft)	x 0.305 = Metres (m)	x 3.281 = Feet (ft)
Miles	x 1.609 = Kilometres (km)	x 0.621 = Miles

Volume (capacity)

Cubic inches (cu in; in³)	x 16.387 = Cubic centimetres (cc; cm³)	x 0.061 = Cubic inches (cu in; in³)
Imperial pints (Imp pt)	x 0.568 = Litres (l)	x 1.76 = Imperial pints (Imp pt)
Imperial quarts (Imp qt)	x 1.137 = Litres (l)	x 0.88 = Imperial quarts (Imp qt)
Imperial quarts (Imp qt)	x 1.201 = US quarts (US qt)	x 0.833 = Imperial quarts (Imp qt)
US quarts (US qt)	x 0.946 = Litres (l)	x 1.057 = US quarts (US qt)
Imperial gallons (Imp gal)	x 4.546 = Litres (l)	x 0.22 = Imperial gallons (Imp gal)
Imperial gallons (Imp gal)	x 1.201 = US gallons (US gal)	x 0.833 = Imperial gallons (Imp gal)
US gallons (US gal)	x 3.785 = Litres (l)	x 0.264 = US gallons (US gal)

Mass (weight)

Ounces (oz)	x 28.35 = Grams (g)	x 0.035 = Ounces (oz)
Pounds (lb)	x 0.454 = Kilograms (kg)	x 2.205 = Pounds (lb)

Force

Ounces-force (ozf; oz)	x 0.278 = Newtons (N)	x 3.6 = Ounces-force (ozf; oz)
Pounds-force (lbf; lb)	x 4.448 = Newtons (N)	x 0.225 = Pounds-force (lbf; lb)
Newtons (N)	x 0.1 = Kilograms-force (kgf; kg)	x 9.81 = Newtons (N)

Pressure

Pounds-force per square inch (psi; lbf/in²; lb/in²)	x 0.070 = Kilograms-force per square centimetre (kgf/cm²; kg/cm²)	x 14.223 = Pounds-force per square inch (psi; lbf/in²; lb/in²)
Pounds-force per square inch (psi; lbf/in²; lb/in²)	x 0.068 = Atmospheres (atm)	x 14.696 = Pounds-force per square inch (psi; lbf/in²; lb/in²)
Pounds-force per square inch (psi; lbf/in²; lb/in²)	x 0.069 = Bars	x 14.5 = Pounds-force per square inch (psi; lbf/in²; lb/in²)
Pounds-force per square inch (psi; lbf/in²; lb/in²)	x 6.895 = Kilopascals (kPa)	x 0.145 = Pounds-force per square inch (psi; lbf/in²; lb/in²)
Kilopascals (kPa)	x 0.01 = Kilograms-force per square centimetre (kgf/cm²; kg/cm²)	x 98.1 = Kilopascals (kPa)
Millibar (mbar)	x 100 = Pascals (Pa)	x 0.01 = Millibar (mbar)
Millibar (mbar)	x 0.0145 = Pounds-force per square inch (psi; lbf/in²; lb/in²)	x 68.947 = Millibar (mbar)
Millibar (mbar)	x 0.75 = Millimetres of mercury (mmHg)	x 1.333 = Millibar (mbar)
Millibar (mbar)	x 0.401 = Inches of water (inH₂O)	x 2.491 = Millibar (mbar)
Millimetres of mercury (mmHg)	x 0.535 = Inches of water (inH₂O)	x 1.868 = Millimetres of mercury (mmHg)
Inches of water (inH₂O)	x 0.036 = Pounds-force per square inch (psi; lbf/in²; lb/in²)	x 27.68 = Inches of water (inH₂O)

Torque (moment of force)

Pounds-force inches (lbf in; lb in)	x 1.152 = Kilograms-force centimetre (kgf cm; kg cm)	x 0.868 = Pounds-force inches (lbf in; lb in)
Pounds-force inches (lbf in; lb in)	x 0.113 = Newton metres (Nm)	x 8.85 = Pounds-force inches (lbf in; lb in)
Pounds-force inches (lbf in; lb in)	x 0.083 = Pounds-force feet (lbf ft; lb ft)	x 12 = Pounds-force inches (lbf in; lb in)
Pounds-force feet (lbf ft; lb ft)	x 0.138 = Kilograms-force metres (kgf m; kg m)	x 7.233 = Pounds-force feet (lbf ft; lb ft)
Pounds-force feet (lbf ft; lb ft)	x 1.356 = Newton metres (Nm)	x 0.738 = Pounds-force feet (lbf ft; lb ft)
Newton metres (Nm)	x 0.102 = Kilograms-force metres (kgf m; kg m)	x 9.804 = Newton metres (Nm)

Power

Horsepower (hp)	x 745.7 = Watts (W)	x 0.0013 = Horsepower (hp)

Velocity (speed)

Miles per hour (miles/hr; mph)	x 1.609 = Kilometres per hour (km/hr; kph)	x 0.621 = Miles per hour (miles/hr; mph)

Fuel consumption*

Miles per gallon (mpg)	x 0.354 = Kilometres per litre (km/l)	x 2.825 = Miles per gallon (mpg)

Temperature

Degrees Fahrenheit = (°C x 1.8) + 32

Degrees Celsius (Degrees Centigrade; °C) = (°F - 32) x 0.56

It is common practice to convert from miles per gallon (mpg) to litres/100 kilometres (l/100km), where mpg x l/100 km = 282

About the MOT Test

In the UK, all vehicles more than three years old are subject to an annual test to ensure that they meet minimum safety requirements. A current test certificate must be issued before a machine can be used on public roads, and is required before a road fund licence can be issued. Riding without a current test certificate will also invalidate your insurance.

For most owners, the MOT test is an annual cause for anxiety, and this is largely due to owners not being sure what needs to be checked prior to submitting the motorcycle for testing. The simple answer is that a fully roadworthy motorcycle will have no difficulty in passing the test.

This is a guide to getting your motorcycle through the MOT test. Obviously it will not be possible to examine the motorcycle to the same standard as the professional MOT tester, particularly in view of the equipment required for some of the checks. However, working through the following procedures will enable you to identify any problem areas before submitting the motorcycle for the test.

It has only been possible to summarise the test requirements here, based on the regulations in force at the time of printing. Test standards are becoming increasingly stringent, although there are some exemptions for older vehicles. More information about the MOT test can be obtained from the TSO publications, *How Safe is your Motorcycle* and *The MOT Inspection Manual for Motorcycle Testing*.

Many of the checks require that one of the wheels is raised off the ground. If the motorcycle doesn't have a centre stand, note that an auxiliary stand will be required. Additionally, the help of an assistant may prove useful.

Certain exceptions apply to machines under 50 cc, machines without a lighting system, and Classic bikes - if in doubt about any of the requirements listed below seek confirmation from an MOT tester prior to submitting the motorcycle for the test.

Check that the frame number is clearly visible.

> **HAYNES HiNT** *If a component is in borderline condition, the tester has discretion in deciding whether to pass or fail it. If the motorcycle presented is clean and evidently well cared for, the tester may be more inclined to pass a borderline component than if the motorcycle is scruffy and apparently neglected.*

Electrical System

Lights, turn signals, horn and reflector

✔ With the ignition on, check the operation of the following electrical components. **Note:** *The electrical components on certain small-capacity machines are powered by the generator, requiring that the engine is run for this check.*

a) *Headlight and tail light. Check that both illuminate in the low and high beam switch positions.*

b) *Position lights. Check that the front position (or sidelight) and tail light illuminate in this switch position.*

c) *Turn signals. Check that all flash at the correct rate, and that the warning light(s) function correctly. Check that the turn signal switch works correctly.*

d) *Hazard warning system (where fitted). Check that all four turn signals flash in this switch position.*

e) *Brake stop light. Check that the light comes on when the front and rear brakes are independently applied. Models first used on or after 1st April 1986 must have a brake light switch on each brake.*

f) *Horn. Check that the sound is continuous and of reasonable volume.*

✔ Check that there is a red reflector on the rear of the machine, either mounted separately or as part of the tail light lens.

✔ Check the condition of the headlight, tail light and turn signal lenses.

Headlight beam height

✔ The MOT tester will perform a headlight beam height check using specialised beam setting equipment **(see illustration 1)**. This equipment will not be available to the home mechanic, but if you suspect that the headlight is incorrectly set or may have been maladjusted in the past, you can perform a rough test as follows.

✔ Position the bike in a straight line facing a brick wall. The bike must be off its stand, upright and with a rider seated. Measure the height from the ground to the centre of the headlight and mark a horizontal line on the wall at this height. Position the motorcycle 3.8 metres from the wall and draw a vertical

Headlight beam height checking equipment

line up the wall central to the centreline of the motorcycle. Switch to dipped beam and check that the beam pattern falls slightly lower than the horizontal line and to the left of the vertical line **(see illustration 2)**.

3·8 m

90°

90°

H29003

Home workshop beam alignment check

Exhaust System and Final Drive

Exhaust

✔ Check that the exhaust mountings are secure and that the system does not foul any of the rear suspension components.

✔ Start the motorcycle. When the revs are increased, check that the exhaust is neither holed nor leaking from any of its joints. On a linked system, check that the collector box is not leaking due to corrosion.

✔ Note that the exhaust decibel level ("loudness" of the exhaust) is assessed at the discretion of the tester. If the motorcycle was first used on or after 1st January 1985 the silencer must carry the BSAU 193 stamp, or a marking relating to its make and model, or be of OE (original equipment) manufacture. If the silencer is marked NOT FOR ROAD USE, RACING USE ONLY or similar, it will fail the MOT.

Final drive

✔ On chain or belt drive machines, check that the chain/belt is in good condition and does not have excessive slack. Also check that the sprocket is securely mounted on the rear wheel hub. Check that the chain/belt guard is in place.

✔ On shaft drive bikes, check for oil leaking from the drive unit and fouling the rear tyre.

Steering and Suspension

Steering

✔ With the front wheel raised off the ground, rotate the steering from lock to lock. The handlebar or switches must not contact the fuel tank or be close enough to trap the rider's hand. Problems can be caused by damaged lock stops on the lower yoke and frame, or by the fitting of non-standard handlebars.

✔ When performing the lock to lock check, also ensure that the steering moves freely without drag or notchiness. Steering movement can be impaired by poorly routed cables, or by overtight head bearings or worn bearings. The tester will perform a check of the steering head bearing lower race by mounting the front wheel on a surface plate, then performing a lock to

lock check with the weight of the machine on the lower bearing (see illustration 3).

✔ Grasp the fork sliders (lower legs) and attempt to push and pull on the forks (see

Front wheel mounted on a surface plate for steering head bearing lower race check

illustration 4). Any play in the steering head bearings will be felt. Note that in extreme cases, wear of the front fork bushes can be misinterpreted for head bearing play.

✔ Check that the handlebars are securely mounted.

✔ Check that the handlebar grip rubbers are secure. They should by bonded to the bar left end and to the throttle cable pulley on the right end.

Front suspension

✔ With the motorcycle off the stand, hold the front brake on and pump the front forks up and down (see illustration 5). Check that they are adequately damped.

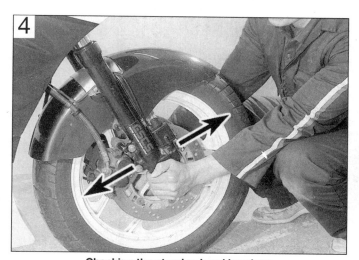

Checking the steering head bearings for freeplay

Hold the front brake on and pump the front forks up and down to check operation

Inspect the area around the fork dust seal for oil leakage (arrow)

Bounce the rear of the motorcycle to check rear suspension operation

Checking for rear suspension linkage play

✔ Inspect the area above and around the front fork oil seals **(see illustration 6)**. There should be no sign of oil on the fork tube (stanchion) nor leaking down the slider (lower leg). On models so equipped, check that there is no oil leaking from the anti-dive units.
✔ On models with swingarm front suspension, check that there is no freeplay in the linkage when moved from side to side.

Rear suspension

✔ With the motorcycle off the stand and an assistant supporting the motorcycle by its handlebars, bounce the rear suspension **(see illustration 7)**. Check that the suspension components do not foul on any of the cycle parts and check that the shock absorber(s) provide adequate damping.
✔ Visually inspect the shock absorber(s) and check that there is no sign of oil leakage from its damper. This is somewhat restricted on certain single shock models due to the location of the shock absorber.
✔ With the rear wheel raised off the ground, grasp the wheel at the highest point and attempt to pull it up **(see illustration 8)**. Any play in the swingarm pivot or suspension linkage bearings will be felt as movement. **Note:** *Do not confuse play with actual suspension movement.* Failure to lubricate suspension linkage bearings can lead to bearing failure **(see illustration 9)**.
✔ With the rear wheel raised off the ground, grasp the swingarm ends and attempt to move the swingarm from side to side and forwards and backwards - any play indicates wear of the swingarm pivot bearings **(see illustration 10)**.

Worn suspension linkage pivots (arrows) are usually the cause of play in the rear suspension

Grasp the swingarm at the ends to check for play in its pivot bearings

Brake pad wear can usually be viewed without removing the caliper. Most pads have wear indicator grooves (1) and some also have indicator tangs (2)

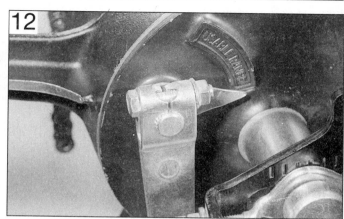

On drum brakes, check the angle of the operating lever with the brake fully applied. Most drum brakes have a wear indicator pointer and scale.

Brakes, Wheels and Tyres

Brakes

✔ With the wheel raised off the ground, apply the brake then free it off, and check that the wheel is about to revolve freely without brake drag.

✔ On disc brakes, examine the disc itself. Check that it is securely mounted and not cracked.

✔ On disc brakes, view the pad material through the caliper mouth and check that the pads are not worn down beyond the limit **(see illustration 11)**.

✔ On drum brakes, check that when the brake is applied the angle between the operating lever and cable or rod is not too great **(see illustration 12)**. Check also that the operating lever doesn't foul any other components.

✔ On disc brakes, examine the flexible hoses from top to bottom. Have an assistant hold the brake on so that the fluid in the hose is under pressure, and check that there is no sign of fluid leakage, bulges or cracking. If there are any metal brake pipes or unions, check that these are free from corrosion and damage. Where a brake-linked anti-dive system is fitted, check the hoses to the anti-dive in a similar manner.

✔ Check that the rear brake torque arm is secure and that its fasteners are secured by self-locking nuts or castellated nuts with split-pins or R-pins **(see illustration 13)**.

✔ On models with ABS, check that the self-check warning light in the instrument panel works.

✔ The MOT tester will perform a test of the motorcycle's braking efficiency based on a calculation of rider and motorcycle weight. Although this cannot be carried out at home, you can at least ensure that the braking systems are properly maintained. For hydraulic disc brakes, check the fluid level, lever/pedal feel (bleed of air if its spongy) and pad material. For drum brakes, check adjustment, cable or rod operation and shoe lining thickness.

Wheels and tyres

✔ Check the wheel condition. Cast wheels should be free from cracks and if of the built-up design, all fasteners should be secure. Spoked wheels should be checked for broken, corroded, loose or bent spokes.

✔ With the wheel raised off the ground, spin the wheel and visually check that the tyre and wheel run true. Check that the tyre does not foul the suspension or mudguards.

✔ With the wheel raised off the ground, grasp the wheel and attempt to move it about the axle (spindle) **(see illustration 14)**. Any play felt here indicates wheel bearing failure.

Brake torque arm must be properly secured at both ends

Check for wheel bearing play by trying to move the wheel about the axle (spindle)

Checking the tyre tread depth

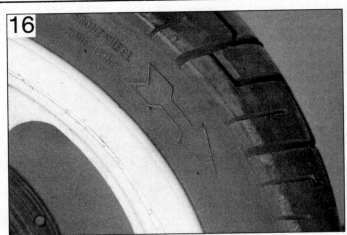

Tyre direction of rotation arrow can be found on tyre sidewall

Castellated type wheel axle (spindle) nut must be secured by a split pin or R-pin

Two straightedges are used to check wheel alignment

✔ Check the tyre tread depth, tread condition and sidewall condition **(see illustration 15)**.
✔ Check the tyre type. Front and rear tyre types must be compatible and be suitable for road use. Tyres marked NOT FOR ROAD USE, COMPETITION USE ONLY or similar, will fail the MOT.

✔ If the tyre sidewall carries a direction of rotation arrow, this must be pointing in the direction of normal wheel rotation **(see illustration 16)**.
✔ Check that the wheel axle (spindle) nuts (where applicable) are properly secured. A self-locking nut or castellated nut with a split-pin or R-pin can be used **(see illustration 17)**.
✔ Wheel alignment is checked with the motorcycle off the stand and a rider seated. With the front wheel pointing straight ahead, two perfectly straight lengths of metal or wood and placed against the sidewalls of both tyres **(see illustration 18)**. The gap each side of the front tyre must be equidistant on both sides. Incorrect wheel alignment may be due to a cocked rear wheel (often as the result of poor chain adjustment) or in extreme cases, a bent frame.

General checks and condition

✔ Check the security of all major fasteners, bodypanels, seat, fairings (where fitted) and mudguards.

✔ Check that the rider and pillion footrests, handlebar levers and brake pedal are securely mounted.

✔ Check for corrosion on the frame or any load-bearing components. If severe, this may affect the structure, particularly under stress.

Sidecars

A motorcycle fitted with a sidecar requires additional checks relating to the stability of the machine and security of attachment and swivel joints, plus specific wheel alignment (toe-in) requirements. Additionally, tyre and lighting requirements differ from conventional motorcycle use. Owners are advised to check MOT test requirements with an official test centre.

Preparing for storage

Before you start

If repairs or an overhaul is needed, see that this is carried out now rather than left until you want to ride the bike again.

Give the bike a good wash and scrub all dirt from its underside. Make sure the bike dries completely before preparing for storage.

Engine

● Remove the spark plug(s) and lubricate the cylinder bores with approximately a teaspoon of motor oil using a spout-type oil can **(see illustration 1)**. Reinstall the spark plug(s). Crank the engine over a couple of times to coat the piston rings and bores with oil. If the bike has a kickstart, use this to turn the engine over. If not, flick the kill switch to the OFF position and crank the engine over on the starter **(see illustration 2)**. If the nature on the ignition system prevents the starter operating with the kill switch in the OFF position,

remove the spark plugs and fit them back in their caps; ensure that the plugs are earthed (grounded) against the cylinder head when the starter is operated **(see illustration 3)**.

⚠ **Warning: It is important that the plugs are earthed (grounded) away from the spark plug holes otherwise there is a risk of atomised fuel from the cylinders igniting.**

> **HAYNES HiNT** *On a single cylinder four-stroke engine, you can seal the combustion chamber completely by positioning the piston at TDC on the compression stroke.*

● Drain the carburettor(s) otherwise there is a risk of jets becoming blocked by gum deposits from the fuel **(see illustration 4)**.

● If the bike is going into long-term storage, consider adding a fuel stabiliser to the fuel in the tank. If the tank is drained completely, corrosion of its internal surfaces may occur if left unprotected for a long period. The tank can be treated with a rust preventative especially for this purpose. Alternatively, remove the tank and pour half a litre of motor oil into it, install the filler cap and shake the tank to coat its internals with oil before draining off the excess. The same effect can also be achieved by spraying WD40 or a similar water-dispersant around the inside of the tank via its flexible nozzle.

● Make sure the cooling system contains the correct mix of antifreeze. Antifreeze also contains important corrosion inhibitors.

● The air intakes and exhaust can be sealed off by covering or plugging the openings. Ensure that you do not seal in any condensation; run the engine until it is hot,

Squirt a drop of motor oil into each cylinder

Flick the kill switch to OFF . . .

. . . and ensure that the metal bodies of the plugs (arrows) are earthed against the cylinder head

Connect a hose to the carburettor float chamber drain stub (arrow) and unscrew the drain screw

Exhausts can be sealed off with a plastic bag

Disconnect the negative lead (A) first, followed by the positive lead (B)

Use a suitable battery charger - this kit also assess battery condition

then switch off and allow to cool. Tape a piece of thick plastic over the silencer end(s) **(see illustration 5)**. Note that some advocate pouring a tablespoon of motor oil into the silencer(s) before sealing them off.

Battery

● Remove it from the bike - in extreme cases of cold the battery may freeze and crack its case **(see illustration 6)**.

● Check the electrolyte level and top up if necessary (conventional refillable batteries). Clean the terminals.
● Store the battery off the motorcycle and away from any sources of fire. Position a wooden block under the battery if it is to sit on the ground.
● Give the battery a trickle charge for a few hours every month **(see illustration 7)**.

Tyres

● Place the bike on its centrestand or an auxiliary stand which will support the motorcycle in an upright position. Position wood blocks under the tyres to keep them off the ground and to provide insulation from damp. If the bike is being put into long-term storage, ideally both tyres should be off the ground; not only will this protect the tyres, but will also ensure that no load is placed on steering head or wheel bearings.
● Deflate each tyre by 5 to 10 psi, no more or the beads may unseat from the rim, making subsequent inflation difficult on tubeless tyres.

Pivots and controls

● Lubricate all lever, pedal, stand and footrest pivot points. If grease nipples are fitted to the rear suspension components, apply lubricant to the pivots.
● Lubricate all control cables.

Cycle components

● Apply a wax protectant to all painted and plastic components. Wipe off any excess, but don't polish to a shine. Where fitted, clean the screen with soap and water.
● Coat metal parts with Vaseline (petroleum jelly). When applying this to the fork tubes, do not compress the forks otherwise the seals will rot from contact with the Vaseline.
● Apply a vinyl cleaner to the seat.

Storage conditions

● Aim to store the bike in a shed or garage which does not leak and is free from damp.
● Drape an old blanket or bedspread over the bike to protect it from dust and direct contact with sunlight (which will fade paint). This also hides the bike from prying eyes. Beware of tight-fitting plastic covers which may allow condensation to form and settle on the bike.

Getting back on the road

Engine and transmission

● Change the oil and replace the oil filter. If this was done prior to storage, check that the oil hasn't emulsified - a thick whitish substance which occurs through condensation.
● Remove the spark plugs. Using a spout-type oil can, squirt a few drops of oil into the cylinder(s). This will provide initial lubrication as the piston rings and bores comes back into contact. Service the spark plugs, or fit new ones, and install them in the engine.

● Check that the clutch isn't stuck on. The plates can stick together if left standing for some time, preventing clutch operation. Engage a gear and try rocking the bike back and forth with the clutch lever held against the handlebar. If this doesn't work on cable-operated clutches, hold the clutch lever back against the handlebar with a strong elastic band or cable tie for a couple of hours **(see illustration 8)**.
● If the air intakes or silencer end(s) were blocked off, remove the bung or cover used.
● If the fuel tank was coated with a rust

Hold clutch lever back against the handlebar with elastic bands or a cable tie preventative, oil or a stabiliser added to the fuel, drain and flush the tank and dispose of the fuel sensibly. If no action was taken with the fuel tank prior to storage, it is advised that the old fuel is disposed of since it will go off over a period of time. Refill the fuel tank with fresh fuel.

Frame and running gear

● Oil all pivot points and cables.
● Check the tyre pressures. They will definitely need inflating if pressures were reduced for storage.
● Lubricate the final drive chain (where applicable).
● Remove any protective coating applied to the fork tubes (stanchions) since this may well destroy the fork seals. If the fork tubes weren't protected and have picked up rust spots, remove them with very fine abrasive paper and refinish with metal polish.
● Check that both brakes operate correctly. Apply each brake hard and check that it's not possible to move the motorcycle forwards, then check that the brake frees off again once released. Brake caliper pistons can stick due to corrosion around the piston head, or on the sliding caliper types, due to corrosion of the slider pins. If the brake doesn't free after repeated operation, take the caliper off for examination. Similarly drum brakes can stick

due to a seized operating cam, cable or rod linkage.
● If the motorcycle has been in long-term storage, renew the brake fluid and clutch fluid (where applicable).
● Depending on where the bike has been stored, the wiring, cables and hoses may have been nibbled by rodents. Make a visual check and investigate disturbed wiring loom tape.

Battery

● If the battery has been previously removal and given top up charges it can simply be reconnected. Remember to connect the positive cable first and the negative cable last.
● On conventional refillable batteries, if the battery has not received any attention, remove it from the motorcycle and check its electrolyte level. Top up if necessary then charge the battery. If the battery fails to hold a charge and a visual checks show heavy white sulphation of the plates, the battery is probably defective and must be renewed. This is particularly likely if the battery is old. Confirm battery condition with a specific gravity check.
● On sealed (MF) batteries, if the battery has not received any attention, remove it from the motorcycle and charge it according to the information on the battery case - if the battery fails to hold a charge it must be renewed.

Starting procedure

● If a kickstart is fitted, turn the engine over a couple of times with the ignition OFF to distribute oil around the engine. If no kickstart is fitted, flick the engine kill switch OFF and the ignition ON and crank the engine over a couple of times to work oil around the upper cylinder components. If the nature of the ignition system is such that the starter won't work with the kill switch OFF, remove the spark plugs, fit them back into their caps and earth (ground) their bodies on the cylinder head. Reinstall the spark plugs afterwards.
● Switch the kill switch to RUN, operate the choke and start the engine. If the engine won't start don't continue cranking the engine - not only will this flatten the battery, but the starter motor will overheat. Switch the ignition off and try again later. If the engine refuses to start, go through the fault finding procedures in this manual. **Note:** If the bike has been in storage for a long time, old fuel or a carburettor blockage may be the problem. Gum deposits in carburettors can block jets - if a carburettor cleaner doesn't prove successful the carburettors must be dismantled for cleaning.
● Once the engine has started, check that the lights, turn signals and horn work properly.
● Treat the bike gently for the first ride and check all fluid levels on completion. Settle the bike back into the maintenance schedule.

This Section provides an easy reference-guide to the more common faults that are likely to afflict your machine. Obviously, the opportunities are almost limitless for faults to occur as a result of obscure failures, and to try and cover all eventualities would require a book. Indeed, a number have been written on the subject.

Successful troubleshooting is not a mysterious 'black art' but the application of a bit of knowledge combined with a systematic and logical approach to the problem. Approach any troubleshooting by first accurately identifying the symptom and then checking through the list of possible causes, starting with the simplest or most obvious and progressing in stages to the most complex.

Take nothing for granted, but above all apply liberal quantities of common sense.

The main symptom of a fault is given in the text as a major heading below which are listed the various systems or areas which may contain the fault. Details of each possible cause for a fault and the remedial action to be taken are given, in brief, in the paragraphs below each heading. Further information should be sought in the relevant Chapter.

1 Engine doesn't start or is difficult to start
- [ ] Starter motor doesn't rotate
- [ ] Starter motor rotates but engine does not turn over
- [ ] Starter works but engine won't turn over (seized)
- [ ] No fuel flow
- [ ] Engine flooded
- [ ] No spark or weak spark
- [ ] Compression low
- [ ] Stalls after starting
- [ ] Rough idle

2 Poor running at low speed
- [ ] Spark weak
- [ ] Fuel/air mixture incorrect
- [ ] Compression low
- [ ] Poor acceleration

3 Poor running or no power at high speed
- [ ] Firing incorrect
- [ ] Fuel/air mixture incorrect
- [ ] Compression low
- [ ] Knocking or pinking
- [ ] Miscellaneous causes

4 Overheating
- [ ] Engine overheats
- [ ] Firing incorrect
- [ ] Fuel/air mixture incorrect
- [ ] Compression too high
- [ ] Engine load excessive
- [ ] Lubrication inadequate
- [ ] Miscellaneous causes

5 Clutch problems
- [ ] Clutch slipping
- [ ] Clutch not disengaging completely

6 Gearchanging problems
- [ ] Doesn't go into gear, or lever doesn't return
- [ ] Jumps out of gear
- [ ] Overshifts

7 Abnormal engine noise
- [ ] Knocking or pinking
- [ ] Piston slap or rattling
- [ ] Valve noise
- [ ] Other noise

8 Abnormal driveline noise
- [ ] Clutch noise
- [ ] Transmission noise
- [ ] Final drive noise

9 Abnormal frame and suspension noise
- [ ] Front end noise
- [ ] Shock absorber noise
- [ ] Brake noise

10 Oil pressure warning light comes on
- [ ] Engine lubrication system
- [ ] Electrical system

11 Excessive exhaust smoke
- [ ] White smoke
- [ ] Black smoke
- [ ] Brown smoke

12 Poor handling or stability
- [ ] Handlebar hard to turn
- [ ] Handlebar shakes or vibrates excessively
- [ ] Handlebar pulls to one side
- [ ] Poor shock absorbing qualities

13 Braking problems
- [ ] Brakes are spongy, don't hold
- [ ] Brake lever or pedal pulsates
- [ ] Brakes drag

14 Electrical problems
- [ ] Battery dead or weak
- [ ] Battery overcharged

1 Engine doesn't start or is difficult to start

Starter motor doesn't rotate

☐ Engine kill switch OFF.

☐ Fuse blown. Check main fuse and ignition circuit fuse (Chapter 9).

☐ Battery voltage low. Check and recharge battery (Chapter 9).

☐ Starter motor defective. Make sure the wiring to the starter is secure. Make sure the starter relay clicks when the start button is pushed. If the relay clicks, then the fault is in the wiring or motor.

☐ Starter relay faulty. Check it according to the procedure in Chapter 9.

☐ Starter switch not contacting. The contacts could be wet, corroded or dirty. Disassemble and clean the switch (Chapter 9).

☐ Wiring open or shorted. Check all wiring connections and harnesses to make sure that they are dry, tight and not corroded. Also check for broken or frayed wires that can cause a short to ground (earth) (see wiring diagram, Chapter 9).

☐ Ignition (main) switch defective. Check the switch according to the procedure in Chapter 9. Renew the switch if it is defective.

☐ Engine kill switch defective. Check for wet, dirty or corroded contacts. Clean or renew the switch as necessary (Chapter 9).

☐ Faulty neutral (gear position), sidestand or clutch switch. Check the wiring to each switch and the switch itself according to the procedures in Chapter 9.

☐ Faulty diode. Check as described in Chapter 9.

Starter motor rotates but engine does not turn over

☐ Starter motor clutch defective. Inspect and repair or renew (Chapter 2).

☐ Damaged idler or starter gears. Inspect and renew the damaged parts (Chapter 2).

Starter works but engine won't turn over (seized)

☐ Seized engine caused by one or more internally damaged components. Failure due to wear, abuse or lack of lubrication. Damage can include seized valves, followers, camshafts, pistons, crankshaft, connecting rod bearings, or transmission gears or bearings. Refer to Chapter 2 for engine disassembly.

No fuel flow

☐ No fuel in tank.

☐ Fuel tank breather hose obstructed.

☐ Fuel valve not opening (carburettor models). Check the valve (Chapter 4).

☐ Fuel pump faulty, or strainer and/or filter is blocked (see Chapter 4).

☐ Fuel line clogged. Pull the fuel line loose and carefully blow through it.

☐ Float needle valve (carburettor models) or injector (injection models) clogged. For all of the valves to be clogged, either a very bad batch of fuel with an unusual additive has been used, or some other foreign material has entered the tank. Many times after a machine has been stored for many months without running, the fuel turns to a varnish-like liquid and forms deposits on the components.

Engine flooded

☐ Float height too high (carburettor models). Check as described in Chapter 4.

☐ Float needle valve worn or stuck open (carburettor models). A piece of dirt, rust or other debris can cause the valve to seat improperly, causing excess fuel to be admitted to the float chamber. In this case, the float chamber should be cleaned and the needle valve and seat inspected. If the needle and seat are worn, then the leaking will persist and the parts should be renewed (Chapter 4).

☐ Starting technique incorrect. Under normal circumstances (ie, if all the carburettor functions or fuel injection system are sound) the machine should start with little or no throttle. When the engine is cold, the choke should be operated and the engine started without opening the throttle. When the engine is at operating temperature, only a very slight amount of throttle should be necessary.

No spark or weak spark

☐ Ignition switch OFF.

☐ Engine kill switch turned to the OFF position.

☐ Battery voltage low. Check and recharge the battery as necessary (Chapter 9).

☐ Spark plugs dirty, defective or worn out. Locate reason for fouled plugs using spark plug condition chart on the inside rear cover and follow the plug maintenance procedures (Chapter 1).

☐ Spark plug caps or secondary (HT) wiring faulty (GSX-R750T and V models). Check condition. Renew either or both components if cracks or deterioration are evident (Chapter 5).

☐ Spark plug cap/coil defective (GSX-R600 and GSX-R750W and X models). Test and renew if necessary (Chapter 5).

☐ Spark plug caps not making good contact. Make sure that the plug caps fit snugly over the plug ends.

☐ Electronic control unit defective. Check the unit, referring to Chapter 5 for details.

☐ Pulse generator coil (crankshaft position sensor on fuel injected models) defective. Check the unit, referring to Chapter 5 for details.

☐ Ignition HT coils defective. Check the coils, referring to Chapter 5.

☐ Ignition or kill switch shorted. This is usually caused by water, corrosion, damage or excessive wear. The switches can be disassembled and cleaned with electrical contact cleaner. If cleaning does not help, renew the switches (Chapter 9).

☐ Wiring shorted or broken between:
  a) Ignition (main) switch and engine kill switch (or blown fuse)
  b) Electronic control unit and engine kill switch
  c) Electronic control unit and ignition HT coils
  d) Ignition HT coils and spark plugs (GSX-R750T and V models)
  e) Electronic control unit and pulse generator

☐ Make sure that all wiring connections are clean, dry and tight. Look for chafed and broken wires (Chapters 5 and 9).

1 Engine doesn't start or is difficult to start (continued)

Compression low

☐ Spark plugs loose. Remove the plugs and inspect their threads. Reinstall and tighten to the specified torque (Chapter 1).

☐ Cylinder head not sufficiently tightened down. If a cylinder head is suspected of being loose, then there's a chance that the gasket or head is damaged if the problem has persisted for any length of time. The head bolts should be tightened to the proper torque in the correct sequence (Chapter 2).

☐ Improper valve clearance. This means that the valve is not closing completely and compression pressure is leaking past the valve. Check and adjust the valve clearances (Chapter 1).

☐ Cylinder and/or piston worn. Excessive wear will cause compression pressure to leak past the rings. This is usually accompanied by worn rings as well. A top-end overhaul is necessary (Chapter 2).

☐ Piston rings worn, weak, broken, or sticking. Broken or sticking piston rings usually indicate a lubrication or carburation problem that causes excess carbon deposits or seizures to form on the pistons and rings. Top-end overhaul is necessary (Chapter 2).

☐ Piston ring-to-groove clearance excessive. This is caused by excessive wear of the piston ring lands. Piston renewal is necessary (Chapter 2).

☐ Cylinder head gasket damaged. If a head is allowed to become loose, or if excessive carbon build-up on the piston crown and combustion chamber causes extremely high compression, the head gasket may leak. Retorquing the head is not always sufficient to restore the seal, so gasket renewal is necessary (Chapter 2).

☐ Cylinder head warped. This is caused by overheating or improperly tightened head bolts. Machine shop resurfacing or head renewal is necessary (Chapter 2).

☐ Valve spring broken or weak. Caused by component failure or wear; the springs must be renewed (Chapter 2).

☐ Valve not seating properly. This is caused by a bent valve (from over-revving or improper valve adjustment), burned valve or seat (improper carburation) or an accumulation of carbon deposits on the seat (from carburation or lubrication problems). The valves must be cleaned and/or renewed and the seats serviced if possible (Chapter 2).

Stalls after starting

☐ Improper choke action (carburettor models). Make sure the choke linkage shaft is getting a full stroke and staying in the out position (Chapter 4).

☐ Ignition malfunction. See Chapter 5.

☐ Carburettor or fuel injection system malfunction. See Chapter 4.

☐ Fuel contaminated. The fuel can be contaminated with either dirt or water, or can change chemically if the machine is allowed to sit for several months or more. Drain the tank and fuel system components (Chapter 4).

☐ Inlet air leak. Check for loose carburettor/throttle body-to-inlet manifold connections, loose or missing vacuum gauge adapter screws, caps or hoses (Chapter 4).

☐ Engine idle speed incorrect. Turn idle adjusting screw until the engine idles at the specified rpm (Chapter 1).

Rough idle

☐ Ignition malfunction. See Chapter 5.

☐ Idle speed incorrect. See Chapter 1.

☐ Carburettors or throttle bodies not synchronised. Adjust them with vacuum gauge or manometer set as described in Chapter 1.

☐ Carburettor or fuel injection system malfunction. See Chapter 4.

☐ Fuel contaminated. The fuel can be contaminated with either dirt or water, or can change chemically if the machine is allowed to sit for several months or more. Drain the tank and float chambers or fuel rail (Chapter 4).

☐ Inlet air leak. Check for loose carburettor/throttle body-to-inlet manifold connections, loose or missing vacuum gauge adapter screws, caps or hoses, or loose carburettor tops (Chapter 4).

☐ Air filter clogged. Renew the air filter element (Chapter 1).

2 Poor running at low speeds

Spark weak

☐ Battery voltage low. Check and recharge battery (Chapter 9).
☐ Spark plugs fouled, defective or worn out. Refer to Chapter 1 for spark plug maintenance.
☐ Spark plug caps or secondary (HT) wiring faulty (GSX-R750T and V models). Check condition. Renew either or both components if cracks or deterioration are evident (Chapter 5).
☐ Spark plug cap/coil defective (GSX-R600 and GSX-R750W and X models). Test and renew if necessary (Chapter 5).
☐ Spark plug caps not making contact.
☐ Incorrect spark plugs. Wrong type, heat range or cap configuration. Check and install correct plugs listed in Chapter 1.
☐ Electronic control unit defective. See Chapter 5.
☐ Pulse generator coil (crankshaft position sensor on GSX-R750W and X models) defective. See Chapter 5.
☐ Ignition HT coils defective. See Chapter 5.

Fuel/air mixture incorrect

☐ Pilot screws out of adjustment (Chapter 4). Pilot jet or air passage clogged. Remove and overhaul the carburettors/throttle bodies (Chapter 4).
☐ Fuel injector clogged or fuel injection system malfunction (see Chapter 4).
☐ Air bleed holes clogged. Remove carburettor and blow out all passages (Chapter 4).
☐ Air filter clogged, poorly sealed or missing (Chapter 1).
☐ Air filter housing poorly sealed. Look for cracks, holes or loose clamps and renew or repair defective parts.
☐ Fuel level too high or too low (carburettor models). Check the float height (Chapter 4).
☐ Fuel tank breather hose obstructed.
☐ Carburettor/throttle body inlet manifolds loose. Check for cracks, breaks, tears or loose clamps. Renew the rubber inlet manifold joints if split or perished.

Compression low

☐ Spark plugs loose. Remove the plugs and inspect their threads. Reinstall and tighten to the specified torque (Chapter 1).
☐ Cylinder heads not sufficiently tightened down. If a cylinder head is suspected of being loose, then there's a chance that the gasket and head are damaged if the problem has persisted for any length of time. The head bolts should be tightened to the proper torque in the correct sequence (Chapter 2).
☐ Improper valve clearance. This means that the valve is not closing completely and compression pressure is leaking past the valve. Check and adjust the valve clearances (Chapter 1).
☐ Cylinder and/or piston worn. Excessive wear will cause compression pressure to leak past the rings. This is usually accompanied by worn rings as well. A top-end overhaul is necessary (Chapter 2).
☐ Piston rings worn, weak, broken, or sticking. Broken or sticking piston rings usually indicate a lubrication or carburation problem that causes excess carbon deposits or seizures to form on the pistons and rings. Top-end overhaul is necessary (Chapter 2).
☐ Piston ring-to-groove clearance excessive. This is caused by excessive wear of the piston ring lands. Piston renewal is necessary (Chapter 2).
☐ Cylinder head gasket damaged. If a head is allowed to become loose, or if excessive carbon build-up on the piston crown and combustion chamber causes extremely high compression, the head gasket may leak. Retorquing the head is not always sufficient to restore the seal, so gasket renewal is necessary (Chapter 2).
☐ Cylinder head warped. This is caused by overheating or improperly tightened head bolts. Machine shop resurfacing or head renewal is necessary (Chapter 2).
☐ Valve spring broken or weak. Caused by component failure or wear; the springs must be renewed (Chapter 2).
☐ Valve not seating properly. This is caused by a bent valve (from over-revving or improper valve adjustment), burned valve or seat (improper carburation) or an accumulation of carbon deposits on the seat (from carburation, lubrication problems). The valves must be cleaned and/or renewed and the seats serviced if possible (Chapter 2).

Poor acceleration

☐ Carburettors/throttle bodies leaking or dirty. Overhaul them (Chapter 4).
☐ Timing not advancing. The pulse generator coil (crankshaft position sensor on GSX-R750W and X models) or the electronic control module may be defective. If so, they must be renewed.
☐ Carburettors/throttle bodies not synchronised. Adjust them with a vacuum gauge set or manometer (Chapter 1).
☐ Engine oil viscosity too high. Using a heavier oil than that recommended in Chapter 1 can damage the oil pump or lubrication system and cause drag on the engine.
☐ Brakes dragging. Usually caused by debris which has entered the brake piston seals, or from a warped disc or bent axle. Repair as necessary (Chapter 7).

3 Poor running or no power at high speed

Firing incorrect

☐ Air filter restricted. Clean or renew filter (Chapter 1).
☐ Spark plugs fouled, defective or worn out. See Chapter 1 for spark plug maintenance.
☐ Spark plug caps or secondary (HT) wiring faulty (GSX-R750T and V models). Check condition. Renew either or both components if cracks or deterioration are evident (Chapter 5).
☐ Spark plug cap/coil defective (GSX-R600 and GSX-R750W and X models). Test and renew if necessary (Chapter 5).
☐ Spark plug caps not in good contact. See Chapter 5.
☐ Incorrect spark plugs. Wrong type, heat range or cap configuration. Check and install correct plugs listed in Chapter 1.
☐ Electronic control unit defective. See Chapter 5.
☐ Ignition HT coils defective. See Chapter 5.

Fuel/air mixture incorrect

☐ Main jet or fuel injector clogged or wrong size. Dirt, water or other contaminants can clog them. Clean the fuel strainer and/or filter, and the carburettors or injectors (Chapter 4). The standard jetting is for sea level atmospheric pressure and oxygen content.
☐ Fuel injector clogged or fuel injection system malfunction (see Chapter 4).
☐ Carburettor throttle shaft-to-carburettor body clearance excessive.
☐ Carburettor air bleed holes clogged. Remove and overhaul carburettors (Chapter 4).
☐ Air filter clogged, poorly sealed, or missing (Chapter 1).
☐ Air filter housing poorly sealed. Look for cracks, holes or loose clamps, and renew or repair defective parts.
☐ Carburettor fuel level too high or too low. Check the float height (Chapter 4).
☐ Fuel tank breather hose obstructed.
☐ Carburettor/throttle body inlet manifolds loose. Check for cracks, breaks, tears or loose clamps. Renew the rubber inlet manifolds if they are split or perished (Chapter 4).

Compression low

☐ Spark plugs loose. Remove the plugs and inspect their threads. Reinstall and tighten to the specified torque (Chapter 1).
☐ Cylinder heads not sufficiently tightened down. If a cylinder head is suspected of being loose, then there's a chance that the gasket and head are damaged if the problem has persisted for any length of time. The head bolts should be tightened to the proper torque in the correct sequence (Chapter 2).
☐ Improper valve clearance. This means that the valve is not closing completely and compression pressure is leaking past the valve. Check and adjust the valve clearances (Chapter 1).
☐ Cylinder and/or piston worn. Excessive wear will cause compression pressure to leak past the rings. This is usually accompanied by worn rings as well. A top-end overhaul is necessary (Chapter 2).
☐ Piston rings worn, weak, broken, or sticking. Broken or sticking piston rings usually indicate a lubrication or carburation problem that causes excess carbon deposits or seizures to form on the pistons and rings. Top-end overhaul is necessary (Chapter 2).
☐ Piston ring-to-groove clearance excessive. This is caused by excessive wear of the piston ring lands. Piston renewal is necessary (Chapter 2).
☐ Cylinder head gasket damaged. If a head is allowed to become loose, or if excessive carbon build-up on the piston crown and combustion chamber causes extremely high compression, the head gasket may leak. Retorquing the head is not always sufficient to restore the seal, so gasket renewal is necessary (Chapter 2).
☐ Cylinder head warped. This is caused by overheating or improperly tightened head bolts. Machine shop resurfacing or head renewal is necessary (Chapter 2).
☐ Valve spring broken or weak. Caused by component failure or wear; the springs must be renewed (Chapter 2).
☐ Valve not seating properly. This is caused by a bent valve (from over-revving or improper valve adjustment), burned valve or seat (improper carburation) or an accumulation of carbon deposits on the seat (from carburation or lubrication problems). The valves must be cleaned and/or renewed and the seats serviced if possible (Chapter 2).

Knocking or pinking

☐ Carbon build-up in combustion chamber. Use of a fuel additive that will dissolve the adhesive bonding the carbon particles to the crown and chamber is the easiest way to remove the build-up. Otherwise, the cylinder head will have to be removed and decarbonised (Chapter 2).
☐ Incorrect or poor quality fuel. Old or improper grades of fuel can cause detonation. This causes the piston to rattle, thus the knocking or pinking sound. Drain old fuel and always use the recommended fuel grade.
☐ Spark plug heat range incorrect. Uncontrolled detonation indicates the plug heat range is too hot. The plug in effect becomes a glow plug, raising cylinder temperatures. Install the proper heat range plug (Chapter 1).
☐ Improper air/fuel mixture. This will cause the cylinders to run hot, which leads to detonation. Clogged jets or an air leak can cause this imbalance. See Chapter 4.

Miscellaneous causes

☐ Throttle valve doesn't open fully. Adjust the throttle grip freeplay (Chapter 1).
☐ Clutch slipping. May be caused by loose or worn clutch components. Refer to Chapter 2 for clutch overhaul procedures.
☐ Timing not advancing.
☐ Engine oil viscosity too high. Using a heavier oil than the one recommended in Chapter 1 can damage the oil pump or lubrication system and cause drag on the engine.
☐ Brakes dragging. Usually caused by debris which has entered the brake piston seals, or from a warped disc or bent axle. Repair as necessary.

4 Overheating

Engine overheats

- ☐ Coolant level low. Check and add coolant (Chapter 1).
- ☐ Leak in cooling system. Check cooling system hoses and radiator for leaks and other damage. Repair or renew parts as necessary (Chapter 3).
- ☐ Thermostat sticking open or closed. Check and renew as described in Chapter 3.
- ☐ Faulty radiator cap. Remove the cap and have it pressure tested.
- ☐ Coolant passages clogged. Have the entire system drained and flushed, then refill with fresh coolant.
- ☐ Water pump defective. Remove the pump and check the components (Chapter 3).
- ☐ Clogged radiator fins. Clean them by blowing compressed air through the fins from the backside.
- ☐ Cooling fan or fan switch fault (Chapter 3).

Firing incorrect

- ☐ Spark plugs fouled, defective or worn out. See Chapter 1 for spark plug maintenance.
- ☐ Incorrect spark plugs.
- ☐ Electronic control unit defective. See Chapter 5.
- ☐ Faulty ignition HT coils (Chapter 5).

Fuel/air mixture incorrect

- ☐ Main jet or fuel injector clogged. Dirt, water or other contaminants can clog them. Clean the fuel strainer and/or filter, and the carburettors or injectors (Chapter 4). The standard jetting is for sea level atmospheric pressure and oxygen content.
- ☐ Fuel injection system malfunction (see Chapter 4).
- ☐ Throttle shaft-to-carburettor body clearance excessive. Refer to Chapter 4.
- ☐ Carburettor air bleed holes clogged. Remove and overhaul carburettors (Chapter 4).
- ☐ Air filter clogged, poorly sealed, or missing (Chapter 1).
- ☐ Air filter housing poorly sealed. Look for cracks, holes or loose clamps, and renew or repair defective parts.
- ☐ Carburettor fuel level too high or too low. Check the float height (Chapter 4).
- ☐ Fuel tank breather hose obstructed.

- ☐ Carburettor/throttle body inlet manifolds loose. Check for cracks, breaks, tears or loose clamps. Renew the rubber inlet manifolds if they are split or perished (Chapter 4).

Compression too high

- ☐ Carbon build-up in combustion chamber. Use of a fuel additive that will dissolve the adhesive bonding the carbon particles to the piston crown and chamber is the easiest way to remove the build-up. Otherwise, the cylinder head will have to be removed and decarbonised (Chapter 2).
- ☐ Improperly machined head surface or installation of incorrect gasket during engine assembly.

Engine load excessive

- ☐ Clutch slipping. Can be caused by damaged, loose or worn clutch components. Refer to Chapter 2 for overhaul procedures.
- ☐ Engine oil level too high. The addition of too much oil will cause pressurisation of the crankcase and inefficient engine operation. Check Specifications and drain to proper level (Chapter 1).
- ☐ Engine oil viscosity too high. Using a heavier oil than the one recommended in Chapter 1 can damage the oil pump or lubrication system as well as cause drag on the engine.
- ☐ Brakes dragging. Usually caused by debris which has entered the brake piston seals, or from a warped disc or bent axle. Repair as necessary.

Lubrication inadequate

- ☐ Engine oil level too low. Friction caused by intermittent lack of lubrication or from oil that is overworked can cause overheating. The oil provides a definite cooling function in the engine. Check the oil level (Chapter 1).
- ☐ Poor quality engine oil or incorrect viscosity or type. Oil is rated not only according to viscosity but also according to type. Some oils are not rated high enough for use in this engine. Check the Specifications section and change to the correct oil (Chapter 1).

Miscellaneous causes

- ☐ Modification to exhaust system. Most aftermarket exhaust systems cause the engine to run leaner, which make them run hotter. When installing an accessory exhaust system, always rejet the carburettors.

5 Clutch problems

Clutch slipping

- ☐ Insufficient clutch cable freeplay. Check and adjust (Chapter 1).
- ☐ Friction plates worn or warped. Overhaul the clutch assembly (Chapter 2).
- ☐ Plain plates warped (Chapter 2).
- ☐ Clutch diaphragm springs broken or weak. Old or heat-damaged (from slipping clutch) springs should be renewed (Chapter 2).
- ☐ Clutch release mechanism defective. Renew any defective parts (Chapter 2).
- ☐ Clutch centre or housing unevenly worn. This causes improper engagement of the plates. Renew the damaged or worn parts (Chapter 2).

Clutch not disengaging completely

- ☐ Excessive clutch cable freeplay. Check and adjust (Chapter 1).
- ☐ Clutch plates warped or damaged. This will cause clutch drag, which in turn will cause the machine to creep. Overhaul the clutch assembly (Chapter 2).

- ☐ Clutch diaphragm spring fatigued or broken. Check and renew the spring (Chapter 2).
- ☐ Engine oil deteriorated. Old, thin, worn out oil will not provide proper lubrication for the plates, causing the clutch to drag. Renew the oil and filter (Chapter 1).
- ☐ Engine oil viscosity too high. Using a heavier oil than recommended in Chapter 1 can cause the plates to stick together, putting a drag on the engine. Change to the correct weight oil (Chapter 1).
- ☐ Clutch housing guide seized on mainshaft. Lack of lubrication, severe wear or damage can cause the guide to seize on the shaft. Overhaul of the clutch, and perhaps transmission, may be necessary to repair the damage (Chapter 2).
- ☐ Clutch release mechanism defective. Overhaul the clutch cover components (Chapter 2).
- ☐ Loose clutch centre nut. Causes housing and centre misalignment putting a drag on the engine. Engagement adjustment continually varies. Overhaul the clutch assembly (Chapter 2).

6 Gearchanging problems

Doesn't go into gear or lever doesn't return

- ☐ Clutch not disengaging. See above.
- ☐ Selector fork(s) bent or seized. Often caused by dropping the machine or from lack of lubrication. Overhaul the transmission (Chapter 2).
- ☐ Gear(s) stuck on shaft. Most often caused by a lack of lubrication or excessive wear in transmission bearings and bushings. Overhaul the transmission (Chapter 2).
- ☐ Selector drum binding. Caused by lubrication failure or excessive wear. Renew the drum and bearing (Chapter 2).
- ☐ Gearchange lever return spring weak or broken (Chapter 2).
- ☐ Gearchange lever broken. Splines stripped out of lever or shaft, caused by allowing the lever to get loose or from dropping the machine. Renew necessary parts (Chapter 2).

- ☐ Gearchange mechanism stopper arm broken or worn. Full engagement and rotary movement of selector drum results. Renew the arm (Chapter 2).

Jumps out of gear

- ☐ Selector fork(s) worn. Overhaul the transmission (Chapter 2).
- ☐ Gear groove(s) worn. Overhaul the transmission (Chapter 2).
- ☐ Gear dogs or dog slots worn or damaged. The gears should be inspected and renewed. No attempt should be made to service the worn parts.

Overshifts

- ☐ Stopper arm spring weak or broken (Chapter 2).
- ☐ Gearshift shaft return spring post broken or distorted (Chapter 2).

7 Abnormal engine noise

Knocking or pinking

☐ Carbon build-up in combustion chamber. Use of a fuel additive that will dissolve the adhesive bonding the carbon particles to the piston crown and chamber is the easiest way to remove the build-up. Otherwise, the cylinder head will have to be removed and decarbonised (Chapter 2).

☐ Incorrect or poor quality fuel. Old or improper fuel can cause detonation. This causes the pistons to rattle, thus the knocking or pinking sound. Drain the old fuel and always use the recommended grade fuel (Chapter 4).

☐ Spark plug heat range incorrect. Uncontrolled detonation indicates that the plug heat range is too hot. The plug in effect becomes a glow plug, raising cylinder temperatures. Install the proper heat range plug (Chapter 1).

☐ Improper air/fuel mixture. This will cause the cylinders to run hot and lead to detonation. Clogged jets/injectors or an air leak can cause this imbalance. See Chapter 4.

Piston slap or rattling

☐ Cylinder-to-piston clearance excessive. Caused by improper assembly. Inspect and overhaul top-end parts (Chapter 2).

☐ Connecting rod bent. Caused by over-revving, trying to start a badly flooded engine or from ingesting a foreign object into the combustion chamber. Renew the damaged parts (Chapter 2).

☐ Piston pin or piston pin bore worn or seized from wear or lack of lubrication. Renew damaged parts (Chapter 2).

☐ Piston ring(s) worn, broken or sticking. Overhaul the top-end (Chapter 2).

☐ Piston seizure damage. Usually from lack of lubrication or overheating. Renew the pistons and cylinder block, as necessary (Chapter 2).

☐ Connecting rod upper or lower end clearance excessive. Caused by excessive wear or lack of lubrication. Renew worn parts.

Valve noise

☐ Incorrect valve clearances. Adjust the clearances by referring to Chapter 1.

☐ Valve spring broken or weak. Check and renew weak valve springs (Chapter 2).

☐ Camshaft or cylinder head worn or damaged. Lack of lubrication at high rpm is usually the cause of damage. Insufficient oil or failure to change the oil at the recommended intervals are the chief causes. Since there are no replaceable bearings in the head, the head itself will have to be renewed if there is excessive wear or damage (Chapter 2).

Other noise

☐ Cylinder head gasket leaking.

☐ Exhaust pipe leaking at cylinder head connection. Caused by improper fit of pipe(s) or loose exhaust flange. All exhaust fasteners should be tightened evenly and carefully. Failure to do this will lead to a leak.

☐ Crankshaft runout excessive. Caused by a bent crankshaft (from over-revving) or damage from an upper cylinder component failure. Can also be attributed to dropping the machine on either of the crankshaft ends.

☐ Engine mounting bolts loose. Tighten all engine mount bolts (Chapter 2).

☐ Crankshaft bearings worn (Chapter 2).

☐ Cam chain rattle, due to worn chain or defective tensioner. Also worn chain tensioner/guide blades. Renew according to the procedure in Chapter 2.

8 Abnormal driveline noise

Clutch noise

☐ Clutch housing/friction plate clearance excessive (Chapter 2).

☐ Wear between the clutch housing splines and input shaft splines (Chapter 2).

☐ Worn release bearing (Chapter 2).

Transmission noise

☐ Bearings worn. Also includes the possibility that the shafts are worn. Overhaul the transmission (Chapter 2).

☐ Gears worn or chipped (Chapter 2).

☐ Metal chips jammed in gear teeth. Probably pieces from a broken clutch, gear or selector mechanism that were picked up by the gears. This will cause early bearing failure (Chapter 2).

☐ Engine oil level too low. Causes a howl from transmission. Also affects engine power and clutch operation (Chapter 1).

Final drive noise

☐ Chain not adjusted properly or excessively worn (Chapter 1).

☐ Front or rear sprocket loose. Tighten fasteners (Chapter 6).

☐ Sprockets worn. Renew sprockets (Chapter 6).

☐ Rear sprocket warped. Renew sprockets (Chapter 6).

☐ Rubber dampers in rear wheel worn (Chapter 6).

9 Abnormal frame and suspension noise

Front end noise

☐ Low fluid level or improper viscosity oil in forks. This can sound like spurting and is usually accompanied by irregular fork action (Chapter 6).

☐ Spring weak or broken. Makes a clicking or scraping sound. Fork oil, when drained, will have a lot of metal particles in it (Chapter 6).

☐ Steering head bearings loose or damaged. Clicks when braking. Check and adjust or renew as necessary (Chapters 1 and 6).

☐ Fork yokes loose. Make sure all clamp pinch bolts are tightened to the specified torque (Chapter 6).

☐ Forks bent. Good possibility if machine has been dropped. Renew forks (Chapter 6).

☐ Front axle bolt or axle clamp bolts loose. Tighten them to the specified torque (Chapter 7).

☐ Loose or worn wheel bearings. Check and renew as needed (Chapters 1 and 7).

Shock absorber noise

☐ Fluid level incorrect. Indicates a leak caused by defective seal. Shock will be covered with oil. Renew shock or seek advice on repair from a suspension specialist (Chapter 6).

☐ Defective shock absorber with internal damage. This is in the body of the shock and can't be remedied. The shock must be renewed or rebuilt (Chapter 6).

☐ Bent or damaged shock body. Renew the shock (Chapter 6).

☐ Loose or worn suspension linkage components. Check and renew as necessary (Chapter 6).

Brake noise

☐ Squeal caused by pad shim not installed or positioned correctly (where fitted) (Chapter 7).

☐ Squeal caused by dust on brake pads. Usually found in combination with glazed pads. Clean using brake cleaning solvent (Chapter 7).

☐ Contamination of brake pads. Oil, brake fluid or dirt causing brake to chatter or squeal. Clean or renew pads (Chapter 7).

☐ Pads glazed. Caused by excessive heat from prolonged use or from contamination. Do not use sandpaper, emery cloth, carborundum cloth or any other abrasive to roughen the pad surfaces as abrasives will stay in the pad material and damage the disc. A very fine flat file can be used, but pad renewal is suggested as a cure (Chapter 7).

☐ Disc warped. Can cause a chattering, clicking or intermittent squeal. Usually accompanied by a pulsating lever and uneven braking. Renew the disc (Chapter 7).

☐ Loose or worn wheel bearings. Check and renew as needed (Chapters 1 and 7).

10 Oil pressure warning light comes on

Engine lubrication system

☐ Engine oil pump defective, blocked oil strainer gauze or failed pressure regulator. Carry out an oil pressure check (Chapter 1).

☐ Engine oil level low. Inspect for leak or other problem causing low oil level and add recommended oil (Daily (pre-ride) checks).

☐ Engine oil viscosity too low. Very old, thin oil or an improper weight of oil used in the engine. Change to correct oil (Chapter 1).

☐ Camshaft or crankshaft journals worn. Excessive wear causing drop in oil pressure. Abnormal wear could be caused by oil starvation at high rpm from low oil level or improper weight or type of oil (Chapter 1).

Electrical system

☐ Oil pressure switch defective. Check the switch according to the procedure in Chapter 9. Renew it if it is defective.

☐ Oil pressure warning light circuit or display defective. Check for pinched, shorted, disconnected or damaged wiring (Chapter 9).

11 Excessive exhaust smoke

White smoke

☐ Piston oil ring worn. The ring may be broken or damaged, causing oil from the crankcase to be pulled past the piston into the combustion chamber. Renew the rings (Chapter 2).

☐ Cylinders worn, cracked, or scored. Caused by overheating or oil starvation. Install a new cylinder block (Chapter 2).

☐ Valve oil seal damaged or worn. Renew oil seals (Chapter 2).

☐ Valve guide worn. Perform a complete valve job (Chapter 2).

☐ Engine oil level too high, which causes the oil to be forced past the rings. Drain oil to the proper level (Daily (pre-ride) checks).

☐ Head gasket broken between oil return and cylinder. Causes oil to be pulled into the combustion chamber. Renew the head gasket and check the head for warpage (Chapter 2).

☐ Abnormal crankcase pressurisation, which forces oil past the rings. Clogged breather is usually the cause.

Black smoke

☐ Air filter clogged. Clean or renew the element (Chapter 1).

☐ Carburettor main jet too large or loose. Compare the jet size to the Specifications (Chapter 4).

☐ Choke cable or linkage shaft stuck (carburettor models), causing fuel to be pulled through choke circuit (Chapter 4).

☐ Fuel level too high (carburettor models). Check and adjust the float height(s) as necessary (Chapter 4).

☐ Float needle valve held off needle seat (Carburettor models). Clean the float chambers and fuel line and renew the needles and seats if necessary (Chapter 4).

☐ Fuel injection system malfunction (Chapter 4).

Brown smoke

☐ Main jet too small or clogged (carburettor models). Lean condition caused by wrong size main jet or by a restricted orifice. Clean float chambers and jets and compare jet size to Specifications (Chapter 4).

☐ Fuel flow insufficient (carburettor models). Float needle valve stuck closed due to chemical reaction with old fuel. Float height incorrect. Restricted fuel line. Clean line and float chamber and adjust floats if necessary (Chapter 4).

☐ Fuel pump faulty (Chapter 4).

☐ Carburettor/throttle body inlet manifold clamps loose (Chapter 4).

☐ Air filter poorly sealed or not installed (Chapter 1).

☐ Fuel injection system malfunction (Chapter 4).

12 Poor handling or stability

Handlebar hard to turn

☐ Steering head bearing adjuster nut too tight. Check adjustment as described in Chapter 1.

☐ Bearings damaged. Roughness can be felt as the bars are turned from side-to-side. Renew bearings (Chapter 6).

☐ Races dented or worn. Denting results from wear in only one position (eg, straight ahead), from a collision or hitting a pothole or from dropping the machine. Renew bearings (Chapter 6

☐ Steering stem lubrication inadequate. Causes are grease getting hard from age or being washed out by high pressure car washes. Disassemble steering head and repack bearings (Chapter 6).

☐ Steering stem bent. Caused by a collision, hitting a pothole or by dropping the machine. Renew damaged part. Don't try to straighten the steering stem (Chapter 6).

☐ Front tyre air pressure too low (Chapter 1).

Handlebar shakes or vibrates excessively

☐ Tyres worn or out of balance (Chapter 7).

☐ Swingarm bearings worn. Renew worn bearings (Chapter 6).

☐ Failed steering damper.

☐ Wheel rim(s) warped or damaged. Inspect wheels for runout (Chapter 7).

☐ Wheel bearings worn. Worn front or rear wheel bearings can cause poor tracking. Worn front bearings will cause wobble (Chapters 1 and 7).

☐ Handlebar clamp bolts loose (Chapter 6).

☐ Fork yoke bolts loose. Tighten them to the specified torque (Chapter 6).

☐ Engine mounting bolts loose. Will cause excessive vibration with increased engine rpm (Chapter 2).

Handlebar pulls to one side

☐ Frame bent. Definitely suspect this if the machine has been dropped. May or may not be accompanied by cracking near the bends. Renew the frame (Chapter 6).

☐ Wheels out of alignment. Caused by improper location of axle spacers or from bent steering stem or frame (Chapter 6).

☐ Swingarm bent or twisted. Renew the arm (Chapter 6).

☐ Steering stem bent. Caused by impact damage or by dropping the motorcycle. Renew the steering stem (Chapter 6).

☐ Forks bent. Disassemble the forks and renew the damaged parts (Chapter 6).

☐ Fork oil level uneven. Check and add or drain as necessary (Chapter 6).

Poor shock absorbing qualities

☐ Too hard:
  a) Fork oil level excessive (Chapter 6).
  b) Fork oil viscosity too high. Use a lighter oil (see the Specifications in Chapter 6).
  c) Fork tube bent. Causes a harsh, sticking feeling (Chapter 6).
  d) Shock shaft or body bent or damaged (Chapter 6).
  e) Fork internal damage (Chapter 6).
  f) Shock internal damage.
  g) Tyre pressure too high (Chapter 1).
  h) Suspension settings incorrect.

☐ Too soft:
  a) Fork or shock oil insufficient and/or leaking (Chapter 6).
  b) Fork oil level too low (Chapter 6).
  c) Fork oil viscosity too light (Chapter 6).
  d) Fork springs weak or broken (Chapter 6).
  e) Shock internal damage or leakage (Chapter 6).
  f) Suspension settings incorrect.

13 Braking problems

Brakes are spongy, don't hold

- ☐ Air in brake line. Caused by inattention to master cylinder fluid level or by leakage. Locate problem and bleed brakes (Chapter 7).
- ☐ Pad or disc worn (Chapters 1 and 7).
- ☐ Brake fluid leak. See paragraph 1.
- ☐ Contaminated pads. Caused by contamination with oil, grease, brake fluid, etc. Clean or renew pads. Clean disc thoroughly with brake cleaner (Chapter 7).
- ☐ Brake fluid deteriorated. Fluid is old or contaminated. Drain system, replenish with new fluid and bleed the system (Chapter 7).
- ☐ Master cylinder internal parts worn or damaged causing fluid to bypass (Chapter 7).
- ☐ Master cylinder bore scratched by foreign material or broken spring. Repair or renew master cylinder (Chapter 7).
- ☐ Disc warped. Renew disc (Chapter 7).

Brake lever or pedal pulsates

- ☐ Disc warped. Renew disc (Chapter 7).
- ☐ Axle bent. Renew axle (Chapter 7).
- ☐ Brake caliper bolts loose (Chapter 7).
- ☐ Wheel warped or otherwise damaged (Chapter 7).
- ☐ Wheel bearings damaged or worn (Chapters 1 and 7).

Brakes drag

- ☐ Master cylinder piston seized. Caused by wear or damage to piston or cylinder bore (Chapter 7).
- ☐ Lever balky or stuck. Check pivot and lubricate (Chapter 7).
- ☐ Brake caliper piston seized in bore. Caused by corrosion or ingestion of dirt past deteriorated seal (Chapter 7).
- ☐ Brake pad damaged. Pad material separated from backing plate. Usually caused by faulty manufacturing process or from contact with chemicals. Renew pads (Chapter 7).
- ☐ Pads improperly installed (Chapter 7).

14 Electrical problems

Battery dead or weak

- ☐ Battery faulty. Caused by sulphated plates which are shorted through sedimentation. Also, broken battery terminal making only occasional contact (Chapter 9).
- ☐ Battery cables making poor contact (Chapter 9).
- ☐ Load excessive. Caused by addition of high wattage lights or other electrical accessories.
- ☐ Ignition (main) switch defective. Switch either grounds (earths) internally or fails to shut off system. Renew the switch (Chapter 9).
- ☐ Regulator/rectifier defective (Chapter 9).
- ☐ Alternator stator coil open or shorted (Chapter 9).

- ☐ Charging system fault. Check for current leakage (Chapter 9).
- ☐ Wiring faulty. Wiring grounded (earthed) or connections loose in ignition, charging or lighting circuits (Chapter 9).

Battery overcharged

- ☐ Regulator/rectifier defective. Overcharging is noticed when battery gets excessively warm (Chapter 9).
- ☐ Battery defective. Renew battery with a new one (Chapter 9).
- ☐ Battery amperage too low, wrong type or size. Install manufacturer's specified amp-hour battery to handle charging load (Chapter 9).

Checking engine compression

● Low compression will result in exhaust smoke, heavy oil consumption, poor starting and poor performance. A compression test will provide useful information about an engine's condition and if performed regularly, can give warning of trouble before any other symptoms become apparent.

● A compression gauge will be required, along with an adapter to suit the spark plug hole thread size. Note that the screw-in type gauge/adapter set up is preferable to the rubber cone type.

● Before carrying out the test, first check the valve clearances as described in Chapter 1.

1 Run the engine until it reaches normal operating temperature, then stop it and remove the spark plug(s), taking care not to scald your hands on the hot components.

2 Install the gauge adapter and compression gauge in No. 1 cylinder spark plug hole (see illustration 1).

Screw the compression gauge adapter into the spark plug hole, then screw the gauge into the adapter

3 On kickstart-equipped motorcycles, make sure the ignition switch is OFF, then open the throttle fully and kick the engine over a couple of times until the gauge reading stabilises.

4 On motorcycles with electric start only, the procedure will differ depending on the nature of the ignition system. Flick the engine kill switch (engine stop switch) to OFF and turn the ignition switch ON; open the throttle fully and crank the engine over on the starter motor for a couple of revolutions until the gauge reading stabilises. If the starter will not operate with the kill switch OFF, turn the ignition switch OFF and refer to the next paragraph.

5 Install the spark plugs back into their suppressor caps and arrange the plug electrodes so that their metal bodies are earthed (grounded) against the cylinder head; this is essential to prevent damage to the ignition system as the engine is spun over (see illustration 2). Position the plugs well

All spark plugs must be earthed (grounded) against the cylinder head

away from the plug holes otherwise there is a risk of atomised fuel escaping from the combustion chambers and igniting. As a safety precaution, cover the top of the valve cover with rag. Now turn the ignition switch ON and kill switch ON, open the throttle fully and crank the engine over on the starter motor for a couple of revolutions until the gauge reading stabilises.

6 After one or two revolutions the pressure should build up to a maximum figure and then stabilise. Take a note of this reading and on multi-cylinder engines repeat the test on the remaining cylinders.

7 The correct pressures are given in Chapter 1 Specifications. If the results fall within the specified range and on multi-cylinder engines all are relatively equal, the engine is in good condition. If there is a marked difference between the readings, or if the readings are lower than specified, inspection of the top-end components will be required.

8 Low compression pressure may be due to worn cylinder bores, pistons or rings, failure of the cylinder head gasket, worn valve seals, or poor valve seating.

9 To distinguish between cylinder/piston wear and valve leakage, pour a small quantity of oil into the bore to temporarily seal the piston rings, then repeat the compression tests (see illustration 3). If the readings show

Bores can be temporarily sealed with a squirt of motor oil

a noticeable increase in pressure this confirms that the cylinder bore, piston, or rings are worn. If, however, no change is indicated, the cylinder head gasket or valves should be examined.

10 High compression pressure indicates excessive carbon build-up in the combustion chamber and on the piston crown. If this is the case the cylinder head should be removed and the deposits removed. Note that excessive carbon build-up is less likely with the used on modern fuels.

Checking battery open-circuit voltage

Warning: The gases produced by the battery are explosive - never smoke or create any sparks in the vicinity of the battery. Never allow the electrolyte to contact your skin or clothing - if it does, wash it off and seek immediate medical attention.

Measuring open-circuit battery voltage

Float-type hydrometer for measuring battery specific gravity

● Before any electrical fault is investigated the battery should be checked.

● You'll need a dc voltmeter or multimeter to check battery voltage. Check that the leads are inserted in the correct terminals on the meter, red lead to positive (+ve), black lead to negative (-ve). Incorrect connections can damage the meter.

● A sound fully-charged 12 volt battery should produce between 12.3 and 12.6 volts across its terminals (12.8 volts for a maintenance-free battery). On machines with a 6 volt battery, voltage should be between 6.1 and 6.3 volts.

1 Set a multimeter to the 0 to 20 volts dc range and connect its probes across the battery terminals. Connect the meter's positive (+ve) probe, usually red, to the battery positive (+ve) terminal, followed by the meter's negative (-ve) probe, usually black, to the battery negative terminal (-ve) (see illustration 4).

2 If battery voltage is low (below 10 volts on a 12 volt battery or below 4 volts on a six volt battery), charge the battery and test the voltage again. If the battery repeatedly goes flat, investigate the motorcycle's charging system.

Checking battery specific gravity (SG)

 Warning: The gases produced by the battery are explosive - never smoke or create any sparks in the vicinity of the battery. Never allow the electrolyte to contact your skin or clothing - if it does, wash it off and seek immediate medical attention.

● The specific gravity check gives an indication of a battery's state of charge.

● A hydrometer is used for measuring specific gravity. Make sure you purchase one

which has a small enough hose to insert in the aperture of a motorcycle battery.

● Specific gravity is simply a measure of the electrolyte's density compared with that of water. Water has an SG of 1.000 and fully-charged battery electrolyte is about 26% heavier, at 1.260.

● Specific gravity checks are not possible on maintenance-free batteries. Testing the open-circuit voltage is the only means of determining their state of charge.

1 To measure SG, remove the battery from the motorcycle and remove the first cell cap. Draw

Digital multimeter can be used for all electrical tests

Battery-powered continuity tester

some electrolyte into the hydrometer and note the reading (see illustration 5). Return the electrolyte to the cell and install the cap.

2 The reading should be in the region of 1.260 to 1.280. If SG is below 1.200 the battery needs charging. Note that SG will vary with temperature; it should be measured at 20°C (68°F). Add 0.007 to the reading for every 10°C above 20°C, and subtract 0.007 from the reading for every 10°C below 20°C. Add 0.004 to the reading for every 10°F above 68°F, and subtract 0.004 from the reading for every 10°F below 68°F.

3 When the check is complete, rinse the hydrometer thoroughly with clean water.

Checking for continuity

● The term continuity describes the uninterrupted flow of electricity through an electrical circuit. A continuity check will determine whether an open-circuit situation exists.

● Continuity can be checked with an ohmmeter, multimeter, continuity tester or battery and bulb test circuit (see illustrations 6, 7 and 8).

Battery and bulb test circuit

Continuity check of front brake light switch using a meter - note split pins used to access connector terminals

Continuity check of rear brake light switch using a continuity tester

● All of these instruments are self-powered by a battery, therefore the checks are made with the ignition OFF.

● As a safety precaution, always disconnect the battery negative (-ve) lead before making checks, particularly if ignition switch checks are being made.

● If using a meter, select the appropriate ohms scale and check that the meter reads infinity (∞). Touch the meter probes together and check that meter reads zero; where necessary adjust the meter so that it reads zero.

● After using a meter, always switch it OFF to conserve its battery.

Switch checks

1 If a switch is at fault, trace its wiring up to the wiring connectors. Separate the wire connectors and inspect them for security and condition. A build-up of dirt or corrosion here will most likely be the cause of the problem - clean up and apply a water dispersant such as WD40.

2 If using a test meter, set the meter to the ohms x 10 scale and connect its probes across the wires from the switch **(see illustration 9)**. Simple ON/OFF type switches, such as brake light switches, only have two wires whereas combination switches, like the ignition switch, have many internal links. Study the wiring diagram to ensure that you are connecting across the correct pair of wires. Continuity (low or no measurable resistance - 0 ohms) should be indicated with the switch ON and no continuity (high resistance) with it OFF.

3 Note that the polarity of the test probes doesn't matter for continuity checks, although care should be taken to follow specific test procedures if a diode or solid-state component is being checked.

4 A continuity tester or battery and bulb circuit can be used in the same way. Connect its probes as described above **(see illustration 10)**. The light should come on to indicate continuity in the ON switch position, but should extinguish in the OFF position.

Wiring checks

● Many electrical faults are caused by damaged wiring, often due to incorrect routing or chaffing on frame components.

● Loose, wet or corroded wire connectors can also be the cause of electrical problems, especially in exposed locations.

1 A continuity check can be made on a single length of wire by disconnecting it at each end and connecting a meter or continuity tester across both ends of the wire **(see illustration 11)**.

2 Continuity (low or no resistance - 0 ohms) should be indicated if the wire is good. If no continuity (high resistance) is shown, suspect a broken wire.

Checking for voltage

● A voltage check can determine whether current is reaching a component.

● Voltage can be checked with a dc voltmeter, multimeter set on the dc volts scale, test light or buzzer **(see illustrations 12 and 13)**. A meter has the advantage of being able to measure actual voltage.

● When using a meter, check that its leads are inserted in the correct terminals on the meter, red to positive (+ve), black to negative (-ve). Incorrect connections can damage the meter.

● A voltmeter (or multimeter set to the dc volts scale) should always be connected in parallel (across the load). Connecting it in series will destroy the meter.

● Voltage checks are made with the ignition ON.

Continuity check of front brake light switch sub-harness

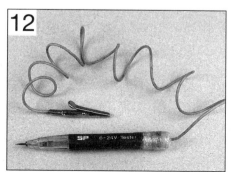

A simple test light can be used for voltage checks

A buzzer is useful for voltage checks

Checking for voltage at the rear brake light power supply wire using a meter . . .

1 First identify the relevant wiring circuit by referring to the wiring diagram at the end of this manual. If other electrical components share the same power supply (ie are fed from the same fuse), take note whether they are working correctly - this is useful information in deciding where to start checking the circuit.
2 If using a meter, check first that the meter leads are plugged into the correct terminals on the meter (see above). Set the meter to the dc volts function, at a range suitable for the battery voltage. Connect the meter red probe (+ve) to the power supply wire and the black probe to a good metal earth (ground) on the motorcycle's frame or directly to the battery negative (-ve) terminal **(see illustration 14)**. Battery voltage should be shown on the meter

A selection of jumper wires for making earth (ground) checks

. . . or a test light - note the earth connection to the frame (arrow)

with the ignition switched ON.
3 If using a test light or buzzer, connect its positive (+ve) probe to the power supply terminal and its negative (-ve) probe to a good earth (ground) on the motorcycle's frame or directly to the battery negative (-ve) terminal **(see illustration 15)**. With the ignition ON, the test light should illuminate or the buzzer sound.
4 If no voltage is indicated, work back towards the fuse continuing to check for voltage. When you reach a point where there is voltage, you know the problem lies between that point and your last check point.

Checking the earth (ground)

● Earth connections are made either directly to the engine or frame (such as sensors, neutral switch etc. which only have a positive feed) or by a separate wire into the earth circuit of the wiring harness. Alternatively a short earth wire is sometimes run directly from the component to the motorcycle's frame.
● Corrosion is often the cause of a poor earth connection.
● If total failure is experienced, check the security of the main earth lead from the

negative (-ve) terminal of the battery and also the main earth (ground) point on the wiring harness. If corroded, dismantle the connection and clean all surfaces back to bare metal.
1 To check the earth on a component, use an insulated jumper wire to temporarily bypass its earth connection **(see illustration 16)**. Connect one end of the jumper wire between the earth terminal or metal body of the component and the other end to the motorcycle's frame.
2 If the circuit works with the jumper wire installed, the original earth circuit is faulty. Check the wiring for open-circuits or poor connections. Clean up direct earth connections, removing all traces of corrosion and remake the joint. Apply petroleum jelly to the joint to prevent future corrosion.

Tracing a short-circuit

● A short-circuit occurs where current shorts to earth (ground) bypassing the circuit components. This usually results in a blown fuse.

● A short-circuit is most likely to occur where the insulation has worn through due to wiring chafing on a component, allowing a direct path to earth (ground) on the frame.

1 Remove any bodypanels necessary to access the circuit wiring.
2 Check that all electrical switches in the circuit are OFF, then remove the circuit fuse and connect a test light, buzzer or voltmeter (set to the dc scale) across the fuse terminals. No voltage should be shown.
3 Move the wiring from side to side whilst observing the test light or meter. When the test light comes on, buzzer sounds or meter shows voltage, you have found the cause of the short. It will usually shown up as damaged or burned insulation.
4 Note that the same test can be performed on each component in the circuit, even the switch.

A

ABS (Anti-lock braking system) A system, usually electronically controlled, that senses incipient wheel lockup during braking and relieves hydraulic pressure at wheel which is about to skid.

Aftermarket Components suitable for the motorcycle, but not produced by the motorcycle manufacturer.

Allen key A hexagonal wrench which fits into a recessed hexagonal hole.

Alternating current (ac) Current produced by an alternator. Requires converting to direct current by a rectifier for charging purposes.

Alternator Converts mechanical energy from the engine into electrical energy to charge the battery and power the electrical system.

Ampere (amp) A unit of measurement for the flow of electrical current. Current = Volts ÷ Ohms.

Ampere-hour (Ah) Measure of battery capacity.

Angle-tightening A torque expressed in degrees. Often follows a conventional tightening torque for cylinder head or main bearing fasteners **(see illustration)**.

Angle-tightening cylinder head bolts

Antifreeze A substance (usually ethylene glycol) mixed with water, and added to the cooling system, to prevent freezing of the coolant in winter. Antifreeze also contains chemicals to inhibit corrosion and the formation of rust and other deposits that would tend to clog the radiator and coolant passages and reduce cooling efficiency.

Anti-dive System attached to the fork lower leg (slider) to prevent fork dive when braking hard.

Anti-seize compound A coating that reduces the risk of seizing on fasteners that are subjected to high temperatures, such as exhaust clamp bolts and nuts.

API American Petroleum Institute. A quality standard for 4-stroke motor oils.

Asbestos A natural fibrous mineral with great heat resistance, commonly used in the composition of brake friction materials. Asbestos is a health hazard and the dust created by brake systems should never be inhaled or ingested.

ATF Automatic Transmission Fluid. Often used in front forks.

ATU Automatic Timing Unit. Mechanical device for advancing the ignition timing on early engines.

ATV All Terrain Vehicle. Often called a Quad.

Axial play Side-to-side movement.

Axle A shaft on which a wheel revolves. Also known as a spindle.

B

Backlash The amount of movement between meshed components when one component is held still. Usually applies to gear teeth.

Ball bearing A bearing consisting of a hardened inner and outer race with hardened steel balls between the two races.

Bearings Used between two working surfaces to prevent wear of the components and a build-up of heat. Four types of bearing are commonly used on motorcycles: plain shell bearings, ball bearings, tapered roller bearings and needle roller bearings.

Bevel gears Used to turn the drive through 90°. Typical applications are shaft final drive and camshaft drive **(see illustration)**.

Bevel gears are used to turn the drive through 90°

BHP Brake Horsepower. The British measurement for engine power output. Power output is now usually expressed in kilowatts (kW).

Bias-belted tyre Similar construction to radial tyre, but with outer belt running at an angle to the wheel rim.

Big-end bearing The bearing in the end of the connecting rod that's attached to the crankshaft.

Bleeding The process of removing air from an hydraulic system via a bleed nipple or bleed screw.

Bottom-end A description of an engine's crankcase components and all components contained there-in.

BTDC Before Top Dead Centre in terms of piston position. Ignition timing is often expressed in terms of degrees or millimetres BTDC.

Bush A cylindrical metal or rubber component used between two moving parts.

Burr Rough edge left on a component after machining or as a result of excessive wear.

C

Cam chain The chain which takes drive from the crankshaft to the camshaft(s).

Canister The main component in an evaporative emission control system (California market only); contains activated charcoal granules to trap vapours from the fuel system rather than allowing them to vent to the atmosphere.

Castellated Resembling the parapets along the top of a castle wall. For example, a castellated wheel axle or spindle nut.

Catalytic converter A device in the exhaust system of some machines which converts certain pollutants in the exhaust gases into less harmful substances.

Charging system Description of the components which charge the battery, ie the alternator, rectifer and regulator.

Circlip A ring-shaped clip used to prevent endwise movement of cylindrical parts and shafts. An internal circlip is installed in a groove in a housing; an external circlip fits into a groove on the outside of a cylindrical piece such as a shaft. Also known as a snap-ring.

Clearance The amount of space between two parts. For example, between a piston and a cylinder, between a bearing and a journal, etc.

Coil spring A spiral of elastic steel found in various sizes throughout a vehicle, for example as a springing medium in the suspension and in the valve train.

Compression Reduction in volume, and increase in pressure and temperature, of a gas, caused by squeezing it into a smaller space.

Compression damping Controls the speed the suspension compresses when hitting a bump.

Compression ratio The relationship between cylinder volume when the piston is at top dead centre and cylinder volume when the piston is at bottom dead centre.

Continuity The uninterrupted path in the flow of electricity. Little or no measurable resistance.

Continuity tester Self-powered bleeper or test light which indicates continuity.

Cp Candlepower. Bulb rating commonly found on US motorcycles.

Crossply tyre Tyre plies arranged in a criss-cross pattern. Usually four or six plies used, hence 4PR or 6PR in tyre size codes.

Cush drive Rubber damper segments fitted between the rear wheel and final drive sprocket to absorb transmission shocks **(see illustration)**.

Cush drive rubbers dampen out transmission shocks

D

Degree disc Calibrated disc for measuring piston position. Expressed in degrees.

Dial gauge Clock-type gauge with adapters for measuring runout and piston position. Expressed in mm or inches.

Diaphragm The rubber membrane in a master cylinder or carburettor which seals the upper chamber.

Diaphragm spring A single sprung plate often used in clutches.

Direct current (dc) Current produced by a dc generator.

Decarbonisation The process of removing carbon deposits - typically from the combustion chamber, valves and exhaust port/system.

Detonation Destructive and damaging explosion of fuel/air mixture in combustion chamber instead of controlled burning.

Diode An electrical valve which only allows current to flow in one direction. Commonly used in rectifiers and starter interlock systems.

Disc valve (or rotary valve) A induction system used on some two-stroke engines.

Double-overhead camshaft (DOHC) An engine that uses two overhead camshafts, one for the intake valves and one for the exhaust valves.

Drivebelt A toothed belt used to transmit drive to the rear wheel on some motorcycles. A drivebelt has also been used to drive the camshafts. Drivebelts are usually made of Kevlar.

Driveshaft Any shaft used to transmit motion. Commonly used when referring to the final driveshaft on shaft drive motorcycles.

E

Earth return The return path of an electrical circuit, utilising the motorcycle's frame.

ECU (Electronic Control Unit) A computer which controls (for instance) an ignition system, or an anti-lock braking system.

EGO Exhaust Gas Oxygen sensor. Sometimes called a Lambda sensor.

Electrolyte The fluid in a lead-acid battery.

EMS (Engine Management System) A computer controlled system which manages the fuel injection and the ignition systems in an integrated fashion.

Endfloat The amount of lengthways movement between two parts. As applied to a crankshaft, the distance that the crankshaft can move side-to-side in the crankcase.

Endless chain A chain having no joining link. Common use for cam chains and final drive chains.

EP (Extreme Pressure) Oil type used in locations where high loads are applied, such as between gear teeth.

Evaporative emission control system Describes a charcoal filled canister which stores fuel vapours from the tank rather than allowing them to vent to the atmosphere. Usually only fitted to California models and referred to as an EVAP system.

Expansion chamber Section of two-stroke engine exhaust system so designed to improve engine efficiency and boost power.

F

Feeler blade or gauge A thin strip or blade of hardened steel, ground to an exact thickness, used to check or measure clearances between parts.

Final drive Description of the drive from the transmission to the rear wheel. Usually by chain or shaft, but sometimes by belt.

Firing order The order in which the engine cylinders fire, or deliver their power strokes, beginning with the number one cylinder.

Flooding Term used to describe a high fuel level in the carburettor float chambers, leading to fuel overflow. Also refers to excess fuel in the combustion chamber due to incorrect starting technique.

Free length The no-load state of a component when measured. Clutch, valve and fork spring lengths are measured at rest, without any preload.

Freeplay The amount of travel before any action takes place. The looseness in a linkage, or an assembly of parts, between the initial application of force and actual movement. For example, the distance the rear brake pedal moves before the rear brake is actuated.

Fuel injection The fuel/air mixture is metered electronically and directed into the engine intake ports (indirect injection) or into the cylinders (direct injection). Sensors supply information on engine speed and conditions.

Fuel/air mixture The charge of fuel and air going into the engine. See **Stoichiometric ratio**.

Fuse An electrical device which protects a circuit against accidental overload. The typical fuse contains a soft piece of metal which is calibrated to melt at a predetermined current flow (expressed as amps) and break the circuit.

G

Gap The distance the spark must travel in jumping from the centre electrode to the side electrode in a spark plug. Also refers to the distance between the ignition rotor and the pickup coil in an electronic ignition system.

Gasket Any thin, soft material - usually cork, cardboard, asbestos or soft metal - installed between two metal surfaces to ensure a good seal. For instance, the cylinder head gasket seals the joint between the block and the cylinder head.

Gauge An instrument panel display used to monitor engine conditions. A gauge with a movable pointer on a dial or a fixed scale is an analogue gauge. A gauge with a numerical readout is called a digital gauge.

Gear ratios The drive ratio of a pair of gears in a gearbox, calculated on their number of teeth.

Glaze-busting see **Honing**

Grinding Process for renovating the valve face and valve seat contact area in the cylinder head.

Gudgeon pin The shaft which connects the connecting rod small-end with the piston. Often called a piston pin or wrist pin.

H

Helical gears Gear teeth are slightly curved and produce less gear noise that straight-cut gears. Often used for primary drives.

Installing a Helicoil thread insert in a cylinder head

Helicoil A thread insert repair system. Commonly used as a repair for stripped spark plug threads **(see illustration)**.

Honing A process used to break down the glaze on a cylinder bore (also called glaze-busting). Can also be carried out to roughen a rebored cylinder to aid ring bedding-in.

HT (High Tension) Description of the electrical circuit from the secondary winding of the ignition coil to the spark plug.

Hydraulic A liquid filled system used to transmit pressure from one component to another. Common uses on motorcycles are brakes and clutches.

Hydrometer An instrument for measuring the specific gravity of a lead-acid battery.

Hygroscopic Water absorbing. In motorcycle applications, braking efficiency will be reduced if DOT 3 or 4 hydraulic fluid absorbs water from the air - care must be taken to keep new brake fluid in tightly sealed containers.

I

lbf ft Pounds-force feet. An imperial unit of torque. Sometimes written as ft-lbs.

lbf in Pound-force inch. An imperial unit of torque, applied to components where a very low torque is required. Sometimes written as in-lbs.

IC Abbreviation for Integrated Circuit.

Ignition advance Means of increasing the timing of the spark at higher engine speeds. Done by mechanical means (ATU) on early engines or electronically by the ignition control unit on later engines.

Ignition timing The moment at which the spark plug fires, expressed in the number of crankshaft degrees before the piston reaches the top of its stroke, or in the number of millimetres before the piston reaches the top of its stroke.

Infinity (∞) Description of an open-circuit electrical state, where no continuity exists.

Inverted forks (upside down forks) The sliders or lower legs are held in the yokes and the fork tubes or stanchions are connected to the wheel axle (spindle). Less unsprung weight and stiffer construction than conventional forks.

J

JASO Quality standard for 2-stroke oils.

Joule The unit of electrical energy.

Journal The bearing surface of a shaft.

K

Kickstart Mechanical means of turning the engine over for starting purposes. Only usually fitted to mopeds, small capacity motorcycles and off-road motorcycles.

Kill switch Handebar-mounted switch for emergency ignition cut-out. Cuts the ignition circuit on all models, and additionally prevent starter motor operation on others.

km Symbol for kilometre.

kmh Abbreviation for kilometres per hour.

L

Lambda (λ) sensor A sensor fitted in the exhaust system to measure the exhaust gas oxygen content (excess air factor).

Lapping see **Grinding**.
LCD Abbreviation for Liquid Crystal Display.
LED Abbreviation for Light Emitting Diode.
Liner A steel cylinder liner inserted in a aluminium alloy cylinder block.
Locknut A nut used to lock an adjustment nut, or other threaded component, in place.
Lockstops The lugs on the lower triple clamp (yoke) which abut those on the frame, preventing handlebar-to-fuel tank contact.
Lockwasher A form of washer designed to prevent an attaching nut from working loose.
LT Low Tension Description of the electrical circuit from the power supply to the primary winding of the ignition coil.

M

Main bearings The bearings between the crankshaft and crankcase.
Maintenance-free (MF) battery A sealed battery which cannot be topped up.
Manometer Mercury-filled calibrated tubes used to measure intake tract vacuum. Used to synchronise carburettors on multi-cylinder engines.
Micrometer A precision measuring instrument that measures component outside diameters **(see illustration)**.

Tappet shims are measured with a micrometer

MON (Motor Octane Number) A measure of a fuel's resistance to knock.
Monograde oil An oil with a single viscosity, eg SAE80W.
Monoshock A single suspension unit linking the swingarm or suspension linkage to the frame.
mph Abbreviation for miles per hour.
Multigrade oil Having a wide viscosity range (eg 10W40). The W stands for Winter, thus the viscosity ranges from SAE10 when cold to SAE40 when hot.
Multimeter An electrical test instrument with the capability to measure voltage, current and resistance. Some meters also incorporate a continuity tester and buzzer.

N

Needle roller bearing Inner race of caged needle rollers and hardened outer race. Examples of uncaged needle rollers can be found on some engines. Commonly used in rear suspension applications and in two-stroke engines.
Nm Newton metres.
NOx Oxides of Nitrogen. A common toxic pollutant emitted by petrol engines at higher temperatures.

O

Octane The measure of a fuel's resistance to knock.
OE (Original Equipment) Relates to components fitted to a motorcycle as standard or replacement parts supplied by the motorcycle manufacturer.
Ohm The unit of electrical resistance. Ohms = Volts ÷ Current.
Ohmmeter An instrument for measuring electrical resistance.
Oil cooler System for diverting engine oil outside of the engine to a radiator for cooling purposes.
Oil injection A system of two-stroke engine lubrication where oil is pump-fed to the engine in accordance with throttle position.
Open-circuit An electrical condition where there is a break in the flow of electricity - no continuity (high resistance).
O-ring A type of sealing ring made of a special rubber-like material; in use, the O-ring is compressed into a groove to provide the sealing action.
Oversize (OS) Term used for piston and ring size options fitted to a rebored cylinder.
Overhead cam (sohc) engine An engine with single camshaft located on top of the cylinder head.
Overhead valve (ohv) engine An engine with the valves located in the cylinder head, but with the camshaft located in the engine block or crankcase.
Oxygen sensor A device installed in the exhaust system which senses the oxygen content in the exhaust and converts this information into an electric current. Also called a Lambda sensor.

P

Plastigauge A thin strip of plastic thread, available in different sizes, used for measuring clearances. For example, a strip of Plastigauge is laid across a bearing journal. The parts are assembled and dismantled; the width of the crushed strip indicates the clearance between journal and bearing.
Polarity Either negative or positive earth (ground), determined by which battery lead is connected to the frame (earth return). Modern motorcycles are usually negative earth.
Pre-ignition A situation where the fuel/air mixture ignites before the spark plug fires. Often due to a hot spot in the combustion chamber caused by carbon build-up. Engine has a tendency to 'run-on'.
Pre-load (suspension) The amount a spring is compressed when in the unloaded state. Preload can be applied by gas, spacer or mechanical adjuster.
Premix The method of engine lubrication on older two-stroke engines. Engine oil is mixed with the petrol in the fuel tank in a specific ratio. The fuel/oil mix is sometimes referred to as "petroil".
Primary drive Description of the drive from the crankshaft to the clutch. Usually by gear or chain.
PS Pfedestärke - a German interpretation of BHP.
PSI Pounds-force per square inch. Imperial measurement of tyre pressure and cylinder pressure measurement.
PTFE Polytetrafluroethylene. A low friction substance.

Pulse secondary air injection system A process of promoting the burning of excess fuel present in the exhaust gases by routing fresh air into the exhaust ports.

Q

Quartz halogen bulb Tungsten filament surrounded by a halogen gas. Typically used for the headlight **(see illustration)**.

Quartz halogen headlight bulb construction

R

Rack-and-pinion A pinion gear on the end of a shaft that mates with a rack (think of a geared wheel opened up and laid flat). Sometimes used in clutch operating systems.
Radial play Up and down movement about a shaft.
Radial ply tyres Tyre plies run across the tyre (from bead to bead) and around the circumference of the tyre. Less resistant to tread distortion than other tyre types.
Radiator A liquid-to-air heat transfer device designed to reduce the temperature of the coolant in a liquid cooled engine.
Rake A feature of steering geometry - the angle of the steering head in relation to the vertical **(see illustration)**.

Steering geometry

Rebore Providing a new working surface to the cylinder bore by boring out the old surface. Necessitates the use of oversize piston and rings.

Rebound damping A means of controlling the oscillation of a suspension unit spring after it has been compressed. Resists the spring's natural tendency to bounce back after being compressed.

Rectifier Device for converting the ac output of an alternator into dc for battery charging.

Reed valve An induction system commonly used on two-stroke engines.

Regulator Device for maintaining the charging voltage from the generator or alternator within a specified range.

Relay A electrical device used to switch heavy current on and off by using a low current auxiliary circuit.

Resistance Measured in ohms. An electrical component's ability to pass electrical current.

RON (Research Octane Number) A measure of a fuel's resistance to knock.

rpm revolutions per minute.

Runout The amount of wobble (in-and-out movement) of a wheel or shaft as it's rotated. The amount a shaft rotates 'out-of-true'. The out-of-round condition of a rotating part.

S

SAE (Society of Automotive Engineers) A standard for the viscosity of a fluid.

Sealant A liquid or paste used to prevent leakage at a joint. Sometimes used in conjunction with a gasket.

Service limit Term for the point where a component is no longer useable and must be renewed.

Shaft drive A method of transmitting drive from the transmission to the rear wheel.

Shell bearings Plain bearings consisting of two shell halves. Most often used as big-end and main bearings in a four-stroke engine. Often called bearing inserts.

Shim Thin spacer, commonly used to adjust the clearance or relative positions between two parts. For example, shims inserted into or under tappets or followers to control valve clearances. Clearance is adjusted by changing the thickness of the shim.

Short-circuit An electrical condition where current shorts to earth (ground) bypassing the circuit components.

Skimming Process to correct warpage or repair a damaged surface, eg on brake discs or drums.

Slide-hammer A special puller that screws into or hooks onto a component such as a shaft or bearing; a heavy sliding handle on the shaft bottoms against the end of the shaft to knock the component free.

Small-end bearing The bearing in the upper end of the connecting rod at its joint with the gudgeon pin.

Spalling Damage to camshaft lobes or bearing journals shown as pitting of the working surface.

Specific gravity (SG) The state of charge of the electrolyte in a lead-acid battery. A measure of the electrolyte's density compared with water.

Straight-cut gears Common type gear used on gearbox shafts and for oil pump and water pump drives.

Stanchion The inner sliding part of the front forks, held by the yokes. Often called a fork tube.

Stoichiometric ratio The optimum chemical air/fuel ratio for a petrol engine, said to be 14.7 parts of air to 1 part of fuel.

Sulphuric acid The liquid (electrolyte) used in a lead-acid battery. Poisonous and extremely corrosive.

Surface grinding (lapping) Process to correct a warped gasket face, commonly used on cylinder heads.

T

Tapered-roller bearing Tapered inner race of caged needle rollers and separate tapered outer race. Examples of taper roller bearings can be found on steering heads.

Tappet A cylindrical component which transmits motion from the cam to the valve stem, either directly or via a pushrod and rocker arm. Also called a cam follower.

TCS Traction Control System. An electronically-controlled system which senses wheel spin and reduces engine speed accordingly.

TDC Top Dead Centre denotes that the piston is at its highest point in the cylinder.

Thread-locking compound Solution applied to fastener threads to prevent slackening. Select type to suit application.

Thrust washer A washer positioned between two moving components on a shaft. For example, between gear pinions on gearshaft.

Timing chain See **Cam Chain.**

Timing light Stroboscopic lamp for carrying out ignition timing checks with the engine running.

Top-end A description of an engine's cylinder block, head and valve gear components.

Torque Turning or twisting force about a shaft.

Torque setting A prescribed tightness specified by the motorcycle manufacturer to ensure that the bolt or nut is secured correctly. Undertightening can result in the bolt or nut coming loose or a surface not being sealed. Overtightening can result in stripped threads, distortion or damage to the component being retained.

Torx key A six-point wrench.

Tracer A stripe of a second colour applied to a wire insulator to distinguish that wire from another one with the same colour insulator. For example, Br/W is often used to denote a brown insulator with a white tracer.

Trail A feature of steering geometry. Distance from the steering head axis to the tyre's central contact point.

Triple clamps The cast components which extend from the steering head and support the fork stanchions or tubes. Often called fork yokes.

Turbocharger A centrifugal device, driven by exhaust gases, that pressurises the intake air. Normally used to increase the power output from a given engine displacement.

TWI Abbreviation for Tyre Wear Indicator. Indicates the location of the tread depth indicator bars on tyres.

U

Universal joint or U-joint (UJ) A double-pivoted connection for transmitting power from a driving to a driven shaft through an angle. Typically found in shaft drive assemblies.

Unsprung weight Anything not supported by the bike's suspension (ie the wheel, tyres, brakes, final drive and bottom (moving) part of the suspension).

V

Vacuum gauges Clock-type gauges for measuring intake tract vacuum. Used for carburettor synchronisation on multi-cylinder engines.

Valve A device through which the flow of liquid, gas or vacuum may be stopped, started or regulated by a moveable part that opens, shuts or partially obstructs one or more ports or passageways. The intake and exhaust valves in the cylinder head are of the poppet type.

Valve clearance The clearance between the valve tip (the end of the valve stem) and the rocker arm or tappet/follower. The valve clearance is measured when the valve is closed. The correct clearance is important - if too small the valve won't close fully and will burn out, whereas if too large noisy operation will result.

Valve lift The amount a valve is lifted off its seat by the camshaft lobe.

Valve timing The exact setting for the opening and closing of the valves in relation to piston position.

Vernier caliper A precision measuring instrument that measures inside and outside dimensions. Not quite as accurate as a micrometer, but more convenient.

VIN Vehicle Identification Number. Term for the bike's engine and frame numbers.

Viscosity The thickness of a liquid or its resistance to flow.

Volt A unit for expressing electrical "pressure" in a circuit. Volts = current x ohms.

W

Water pump A mechanically-driven device for moving coolant around the engine.

Watt A unit for expressing electrical power. Watts = volts x current.

Wear limit see **Service limit**

Wet liner A liquid-cooled engine design where the pistons run in liners which are directly surrounded by coolant **(see illustration)**.

Wet liner arrangement

Wheelbase Distance from the centre of the front wheel to the centre of the rear wheel.

Wiring harness or loom Describes the electrical wires running the length of the motorcycle and enclosed in tape or plastic sheathing. Wiring coming off the main harness is usually referred to as a sub harness.

Woodruff key A key of semi-circular or square section used to locate a gear to a shaft. Often used to locate the alternator rotor on the crankshaft.

Wrist pin Another name for gudgeon or piston pin.

Note: *References throughout this index are in the form – "Chapter number" • "page number"*